BEYOND METHOD

From the Library of

Julie Christen-Heyles

BEYOND METHOD

Strategies for Social Research

edited by

Gareth Morgan

SAGE PUBLICATIONS
Beverly Hills / London / New Delhi

For information address:

SAGE Publications, Inc.
275 South Beverly Drive
Beverly Hills, California 90212

SAGE Publications India Pvt. Ltd.
C-236 Defence Colony
New Delhi 110 024, India

SAGE Publications Ltd
28 Banner Street
London EC1Y 8QE, England

Printed in the United States of America

Library of Congress Cataloging in Publication Data

Main entry under title:

Beyond method.

   Bibliography: p.
   1. Social sciences—Research—Addresses, essays, lectures. I. Morgan, Gareth.
H62.B474   1983   300'.72   82-25082
ISBN 0-8039-1973-5
ISBN 0-8039-2078-4 (pbk.)

FIRST PRINTING

Contents

Preface

My aim in producing this volume is to advance the cause of a reflective social science. As Jacques Ellul has observed, we live in an age that celebrates technique. This is particularly evident in the social sciences, where concern for methodology dominates. While methodological sophistication provides an important basis for the technical conduct of research, this is insufficient to establish a social science that is substantially rational in the sense that its practitioners are able to observe and question what they are doing and why they are doing it, and thus to make informed choices about the means and consequences of their research. For this, a much broader and self-reflective stance is required. A knowledge of technique needs to be complemented by an appreciation of the nature of research as a distinctively human process through which researchers *make* knowledge. Such appreciation stands in contrast to the more common view of research as a neutral, technical process through which researchers simply reveal or discover knowledge. Such appreciation requires that we reframe understanding and debate about research in a way that goes beyond considerations of method alone.

This is precisely what this volume attempts to achieve. I have designed it in a way that counterposes the logics of twenty-one different approaches to research, to generate constructive debate about the wide range of choice facing the social researcher. The research strategies represented have been selected to create a microcosm of social science perspectives within the context of a single volume. The idea here is to help the reader attain an approximate grasp on social science as a whole, and thus address the diversity and contradiction that make the selection of a research strategy such a problematic and value-laden affair. While most of the contributors focus on the study of formal organization as a means of illustrating their favored research strategy, the volume is of direct relevance to all social science disciplines.

The opportunity for reflection offered by this volume encourages the social researcher to examine what he or she is doing within the context of available options. In this way, it facilitates a reflective distancing from one's favored perspective, to appreciate how it differs from rival approaches, and to take heed of the possibilities that are open to one in engaging in a particular research study. Second, it encourages the researcher to engage in a reflective style of research that is ever sensitive to the assumptions and implications of all aspects of the research process, and how these influence what is learned about the phenomenon being investigated. Third, it encourages the researcher to respond in an intelligent and constructive way to the existence and knowledge claims of rival modes of research practice and to the contributions that each offers. Such considerations offer the possibility of developing a social science that can be liberative as well as functional, guided by a sense of what is possible as much as by what is actual, and which is recognized as being as much a political, moral, and ethical activity, as it is a technical one.

In accordance with the overall spirit of the volume, all contributors reflect on the nature of their research practice in a manner designed to reveal underlying assumptions, so that the rationale of their view is made clear. I am grateful to them for agreeing to collaborate in this way, and in particular, for the open and constructive way in which they have responded to the editorial constraints and demands that the production of this volume has required. Special thanks are due to Ken Benson, Bob Cooper, Cynthia McSwain, Linda Smircich, Bill Torbert, Steve Turner, Orion White, and Tom Wilson, who gave special advice and support on crucial occasions, and to the other authors, who along with those mentioned above, were able to join the project workshop held at York University in August 1981. These were Michel Bougon, Mino Carchedi, Lynda Glennon, Gareth Jones, William Outhwaite, Derek Pugh, and Gerald Susman.

Thanks are due to many members of York University for valuable administrative and financial assistance, especially to Dean Wallace Crowston for his help and encouragement, and to Vicki Keller for excellent secretarial support. I'd also like to thank Leona Andrews and Gisela Birmingham for their help in typing sections of the manuscript, and Pat Bradshaw and Clement Hammah for their valuable contributions. My new friends at Sage Publications have proved indispensible and adventurous partners in making the publication of this manuscript a reality.

— *Gareth Morgan*
Toronto, Canada

—I—

INTRODUCTION

1

RESEARCH AS ENGAGEMENT

A Personal View

Gareth Morgan
York University

My formal interest in what I now see as the problem of knowledge and its social construction stems from problems encountered as a young, eager, organizational researcher. Indeed, I can pinpoint the very day in 1972 when I was struck by the realization that the conduct of empirical research was much more problematic than as presented in the textbooks, and that the results of such research must be much less solid than appeared from a reading of the scientific reports presented in journals and scholarly manuscripts.

I was conducting research on the organization and management of an English new town development corporation at the time. I had just completed a questionnaire survey of staff attitudes toward the organization in which they worked and was reflecting on the statistical results of the data analysis. From one point of view, the statistics provided a very high level of support for the general hypothesis I was interested in testing, but they were also open to alternative interpretations. I had been influenced by debates within organization theory between "systems theorists" and proponents of an "action frame of reference" (Silverman, 1970), and by the view that science progresses most rapidly when we attempt to refute our theories and hypotheses rather than seek to confirm them (Popper, 1958). Bringing these ideas together, I found that I could use my data to support and refute in some degree most of the rival theories and hypotheses that I cared to generate. From one point of view I could support or reject a systems view of the organization that attributed satisfaction with the management of the corporation to congruence between task, human, and managerial variables; from the standpoint of an action frame of reference, many other explanations appeared equally plausible.

The conclusions to be drawn from my study seemed to depend on the stance adopted toward my data and on how critical my interpretation was to be. Even where the data generated correlation coefficients that were highly significant in a statistical sense, I could identify data from supplementary sources (e.g., interviews and observations) that made them highly problematic. I remember pondering the question, "What lies on the other side of the correlation coefficients?" It occurred to me that the coefficients I was examining were both affirmational and negational. While supporting a hypothesis they simultaneously negated it by identifying the basis for a counterexplanation in terms of what was unexplained — the affirmational 0.45 identified a problematic 0.55!

I was unsatisfied with any solution to this problem that placed faith in a "null hypothesis," and in the idea that the data were interesting and the hypothesis sound because they beat the laws of chance. Recourse to alternative theories and alternative sources of data to explain the problematic "other side" added to my disquiet, for they frequently pointed toward the appropriateness of rival explanations of the total situation being researched. The conclusions to be drawn from a particular piece of data depended very much on the frameworks through which it was to be interpreted. The data I had collected seemed to contain many potential meanings, and I vaguely appreciated that as a researcher I had the power to realize these different meanings in the way that I presented my results. However, it was a power with which I felt uncomfortable, because I felt that science ultimately was concerned with generating objective forms of knowledge that were independent of the researcher. As a result, I searched for a new basis for objectivity, and thus an escape from my dilemma, through the collection of more data in new sites and in a search for an integrative theory that would make sense of the contradictory aspects of my research.

I now understand that in this early research experience I had encountered in a crude way what Heisenberg (1958) has described as the "uncertainty principle." In essence, this principle suggests that scientific research involves an interaction between the scientist and the object of investigation, and that what the scientist observes is directly related to the nature of that interaction. This view of science is closely related to Berkeley's (1910) observation that an object gains its objectivity only by being observed, and that objectivity must thus be a property that stems from the observer.

These ideas have the most profound implications for the way we view and conduct science, for they emphasize that science is basically a process of interaction, or better still, of *engagement*. Scientists engage a subject of study by interacting with it through means of a particular frame of reference, and what is observed and discovered in the object (i.e., its objectivity) is as much a product of this interaction and the protocol and technique through which it is operationalized as it is of the object itself. Moreover, since it is possible to engage an object of study in different ways — just as we might engage an apple by looking at it, feeling it, or eating it — we can see that the same object is capable of yielding many different kinds of knowledge. This leads us to see knowledge as a potentiality resting in an object of investigation and to see science as being concerned with the realization of potentialities — of possible knowledges.

This view emphasizes the importance of understanding the frameworks through which scientists engage their object of investigation and of understanding the possible modes of engagement. Most of my recent research work has been devoted to this task; the problems encountered in interpreting the results of my new town research gradually led to systematic analysis of the different theoretical frameworks that can be used for social analysis, with particular reference to the study of organization. *Sociological Paradigms and Organizational Analysis* (Burrell and Morgan, 1979) approaches the problem by demonstrating how different approaches to social analysis are built on sets of assumptions that are rarely made explicit, yet which exert a decisive influence on the nature of theory and research. My recent work on the impact of metaphor on theory construction (Morgan, 1980; Morgan and Smircich, 1980) develops this theme, illustrating how different images of a subject guide and prefigure, and hence shape, what is seen.

The present volume furthers the task by bringing together the views of social scientists who advocate different approaches for engaging and understanding social life. Its aim is to widen and deepen understanding of the nature of contemporary research practice and its possibilities and to initiate constructive debate about the implications of this diversity. The existence of different strategies for social research, drawing on different ground assumptions, and generating different kinds of knowledge, poses intriguing problems regarding the way we should view or evaluate the research process. Science has traditionally cast this issue as one hinging on the problem of objectivity, emphasizing the importance of disciplined observation and value-free inquiry as a means of generating "objective" knowledge.

The position presented in this work challenges this notion of objectivity, for it emphasizes the crucial link between observer and observed, and by implication, questions the very possibility of neutral observation or evaluation. The view of research as engagement emphasizes that researcher and researched must be seen as part of a whole and, therefore, questions the idea that it is possible to stand outside the research process and evaluate it in any absolute way. As an alternative, the conclusions to this work suggest an approach that replaces the idea that we should be concerned with the neutral evaluation of research with the idea that we should be more concerned with exploring research diversity and its consequences through a model based on the idea of reflective discourse, or "conversation."

Significantly, this conclusion is a direct product of the way the overall project has evolved. Originally, the aims of the project were quite simple — to illustrate the rationale and nature of a variety of approaches to organizational research. The basic idea was to produce a volume that would stand as a methodological equivalent to *Sociological Paradigms and Organizational Analysis.* In conversation and debate with readers of that work I was impressed by the argument that it was all very well to talk about the nature of different theoretical perspectives, but that there was no guidance as to how they could be implemented in actual research practice. In response, I decided to invite researchers favoring different paradigms to collaborate on a project designed to reveal the logic of their various research perspectives and to illustrate their uses in practice. Using the framework discussed in Chapter 2 as a means of unifying the project, I aimed to create a volume that would satisfy demands for methodological guidance in a way that got beyond a discussion of methodology alone by emphasizing the essential links between theory and method. I hoped that this approach would aid understanding and development of the different styles of research represented in the volume, especially those unfamiliar.

Once in progress, the project gained a momentum of its own. Issues that I had tended to gloss over in the planning stages called for increasing attention. In particular, there was the problem of how to close the project. While it was possible just to present the different research perspectives for consideration, their juxtaposition seemed to raise a number of issues calling for at least some comment. For example, there was the question as to how the reader could come to some conclusion regarding the contrary nature, significance, and claims of the different perspectives. Using the work of Gödel (1962) as a metaphor for framing this issue, I realized that there was a major problem here: There was no obvious point of reference outside the system of thought represented in the volume from which the different perspectives could be described and evaluated. As Gödel has shown in relation to mathematics, there is a fallacy in the idea that the propositions of a system of thought can be proved, disproved, or evaluated on the basis of axioms within that system. Translated into terms relevant to the present project, this means that it is not possible to judge the validity or contribution of different research perspectives in terms of the ground assumptions of any one set of those perspectives, since the process is self-justifying. Hence the attempts in much social science debate to judge the utility of different research strategies in terms of universal criteria based on the importance of generalizability, predictability and control, explanation of variance, meaningful understanding, or whatever are inevitably flawed: These criteria inevitably favor research strategies consistent with the assumptions that generate such criteria as meaningful guidelines for the evaluation of research. It is simply inadequate to attempt to justify a particular style of research in terms of assumptions that give rise to that style of research. As will become evident from reading of the chapters in this volume and from our discussion in the concluding chapter, different research perspectives make different kinds of knowledge claims, and the criteria as to what counts as significant knowledge vary from one to another.

Given that it did not seem possible to evaluate the claims and contributions of the different research perspectives from an independent point of reference, I concluded that an alternative approach to the problem was required. It seemed necessary to devise some new means of exploring the diversity and its implications, in a way that would replace a concern for evaluation with a general concern for appreciating the merits and significance of the different points of view. To achieve this, I decided to organize a workshop of contributors to the project, structured in a way that would encourage constructive debate about the issues the project raised. In order to overcome the fallacy of trying to evaluate the different perspectives from a single perspective within the system, I decided that it would be appropriate to try to create a dialectic between a number of such points of view. Using the analysis of paradigms offered by Burrell and Morgan (1979) as a framework for generating different approaches to the problem, it seemed that at least four issues were worthy of attention.

(1) Was it possible to learn something from the assumptions underlying the different research perspectives? Although each perspective offered a logically coherent and internally consistent argument for conducting research in a particular way, this argument was ulti-

mately derived from the ground assumptions on which it was based. Was it possible to raise and debate these assumptions? Was it possible to adopt a *functionalist* standpoint and to determine their appropriateness or accuracy as a means of deciding on the relative merits of the various research strategies?

(2) Was it possible to view the different research strategies from an *interpretive* standpoint, as modes of discourse, and attempt to translate them into a common language in order to assess the nature of their differences and the possibility of achieving some form of integration?

(3) Was it possible to view the different strategies from a *radical humanist* standpoint as having ideological, ethical, moral, political, and psychoanalytic significance and to examine and assess their nature and implications from these points of view?

(4) Was it possible to analyze the different perspectives from a *radical structuralist* standpoint, treating the world of empirical reality as the product of deep-seated generative mechanisms, and to determine the extent to which different research strategies provide structural modes of understanding, rather than confine themselves to the analysis of surface data?

My original plan was to invite four social scientists to explore the possibility of analyzing research strategies in terms of one or another of the above perspectives and provide critiques of the various research strategies represented in the project. These analyses and critiques would have been used to focus workshop discussion and create a means of exploring differences among the various points of view. The aim was to see whether it was possible to create a collaborative atmosphere and reach some consensus as to the issues that needed to be addressed in considering the merits and consequences of the different research perspectives. However, full realization of the plan was disrupted by a problem in funding the project; the agencies approached were unable to help or were simply unimpressed by the need or potential worth of such a workshop. York University rescued the project, creating the opportunity for sixteen members to meet in Toronto to explore the significance of their different points of view. The idea of generating four independent analyses of the research perspectives could not be realized, given the new constraints, so it fell to me as organizer of the workshop to offer the four themes as a possible agenda, allowing the precise structure and content of the workshop to evolve through discussion, in accord with its open, collaborative intent.

The situation created by this turn of events was in many ways similar to that depicted in Pirandello's play *Six Characters in Search*

of an Author. I, as organizer of the workshop, had a "play" that I
wanted to stage, but the "players" who attended the workshop were
less interested in the script *I* proposed than they were in realizing the
"characters" *they* wished to play. At the opening session of the
workshop I presented my vision of what the workshop could achieve,
identifying the four themes as a possible means of organizing discussion and some of the issues that could receive detailed attention.
However, there was polite reluctance to accept my definition of
priorities. Most workshop members felt that the more pressing need
was to achieve a deeper and more direct and personal understanding
of the research perspectives represented at the workshop. As a result
it was decided to engage in conversation designed to explore each
other's position. Workshop members presented their views on why
they were engaged in their particular styles of research, which were
further explored through discussion. The workshop thus served to
reproduce, through conversation, the personal biographies that had
led to the adoption of particular philosophical positions and styles of
research practice.

My feeling during the workshop was that the project was drifting
away from my control and was not meeting the objectives I had set for
it. I saw the discussion as producing and reproducing perspectives
characteristic of different paradigms, with the usual problem of people "talking by" one another because they exchanged with each other
on the basis of different frames of reference that were not being made
explicit. In my worst moments I felt that one of the most cynical and
negative reviewers of an unsuccessful funding proposal for the workshop would be proven correct — that the workshop would prove to be
"just talk." While a few workshop members may have agreed with
this feeling when I shared it with them, the overwhelming response to
my view was that the workshop was going extremely well and that a
considerable amount was being achieved. There was a lot of talk, yes,
but it was clarifying and edifying, and it provided a model of what
social scientists should do if they are interested in getting a better
understanding of their own position and those of others. One member
confronted me directly with the view that I was feeling particularly
uncomfortable about the process because my own conceptual
categories and objectives were being "blown apart."

As I look back at the workshop three months later, I believe that
my colleague's analysis of the situation was correct. I appreciate that
in planning and structuring the workshop, I was searching for common ground on which we could build rules for the conduct and debate
of different research perspectives. I realized that there was no one set
of grounds on which this would be possible, but in its place sought to

create some form of unity through a dialectic involving four. By dint of circumstance the workshop found an alternative means for addressing the problems. The need to confront and understand one's position and those of others led to a conversational mode of inquiry that served the purpose of self-edification and raised themes that were in need of attention. The four themes I had identified as the basis of a possible agenda in the end proved to be just four themes among many.

In the concluding chapters of this work, we will explore some of these themes and the idea that the practice of social research can proceed most effectively if we replace the view that science involves a quest for certain knowledge that can be evaluated in an unambiguous way, with the view that it involves modes of human engagement on which we can and should reflect, and about which we can and should converse to improve our understanding and practice. It will be argued that if we understand that science is not simply about the acquisition of knowledge but is a means of expressing ourselves — and of forming, transforming, and generally coping with our world — we can approach this endeavor in a new way. In so doing, we will be able to steer clear of the delusion that it is possible to know in an absolute sense of "being right" and devote our energies to the more constructive process of dealing with the implications of our different ways of knowing.

About the Author

GARETH MORGAN

I grew up in a small town in English-speaking Wales, elder son of "Morgan the Butcher." My interest in developing a critical social science no doubt stems from this early experience. The contradictions of being Welsh have long generated a strong nonconformist tradition and degree of self-reflection, fueled in my case by the "watch-what-you're-doing" gaze of the lay sociologists that discussed local "goings-on" in our shop each morning. Each Welsh town has its "Mrs. News of the World," miraculously everywhere, always, hawk-eyed and elephant-memoried. Our town had many of them.

My escape was to London, the LSE, books, economics, political thought, and on to a promising career as an accountant in local government. All this was put in new perspective by events of the late 1960s, spent studying public administration in Texas, amidst the contradictions of flower-power and cowboys, rallies and lectures, accounting, computers, and humanistic visions of a new utopia. From there I embarked on a university career at Lancaster, teaching organization theory and engaging in the research that has led me to the issues examined in the present volume.

Most of my work as a social scientist now rests trying to understand how our assumptions shape ourselves and our society, since I believe that in challenging and changing these assumptions we have a chance of changing society in constructive ways.

2

RESEARCH STRATEGIES

Modes of Engagement

Gareth Morgan
York University

A view of research as engagement stresses that research is not just a question of methodology, for method is but part of a wider process that constitutes and renders a subject amenable to study in a distinctive way. The selection of method implies some view of the situation being studied, for any decision on *how* to study a phenomenon carries with it certain assumptions, or explicit answers to the question, *"What is being studied?"* Just as we select a tennis racquet rather than a golf club to play tennis because we have a prior conception as to what the game of tennis involves, so too in relation to the process of social research; we select or favor particular kinds of methodology because we have implicit or explicit conceptions as to what we are trying to do in our research. An understanding of research as engagement thus emphasizes the importance of understanding the network of assumptions and practices that link the researcher to the phenomenon being investigated.

It is helpful to think about the mode of engagement embodied in these assumptions and practices as reflecting a *logic* or *strategy* of research. When we frame understanding of the research process in these terms, we are encouraged to replace abstract debates about the merits of different kinds of methodology with a consideration of the significance and merits of the different logics of research that are available to the researcher. We are encouraged to see the research process as involving choice between modes of engagement entailing different relationships between theory and method, concept and object, and researcher and researched, rather than simply a choice about method alone.

One of the central ideas underlying the design of this volume is that the logics of different research strategies can be decoded through systematic analysis of the modes of engagement. Figure 2.1 presents a framework for doing this, focusing attention on the way ontological and epistemological premises favor distinctive kinds of research practice. The following chapters illustrate 21 different research strategies in these terms. Each author discusses the core assumptions on which his or her mode of research is based, the epistemological implications of these assumptions, and the kind of methodology through which the overall research strategy can be operationalized. Each chapter thus provides a rationale as to *why* research should be conducted in a particular way and suggests *how* the strategy can be implemented in practice.

As we read through these chapteres we are invited to see and study social life in different ways. The changing images we encounter favor research strategies characteristic of the natural sciences, pragmatism, interpretive anthropology, phenomenology, dramatism, structuralism, critical theory, Jungian analysis, and varieties of Marxian dialectics. The following overview is presented to help the reader obtain an initial grasp on this diversity and to highlight the basic orientation and logic of the different points of view.

Studying structure and process. In Chapter 3, Derek Pugh discusses the logic underlying the Aston Program of organizational research and his concern with furthering the development of a positivist social science. Building from the assumption that organizations and behavior in organizations can be understood as systems of observable regularities characterized by multiple causality, he argues that the aim of the organizational researcher should be to produce generalizable knowledge based on systematic, comparative, and replicative observation and measurement. Pugh draws the distinction between wisdom as a stock of insight, and knowledge as a set of substantiated empirical findings, arguing that it is the scientist's task to advance the latter. Hence his approach to research generates empirical propositions about the nature of organization and tests the extent to which they explain organizational reality. The route to knowledge rests in identifying generalizations based on the explanation and prediction of variance between measures of organizational variables relating to context, structure, performance, and behavior, analyzed through multivariate techniques such as factor analysis. The research strategy advocated utilizes cross-sectional, empirical "snapshots" to identify the structure of organizational reality at given

Constitutive Assumptions (PARADIGMS)	The rationale for a particular research strategy is grounded in a network of implicit or explicit assumptions regarding ontology and human nature that define the researcher's view of the social world. These assumptions provide the foundations of research practice, inclining the researcher to see and interpret the world from one perspective rather than from another. By identifying the researcher's assumptions about human beings and the world in which they live, we can identify the basic paradigm that serves as a foundation of inquiry.
Epistemological Stance (METAPHORS)	Scientific knowledge is shaped by the way researchers attempt to concretize the ground assumptions that underwrite their work. Images of a social phenomenon, usually expressed in terms of a favored metaphor, provide a means of structuring scientific inquiry, guiding attention in distinctive ways. The image favors a particular epistemological stance in suggesting that certain kinds of insight, understanding, and explanation may be more appropriate than are others. Different ground assumptions and the images through which they are grasped and developed thus give rise to different grounds for knowledge about the social world.
Favored Methodology (PUZZLE SOLVING)	The image of a phenomenon to be investigated provides the basis for detailed scientific research concerned to examine, and perhaps operationalize and measure, the extent to which detailed aspects of the image characterize the phenomenon. The image generates specific concepts and methods of study through which knowledge of the phenomenon can be obtained. In effect, methodologies are the puzzle-solving devices that bridge the gap between the image of a phenomenon and the phenomenon itself. Methodologies link the researcher to the situation being studied in terms of rules, procedures, and general protocol that operationalize the network of assumptions embodied in the researcher's paradigm and favored epistemological stance.

The logic of a research strategy is embedded in the links between all the above factors.

SOURCE: Derived from Burrell and Morgan (1979), Morgan (1980), and Morgan and Smircich (1980)

Figure 2.1 A Framework for Analyzing the Logics of Different Research Strategies

points in time, and longitudinal analysis to understand the processes through which structure changes over time. In the analysis of both structure and process, emphasis is placed on the need to produce generalizations about the nature of the empirical world, based as far as possible on the use of replicable methods of observation and measurement. In this way Derek Pugh's logic of research advances the positivist's aim of building a stock of quasi-objective knowledge that specifies the laws, regularities, and relationships between social phenomenon conceptualized and measured as networks of social facts.

Identifying and studying configurations. Chapter 4, by Danny Miller and Henry Mintzberg, builds on similar ontological premises regarding the nature of the social world. Organizations are viewed as concrete empirical phenomena, changing over time as a result of patterns of interdependence between different elements within the organization and between organization and environment. Their view of organization, like Pugh's, draws on an open systems perspective.

The distinguishing yet complementary characteristic of the Miller and Mintzberg chapter stems from the idea that there are different types or species of organization, which share common, nonrandom, internally homogeneous clusterings of organizational attributes. They suggest that the different types can be identified and studied as gestalts, or configurations of organizational variables, that cohere in logical, predictable, and mutually defining ways to generate distinctive organizational states, situations, processes, and modes of transition.

Considerable attention is devoted to the epistemological implications of this view. It is suggested that if there are different configurations of organizational attributes, then research must be oriented toward understanding the internal logic and consistency of the networks of mutual causality that define these configurations. This calls for a style of research that is as much concerned with synthesis (i.e., of understanding holistically) as it is with analysis (i.e., of understanding in terms of parts and relationships between parts). As a result, the authors argue for research that balances the kind of aesthetic insight required to interpret a work of art with the traditional positivist concern for a science that allows us to predict empirical relationships.

Miller and Mintzberg also use the idea of configuration to emphasize the dangers of overgeneralization in organizational research. In particular, they show how the existence of different types of organization makes a search for universal or widely based causal relationships between narrow sets of variables unrealistic. Such studies run the danger of mixing the characteristics of different configurations and of ignoring their logics. Because of these problems, they suggest that the development of taxonomies that distinguish among configurations provides an essential basis for effective organization theory and research.

Quasi-Experimentation. In Chapter 5, Tom Cook examines the logic of quasi-experimentation, a research strategy designed to investigate causal relationships in situations in which the methods of classical experimentation are inappropriate or difficult to apply. As Cook argues, the use of experimentation in social research has traditionally been based on models and methods derived from physics and chemistry, which because of their "closed" nature, are inappropriate for studying the "open systems" found in social life. The limitations of experimental method, particularly for studying phenomena where there may be spontaneous change and maturation over extended periods of time, or where the meaning and significance of a phenomenon is intimately tied to context, provide the rationale for quasi-experimentation as a mode of field research that adapts aspects of the experimental method for the study of open systems.

As Cook argues, quasi-experimentation has, for the most part, developed on the basis of an ontology that reflects its origins in agricultural research. This ontology presumes that we live in a world of real objects and relationships that are lawfully interrelated by a force called *causation*. It follows from these assumptions that we can use experiments and quasi-experiments to discover these lawful relationships. However, Cook is cautious about using the notion of cause to explain these relationships, for no matter how much we observe empirical regularity in the world, we can never be sure that covariation signifies causation. In addition, as most researchers now recognize, in open systems we typically find configurations of multiple interdependencies rather than discrete linear relations, which makes the notion of causation problematic. As Wilden (1972: 39) has suggested, there are always causes that cause causes to cause causes. Given these considerations, Cook offers quasi-experimentation as a method for studying and probing empirical relations in a way that may generate useful, yet always tentative, knowledge and explanations about relations in social life. Whereas the emphasis in traditional experimental and quasi-experimental research has been on a search for explanations that provide a basis for effective prediction and control, Cook's objectives for research are more modest. Adopting an epistemological position that has much in common with the pragmatist view that knowledge is primarily of significance because of its action consequences, he argues in favor of using quasi-experimentation to obtain knowledge about relationships that can be manipulated and changed.

Action research. The idea that knowledge should be judged with reference to criteria based on action and usefulness is explored further in the research strategy presented in Chapter 6. Here, Gerald

Susman sets out the rationale for "action research," which attempts to combine the practical concerns of people in problem situations with the goals of social science. The aim is to link knowledge, action, and its practical consequences in a way that allows generalization beyond the immediate situation in which such action occurs. In this way, action research attempts to link theory and practice, thinking and doing, in a mode of inquiry that is both practical and scientific.

Susman builds from the idea that though we live in a world of real events and things, we can only know that world through the mediation of language and conceptual frameworks that are historically and culturally specific. As a result, all knowledge and understanding is necessarily partial, tentative, and indirect. This epistemological position is used to provide the rationale for action research as a mode of inquiry that starts by advocating certain models and beliefs as a framework for dealing with a problematic aspect of reality, uses observation and reasoning to draw out the consequences of this framework of analysis, and then proceeds to test it through action designed to see whether the anticipated consequences ensue. Knowledge is gained and refined by acting on beliefs, observing consequences, and redefining beliefs in light of consequences. The approach thus harnesses aspects of experimental methodology within a problem-solving approach to test the appropriateness of specific models and beliefs. The aim is not to arrive at a set of models and beliefs that correspond with reality; rather, it is to find a set that provides tools for dealing with reality. The action research perspective thus appeals to a philosophy of knowledge that has more in common with pragmatism than it does with positivism. Knowledge is viewed as a means of "coming to terms" with the world, rather than as a means of representing or creating the world.

Since action research sets out to test the action consequences of the premises from which it starts, it is clear that different theoretical frameworks can provide different starting points. In order to provide a concrete illustration, Susman adopts the premises of sociotechnical systems theory and illustrates how action research proceeds through an interactive cycle of diagnosis, action planning, action taking, evaluation, and the specification of learning. The approach illustrates how action research starts and ends in a concrete setting, transforming that setting in accordance with the conceptual frameworks that are used to represent the situation and problem that provide the focus for study.

Organizational learning. In Chapter 7, Donald Schön outlines a research strategy designed to investigate organizations as learning systems. Learning at both individual and collective levels is characterized as a process that continually changes in response to self-observation of performance, materials, tools, and context of operations, guided by values and norms embedded in purposes. His analysis draws on a cybernetic perspective that views values and norms as reference points for a continuous process of error detection and correction, which provides a basis for "organizing" and for regulated activity as an outcome. Two kinds of learning are identified: "single loop" and "double loop." In the former, action strategies are changed to accommodate system errors, but the norms that guide and regulate the system remain intact. In the latter, the norms are questioned and changed, so that the system operates with reference to different ground assumptions. The most significant kinds of organizational learning always involve a change in theory in use mediated by some form of inquiry.

This conception of organizational learning provides the basis for a research strategy that attempts to investigate systematically the relationship between successive states of theory in use and the modes of inquiry that bring such changes about. This includes a variety of empirical research methods involving the observation of practice, the reconstruction of organizational history, the exploration of how people think about their activities, and investigation of the general relationship between theory and practice in any given situation. The concern is with tracing the pattern of thinking, inquiry, and action that gives rise to organizational change and to determine the quality of inquiry adopted.

Interpretive interactionism. In Chapter 8, Norman Denzin outlines the logic of a research strategy based on the idea that human beings construct and organize their everyday life through intertwined streams of consciousness — phenomenological and interactional. Humans are seen as reflexive, intentional actors, constructing and reconstructing a world rich in meaning, motive, emotion, and feeling through interaction with others. They draw on structures of experience crystalized in linguistic, economic, political, and other social practices that at times are taken for granted, and at others, are made problematic. These practices provide frames of experience against which ongoing activity can be mobilized and made sensible through symbolic actions and interactions that are simultaneously individual and social. Personal and social history are seen as intertwined, unfolding as a result of actions that situate a person in a lived world that is in effect made by them, yet is not entirely of their own making. In this way social life combines the dimensions of self and other, intentional action and social constraint, to produce social relations that manifest themselves as recurring structural forms.

Denzin develops this view of social life to argue that social science should be concerned with providing interpretive reports of the way phenomenological and interactional processes combine in "constitutive practices" that make the world both meaningful and understandable to those involved in those practices. The task of social analysis becomes one of presenting and interpreting life as a sequence of symbolic interaction, in a way that shows precisely *how* individuals express and construct their presence in the world. The only facticity that interpretive inquiry can presuppose is the individual's presence in the lived world. Analysis must proceed from there, to show how every slice of social life carries its own logic, sense of order, and structure of meaning.

As a consequence Denzin argues that the interpretive researcher must participate in, and use concepts that belong to, the situation being studied, in order to reveal its nature. The idea that generalization should be a goal of interpretive inquiry is rejected, as is the use of "second-order" analytical constructs. The approach must be to treat every human situation as novel, emergent, and filled with multiple and often contradictory meanings that cannot be understood through observation at a distance.

Life history methodology. In Chapter 9, Gareth Jones also explores the implications of a phenomenological approach to symbolic interaction using the concept of life history as a framework for analysis. Jones builds on the idea that the ability of human beings to act as competent members of a particular cultural milieu is acquired as part of an evolving life experience. We are born into a world that is rich in symbolic significance, but which remains inaccessible to us until we learn to enter, and relate to, it through communication with others. Like Denzin, Jones argues that the symbolic world serves as both resource and constraint — central for the process of communication and the full development of consciousness, yet also presenting the individual with what amounts to a previously constituted reality, which may exert a confining hold on the way individuals are able to express and develop themselves. Individuals are viewed as seeking to enter a world that is rational in the sense of being underwritten by a system of shared meaning, while seeking to use and shape that world for expressing and developing themselves.

This view of human action and development is used to justify an epistemology that suggests that understanding of the social world must be grounded in an understanding of the processes through which humans enter, sustain, and change their world by means of rational and expressive action. Jones argues that a life history methodology is particularly appropriate for this task since the way an individual learns to become a member of an organization, a profession, a family, or whatever is an episode in life history that can be understood in terms of the generic processes that define relations between humans and their world.

Life history methodology favors a qualitative style of research that attempts to build explanatory schemes from the experience, accounts, and reconstructions of those involved in the situations being studied. In line with its view of the tensions that exist between the expressive and rational aspects of human action, this method adopts a dialectical style of inquiry that deliberately explores the relation between the theoretical constructions brought to the research by the researcher, and those found in the situation being studied. The aim of analysis is to arrive at an effective interpretation that recognizes the tensions between competing interpretations, and that no one construction is likely to be right or wrong — merely better or worse than others.

Studying organizations as cultures. In Chapter 10, Linda Smircich approaches the study of social organization by focusing on how individuals create and use shared modes of interpretation as a basis for unified action. Her thesis is that organized activity depends on shared meaning and that the study of organization must reveal how this occurs. Adopting a phenomenological approach to symbolic interaction similar to that of Denzin and Jones, she is interested in studying the interpretive processes through which individuals frame and construct the significance of actions, events, words, concepts, and facts in ways that are always context specific. Meaning is always relational in that it depends as much on the context of interpretation as it does on the specific phenomenon to which meaning is assigned. Organized activity is seen as depending on the existence of shared schemes or contexts of interpretation, which allow actions to be aligned in a coherent way.

Smircich uses the image of "culture" as an epistemological device for marshaling the insights stemming from this perspective. As anthropologists have shown, different social cultures are held together as elaborate systems of meaning by individuals who construct and use language, ideology, myth, ritual, and other forms of symbolic action to forge patterns of collective activity that endure over time. Formal organization can be studied in similar terms, using the methods of interpretive anthropology to throw light on the coherent themes, or patterns of meaning, embedded in the symbolic actions that define the character of everyday organizational life.

The style of research required for this purpose is one of "empathic ethnography." An attempt is made to get inside the situation being studied and reconstruct it from the members' point of view. This calls for an open-ended, inductive approach to research, whereby the researcher consciously adopts the role of learner and attempts through observation, interview, and examination of documentary evidence to understand the shared and divergent patterns of meaning that underlie interactions.

Uncovering cognitive maps. The interpretive concern with understanding how humans construct and view their world is explored further by Michel Bougon. In Chapter 11 he develops an approach to research that specifically attempts to document human visions of reality in a way that minimizes the influence of the researcher on the research process. In an almost literal sense, his research strategy attempts to "get inside" the heads of other people in order to document how they see their world.

Bougon's approach is inspired by a concern with understanding how individuals transform day-to-day experience into knowledge. His explanation of this process develops an essentially behavioristic vision of the human as a locus of sense experience, but within the context of a phenomenological mode of interpretation stressing that humans ultimately construct their reality through "schema" that project specific form on that experience. These schema are viewed as pattern recognition devices, located in and sustained by the arrangement of neurons in the human cortex.

For Bougon, the locus of what humans experience as reality is thus found in the brain. Reality as experienced in everyday life is viewed as having no independent or external existence since, although rooted in sense data, it is ultimately shaped and made sensible through cognitive processes. Bougon's work systematically encourages us to link ideas and findings in the field of brain research with those of modern phenomenology, to create explanations of social reality that recognize that humans construct a social world through processes that are ultimately biological.

The importance Bougon places on the role of schema in the process of reality construction leads to his interest in the discovery of "cognitive maps." He suggests that it is possible to map the knowledge structures through which people enact their realities in a way that can contribute insight to many of the issues with which social researchers have traditionally been concerned. The problems of understanding structures of human motivation, of decoding how humans organize themselves on the basis of shared meaning, and of how configurations of reality are created, sustained, and changed can all be analyzed from this point of view.

Bougon's suggestion that social researchers should study cognitive maps poses an intriguing question. How can the researcher discover what is inside the head of another person without influencing what he or she discovers? The research process runs the risk of contamination because the researcher's own cognitive map may influence what is discovered and how it is interpreted. Bougon presents a solution to this problem in the form a "self-Q" technique that essentially attempts to pass control of the research process from the researcher to the person being researched. The research "subject" is invited to ask him- or herself questions regarding the phenomenon to be investigated. In posing these questions, elements of the person's cognitive map are revealed and documented by the very person being researched. The research technique uses the idea of "projection" as a means of studying how human beings project, externalize, and structure their everyday realities.

Reading organization. One of the prominent themes in modern social thought focuses on the idea that social life can be viewed as a form of language or text, to be interpreted and understood in terms of some underlying structure or network of rules. In Chapter 12, Steve Turner explores the implications of one such perspective, using the ideas of Lévi-Strauss and Jacques Derrida as a point of departure. The basic premise underlying his chapter is that human beings strive continually to bridge the gulf that exists between the realm of subjective mind and the external world, and do so through various kinds of social constructions, or enactments, that are mythological in character. In Lévi-Strauss's view, these myths follow a common pattern in a wide variety of different settings, for the structuring of reality they present is as much a product of the generative capacities of the human mind as it is of the external world to which they relate. Our myths represent the real, but never grasp it, since we never succeed in entering the external world on its own terms.

These ideas point toward the potential of an interpretive social science concerned with analyzing or reading social life as myth. This encourages us to understand how people "read" and make sense of their lives in ways that are meaningful to them, and how the social scientist is engaged merely in generating yet other readings of the situations studied. These different readings may be interesting and useful but may have no ultimate claim to special authority. They are simply different orderings of a "reality" that can always be read in many different ways. This approach for understanding and analyzing social life can be described as "structuralist" in the sense that it attempts to discover an underlying order in human affairs. However, it is a structuralism that emphasizes that "structure" emanates from the human mind and that the ordering of reality that it produces is but one among many possible orderings.

In developing his approach to structuralism, Turner focuses attention on the idea that we can always read social organization in a way that relates the surface detail to an intelligible whole. In this process, the concepts, accounts, and explanations of members of a situation are treated as fragments of a wider, more comprehensive mythic structure of the total situation, but they are not allowed to dominate analysis. In this, Turner differs from interpretive social scientists who limit their task to revealing situations from members' points of view, since he argues that analysis must systematically attempt to avoid being trapped by the preconceptions that underlie such accounts.

Organization as otherness. In Chapter 13, Robert Cooper develops an approach to social analysis that treats all human organization as an expression of "otherness." His essay investigates how human beings organize their everyday world through the "other" — a dialectical structure of "in-one-anotherness" in which one aspect of experience is always mediated by another. For Cooper, the other is a basic ontological form. Indeed, it is identified as *the* form that organizes human experience.

Cooper's essay is best understood as an exercise in structural phenomenology. His argument seeks to reveal the genesis of organization in an archetypal mode of consciousness that structures experience through a process involving simultaneous conjunction and disjunction. For example, we recognize a page in this volume as a "page" through a process that recognizes two sides that are simultaneously joined, yet stand apart. The page is recognized as a page by creating fixed points of reference in a reversible structure. The page expresses the logic of otherness in that the sides of the page are "in one another." The recognition of one side exists only in relation to the other.

Cooper argues that the dialectical logic of this process, formulated in the concept of "other," provides a key for decoding the underlying structure of all aspects of social life. The other is, in effect, viewed as a latent organizing principle to which the details of human life lend manifest, visible form. Cooper argues that much of the work of social theorists such as Freud, Heidegger, Lacan, Lévi-Strauss, G. H. Mead, and Merleau-Ponty illustrates how the other operates as a basic structure of experience, shaping the realms of conscious and unconscious mind, symbolic interaction, human communication, and linguistic and social structure.

This line of reasoning suggests that social analysis should follow the logic of "otherness." If the world of human organization is constructed through the other, then the other provides an obvious methodology through which it can be deconstructed or analyzed. In effect, Cooper advocates an approach to social analysis that parallels M. C. Escher's approach to art. The analogy of an Escher lithograph such as *Ascending and Descending* (1960) or *Waterfall* (1961), or the wood engraving *Mobius Strip* (1961), which presents aspects of everyday reality in terms of a circular structure of relations that return to their point of origin, illustrates the logic of Cooper's approach to social analysis well. The other, as a method of analysis, seeks to break free of the fixed perspectives in social science that punctuate reality into a series of discrete, linear, relations.

This approach to social analysis has concrete implications for the way we conceptualize organization as a phenomenon. Organization emerges as a process characterized by otherness, which assumes a fixed empirical or literal form, only when human beings attempt to fix reality in a way that banishes self-contradiction and inconsistency. The structure thus produced is always but an expression of otherness, and thus always part of a wider structure of relations.

Dramatism and demystification. In Chapter 14, Iain Mangham and Michael Overington explore the implications of dramatism as a metaphor for social analysis. Their argument builds on the premise that human beings are actors who play characters, and that social life is theater. This characterization defines a basic ontology that suggests that human beings are works of dramatic art, and their actions intelligible in terms of a dramatistic pentad (Burke, 1969a) defining relations between act, scene, agent, agency, and purpose. This means that human action is based on a motivational structure that integrates what is done, when or where, who does it, how, and why. This pentad is viewed as defining fundamental dimensions of human existence, in that we, as reflexive human actors, are capable of being aware of our acting and the relations that exist among the elements of the pentad in our daily lives. Life is thus theater in the fullest sense. We realize our lives through action that is inherently dramatic — not in a superficial sense that suggests that we have a choice as to whether we engage in role playing or impression management, but in an existential sense that suggests that, of necessity, we manage ourselves by means of a theatrical consciousness that is aware of, and preserves a distinction between, ourselves and our roles. Life *is* theater, in the tradition pioneered by Evreinoff (1927) and Pirandello (1952). Theater as we know it in its modern institutionalized sense is but a reflection and model of reality, rather than a departure from it.

Mangham and Overington develop the ideas of Berthold Brecht to suggest that, like visitors to a theater, we can become compliant, uncritical participants and audiences in the drama of everyday life.

This is characterized as a state of "mystification," in which we become preoccupied or hypnotized by a particular element of the pentad (e.g., by the power of situations [scenes], methods [agency], and so on) so that we are blind to what is happening and to alternative courses of action. In order to overcome such mystification it is necessary for participants in a situation to develop a critical consciousness that demystifies through awareness of the relationships among elements of the pentad defining that situation.

Dramatism thus provides an epistemology and method for social analysis, suggesting that all explanations of human action must take account of relations between *all* elements of the pentad and that social analysis should be primarily concerned with demystification. The metaphor is offered as a means of stripping what is familiar and taken for granted of its naturalness, so that it can be seen and understood as expressing a particular relation among elements of the pentad.

Critical organization theory. In Chapter 15, John Forester examines the implications of Jürgen Habermas's approach to "critical theory" for studying organization. He builds his analysis on the ontological assumption that the basis of human society is grounded in the process of communicative interaction — the ability of human beings to reflect on themselves and others and to engage in various forms of discourse as a means of "making sense together." Forester argues that this process of communicative interaction, and the social setting in which it occurs, may be subject to systematic distortions that deceive, mislead, manipulate, or mystify those involved in communicative interaction.

This mode of analysis has important implications for the study of organization since certain organizational arrangements may systematically hinder members' involvement in free and open discourse by distorting their ability to check the truth, legitimacy, sincerity, or clarity claims made on them in everyday organizational life. His analysis encourages us to reformulate our understanding of organization in a way that emphasizes its moral and political significance. In the true tradition of critical theory, it invites us to examine routine aspects of daily life that are typically taken for granted and to understand their role in producing and reproducing a pattern of social life that runs counter to the ideal of a democratic society in which humans have free and equal opportunity to shape their lives together.

This research perspective calls for the use of various interpretive research methodologies to analyze the social construction of power relationships, together with more structural modes of analysis to reveal the nature of the social, political, and economic contexts within which such activities are set. The distinctive nature of the research strategy in practice stems from the critical stance from which such techniques are used. Whereas much phenomenological and structuralist research is content to understand the construction of social life, critical theory is firmly committed to providing a thorough-going critique of the distortions that characterize such constructions. The point is not only to understand the nature of social life, but to change it.

A counterstructure for social research. The idea that human beings may be dominated by processes of distorted communication is further explored in Chapter 16. Here, Tom Wilson focuses on the relationship between social scientists and their subjects, arguing that the structure and methods of contemporary research systematically repress and distort the possibility of achieving free and "open" inquiry, and advocating an alternative structure for the conduct of research.

Wilson builds his argument on the view that as a form of social interaction, social science reflects and reproduces the bureaucratic-meritocratic mode of rational domination that characterizes the advanced societies. He argues that while the ideas of "rationality" and "domination" have traditionally been seen as opposing notions, modern bureaucratic and meritocratic organization structures have increasingly attempted to fuse them in a way that institutionalizes "reason" and "knowledge" as a basis of authority and rule. The institutions and methods of modern social science provide preeminent examples of this process in action, where the values of professionalism and scientism are joined together in a formal quest for "knowledge," which, in reality, turns out to be a means for expressing and sustaining hierarchical domination. Wilson argues that this structure of domination is evident in the way social science practice enacts a division of labour between researcher and researched, in a relationship that is either exploitative or "caretaking" in nature. Research practice typically assumes that the researcher has a greater capacity for reason and/or access to knowledge than do those being researched, and that research subjects can be treated as "objects" of investigation. Wilson argues that the net effect is to create a pattern of repressed and distorted communication in which the researcher can engage more or less unchallenged in a social science that serves the needs of the status quo. The "anti-method" proposed by Wilson deliberately seeks to subvert this practice in a way that will help establish a less-distorted, more open mode of research that offers the possibility of merging nonviolent and incremental processes of interaction with significant social change.

Feminist methodology. In Chapter 17, Lynda Glennon challenges the dualism that underlies many modern conceptions of gender to advocate a dialectical approach to research that can provide a basis for securing radical social change. Glennon argues that the conventional distinctions between male and female are socially constructed ones, reflecting and sustaining the dualistic mode of thinking that has become a feature of our age. In almost every sphere of life, this dualism renders understanding and action possibilities in a binary fashion placing an emphasis on *either/or*. Glennon argues that this has often been the case within the feminist movement, which often adopts dualistic solutions to the problems observed. Thus feminists often find themselves taking stands on gender issues that reinforce distinctions between male and female. Of the four kinds of feminism identified in her chapter, Glennon advocates a "synthesism," which strives to achieve a dialectical interplay between the attributes now typically polarized as male and female.

Developed as a research strategy, synthesism replaces the dualism that separates fact from value, objective and subjective, logic and intuition, researcher and researched, with an action-based approach that attempts to transform as well as understand the situations being studied. Within the context of feminist concerns, for example, the aim and style of research focuses on the need to challenge and reorient the dualistic thinking sustaining conceptions of male and female, work and leisure, and the rational and expressive aspects of human activity generally. The concern is with treating these binary constructions as constructions rather than as ontological givens and to demonstrate how understanding and action can be reformulated in a way that transcends the constraints that such dualism creates.

Glennon's chapter calls, in effect, for a restructuring of thought, knowledge, and action in accord with the dialectical nature and values of synthesism and outlines the elements of a research strategy for moving towards this end. While developed and presented within the context of debates within feminism, its relevance is by no means confined to problems and issues falling within this domain.

Initiating collaborative inquiry. In Chapter 18, Bill Torbert outlines a research strategy concerned with using and enhancing the self-transforming capacities of human beings in a process of institutional self-study. His argument builds on the premise that the essence of human being rests in a capacity for intentional action that can attend to four territories of experience simultaneously: (a) the visible, outside world, (b) one's own action as sensed by oneself, (c) the process of thinking or mapping one's world, and (d) the attention that can focus on any of the other three territories, or encompass all, including itself, at once. In much of modern life the attention given to each of these four territories is very uneven and at times nonexistent. For example, individuals may be held in awe by the realm of objective facts or be preoccupied with a process of subjective introspection.

Bureaucratic institutions draw firm distinctions between what is public and private and foster instrumental patterns of thought and action that link subject and object worlds in a narrow manner. Traditional approaches to science build on a similar dualism, attempting to link thought and empirical reality, but ignoring the other relevant territories of experience. As a result, our knowledge and experience of the world is fragmented and channeled in narrow and confining ways.

Torbert argues that it is possible to develop an integrated mode of being, knowing, and doing that is able to attend to the four territories of experience and deal with their incongruities in a way that links intuition, theory, practice, and effects. In so doing, humans are able to develop their capacity to engage in intentional, constitutive actions that shape and change themselves and their social context. In this way, Bill Torbert develops the implications of a critical, phenomenological approach for understanding human action to provide the basis for a process of self-study, which, when applied in a context of collaborative inquiry, sets the basis for an effective system of individual, group, and organizational development. Theory and practice are united in a form of action-learning relevant to every aspect of social life.

Organization as transformation. The idea that individuals have a capacity for reflective self-transformation is further explored in Chapter 19, in which Orion White and Cynthia McSwain outline the elements of a transformational approach to social analysis. Their argument builds on the premise that all aspects of social life are manifestations of the unconscious. Drawing on the work of Carl Jung, they argue that human beings are representations of both a physical and psychological reality, physical energy being transformed into patterns of physical growth and development, and psychic energy into patterns of spiritual and social development. Institutionalized social structure, ongoing social relations, as well as patterns of thought and individual action, are viewed as projections or analogues of the unconscious mind. White and McSwain believe that the course of individual and social development is much influenced by our ability to deal with this realization and to influence the process whereby unconscious energy is transformed into different facets of social life.

It follows from this perspective that in our search for knowledge, we evoke significant images of reality rather than grasp or represent a reality in any absolute sense. Anything that evokes or is "interesting" thus stands as a form of knowledge, for interest draws energy from the unconscious and is significant in itself.

White and McSwain argue that the transformational approach to research suggests a "conservative anarchism" in relation to methodology, in that any method of interest to the researcher has a role to play in research. The crucial methodological consideration concerns the stance or posture adopted by the researcher; it should allow reflection on the nature and significance of the way the research is being constructed so that the research design can evolve in the light of experience. In effect, the transformational perspective invites social researchers to continue in the practices in which they are engaged but to adopt a mode of involvement that stands to traditional research practice, as Zen archery stands to the instrumental use of a bow and arrow for the purpose of hitting a target. White and McSwain suggest that research attitudes that are open to recognizing the influence of the unconscious on research practice will themselves lead to new modes of perception that allow us to address and reconstitute our understanding of issues, permitting us to deal with their genesis in the unconscious.

Organization and praxis. In Chapter 20, Wolf Heydebrand addresses the issue of transformation from a Marxian perspective. His analysis builds on the view of social reality as a concrete process of historical emergence, in which human activity continuously produces and reproduces the material, social, and cultural world. The organizational relations of production and reproduction are understood as a concrete dialectical totality or unified whole, described by Marx (1904: 293) as "a combination of many objects with different destinations, i.e., a unity of diverse elements." Although reality as objective historical existence can be represented subjectively in symbolic form, this does not mean that subject and object worlds exist as separate realms. The objective world is internalized in the subjective reality of individuals, just as the subjective reality underlying human action influences the way objective reality is shaped. In a similar way, the present and future are always interdependent with the past, in the sense that humans create their present and future under conditions created in the past. The concept of totality attempts to grasp this spatiotemporal wholeness or, to use Cooper's phrase (Chapter 13), state of in-one-anotherness. Society is not just an assemblage of individuals or parts — it is a totality that comprises various contradictory tendencies in a historically specific form.

The concept of totality provides a unique perspective for understanding the process of innovation and social change. It now becomes possible to distinguish between innovations that rearrange the structure of relations within a given totality and innovations that transform the totality itself. It is this latter kind of change that Heydebrand characterizes as "praxis" — a process in which humans collectively attempt to overcome resistance and engage in mutual transformation of subject and object — self and other — to bring into being a completely new structure of relations: a new totality.

Heydebrand argues that the capacity for praxis as collective self-transformation is rooted in the capacity for symbolic interaction that allows humans to recognize the constraints under which they live and mobilize action designed to change these constraints. The capacity for symbolic interaction is seen as a potential capacity for self-organization that seeks to minimize external domination in favor of self-determination. Whether this capacity is realized in practice depends in large part on the process of ideological struggle through which human beings become aware of their place in history and their role in producing themselves and the social arrangements under which they live.

Epistemologically, this perspective suggests that praxis, as a form of knowledge or consciousness, contains within itself and transcends three other broad forms of knowledge: subjectivism, objectivism, and criticism. It is a knowledge that embraces relations between subject and object, theory and practice, and thought and action within a transformational process that allows humans to engage and change their reality and themselves through understanding, explanation, and critique.

Heydebrand's view of praxis generates a methodology for the study of organization that embraces historical, dialectical, interpretive, and critical modes of inquiry, and in which the role of analyst is merged with that of political actor, since the researcher becomes actively concerned with identifying and advocating strategies for change that facilitate the emergence of capacities for self-organization and transformation. Heydebrand illustrates this approach in relation to his studies of the U.S. judicial system, where competing professional and bureaucratic strategies of reform set the basis for an emergent form of organization that may supersede these older forms.

Toward a realist perspective. In Chapter 21, William Outhwaite presents the elements of an approach to social analysis based on the conception of a "realist" philosophy of science that distinguishes among three domains of reality — the empirical, the actual, and the real. The thrust of his analysis is to suggest that our reality is shaped by causal tendencies or generative mechanisms in the domain of the real, and that the domains of the actual and empirical are, in effect, realized tendencies that lend specific form to processes in this other domain.

This view challenges scientific explanations provided by positivist science, arguing that in conducting experiments or empirical surveys, positivists are often merely searching for correlations and laws without any real insight or explanation as to why these events occur. In a similar way, the interpretive researcher who focuses on the social construction of reality often confines attention to superficial and abstract study of the surface of reality, as manifested in consciousness. Both approaches are viewed as seriously lacking in that they fail to explain reality as the manifestation of a complex, deep structure of relations. The "real" nature of these relations may never be evident or realized, but it nonetheless exists, such as when the underlying nature of a situation is disguised by oppositional tendencies that give a surface appearance of stability, rather than one of contradictory pressures for change. From the realist perspective the task of social analysis becomes one of transcending empiricism of both positivist and interpretive persuasion and of explaining reality as the realization or manifestation of a particular network of tendencies and counter-tendencies.

Outhwaite offers a realist strategy for decoding the deep structure of relations that account for a particular phenomenon by focusing on what he describes as a "real definition." This involves attempting to formulate a conception of the way an object is determined by its internal and external relations, as an outcome of interacting tendencies. The surface, "empirical" manifestation of the phenomenon as an entity, or the way it is interpreted and defined in conventional practice, may provide a starting point for this analysis, but no more. The task of analysis must be to explore and explain the tendencies that produce and reproduce the phenomenon as an empirical reality. Outhwaite offers a number of criteria for assessing the validity of the real definitions thus produced, and refers to illustrations of the kind of analysis he has in mind such as in Marx's work on political economy.

A dialectical method for organizational analysis. In Chapter 22, Ken Benson outlines a method of studying organization based on Marxian dialectics. His approach, similar to that of Wolf Heydebrand, is based on the view that the core human activity is productive activity, arguing that human beings produce a world and are in turn produced by it. This process of production is both social and material in that we construct or enact a social world within the context of a material reality that has assumed determinate form as a result of a particular pattern of social history. The ideas, shared meanings, and concrete practices of human beings are all interrelated. They are not dichotomized elements of a world comprising realms of a subjective or objective reality so much as expressions or manifestations of a mode of social organization. Benson sees the dominant mode of social organization as stemming from core practices associated with the production of material goods; changes in these core practices reverberate in their effects throughout the total social formation.

It is thus appropriate to view society at a given point in time as expressing a particular stage in the development of a mode of social organization. Marxian dialectics suggests that this process of historical development can best be understood in terms of an interplay between tendencies and countertendencies generated within the social formation. The tendencies within a mode of social organization are organizing principles that realize themselves in specific kinds of human practice and discourse. They encourage a social formation to develop in predictable directions so long as core aspects of the underlying structure remain in place. However, these developments eventually generate countertendencies, or "contradictions," that threaten the character and existence of the mode of social organization. As Benson shows, these contradictions are of major importance in explaining patterns of development and change since they force a continuing reorganization of the totality. Many social changes arise as piecemeal attempts to sustain the underlying structure of relations in response to the existence of contradictions within a social system. They are, in effect, changes that serve to sustain the status quo. Other, more revolutionary changes occur when the contradictions cannot be contained within the bounds of a particular mode of social organization in this way.

It follows from this dialectical view of social reality that any attempt to understand the workings of a social system must be concerned with relations as a totality. The primary epistemological task becomes one of understanding the core tendencies or organizing principles, their principal contradictions, and how the interplay between them becomes manifest in particular configurations of social practice. Benson's chapter implements important aspects of the realist research strategy discussed by Outhwaite in Chapter 21 and provides a methodology that supplements that offered by Heydebrand in Chapter 20. Benson's dialectical method serves the cause of "praxis" because it can help identify the contradictions that make change probable thus making analysis a tool for guiding emancipatory action.

Class analysis. In Chapter 23, Mino Carchedi develops a Marxian research strategy that uses a materialistic interpretation of the dialectical method as a basis for "class analysis." Like Benson and

Heydebrand, Carchedi starts from the premise that the core human activity is productive activity. He argues that to live and reproduce, people must transform reality, and first of all, material reality. This is achieved through a social division of labor that defines relations among human beings and with the means of production. These "production relations" can be identified as "class relations." Under capitalism, these class relations are antagonistic because they unite, in mutual dependence, struggle, and domination, two antagonistic poles variously characterized as a relation between owners of the means of production and nonowners, exploiters of surplus value and exploited, nonlaborers and laborers. The process of transforming material reality is characterized by a struggle between these opposing forces through which one class attempts to dominate and control the other as a means of producing and reproducing a given mode of social organization and material life.

For Carchedi, an understanding of classes, as expressions or carriers of structural relations, is essential for understanding the nature and significance of knowledge. He argues that all knowledge is class knowledge; it is determined by the place one occupies in the productive process. Both theoretical and practical knowledge stem from transformation of, and one's relations with, the material world. Hence Carchedi's position of nonreflective materialism. Knowledge is not just a reflection of the material world in thought; it is a particular kind of mental transformation of that reality, determined by one's relation with that reality. Since different people occupy different positions in relation to the process of material transformation, there is a basis for different kinds of knowledge. Hence Carchedi's view that the multiple perspectives and world views that lay claim to knowledge must be understood as class-based renderings of reality. Knowledge is produced by and for classes, and like those classes, exists in a struggle for domination. Knowledge is thus in the most fundamental sense "ideological" in that it formulates views of reality and solves problems from class points of view.

Carchedi rejects the idea that it is possible to verify knowledge in an absolute sense through comparison with socially neutral theories or data, but recognizes that there is the possibility of producing a "correct" knowledge from a class standpoint. For example, in line with Marx's own analysis, Carchedi argues that the dominated class is uniquely placed to obtain an objectively "correct" knowledge of social reality and its contradictions. It is the class with the most direct and widest access to the process of material transformation that ultimately produces and reproduces that reality.

It follows from Carchedi's analysis that the social scientist as a producer of class-based knowledge is always a part of the class struggle. Recognizing this, Carchedi advocates using dialectical analysis as a particular means of formulating knowledge from the standpoint of the dominated class — the proletariat — to foster social change.

Like the approaches advocated by Heydebrand, Outhwaite, and Benson, Carchedi's model of dialectical analysis suggests that inquiry should proceed in a way that unravels the relations between elements of a totality to demonstrate how tendencies acquire specific empirical form and to understand the role of specific aspects of empirical reality in the reproduction and change of the totality. Like all the other research strategies in this volume, the model generates a distinctive kind of analytical insight that shapes our understanding of the phenomenon being studied in theoretical and empirical terms. Carchedi's chapter is in itself an exercise in dialectical thinking since his writing and manner of exposition implement the logic of his mode of analysis.

DEALING WITH DIFFERENCE

The reader may well feel boggled by the degree of contrariness and range of issues that are raised in the above review. In my experience this effect grows slowly at first, but eventually overwhelms as the "difference" accumulates. Such diversity begs further simplification and classification in order to make it more manageable and to provide an easy route to understanding. However, this temptation must be resisted, since it will counter one of our main purposes. Classification and simplification can aid understanding, but if interpreted too literally, they exert a confining or diversionary hold on imagination as interest in the classificatory "map" replaces interest in the "territory." Our purpose in this volume is to analyze research strategies in a way that moves us "beyond method," so that we can consider the logics of engagement that link researcher and researched. This also requires that we move "beyond classification," to focus as much attention as possible on the nature of the constitutive processes that characterize research, rather than on the labels used to denote similarities and differences among them.

Our first response to the diversity reflected in the different research strategies should simply be to understand it by decoding the logic and significance of the different points of view. With this understanding, we will be well equipped to address the intriguing issues and problems that this diversity poses and to appreciate the contributions that different strategies can make to social research. The concluding chapters of this work address this task, inviting "conversation" about the themes that unite and separate the various strategies, and about the issues they raise.

— II —

THE RESEARCH STRATEGIES

3

STUDYING ORGANIZATIONAL STRUCTURE AND PROCESS

Derek S. Pugh

The Open University

I am an unreconstructed positivist. It is almost inevitable that this should be so, when we consider my early conditioning. I specialized in science at high school and studied psychology in college at a time (the late forties) when the high-status role model was Clark L. Hull. I never took to Hull, and preferred the much lower status Kurt Lewin, primarily on the grounds that my interest in psychology was as the study of the behavior of humans, not of white rats. I now feel that Hull's attempts to generalize had a greater impact on me than I realized.

I was fortunate in being at a university — Edinburgh — that regarded the fledgling science of psychology as having so recently moved out from under the wing of philosophy that we were all required to take several courses in logic and metaphysics. Thus I had a good grounding in epistemology and even flirted with solipsism — as befits someone learning his philosophy on the same benches as did David Hume.

I eventually came to the conclusion that whatever view I took on the philosophical issues as such, the fact was that in order to pursue

Material included in this chapter excerpted from "The Aston Programme of Research," in A. Van de Ven and W. Joyce (eds.) *Perspectives on Organization Design and Behavior* (New York: John Wiley), pp. 135-140 reprinted by permission. Copyright © 1981 by John Wiley and Sons, Inc.

any substantive study I would need to assume a realist, determinist, positivist approach. Otherwise I would be condemned to spend my time on the metaphysics, without getting round to the physics, or, in my case, to the social psychology. This is still my view.

I work in what Burrell and Morgan (1979) have described as the functionalist paradigm, for the very pragmatic reason that this is the only way I can see of contributing to my substantive discipline — organizational behavior — which I define as the study of the structure and functioning of organizations and the behavior of groups and individuals within them. I do not see how one can study organizational behavior (OB) without making the ontological assumption that people and organizations exist as relatively concrete entities (It *is* after all only an assumption — I have already confessed to being, like Hume himself, a closet solopsist). Otherwise, one can only contribute to what I will call meta-OB (by analogy with metaphysics) on the issue of whether and in what way organizations exist, as do the interpretive theorists. The answer to this question is largely irrelevant to OB, for it involves what Gilbert Ryle would call a "category error." It is all very well for a nuclear physicist to see a materials engineer looking at a steel bar and to tell him: "That's really a series of pulsating energy waves." But the engineer might fairly reply, "I was calculating the stresses and strains to see how it holds up the roof." The nuclear physicist's comment is irrelevant to the task at hand. So too in relation to the practice of OB. It is all very well for theorists to question the ontological status of organization, but it does not advance the functionalist aim of conducting research that increases our knowledge of the way organizations are structured and the way individuals and groups behave. Functionalist theorists may be able to learn something from theorists working in other paradigms and use it for their own purposes of understanding organizations. But they must not be deflected from the main task of furthering their own specific discipline. I always find it strange when sociologists say, in an accusatory way, of those of us working on the "Aston approach" that we only use a part of Weber's ideas and take them out of his context anyway. Well, of course — we are not in the business of developing Weber, but of drawing from him and many others to fashion our own approach to our particular subject of study. Ideas are not diminished if only part is taken — the whole still remains if others wish to build on that. I regard the openness of the functionalist paradigm, and the willingness of its practitioners to draw on (steal?) concepts from other approaches, as a strength.

SIX PRIOR PHILSOSPHICAL BELIEFS

My view as to the nature of acceptable OB research is based on the following assumptions.

The first concerns *metaphysics*. While I accept that what we normally call "data" (i.e., givens) should more appropriately be called "capta" (i.e., takens), I have a prior ontological belief that the OB universe is replete with regularities and a prior epistemological belief that we can manipulate our concepts so that the relevant data/capta expose these. This "appeal to data" is fundamental to the enterprise. The data must be communicable and objective, and I would define objectivity, using a coherence theory of truth, as long-run intersubjective agreement.

The second assumption concerns *ethics*. While I accept that our values affect what we choose to study, and how we develop our concepts to study it, I believe that there is a separation between facts and values, and though facts are value related, they are not value determined. This assumption again underlies the "appeal to data."

These two assumptions lead to the development of a *conceptual framework* of analytical constructs that will be used to focus on and analyze the regularities of the presenting data. Thus, for example, we may be interested in studying the effects of "technology" on "role standardization" and, for the purposes of this analysis, treat the component parts of the framework as real. "Real," not in the sense that you can touch or hear role standardization (you cannot do that to an atomic particle either), but real in that information about the components of the framework can be obtained, relationships delineated, and predictions tested out. The objection that this conceptual approach involves reification and is therefore to be rejected (e.g., Silverman, 1970) seems to me to be mistaken in that it demonstrates a confusion about the ontological status of *any* conceptual or scientific framework — not just a social science one. As far as I am concerned, Hume has convincingly demonstrated that to believe that an other exists is just as much an unquestioned assumption (read "reification") as to believe that an organization exists. Those working in other paradigms may wish to make other assumptions, but the ontological status of these assumptions does not differ from that of the structural functionalist ones. Thus, we have to reify *something* if we are to move from metaphysics to organizational behavior, and this is a matter of research objectives and strategies, not of ontology.

The fourth assumption must therefore concern what is to be the *subject of study*. As stated earlier, I define "organizational behavior" as "the study of the structure and functioning of organizations and the behaviour of groups and individuals within them" (Pugh, 1966). It is a subdiscipline that draws on a variety of human and social science disciplines and interrelates them to illuminate the subject of study. The detailed research working out of this approach is explicated below. What I would emphasize here is my belief in the necessity of studying, and theorizing without regard to what have traditionally been considered discipline boundaries and of adopting an interdisciplinary approach. Thus environment, organization, groups, and individual behaviors should be studied in relation to one another. One of the basic contributions of systems theory is that it has shown the interrelation of the different levels within an overall conceptual approach. By emphasizing that any entity from a living cell to a whole society may be looked at in its own light as an open system or as a subsystem of a larger system that then becomes its environment (see, for example, von Bertalanffy, 1950; Miller, 1965), systems theory has enabled the construction a comprehensive interdisciplinary framework for the study of organizational behavior to be attempted.

The fifth assumption hinges on a distinction that I like to draw between *wisdom*, by which I mean a stock of insight, and *knowledge*, as a set of substantiated findings. Wisdom is much deeper and richer than knowledge is, but it is often riddled with superstition and incompatible beliefs and ideas. Knowledge, generated through systematic, comparative, replicative, scientific study of the empirical world, consists of generalizable propositions that give insight and/or have predictive powers when applied to phenomena other than those on which they are based. Our stock of knowledge is always partial and falls behind wisdom in its claims, but it is able to show some wisdom to be just superstition or unsubstantiated belief. I see the quest for generalizable propositions that can be tested empirically against the facts as central in the construction of a positivist science and the generation of knowledge. Descriptive history is not enough; generalizable analysis is required. Indeed, I see generalization as inevitable in organizational study. Even when it is actually disclaimed (as in specific case history), it is implicitly proposed — otherwise, why would the research be offered to interest us? Indeed, there is a paradox here in that if we attempt to generalize and specify the extent of the generalization, we by this fact limit it. But it we describe a particular process in a particular case, then we inevitably imply a total generality.

The above two assumptions about the focus on organizational behavior and the need for generality combine to give the subdiscipline some distinctive characteristics. Thus, for example, the aim of understanding behavior in organizations is regarded as an object of study in its own right, not as a setting in which to apply accepted sociological and psychological knowledge. More important, OB as a subject is not limited to asking sociological and psychological research questions; it develops its own problematics related to the conceptual frameworks with which it deals, one of which, the Aston Programme, is presented below.

Finally, the *ethical framework* within which this study is undertaken is that of discovering how "to organize better." This does not mean that OB reduces to only a technology, because generalizations are necessary for improved understanding, and the subject must have both its scientific and technological aspects (see Pugh, 1969, for a development of this point — in particular, of the limitations of conceiving the discipline as a technology).

THE ASTON PROGRAMME

These basic prior beliefs underlie the approach to the study of context, structure, performance, and behavior of and in organizations that characterizes what has come to be called the Aston Programme (Pugh and Hickson, 1976; Pugh and Hinings, 1977; Pugh and Payne, 1977; Hickson and McMillan, 1981). This was a program of work begun in the early 1960s when a group of researchers at the Industrial Administration Research Unit of the University of Aston in Birmingham, England, came together to develop the study of organizational behavior on an empirical basis. Their work, which has continued at Aston and elsewhere (at the London Business School and the Universities of Bradford, Birmingham, and Sheffield), has developed a distinctive positivist functionalist approach that is placed in the general context of British work in this field by Pugh et al. (1975).

The view taken at the outset was that there was a considerable amount of case study research describing the functioning of organizations and aspects of the behavior of organizational members, but little in the way of systematic comparisons across organizations to enable the representativeness of case studies, with their specific data base and consequent danger of overgeneralization, to be evaluated. This was perceived to be an important inadequacy in the field, and a strategy was therefore developed to carry out comparative surveys across organizations to explore meaningful, stable relationships that would enable the particular idiosyncrasies of case studies to be placed in perspective. These studies would begin on a cross-sectional basis and would then be developed longitudinally to enable the process of stability and change to be investigated. The group was interdisciplinary in its orientation, including sociologists and psychologists, and sought to carry out studies of group and individual behavior in relation to the organizational setting in which they occurred — and not neglecting such settings as had previously been the case.

The general research strategy adopted may be summarized as being based on five specific assumptions:

(1) In order to find out which organizational problems are specific to particular kinds of organizations and which are common to all organizations, comparative studies are needed that include organizations of many types.

(2) Meaningful comparisons can only be made when there is a common standard for comparison — preferably measurement.

(3) The nature of an organization will be influenced by its objectives and environments, so these must be taken into account.

(4) Study of the work behavior of individuals or groups should be related to study of the characteristics of the organization in which the behavior occurs.

(5) Studies of organizational processes of stability and change should be undertaken in relation to a framework of significant variables and relationships established through comparative studies.

We set out to generalize and develop this study of work organization and behavior through consideration of the interdependence of three conceptually distinct levels focusing on: (1) organizational structure and functioning, (2) group composition and interaction, and (3) individual personality and behavior. Our aim was to engage in systematic study of a particular level of analysis and its interrelations (e.g., of group composition and interaction and its relation to particular organizational structures).

The studies began by focusing on the organizational level. When these had reached an appropriate point at which the comparative organizational measures could be used to specify those aspects of the organization that could be used as context for the next level of analysis, the group studies were inaugurated. The plan was that these would then run parallel with the organizational-level studies. Similarly, when the group-level studies were sufficiently specified to be able to act as input variables for individual-level analysis, then this final level of causality from the larger to the smaller unit would be implemented. But this is clearly a great oversimplification and, as will be discussed later, a full analysis will have to take account of two-way interactions and feedback loops. Studies of this type cannot be done on a cross-sectional basis but must be longitudinal taking account of dynamic processes over time. Only in this way will data on rival causal hypotheses be obtained (Pugh and Hickson, 1972). Such processual studies will be carried out within a framework of established, meaningful, stable relationships identified through the cross-sectional phase.

Figure 3.1 presents a simple model that we developed early in the studies to identify relevant variables and their relationships within and between the different levels of analysis. Our approach was to develop measures of the different aspects of context, structure, performance, and behavior, and to obtain external validity by testing acceptable hypotheses about the relationships between them. The argument was that if we could postulate relationships between the four boxes shown in Figure 3.1 and obtain data to support our hypotheses, we would have gone a considerable way toward demonstrating that our scales measured those aspects of structure and behavior that were relevant to organizational functioning.

Further, if we could predict to a considerable degree from a knowledge of an organization's context what its structural scores would be, we would have evidence that its scores were meaningful. Again, if we could demonstrate that in given contexts an organization's structural scores would be directly related to its performance, then we had that much more confidence in our conceptual framework. It is this concept of validity as a demonstrated link of data supporting conceptually defined hypothetical relationships that lies at the epistemological basis of our endeavor.

As the studies have progressed, the relatively simple model presented in Figure 3.1 has been elaborated on, resulting in Figure 3.2, which presents a framework outlining the current focus of the studies from a systems point of view (Pugh and Payne, 1977). The major units of analysis are the organization departments or major segments of organizations, small groups or teams, and the individual. The conversion process linking context and performance has been divided into "aims and resources" and "structure and processes" to emphasize that the behavior that takes place and the attitudes that are developed are a result of an interaction among these factors. The behavior and attitudes are a result of the attempt to achieve aims, given the de-

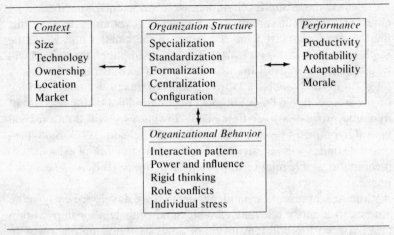

Figure 3.1 A Scheme for Organizational Functioning

mands, opportunities, and constraints of the environment in which the unit of analysis (the system) is functioning. There are two-way arrows linking the boxes marked "aims and resources" and "structure and processes," for we consider that the available resources tend to determine the structure and processes that occur, but that there is a continual interaction between these processes and the aims, tasks, and the use to which resources are put. The lists of variables in the boxes are not meant to be exhaustive, but to represent some of the major features that have been studied.

Figure 3.2 also attempts to convey the fact that individuals and groups are part of a larger system, and that the larger system forms part of the environment of these subsystems. The dotted arrows down the left-hand side are intended to convey this. The research implication is highlighted by Katz and Kahn (1966): "The first step [in research] should always be to go to the next higher level of system organization, to study the dependence of the system in question upon the super-system of which it is a part, for the super system sets the limits of the variance of behaviour of the dependent systems."

The dotted arrows up the right side of the diagram indicate that lower-level systems also can have the effects on the suprasystems. An individual in the form of a chief executive can have considerable effects on the structure and processes of the organization as a whole. This illustrates nicely the interdependence between the various systems within organizations and allows us to stress the need for explanations that combine structural, group, and individual frameworks.

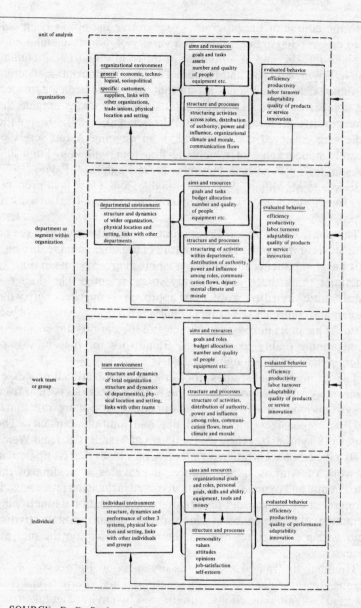

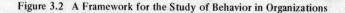

SOURCE: D. D. Pugh and R. Payne (eds.) *Organizational Behavioral in Its Context* (1977) Saxon House/Gower of Aldershot and Brookfield, Vermont, p. viii. Reprinted by permission.

Figure 3.2 A Framework for the Study of Behavior in Organizations

In the course of the program, comparative data have been collected on over 300 organizations in a variety of industrial and nonindustrial contexts, and in a number of different countries, including Britain, Egypt, Finland, and Poland. The fact that the data-collecting instruments are available has meant that there have been a considerable number of replications and extensions by persons outside the Aston group (e.g., Routamaa, 1980; Wheeler et al., 1980). Most of the studies are collected and reprinted in an ongoing Aston series of research monographs, of which the first four volumes (Pugh and Hickson, 1976; Pugh and Hinings, 1977; Pugh and Payne, 1977; Hickson and McMillan, 1981) are available, and a fifth is in preparation. They form the most convenient source of material on the work of the program.

The phase of the Aston Programme discussed above focuses on the analysis of the context and structure of organizational reality on a static basis, producing empirical snapshots at given points in time. (I sometimes think that I am the only social scientist who does not regard "static" as a dirty word.) The approach is consistent with what Morgan and Smircich (1980) have characterized as "extreme objectivism." One of its purposes is to measure the various dimensions of organizational reality to provide a framework for the analysis of system dynamics on a longitudinal basis.

These longitudinal studies, focusing on organizational processes represent a crucial second stage of the Aston project. As is clear from the systems model discussed earlier, our conception of organization is one that emphasizes interdependence and multiple causality. The framework synthesizes the cyberneticism of March (1981) and Weick (1979) with the concentration on affective processes that is apparent in the work of Argyris (1957). Hence, it provides a melding of the instrumental and expressive factors involved in decision processes. It is congruent with our wider paradigm that organizational functioning is a multilevel phenomenon in which specific organizational activities occur within a wider set of parameters that condition the internal processes.

The analytic framework regards organizational processes as an ongoing stream of events, activities, interactions, interpersonal feelings, and individual reactions, conditioned by environmental, structural, and interpersonal relationships, to produce outcome conditions that may modify or reinforce the initial state of organizational functioning. The framework has been used as a means of studying decision processes over time in the top management groups of three organizations (Pugh et al., 1976, presents an initial report). Recurring issues have been identified, the processes of their development traced, and their effects on the authority structure examined. Using this framework of analysis, we consider the processes concerned with each decision issue on a comparative basis. Thus, for example, the processes involved in the issue of product quality in each of the three firms have been analyzed in these terms, and comparisons made. Certain emerging patterns are beginning to develop that are characteristic of the three organizations.

The analysis of processes can illuminate prevailing structural, cultural, technical, and learning patterns within the organizations. This concentration on actual processes can shed light on these features as revealingly as can approaches that proceed through questionnaire surveys of sets of employees. By focusing on the dynamic aspect, it begins to illuminate the issues of how cultures reproduce themselves and of how structures came to be as they are and are maintained through time.

It is clear that this study moves our work toward improving the complexity of explanatory models. It is indeed only with processual data analyzed at a systems level that the framework in Figure 3.2 can really be exploited. In terms of the Morgan and Smircich (1980) analysis of approaches to research, this longitudinal phase of the Aston project focuses on "processual analysis." I prefer this term to "historical analysis" because of the necessity for generalization. As in the case of static research, the analysis of process is underwritten by a quest to establish the substantial knowledge that characterizes positivist science and the functionalist paradigm. In the study of process I continue to ask such questions as what factors (e.g., in the system, in the person, in the values), in what way, affect how the manager, as actor, behaves?

Using an approach that covers both structure and process emphasizes our view that an understanding of organizational reality cannot rest solely on either the explication of structural characteristics and constraints or the explication of the constructions of the individual actors. Organizational theorists should concentrate on the interplays between them. Thus the approach is concerned both with systems constraints and individual social action, attempting to bring them together in an overall framework (see Ranson et al., 1980). The overall strategy of the Aston approach is to conduct nomothetic studies to produce generalizable concepts and relationships, and then to conduct ideographic studies moderated by, and developing from, a generalized framework that can give proper balance to the common and specific aspects of a particular organization's functioning.

About the Author

DEREK S. PUGH

After initial training as a psychologist, I joined an interdisciplinary research group, the University of Edinburgh Social Sciences Research Centre. There I discovered sociology, but more important, I came away with a deep feeling of the abitrariness of discipline boundaries. I can easily be provoked into maintaining that disciplines are merely the restrictive work practices of academics, and that what matters is that the subject of study should be illuminated in as many ways and with as many conceptual research schemes as possible. It is this sort of approach that has led me to be regarded as a psychologist by sociologists and a sociologist by psychologists. My academic career has thus eschewed "old-fashioned" discipline affiliation. Over the past three decades I have held teaching posts in public health, human relations, industrial administration, organizational behaviour, and (since January 1983) systems. This, of course, is a source of considerable academic flexibility, and in my current group we have research in progress on water conservation systems, catastrophic systems failures (such as the Three Mile Island incident) and the functioning of worker cooperatives.

— 4 —

THE CASE FOR CONFIGURATION

Danny Miller

*Ecole des Hautes Etudes Commerciales
and McGill University*

Henry Mintzberg

McGill University

Debates abound in the literature of management and organization theory. Are bureaucracies centralized? Does the proportion of administrative personnel increase with organizational size? Does structure follow strategy? Is size or technical system the key determinant of structure? None of these issues ever seems to get resolved.

It is generally accepted that we best understand our world by first doing analysis and then synthesis. We divide things up into components, and then we put them back together again into some form of intelligible composite. Our contention in this chapter is that the methods traditionally favored in the study of organizations, and perhaps in the social sciences in general, encourage analysis in the absence of synthesis. Specifically, they tend to focus on continuous relationships among few variables in search of simple causation. We wish to advocate an approach here that favors synthesis, developing or isolating composites that take the form of what we have called "gestalts," "archetypes," and "configurations." These can be defined as commonly occurring clusters of attributes — in the case of our own research, states and processes of the organization as well as characteristics of its situation — that are internally consistent, such that the presence of some attributes can lead to the reliable prediction of others. We believe that much of the confusion in the literature can be resolved by greater emphasis on synthesis, and that configurations not only more clearly but also more accurately describe organizational phenomena.

We open the chapter with a brief review of one well-known debate in the literature of organization theory, first discussed from the perspective of simple causation, or analysis, and then from that of configuration, or synthesis. We then discuss briefly what we believe to be the major problems with the analytic approach and proceed to describe that of synthesis as it has emerged in our own research. This is followed by a presentation of some evidence and discussion of a number of logical arguments to support our contention that organizations are more clearly and accurately described in terms of configuration.

CONFUSION IN ANALYSIS

In 1957, C. Northcote Parkinson, with his tongue firmly planted in his cheek, proposed his "first law": "Work expands so as to fill the time available for its completion" (1957: 33). Since then, sociologists have been struggling over the interpretation of the statement — that the proportion of administrators in an organization increases as it grows. Their approach was simple: to run statistical analyses of data on organization size and A/P ratio (administrative to production personnel).

But there were problems from the outset. Two of the initial studies (Terrien and Mills, 1955; Anderson and Warkov, 1961) produced diametrically opposed results. When Rushing (1967) reviewed twelve studies a number of years later, he found two that showed A/P increasing with organization size, six that showed it decreasing, and four that showed no significant changes. The debate continued, with more results but no resolution. Pondy (1969) found the A/P ratio to range from 9 percent in the logging industry to 131 percent in drugs, throwing into doubt the utility of generalizing across industries. Nevertheless, two years later Blau and Schoenherr published a book entitled *The Structure of Organizations*, based on a study of employment security agencies, that concluded that "organizations exhibit an economy of scale in management overhead" (1971: 309) that proceeds at a decelerating rate no matter what their size. One would presumably have to infer that even if General Motors acquired the entire U.S. economy, it could manage it without ever having to increase its proportion of administrators. Finally, Child (1973) went to great efforts to break down the component parts of A and P and to include a variety of possible intervening variables (such as spatial dispersion and technological complexity). He concluded that no conclusions could be drawn about A/P in general, the A being composed of too many diverse groups. The history of the debate over whether or not bureaucracies are centralized is just as inconclusive (see Mintzberg, 1979: 195-196), and so are many other debates in the literature.

Let us try another tack. Imagine that the structural parameters of organizations cluster into five configurations, described by Mintzberg (1979). The *simple structure* — in which the chief executive officer retains personal control of all major decisions so that few other managers or staff specialists are required — exhibits a low A/P and is nonbureaucratic and highly centralized (where bureaucracy is taken to mean an emphasis on standardization, and decentralization, the dispersal of decision-making power). In contrast, the *machine bureaucracy* — dominated by rules and regulations, with a fully developed line hierarchy and staff contingent — exhibits a rather high A/P and is highly bureaucratic and rather centralized. In the *professional bureaucracy,* a good deal of the power is held by operating professionals who serve their clients individually through rather standardized programs. Hence the structure is quite decentralized and bureaucratic in that it has a high degree of standardization in its operating procedures. It has a fairly high A/P ratio because of the size of the support staff used to back up the expensive professionals, although line managers and staff analysts are relatively few due to the minimal need for direct supervision or formalization. In a fourth configuration, the *divisionalized form,* the organization splits itself into semi-autonomous, market-based units, monitored from a headquarters by performance control systems. As we have argued elsewhere (Mintzberg, 1979: 384-387), these systems drive the divisions toward machine bureaucratic structure; in other words, toward bureaucratization coupled with centralization (at least at the division level). The A/P also emerges as fairly high within the divisions, while company-wide A/P is bolstered by the added administrative personnel at the headquarters. Finally, in a configuration called *adhocracy,* line managers, staff specialists, and often operating personnel as well, combine in fluid project teams to innovate. Here the degree of bureaucratization tends to be low, the degree of decentralization high, and the A/P ratio probably the highest of all, due to the proliferation of staff specialists, of managers (a consequence of matrix structure and small project teams), and in many cases, of automation (which reduces drastically the P in A/P).

Now, assuming this is how the world really works — that at least a good proportion of organizations tend to adopt something close to these various configurations — what would happen if different kinds of organizations were mixed in research samples and then measures taken of A/P, bureaucratization, and centralization? We believe that we already have the answer in the research cited earlier.

SOME CRITICISMS OF THE ANALYTIC APPROACH

The approach to research that we are calling analytic exhibits, in its purest form, six basic attributes. These are listed below with a number of criticisms, most of which have been discussed at length in the literature but merit brief review here as a set.

(1) *The focus is on bivariate relationships, which often gives way to sharply circumscribed multivariate analysis.* The problem with bivariate relationships is that critical intervening variables tend to damage their explanatory power. For example, bureaucracies may be centralized when their operating work is unskilled, decentralized when it is skilled. Specification error may be an easy criticism to make, and it has been made often, but that perhaps reflects a fundamental weakness in the analytic approach to research.

(2) *Relationships are generally assumed to be linear and causation unidirectional.* Discontinuities — changes in kind rather than in degree — upset the assumption of linearity, and sometimes even change the direction of causality. Starbuck (1965) has made a convincing case for metamorphosis in organizations; Klatsky (1970) in fact uses metamorphosis to try to explain the size-A/P relationship, arguing that the curve is U-shaped. Miller (1979) found different orientations to adaptation in different groups of firms, with many of the correlational relationships among variables of strategy making, structure, and environment changing in both direction and significance from one group to another (e.g., those between environmental dynamism and risk taking or innovation and centralization of strategy-making power). The problems of nonlinearity have typically been treated by the use of moderated regression analysis or saturated regression models containing exhaustive interaction terms. But these techniques must be limited to situations in which a relatively small number of variables can substantially explain the phenomenon under study, and in which there are good theoretical reasons for anticipating particular relationships and *specific* moderating influences. But how often do these conditions occur? Given our current knowledge,

which variables are to be selected as the key moderators; in what fashion are they to be described as moderating between dependent and independent variables; indeed, how are we to distinguish between dependent and independent variables in the first place?

(3) Research samples tend to be either very narrow or very broad, from employment security agencies (Blau and Schoenherr, 1971) or stock brokerage offices (Pennings, 1975) in some studies, to a sample "as different as a large tire manufacturing firm and the public baths in Birmingham" in another (Holdaway et al., 1975: 30, in reference to Pugh et al., 1968). The narrow sample can lead to false generalizations, as seems to be the case in the Blau and Schoenherr conclusion about the relationship between size and A/P, while the broad, indiscriminate one, by including what amounts to a conflicting array of relationships, can prove impossible to interpret, as has been the case in the Pugh et al. findings on bureaucratization and centralization. As McKelvey has noted, the latter type of sample "is akin to a biologist wanting to make broad statements about heartbeat rates based on a sample of one elephant, one tiger, one rabbit and an alligator" (1978: 1437-1438).

(4) Measures are generally cross-sectional in nature, that is, taken at only one point in time. But time leads and lags abound in organizations. To take one important example, because structural change normally lags situational change (e.g., Chandler, 1962), it is somewhat a matter of luck whether a cross-sectional study captures the structure that reflects today's situation — which it typically measures — or yesterday's, which it typically does not.

(5) Variables tend to be rather abstract, far removed from organizational occurrences, and the measures of them tend to be general. A/P is the most obvious example. But the nuances and complexities present in organizations often destroy the explanatory power of such variables and measures. The A of A/P can, for example, include everyone from a mailroom clerk and a cost estimator through a production scheduler, laboratory scientist, and personnel manager, to a legal adviser and the chair of the board. And how should one categorize the chef in the corporate cafeteria — A or P? Thus Child (1973) found that different factors were required to explain the rate of growth of different administrative groups. Likewise, much of the centralization-bureaucratization debate has focused on the weaknesses of the measures of decentralization (e.g., Perrow, 1974).

(6) The research typically proceeds from a distance, usually through questionnaires. The detachment of researchers from the context of their research precludes the collection and examination of anecdotal data. How are researchers faced with a set of general

measures of a few rather abstract variables (such as A/P or "decentralization") supposed to probe into causation and interpret the findings? They seem to be lacking some kind of hook — some rich example or specific scenario — on which to hang the results in order to explain them. The overall result is that while data abound, insightful theory remains sparse.

To conclude, had we to name one key weakness in the analytical approach to research, or in the social sciences in general, it would be that researchers have been bent on testing for simple, circumscribed relationships instead of searching for or constructing rich, insightful patterns.

THE PERSPECTIVE OF SYNTHESIS

Corresponding to these attributes of the approach we call "purely analytic" are a set of attributes that favor synthesis as the objective of research. In its purest form, the approach of synthesis combines all five of the attributes discussed below, although the first two are the most critical.

(1) A large number of attributes — ideally of state, process, and situation — are studied simultaneously in order to yield a detailed, holistic, integrated image of reality. We concur with McKelvey (1975) and Pinder and Moore (1979), who argue for studies that employ as inclusive a set of organizational attributes as possible. Thus studies of the organization need not be restricted to attributes of its structure, but can also consider those of its environment, its technical system, its age and size, its power relationships, its leaders, its strategy, its strategy-making procedures, its flow of information and patterns of communication, its performance, and so on.

(2) Data analysis and theory building are geared to finding common natural clusters among the attributes studied, which necessitates careful sample definition. The objective of the research is to derive theoretical typologies or empirical multivariate taxonomies that discriminate among different configurations of the attributes, each revealing its own relationships among the attributes. To achieve this objective, samples have to be carefully defined. Narrow samples can be useful to uncover individual configurations intuitively and to describe them in depth, but the effort must then be made to build typologies or taxonomies across different studies. Alternatively, we can proceed through the use of broad and representative stratified

random samples (McKelvey, 1975), coupled with the use of systematic statistical techniques for generating taxonomies and testing their predictive utility (Miller, 1978, 1981). These can enable us to make precise comparisons across different kinds of organizations.

Since multivariate relationships can vary from one configuration to another, we must first try to find these configurations in the form of dense homogenous clusters of attributes or interrelationships that together form a predictive taxonomy. A relatively small number of categories must encompass a large proportion of the population, and the configurations must be sufficiently restricted (i.e., tightly defined) to afford accurate and meaningful descriptions of their members. A taxonomy will be of value only if it is likely to classify a randomly selected organization from the population using a small number of variables, and to predict accurately many of its other attributes or relationships simply by making reference to class membership.

(3) Causation is viewed in the broadest possible terms. The search is not simply for unidirectional causation between pairs of variables, nor even necessarily for multiple forms of causation. The approach of synthesis is really the search for *networks* of causation. Each configuration has to be considered as a system in which each attribute can influence all of the others by being an indispensable part of an integrated whole. There are no purely dependent or independent variables in a system; over time, everything can depend on everything else. Thus, while large size may encourage bureaucratization or standardization (e.g., Pugh et al., 1968), as may the technical system of mass production (Woodward, 1965), it could also be true that bureaucracies have a propensity to grow larger and to favor mass production. Moreover, from the analytic perspective, debate has raged over whether it is the "imperative" of organizational size or technical system that best explains structure. From the perspective of synthesis, these factors, as well as many others (such as a stable environment), might all be described as part of the system we have called machine bureaucracy.

(4) Time and process are taken into account wherever possible. The approach of synthesis favors longitudinal research, in which processes are studied alongside states, where possible. Results from such studies enable researchers to flesh out their findings, helping them to explain leads and lags, and, in general, providing depth to their understanding of why organizations behave as they do.

(5) Despite efforts to measure and quantify, anecdotal data are gathered to help explain the more systematic findings. Abstract results come to life when put in the context of even one rich, detailed

illustration. We fully realize that the preference for the analytic approach reflects economic and logistic practicalities no less than it does methodological beliefs. In more pointed terms, indirect cross-sectional research is very convenient in a world of publish or perish. That bias could, we believe, be corrected if reviewers paid as much attention to the significance of the conclusions as to the significance of the correlations. But since we anticipate no revolution in the politics of academe, we should point out that research from the perspective of synthesis can be convenient too. For example, published book histories and strings of articles on single organizations have been found to serve as reliable longitudinal data bases, rich in detail and anecdote (Miller and Friesen, 1980a, 1980b, 1982b). In-depth studies of single organizations can also produce significant results, though not in the statistical sense. Such intensive studies can make up for their lack of generality by greater depth of description. And the results of these studies can be cumulative. Given 100 researchers with a set amount of time, each can study, say, 1 organization or 100. The choice then becomes between in-depth data on 100 organizations or superficial data on 10,000. We are not here advocating quantitative or qualitative approaches, in-depth or large-sample studies. We merely wish to emphasize that effective and convenient methodologies can be found to study organizations from the perspective of synthesis.

Of course, as we have already noted, the approach of synthesis can be useful only if configurations do in fact reflect reality, that is, only if common, nonrandom, internally homogeneous clusterings of attributes occur, a relatively small number of which account for a large fraction of the population of organizations. Otherwise, far too many types would be needed to explain that population, and our research methodologies (not to mention our own cognitive faculties) would become hopelessly inadequate. The last section of this chapter presents theoretical arguments and empirical evidence in support of the existence of such configurations in the world of organizations.

WHY CONFIGURATIONS?

Two sets of arguments can be put forward in support of configurations. One argues for their convenience — specifically, their compatibility with human cognition — the other for their existence. Let us consider each in turn.

Configuration and Cognition

Even the most untutored visitor to an art museum is able to glance at a painting, appreciate its form and structure, and take away impressions of its mood, shape, and perhaps theme. The visitor first appraises the stimulus holistically, roaming over the canvas with his or her eyes to take in the extensive qualities of the painting. Afterwards, his or her attention might be directed to appreciating particular areas of the canvas or specific qualities of it — the coarseness of its brushstrokes, the intensity of its hues, the flow of its lines.

In a basic sense, the observer's first impressions are ones of synthesis. That is how he or she first appreciates the painting and comprehends its basic message. The observer is unconsciously effecting a synthesis that employs components or attributes only so far as they merge into a comprehensible whole. Only subsequently might that observer begin to *analyze* the attributes individually, to consider their role in making up that whole.

If we lived in a world controlled by a malevolent deity, he or she might have constituted human beings so that analysis would always have to precede synthesis in cognition, even in the viewing of paintings. He or she might force us to go over a canvas one square inch at a time, and then somehow to combine these myriad fragments to obtain some idea of pattern. In such a world, either paintings would be very small or museums very empty.

To be sure, analysis and synthesis are both necessary phases of scientific activity. Analysis is used to define the components or attributes of a phenomenon and to measure them; synthesis is used to combine these into integrated images, conceptions, or configurations, and to identify patterns and form generalizations. Then analysis returns to enable us to test these generalizations and deduce their logical consequences. But the purpose of science is insight, much as is the purpose of painting. In other words, just as the painter paints to enlighten the observer, so too does the researcher study to enlighten the practitioner. And we believe that the practitioner — in the case of organization theory, the line manager, staff specialist, consultant — perceives much as does the visitor to the museum.

Synthesis forms the basis of the practitioner's perception: It must precede, condition, and inform his or her analysis. Disjointed analysis by itself provides him or her with only glimpses of fragments, whose context-free states obscure their meanings. Findings may be statistically significant, but not conceptually so. They become elusive, float away, inhibit rather than foster understanding. The fewer the fragments, and the more distant one from another on the invisible canvas, the more difficult it is to get a realistic image of that canvas — to make any sense of things.

Our world of organizations is very complex, and the fragments uncovered by research from the perspective of analysis are very distant from one another. Hence the images offered to the practitioner have been very incomplete. No wonder that while the archives of organization theory may be crowded, its museums are almost empty.

Our point is that configurations developed from the perspective of synthesis, by providing relatively composite images of spheres of reality (and remember that no painting tries to depict all of reality), may be more compatible with patterns of human cognition than are linear relationships developed from the perspective of analysis, which seek to explain components more than composites. People deal with a complex world by compartmentalizing it in terms of images or clusters, by putting its many attributes into various envelopes, each of which is a convenient storehouse of related information, with its own label. This is what we mean when we use the words "model," "stereotype," "kind," and "type."

Some Evidence for Configuration

Configurations may, however, be more than just convenient tools for cognition. They may, in fact, more accurately reflect "objective" reality, describing patterns that really do exist in some sense. To develop an earlier point, if this were a continuous world, with all shades of gray more or less equally represented between black and white, the analytic approach would prove more powerful. Alternatively, were there natural clustering around relatively few shades, the approach of synthesis would prove more effective. Let us review some empirical evidence for that clustering.

There has in fact been a thin stream of research that has favored synthesis and developed configurations. We believe that this has proven to be the more insightful research, and, despite its sparseness, that which has been favored by practitioners.

The first such study of note — one that struck a resounding chord for configuration — is that of Joan Woodward (1965). Interestingly, Woodward took an analytic perspective at the outset, developing what she believed to be a continuous scale of technology — ranging from the production of units to customer requirements, through mass production, to the continuous production of fluids. She then attempted to study its relationship to various attributes of structure. Some of these relationships proved to be linear, but a number did not. In other words, viewed in terms of a single scale of technology, Woodward's results proved confusing. (Indeed, the scale itself has proved confusing, with debates raging about what it really means; see Hunt, 1970; Starbuck, 1965, even Reeves and Woodward, 1970). But viewed from the perspective of three basic types of organizations, or configurations, Woodward's conclusion fell neatly into place. Each type demonstrated an integral cluster of attributes, and the more successful firms seemed to conform most strongly to the central tendencies of each cluster. Woodward's descriptions of unit, mass, and process production firms have been widely quoted ever since.

In the same vein, we can mention a number of other studies — all widely cited — that uncovered configurations of attributes of organizational structure and situation. An early one was that of Burns and Stalker (1966), who found "mechanistic" structures in textile firms dealing with stable environments, and "organic" structures in electronics firms operating in dynamic environments. Lawrence and Lorsch (1967) found equivalent structures in container firms facing simple and stable environments and in plastics firms facing complex and dynamic environments, respectively. (Indeed, of interest is the strong apparent equivalence between Woodward's mass producers, Burns and Stalker's mechanistic firms, and Lawrence and Lorsch's container companies, all corresponding to what we earlier called machine bureaucracy, and Woodward's process firms, Burns and Stalker's organic firms, and Lawrence and Lorsch's plastics companies, all corresponding to what we called adhocracy.)

All the typologies discussed above were derived conceptually from empirical data. Some of the research of the same period set out to generate taxonomies — classification schemes derived empirically, normally through multivariate analyses performed on a number of organizational variables. But this research has not met with the same degree of success. A recent paper by Carper and Snizek (1980) summarizes what they believe to be the most frequently cited taxonomies. They complain about the small number of variables used and call for taxonomies based on the simultaneous consideration of multiple measures of many dimensions. McKelvey (1975) also has criticized the samples of the taxonomic studies as being unrepresentative and poorly defined, and also the taxonomies themselves for weaknesses of parsimony and lack of intraclass homogeneity. Too much attention is paid to generating types, in his view, and not enough to establishing their robustness in different data bases or their predictive utility.

Some of these problems have been addressed in more recent research. This research departs from earlier work in its attempt to include in its configurations not only descriptions of state — that is, structure, environment, and sometimes performance — but also descriptions of process, notably the organization's approach to strategy making. For example, the work of Miles and Snow (1978), already frequently cited, has sought to classify organizations on the basis of their strategies, structures, and managerial styles. Though based on empirical data, this study presents a typology derived conceptually. Miller and Friesen (1978) have used a similar orientation to derive taxonomies empirically. In a first study, they collected a diverse sample of 80 business firms using a published case history data base and examined 31 variables of environment, structure, strategy making, and performance. Using a multivariate technique to generate their taxonomy and a related hypothesis-testing method to establish its generality and stability, Miller and Friesen found that ten tightly defined archetypes encompassed 85 percent of their data base. There was much statistically significant clustering in the data. In a second study, Miller and Friesen (1980a) divided 36 lengthy organizational histories, described in detailed books and strings of articles, into briefer intervals of transition. They used 24 variables describing strategy making, structure, environment, and performance to characterize each transition. Transition archetypes were identified using a procedure similar to that of the first study (and then validated through questionnaires sent to companies). Again, predictively useful clustering was found.

The empirical literature carried out from the perspective of synthesis, however sparse, appears to provide evidence for the existence of configurations — not only of state, but of state, situation, and process, even of transition. More intensive research efforts in this regard will, in our opinion, reinforce this conclusion and lead to the development of far richer descriptions of the world of organizations than we have known in the past.

Some Reasons for Configuration

One point remains to be more fully developed here. Why, from the perspective of that world of organizations, should common configurations exist? We propose three main arguments, woven into the following paragraphs, to account for the emergence of organizational configurations.

According to Charles Darwin (1968: 231):

> Species at any one period are not indefinitely variable, and are not linked together by a multitude of intermediate gradations, partly because the process of natural selection will always be very slow and will act, at any one time, only on a very few forms; and partly because the very process of natural selection almost implies the continual supplanting and extinction of preceding and intermediate gradations.

Hannan and Freeman (1977) have argued that formal organizations may be subject to selection processes similar to those of the biological species. Both survive only if they evolve in ways adapted to their environments. Our first argument, then, is that *Darwinian forces may encourage only relatively few organizational forms to survive in the same setting;* their variety and number are circumscribed by the dictates of population ecology.

But which forms survive? Increasingly, researchers and practitioners alike are coming to see the world in "systems" terms. Everything seems to depend on everything else. It used to be fashionable in science and everyday affairs to isolate variables, to catch what has been called the "economist's plague" — holding all other things constant. The trouble is that other things do not remain constant. Things move together because of their interdependencies. And that may be a force for the emergence of configurations in organizations. Our second argument is that *the organization may be driven toward configuration in order to achieve consistency in its internal characteristics, synergy (or mutual complementarity) in its processes, and fit with its situation.* Rather than trying to do everything well, the effective organization may instead concentrate its efforts on a theme and seek to bring all of its elements into line with this. Configuration, in essence, means harmony.

Note the departure here from traditional Darwinian theory, giving rise to the two separate arguments for the emergence of configuration. Our first point argues that it is the environment that causes adaptation in the long run by allowing only a limited number of synergistic and compatible organizational forms to survive. Our second point, not inconsistent with the first but departing from the analogy with the biological species, argues that organizations seek to adapt *themselves* to the dictates of consistency, synergy, and fit. They are able to act "morphogenically." Unlike the biological species, which have to wait generations to adapt, organizations have the capacity to adapt themselves within their own lifetimes (Simon, 1969), for example, by effecting transitions from less to more viable configurations.

And this brings us to our third argument. Were it common for organizations to make such transitions gradually and incrementally, the case for configuration could be weakened. Assuming a reasonable number of organizations in transition between configurations at any one time, and assuming that time spent in transition is time spent out of configuration, so to speak, a random cross-section of organizations might display too much variety, with different ones arrayed along the whole continuum of transition. In other words, clustering would break down, and so would our case for configuration. But *the economics of adaptation, as well as recent empirical evidence, argues for a "quantum" approach to organizational change — long periods of the maintenance of a given configuration punctuated by brief periods of multifaceted transition to a new one.*

Contingency theory has found that organizations must change their internal attributes — structures, strategies, and processes — to cope with changes in their environments (unless, of course, they can more easily alter their environments instead). The question is: What form does that internal change take? Essentially, the organization has two broad choices. It can try to keep up with changes in its environment by changing itself in incremental and perhaps piecemeal fashion. In so doing, the organization maintains environmental fit, but at the expense of internal consistency. Alternately, the organization can delay transition until absolutely necessary, thereby better maintaining internal consistency, but at the price of gradually worsening environmental fit. Either choice can damage configuration — but the latter far less than the former, since the interrelationships among the state characteristics and processes (the means by which the organization functions every day) remain in tact. (The organization can keep attending to that part of the environment — albeit perhaps a diminishing part — that remains compatible with its internal configuration.)

There are a number of reasons why organizations would opt for the maintenance of internal configuration as long as possible, rather than for continual adaptation to the environment. First, an environmental change can sometimes prove to be a temporary blip or an anomaly. The logical tendency, therefore, would be to delay reaction to it, to wait at least until the signals are clear. Second, internal change tends to be costly, involving shifts in established patterns of behavior. It is, therefore, logically resisted or at least delayed so that many changes can be made at the same time. This is especially true when the organization has attained configuration. In the face of a tight integration of structural and process attributes, change in any one means *dis*integration, resulting in discrepancies and disharmonies in the inner workings of the organization. Third, internal change, especially in the face of configuration, is also resisted for ideological, cognitive, and political reasons. When an organization is successful, especially as a result of configuration, the force of internal ideology tends to impute a mythical quality to its structure and processes, evoking an attitude of conformity that can block not just change but even the perception of the need for it (Starbuck et al., 1978). Even leaving ideology aside, those in the organization who developed the existing structures and processes, and the configuration — often the organization's most powerful managers — become enamored of them, blind to their weaknesses, and politically dependent on them. Moreover, the managers of successful organizations, never sure which of the attributes of structure and process lie at the root of that success, will tend to avoid tampering with any one — with any element of their "tried and true" formula, their configuration.

Thus there are a number of reasons why organizations delay adaptation to environmental change, and especially try to retain internal configuration as long as possible. But adaptation must, of course, come eventually. As the environment continues to change and the fit with it worsens, steps must be taken to initiate substantial change in internal structure and process. But to evoke such changes in the face of all the forces discussed above would seem to call for virtual revolution. Thus, when such internal change does come, we would expect it to be pervasive and dramatic, costly and disruptive. The organization would be driven to change many of its attributes concurrently, not only to get all of the disruption over with at one time, but, more important, to try to keep its attributes in complementary alignment. In other words, the organization would logically try to leap to a new configuration. And it would be driven to execute that leap rapidly, to avoid spending too much time in a state of transition. In that state of transition, configuration of state and process is absent: the structure and the workings of the organization lack internal consistency; the organization is no longer suited to its old environment while not yet adapted to its new one. As the most common pattern of effective significant adaptation, therefore, we would expect the following. First, the organization would undergo lengthy periods of the maintenance of a given configuration when possible. Second, these long periods of relative internal calm and harmony would be punctuated occasionally by brief periods of disruption — of something akin to revolution — during which the leap to a new configuration would be made.

Such a pattern has long been recognized in the conceptual literature (e.g., Greiner, 1972; Starbuck, 1965: 486). But recent research has
provided some empirical support for it as well. Miller and Friesen
(1980b) found that there was a tendency for organizations to undergo
two types of periods. In the most common periods of "momentum,"
firms reinforced or extended their past structures and strategy-
making practices. Changes that did occur were extrapolations or
continuations of earlier developments and tended to take place simultaneously across many variables, in our opinion to keep them in some
thematic and functional, that is, configurational, alignment. Less
common but more dramatic were the periods of "revolution." Here
organizations reversed the direction of change in many variables of
strategy making and structure simultaneously, in what seemed to be
an attempt to reach a dramatically different configuration. In another
study, Miller and Friesen (1982a) found that successful firms in their
sample showed a much greater propensity to undergo revolutionary
structural change that was both simultaneous in a number of areas and
extreme. They seemed to be able to move quickly from one effective
configuration to another. Unsuccessful firms favored piecemeal and
incremental approaches, perhaps remaining "between" configurations too long. Theoretical and mathematical arguments for the desirability of revolutionary structural change and its relationship to
performance and configuration are to be found in Miller (1982) and
Friesen and Miller (1981), respectively.

These results provide indirect but encouraging support for the
existence of configurations. They are not, of course, conclusive. But
together with the other evidence and theoretical arguments presented
in this discussion, they do lead us to the conclusion that configurations, molded by selective and adaptive forces and preserved by
economic ones, can be highly functional phenomena for organizations and for the societies that sustain them.

The concept of configuration can help us to overcome the problem
of the blind men, each of whom touched a different part of the
elephant and then argued about the nature of the beast. It can open the
eyes of the researcher to the study of whole beasts, each a logical
combination of its own characteristics, similar to all the members of
its own species, yet fundamentally different from those of other
species. The research that we have discussed in this final section can
point the way. It suggests that systematic study of many organizational attributes, of process as well as of state and situation, ideally
over time and reinforced by anecdotal data — what we have called
research from the perspective of synthesis — can lead to more useful

theories by which to comprehend our complex world of organizations.

About the Authors

DANNY MILLER

Perhaps my interest in organizations stems from my congenital inability to function well within them. At school the curriculum grated, at Dad's shop, the work, and at the Bank, my first and last formal employer, everything. In 1972, I enrolled in a most unstructured Ph.D. program at McGill and fell under the inspired tutelage of Henry Mintzberg and Peter Friesen. Henry kindled my interest in policy and my need to rebel against simple contingency frameworks. Peter convinced me that the rebellion had better have a scientific basis (forgive me!) if it were to amount to anything. I've been hooked on research ever since, pursuing a career on the outer fringes of two rather tolerant organizations.

HENRY MINTZBERG

I was trained as an engineer, a point I tended to dismiss for many years until people began to comment on certain engineering characteristics of my work (e.g., the electrical engineers in the audience were "drooling" when I presented a study of decision making that showed a number of involved feedback loops). Perhaps that is behind my search for order. That probably also explains (if it doesn't justify) my almost total ignorance of philosophy, although this may prove as much a strength as a weakness. From the days of my doctoral studies, my world was ordered into a number of subject areas — managerial work, organizational structure, organizational power, strategic decision making, strategy formation, the role of the policy analyst. Pradip Khandwalla joined our faculty in the early seventies and brought with him the notion of configuration from his thesis, or at least he brought the finding that logical combinations of the elements of structure and situation seemed more likely to explain organizational effectiveness than did selecting the best elements per se. That idea bubbled in my mind for a while, emerged in my book on organizational structure (in the form of five configurations), and has since caused a gestalt shift in my thinking. I now order my world by subjects such as "size and bureaucracy" (essentially why large organizations do us in and what we can do about it), "adhocracy," "missionary," and "lego" (the creation of new configurations). Danny Miller, my first doctoral student, was pursuing similar interests, but with a very different research methodology. This paper with him, first written a number of years ago (1979 or early 1980), stands at the point of my transition.

5

QUASI-EXPERIMENTATION

Its Ontology, Epistemology, and Methodology

Thomas D. Cook

Northwestern University

Quasi-experiments (Campbell and Stanley, 1963) constitute a class of empirical studies with humans that lack two of the usual features of experimentation. They rarely occur inside a laboratory, and they never involve the random assignment of units to the treatments being contrasted. In all other respects, quasi-experiments are like experiments. Their function is to probe causal relations between manipulated independent variables (treatments) and measured outcomes, and their structure involves one or more treatments, measures taken after a treatment, and — usually — more than one unit receiving each treatment.

Campbell differentiated quasi-experiments from pre-experiments as well as experiments. Pre-experiments were characterized by the absence of both pretreatment measures and control groups. Pretest measures are needed if change is to be studied. Control groups are needed because (a) humans spontaneously mature with time, so that observed changes risk being spuriously interpreted as consequences of a treatment when they may instead be due to normal maturational processes; and (b) for many research purposes, it is not desirable to isolate humans from their normal settings where they are exposed to theoretically irrelevant forces whose causal impacts can also masquerade as treatment effects. Campbell's thesis was that, unless random assignment has occurred, designs without pretests and control groups cannot fulfill their cause-probing function in social research and should be called "pre-experimental."

Campbell's severe judgment only concerns research on organisms that spontaneously change and cannot be studied in closed environments. Most research in the natural sciences deals with inert objects that do not change or whose development can be temporarily halted. Such objects are studied in environments that, thanks to sterilized test tubes, lead-lined walls, rubber sheaths enclosing wires, linear accelerators, and the like, keep out all contaminants that have already been identified as possible spurious causes. Thus in the natural science laboratory inert organisms and isolation serve the same cause-probing function that pretests, control groups, and known assignment processes serve in open system research with individually evolving organisms. There is no paradox involved in noting that the experiments in physics and chemistry that most laypersons would label as scientific *par excellence* have a structure that, in the social sciences, Campbell has labeled as "pre-experimental."

Some social science research is based on the closed system model of physics and chemistry, especially in laboratory work in social and personality psychology, where the setting is controlled in order to tailor interventions to theory and to close out irrelevant causal factors. Moreover, since most experiments last about 50 minutes, spontaneous maturation rarely interferes with the interpretation of experimental results. However, this restriction of the ecology and time frame entails that some substantive topics cannot be investigated. It is also possible that, instead of creating the planned "sanitized" ecology, the laboratory may sometimes create a novel environment that respondents seek to understand, confounding their reactions to the planned experimental stimuli with their shared interpretations of the experiment's purpose. Because of this — and because people differ from each other in so many ways before a study begins — laboratory researchers in psychology have had to supplement the experimental isolation favored in chemistry and physics with structural features borrowed mostly from agricultural experimentation (e.g., control groups, random assignment, and the use of multiple units per treatment group).

Agricultural research takes place in relatively open systems because the goal is to discover how seeds will grow outside of a totally controlled world — in a world that approximates how the seeds will actually be grown. This practical goal means that theorists of agricultural research methods have had to develop ways to account for the causal effects of such theoretical irrelevancies as differences between experimental plots — in sunshine, rainfall, soil composition, and so on. The preferred solution stresses the *random* assignment of units to treatments in order to distribute causal irrelevancies equally across the treatment groups, as opposed to trying to keep them out as in the natural science model. However, the agricultural model is not meant to be totally naturalistic. In the model, the researcher needs control over which seeds go where; the experimental station is laid out in miniature plots that are hardly isomorphic with a farmer's fields; and the seeds are tended by the professional agriculturist with a level of attention that few practicing farmers can afford. The agricultural model is based, therefore, on a *modified* open system. Moreover, it was developed for seeds without a consciousness that impels them to give meaning to situations, persons, and events.

The major use of the agricultural model in social research lies in the subfield called "social experimentation" (Riecken and Boruch, 1974). Here, the concern is with testing treatments of long duration that are thought to be relevant to social policy options by assigning them *at random* in naturalistic settings. However, random assignment is not always possible in social research — for ethical, political, and logistical reasons; also, it makes groups equivalent at the beginning of a study but it cannot guarantee that they will remain that way for all of a research project. Consequently, although random assignment is an important tool for field researchers, it is no panacea for those who want to study causal relationships in open systems. Quasi-experiments represent the fallback most frequently advocated, since they are like randomized field experiments in all ways except that treatment assignment is by self-selection or administrator fiat rather than by chance. The roots of quasi-experiments are then, not in the closed system model of the natural sciences, nor in the mixed natural science/agricultural model of laboratory research in psychology. Rather, they lie in an agricultural research model based on open field tests where the researcher tries to modify only as much of the system as is necessary to measure dependent variables. The quasi-experimentalist does not go so far as the social experimentalist who, for the sake of randomization, is prepared to trade off naturalism for control over the assignment process. Nor does he or she usually go as far as the agriculturalist either in laying out a miniature world of simulation or in assuming that the objects of study are without consciousness. Quasi-experimentalists seek to conduct research in the settings to which extrapolation is desired, and they are ever conscious of doing research with active, reactive, and proactive human beings. The task in this chapter is to discuss the ontology, epistemology, and methodology of quasi-experiments. It is not possible to do this without differentiating between the normative and presumed behavioral standards from which such matters could be derived.

One might choose as a nomative standard the writings of Campbell, whose preferences are clear: Quasi-experimentation should be ontologically realist, but also epistemologically fallibilist, critical, and hence postpositivist, and it should pursue publicly specified methods that try both to verify causal relationships and to falsify them through the judicious use of experimental designs, statistical analyses, and a critically appraised common sense that is heavily dependent on past knowledge in a particular substantive area.

Although no one speaks for quasi-experimentation with the authority of Campbell, his is only one voice. Moreover, some critics (e.g., Cronbach, 1980; Dunn, 1982) see the common practice of quasi-experimentation as less critical and more positivist than Campbell would like. They believe that "threats to validity" lead practitioners into an uncritical and mechanical acceptance of the proper way to do research that underplays background knowledge and unnecessarily restricts the criteria by which research is judged. Both Cronbach and Dunn have their normative disagreements with Campbell, but they pale when compared to their disagreements with what they see as the current, modal practice of quasi-experimentation.

It is difficult to decide whether to explicate the normative ontological and epistemological foundations of quasi-experimentation or those that critics claim are the foundations of its model practitioner. After much reflection, I decided to deal only with the normative. There were three reasons for this. First, it is encumbant on us to discuss methods at their best, provided that, with sufficient care and training, they can be implemented well — as I am convinced quasi-experimental methods can be. Second, I do not know how prevalent are the assumptions and methods that critics attribute to practitioners of quasi-experimental research, and it may not be fruitful to discuss what may be events of low frequency. Third, in dealing with quasi-experimentation in Campbell's normative mode we have to discuss those of the critics' objections that pertain to his normative position. These objections are especially important, for they touch on what may be generic attributes (and limitations) of quasi-experimentation.

THE ONTOLOGY OF QUASI-EXPERIMENTATION

Ontology and Causation

It would seem logical to develop methods only after deciding on the ontological assumptions one wants to make about the world, determining how one can know about such a world, and then deciding which questions are worth asking about that world. This may not be how most methods — including quasi-experimentation — were developed. Indeed, given its origins in agriculture, it is likely that quasi-experimentation came to adopt whatever ontological assumptions buttressed agricultural work in the 1920s and 1930s, updating them as their limitations became clearer. These were overwhelmingly realist assumptions, built on the supposition that an external world of objects exists, that these objects are lawfully interrelated, and that the relationships are mediated by a real force in objects that is called *causation*. Later, as genetics and particle physics advanced, the external world came increasingly to be seen as probabilistic, requiring nondeterministic explanatory laws. In ascribing to such ontological assumptions, agriculture was probably no different from any of the other natural sciences of the time.

Although most of the important points to be made about quasi-experimentation are epistemological, some ontological issues have to be discussed. Cronbach operates from an ontological position that assumes that real causal forces exist in systemic configurations rather than as simple univariate causes and effects. The world of multivariate causal interdependency that he postulates is what McGuire (1968) has amusingly called a "pretzel-shaped" reality. It is characterized by multiple causal paths, both linear and reciprocal, that converge on some outcome. Lawful statements of causation require full knowledge of this system of variables so that total prediction of the outcome can be achieved. From his belief in the systemic organization of causal connections and the utility of causal explanations of this type, Cronbach questions whether the experimentalists' isolation and manipulation of a small set of specific causal agents is sensitive to the real nature of causal agency, which depends on complex patterns of influence between multiple events and also involves characteristics of respondents, settings, and times. Cronbach is therefore unwilling to make an ontological assumption he attributes to social experimentalists: that manipulating one thing will inevitably make another thing happen.

Quasi-experimentalists might respond to this criticism in several ways. First, they could contend that ontological roots have been attributed to quasi-experimentation that it does not have. Quasi-experimentation does not aspire to describe or model a complete causal system in order to achieve perfect prediction and understanding of the behaviors that occur within the system. Rather, the goal is to identify manipulanda that can make a difference to specific outcomes, even if these involve only a small part of a larger system. Let me describe the difference with examples. We have very dependable information about the causal relationship between aspirin and headaches, but little causal understanding of why aspirin is generally so effective or of the conditions under which it is inevitably effective. At two years of age, a child has knowledge that flicking a light switch causes the light to go on, but he or she has no dependable knowledge of why the switch affected the light, and he or she cannot do much to light his or her room if the bulb is burned out. Quasi-experimentation is moot on the issue of the multivariate complexity required for complete causal understanding, complete causal explanation, and total prediction. It seeks only to discover those parts of the real world in which causal relationships exist and in which manipulating one thing predictably causes another to change. The total set of contextual dependencies on which such causal relationships depend, and the micro-mediating processes that bring them about, are issues to which quasi-experimentation speaks only indirectly.

In any case, it is possible to argue that, even if causal understanding of nature requires complexly interdependent causal systems, quasi-experiments can be modified so as to better approximate such understanding. The ability to use quasi-experimental structures for probing complex causal systems depends on the availability of relevant substantive theory to guide the selection and measurement of factors that are believed to be causally relevant, including historical, situational, and personological variables as well as micro-mediating processes that are supposed to take place after the independent variable has varied and before the more distal causal outcomes of interest have been observed. If theory-guided sampling and measurement are available, one can then undertake causal modeling — the traditional methodology for understanding multivariate causal systems. Quasi-experimentation defines a flexible structure of experimental attributes *to whose sampling and measurement frameworks additions can be made.* Only ingenuity and resources prevent adding to this structure so as to probe issues of causal understanding in addition to testing issues of causal relationship.

The modest type of causation that quasi-experimentalists pursue may be related to the belief that the external world is probabilistically ordered in its essence. If it is, understanding and prediction could never be perfect even with more comprehensive causal knowledge. Yet I suspect that not even a probablistically ordered external world could account for all the discrepancy between the causal knowledge typically gained from quasi-experiments and either predictive accuracy or total causal understanding. Much of the discrepancy is surely attributable to quasi-experimentalists prioritizing on the search for nature's dependable causal levers without first fully understanding why certain levers might function efficiently, or without fully understanding why certain levers have functioned efficiently in the past. In cutting out for analysis such a small portion of the presumed lawful world, quasi-experimentalists do not deny an external world of complex causal systems nor do they deny the utility of full understanding. Their apparent ontological modesty is tactical, built on the assumption that within this world causal levers exist that will often, but not invariably, bring about changes that are useful for practical action and the development of grounded social theory.

In this, quasi-experimentation is unlike most of science. Science uses experiments to enhance the explanatory power of theories through the more exact specification of unique mediating processes or through the discovery of unique phenomena deduced from a theory but not deducible from any other known theory. In such experiments there is no presumption of observing causal forces in the typical settings of their operation. Indeed, the whole purpose of laboratory experiments is to modify the normal operations of the external world so as to isolate forces normally correlated with each other or to create novel combinations of forces that do not occur in Nature. The laboratory experiment depends for its utility on the extraordinary combination of ordinary forces; and verisimilitude is of no immediate concern. Quasi-experimentation, on the other hand, probes individual manipulanda that are presumed to have immediate implications for modifying the external world. The testing of causal laws, the generation of causal understanding, are not its strong points.

The crucial issue is whether dependable predictions can be gained by quasi-experimentalists who emphasize only those levers in complex causal systems that they are willing to postulate exist. The traditional scientist would argue "no," and the quasi-experimentalist would argue "often enough to make the strategy viable." There is no difference here in causal ontology; there is a difference, though, in the sections of the presumed real world of causal forces that the researcher should prioritize on — the full system as it is presumed to be, or a few manipulanda within it.

Human Cognition and Motivation

It is by now commonplace to observe that cognitive and motivational constructs play major roles in the social sciences in the form of intentions, preferences, meanings, understandings, and desires. It is also commonplace to observe that, with the exception of some biologists, most of the natural sciences do not deal with such matters. From this follows doubt about whether the methods developed in the natural sciences for an external world devoid of human cognition and motivation are relevant to the world of humans that obviously requires cognitive and motivational concepts for anything approaching a full understanding or explanation of behavior. If quasi-experimentalists claim to be ontological realists, the issue then arises of specifying just how cognitions and motives are assumed to be "real" parts of the external world instead of constructions invented by humans.

On being confronted with this issue, most quasi-experimentalists would probably disagree with its unstated premise about the priority of full causal explanations for social behavior. Instead, quasi-experimentalists seek knowledge about dependable but probabilistic causal relationships between manipulanda and outcomes, knowing that understanding and prediction will be enhanced by learning why particular consequences have come about and knowing further that human perceptions and interpretations will figure among the required explanatory constructs. However, quasi-experimentalists console themselves by noting that prediction and explanation can be advanced within their modest cause-probing context through adding to the sampling and measurement frameworks of a study, and by also noting that one rarely manipulates in direct fashion an intention or motive even when the theoretical rationale for a particular manipulation depends on it influencing cognitions and motivations prior to affecting the outcomes of explicit interest.

A second response of quasi-experimentalists is to claim that its methods continue to be relevant even if the world does not exist other than in the meanings of individuals and in the shared meanings of groups. An observation made by some idealists is that humans seem to have a powerful need to generate causal understandings of events and people, and that they generate these understandings through a process that is superficially akin to scientific inference. That is, they observe concomitances between variables, note temporal precedences where these are clear, and sometimes go about the task of ruling out alternative interpretations. Such processes are less systematic than in science, particularly because in ordinary knowing induction plays a larger role, and the extensive searching for alternative interpretations and for ways of testing their viability plays a smaller role (see the next section on Epistemology). Nonetheless, there is nothing *in principle* to prevent individual knowers from recreating in their heads, or with the aid of simple jottings on paper or blackboards, the processes followed by quasi-experimental researchers, including the use of pretests, control groups, and the like. Are we not capable of thinking: "Did Bob's new job cause him to become more self-disciplined? He took the job last summer, didn't he? He certainly seems to be more self-disciplined since then. Bill recently took the same job. Has he become more self-disciplined, I wonder. Has he changed in any of the other ways Bob has?" Quasi-experiments do not depend for their utility on an external world or on manipulated events and directly observed outcomes. Nor do they necessarily neglect cognitive and motivational constructs. They are structures for probing causal relationships from one variable to another and are extremely plastic where they are carried out (in the head or the field) and in the constructs measured (the behavioral, cognitive, and motivational). They are much less plastic, of course, in their function.

THE EPISTEMOLOGY OF QUASI-EXPERIMENTATION

Much more has been written about the epistemology of quasi-experiments than about their ontology. Recent discussions suggest that quasi-experimentation is buttressed by a postpositivist epistemology with three major pillars. First, objectivity is made a function of intersubjective verifiability across heterogeneous perspectives, and the possibility of theory-neutral measurement is denied. Second, roles are ascribed to both verification and falsification, but the latter is stressed more despite its acknowledged imperfections. And third, the open public discussion of results is emphasized as a means of forcing out the most comprehensive array of currently imaginable alternative interpretations of the findings from a study or a set of related studies. None of these pillars is cast in concrete, and all potential consumers of quasi-experimental research are urged to treat its results as tentative. It could be said, therefore, that quasi-experimentation is probabilist-realist in a fallibilist mode that openly acknowledges the need to debate in truly critical fashion the questions, procedures, and results of studies from a variety of relevant and competing perspectives.

Objectivity

Many quasi-experimentalists would agree with Kuhn (1970) that individual observations are impregnated with the theories of observers. Observations are not pure reproductions of an external reality unsullied by the cognitive and motivational characteristics of knowers. Consequently, any version of objectivity is rejected that is predicated on theory-neutral observations.

Fortunately, this is not the definition of objectivity on which quasi-experiments depend. Most quasi-experimentalists believe that observations are impregnated, not with a single theory, but with multiple theories. Thus, all persons, whatever their preferred theories of physics or theology, make the observation that, on earth, objects tend to fall rather than rise; and all persons, whatever their psychological and sociological preferences, make the observation that external threats tend to increase group cohesiveness. Quasi-experimentalists put most faith in observations that have been reliably repeated across measuring instruments, necessarily fallible, some of which are impregnated with biases presumed to operate in one direction and others with biases operating in a different direction. Such a conception equates objectivity with intersubjective reliability rather than with the infallible measurement of external objects. But it is not any kind of reliability. It is a *critical* reliability based on explicating presumed directions of bias and making sure that biases are involved that operate in all conceivable directions.

The assumption that objectivity is only feasible as critical intersubjective verifiability suggests why quasi-experimental design is associated with multiple operationalism. Quasi-experimentalists reject the positivist notion that constructs are isomorphic with measures, that "IQ is what the IQ test measures." Instead, they see every measure as containing unique variance that is not part of the construct under examination, and as also failing to represent some variance that is part of the construct. From this assumption arises the call for triangulation, for using measures that share the variance presumed to represent the construct of interest but that also have unique sources of theoretically irrelevant variance. The strategy is to test whether a particular pattern of results is obtained *despite* the operation of any potential validity threats located by the unique variance associated with each measure or manipulation.

This same logic is linked to a data analysis strategy based on replication. The preferred strategy is for the analyst to probe whether the same pattern of results occurs despite the irrelevant variance contained in individual data-analytic models and data sets. Just as with single measures or manipulations, quasi-experimentalists are distrustful of results generated from a single data analysis or a single study, however perfect it may appear to be on first reading. Each study is bound to be imbued with the unique perspectives of its investigators, and the hope is to discover a common pattern of results despite the heterogeneity in the models, data, and assumptions of individual researchers.

This discussion highlights the need for a deliberately critical triangulation that self-consciously seeks to make heterogeneous the values of scientists and the inevitable limitations of measurement and of operational specification of research questions. To give a trivial example restricted to measurement, it is hardly useful to have many measures of attitude if all of them are paper and pencil, for there is nothing about most conceptualizations of attitude that restricts them to a paper-and-pencil mode of data collection. A better strategy would be to vary the mode of data collection to include direct behavioral observation, face-to-face interviews, and other data collection methods. To replicate is not to triangulate. The former is usually less self-conscious and critical than is the latter. Nonetheless, triangulation is itself inherently imperfect. To be perfect would require that all the alternative interpretations of a measure or set of measures have been incorporated into tests. Given that this notion can only be tested inductively, it can never be fully justified. However, a consciousness of the need for *critical* triangulation can permit the analyst and his or her commentators to force out more alternative interpretations and to deal in a more complete fashion with those that have been identified to date.

Verification and Falsification

Quasi-experiments serve to *probe* causal relationships. The choice of verb is important, for cause is probed or tested but never proven. It is something inferred and not observed, and the inference necessarily depends on logically imperfect information. Each probe should take two necessary, but individually insufficient, forms. One is based on verifying that the pattern of data conforms with a particular causal hypothesis; and the other is based on falsifying all identified interpretations of the data pattern other than the one that is provisionally preferred.

It is obvious that the covariation of two measures does not verify a causal connection because the logical possibility always holds that other hypotheses may also fit the data. The likelihood of such alternatives is lowest when theoretical predictions have been made that are so exact (i.e., in specifying the angle of the perihelion of a planet) or so counterintuitive that no other plausible theory can currently explain them. Hence the pressures to mathematize theories and to make predictions about outcomes that are novel for the setting under study. A crucial issue in the social sciences is whether our theories permit the numerically precise predictions or the unique outcomes required by a verificationist perspective. An important epistemological issue is whether verification is not itself replete with latent falsification, for one might argue that precise and unique predictions only further causal inference because they reduce the number of alternative interpretations. Another question for epistemologists is whether verification falls short of perfection because, as the history of science repeatedly illustrates, the precise and unique predictions of one generation are often subsumed into different theories in later generations — although the primary observations of the original theory need not be foresaken. Newton's theory provides the most frequently cited illustration of a theory that made precise and empirically verified predictions but was nonetheless superseded by another theory — Einstein's. Precision and uniqueness probe theories but do not prove them; in the social sciences it is doubtful whether too many unique predictions will be forthcoming. After all, humans have for millenia been winnowing unsubstantiated propositions about human nature out of our stock of common sense, leaving us with an edited supply of ideas that have withstood many of the verification (and falsification) tests of the past.

Quasi-experimentalists owe a large debt to Popper (1958, 1968) because of his emphasis on falsification, on trying to infirm hypotheses as well as confirm them. Falsification requires explicating all of the plausible threats to the validity of, say, a causal relationship and then conducting as honest a set of tests as one can to see if these alternatives can be ruled out. If they can, the initial causal relationship is treated as provisionally true, although the possibility has to be acknowledged that it may be superseded in the future. If the alternatives cannot be ruled out, then the analyst remains in public doubt as to what should be considered provisionally true.

Permeating this conception of the role of falsification are two crucial assumptions. The first is that falsification tests are definitive, whereas verification tests are not. The logic for this is that verification, as usually conceived, is based on induction: e.g., "Every person I have met who lives in Llanbedr has a Welsh accent. Therefore, every person in Llanbedr is Welsh or has a Welsh accent." The problem with such an inference is that non-Welsh people can have Welsh accents, and in the future there may be persons in Llanbedr with no trace of a Welsh accent. On the other hand, falsification is based on deductive logic: "If all the people in Llanbedr have Welsh accents, and if I meet one resident who does not have a Welsh accent, then the basic postulate is clearly disproved by the observation of someone without a Welsh accent."

Popper's thesis about the definitiveness of falsification is better grounded in logic than in the practice of science. Scientists do not give up hypotheses or theories if they are infirmed, even a number of times. Most of them disbelieve the first tests and then modify their theory to take account of the disconfirming observation, often by adding on ad hoc qualifications. Rarely is the theory abandoned. Also, Popper's thinking is based on the ability to confront general statements with empirical tests of particulars. But his work has not yet fully grappled with the impossibility of collecting observations that provide convincing "pure" empirical tests of what is false. This is particularly salient in social science research traditions that use statistical tests. There, the dogma is that one cannot prove the null hypothesis. Yet it is by accepting the null hypothesis that one acts as though a particular relationship were nonexistent and so rules out an alternative as "false." Falsification does not offer the practicing scientist a trouble-free route to truth; as with verification, the inferences that scientists draw are necessarily fallible. However, falsification does promote a self-conscious critical attitude that is at least congruent with logic, and that is why quasi-experiments stress it so heavily.

The second assumption of a falsification perspective is that all relevant alternative interpretations have been identified in the theory of quasi-experimentation. Campbell and Stanley (1963) advanced a number of specific alternatives (called "threats to validity"). These represent hypotheses derived from prior experience either about forces whose causal influence is frequently confounded with that of treatments (internal validity) or forces whose operation influences the generality of presumed causal connections (external validity). Dunn (1982) objects to this, mostly because the two types of validity fail to deal with the problem of asking trivial research questions, about which he has generated his own list of threats. Dunn is also concerned — as is Cronbach (1980) — with the primacy given to internal validity in the theory of quasi-experimentation. Internal validity deals with the validity of inferences about whether the relationship between two operations is causal; the worry is that prioritizing on cause within the confines of a single study neglects questions about the transferrability of the findings to other settings, populations, constructs, and versions of a treatment.

These objections are not epistemological in the sense of dealing with how we know. Rather, they are differences about priorities in what is worth knowing. Dunn wants to make the latter explicitly problematic from study to study and seeks to provide a framework for assessing importance. In this, I can imagine no quasi-experimentalist disagreeing. To the charge that the theory of quasi-experimentation has been too uncritical about guiding research questions, many quasi-experimentalists would probably reply, "I take it for granted that researchers can justify the importance of the issues they work on. If techniques exist for raising consciousness on this issue, I would like to learn about them. They may prove to be important adjuncts to quasi-experimentation. But they will probably be relevant to all research, and not just to quasi-experimentation."

Criticism of the primacy of falsifying threats to internal validity can be countered three ways. First, quasi-experimental research does not ignore external validity; Campbell did, after all, invent the term in recognition of the importance of generalizing to specific populations; also, Cook and Campbell (1979) emphasized the related need to generalize *across* different populations. Second, it is an assumption of most experimentalists that the costs of being wrong about causal connections are usually higher than the costs of being wrong about whether a well-corroborated causal finding can be generalized to the population from which the research sample was selected, or even to related populations. This assumption cannot be convincingly tested. Its justification depends on accepting the following argument: "If we state that X causes Y but are wrong, we may then advocate the widespread manipulation of X; if we state that X does not cause Y but are again wrong, then we may abstain from implementing what might have been helpful." On the other hand, if we are correct that X causes Y in a sample of Welshmen from Llangollen, Aberystwyth, and Ruthin, we might feel relatively comfortable in generalizing the causal knowledge to all of Wales or to another northern city with Welsh speakers (e.g., Denbigh) or even to the parts of east-central Wales that have few Welsh speakers and to the parts of south Wales that are heavily industrial. At this point, the issue concerns reasonable common sense, with the parties differing as to what is most commonsensical. The third point to be made in favor of the primacy of internal validity is circular in its logic, but nonetheless of importance. To choose to conduct a quasi-experiment should mean that causal inferences about manipulanda are important, for the sole justification of quasi-experiments is that they permit better probes of causal connections in field settings than do other research designs. Since research questions should dictate method choices and not vice versa, the choice to conduct a quasi-experiment already presupposes a very high priority for internal validity.

Being Public and Critical

The published lists of threats to validity represent attempts to make researchers more critical, to force them to worry about whether particular threats have been ruled out. The lists offer general guidelines, and should not be applied, willy-nilly, to every research project in the anticipation that once all the listed threats have been dealt with "truth" remains. Texts on quasi-experimentation link particular validity threats to particular experimental designs (e.g., Cook and Campbell, 1979), but they also note that the designs and threats are not inevitably linked. In some projects new threats may be uncovered that have not yet been discovered, and sometimes a threat that usually goes with a particular design will be irrelevant in a specific research instance. The validity threats are meant to raise consciousness and not to be checklists that guarantee truth.

The inevitable fallibility of knowledge of the external world, and the recognition that this fallibility results in part from the uniqueness of individual perspectives, should dispose quasi-experimentalists to welcome criticism. They should, of course, strive for the maximal self-criticism, in part guided by common sense, substantive knowledge, experimental design, and knowledge of validity threats. But they should also strive to have their work critically examined by others. I try to teach students in courses on Quasi-Experimentation that "your substantive and methodological enemies are your best friends." This is meant to capture the importance, both of gaining alternative perspectives on one's work and of dealing seriously with these objections. I tell students that if they are inclined to treat a particular threat as "implausible" but their enemies are not, then they should deal with it. I also tell them that their critics are in a special position to point out alternatives that have not yet been identified or adequately dealt with. Public exposure promotes a self-conscious stance of great importance, making for a more *critical* falsification than even the most honest self-criticism can achieve. Although public criticism is vital at all stages of research, with important projects it is inevitable (and desirable) that critical commentary will eventually appear and suggest new limitations of the work or novel interpretations of its findings. Such public debate involves triangulation — not now of methods, but of perspectives on the importance of research questions, on the alternative interpretations that need to be considered, on the adequacy with which the alternatives have been treated, and on the meanings that should be attached to results.

Implicit in this advocacy of public criticism is a realization that, so long as ultimate truth is not accessible, the process of assigning validity is social and partly dependent upon a consensus achieved in debate. This is a process that in some ways is more akin to the assignment of social credibility than scholarly validity. However, the process is social *within limits*, for discussions about research findings are typically disciplined by agreement that some possible threats appear implausible in light of the findings and characteristics of the research design, as well as in light of past findings and our cultural stock of critical common sense. The hypothesis, then, is that public discussion usually determines the degree of temporary legitimacy that is conferred on claimed findings through a process to which the methods of science have usually contributed by rendering implausible some alternative interpretations that might have been offered and by focusing the discussion on the major unresolved issues that remain. However, the degree to which public discussion is critical ultimately depends on the range of relevant perspectives from which the work is publicly examined, and not on the public nature of the discussion per se.

Quasi-experimentation is more dependent on criticism than are other forms of experimentation. This is because fewer threats are dealt with through such omnibus mechanisms as random assignment or the creation of closed testing systems. If random assignment is properly implemented and maintained during a study, researchers do not have to concern themselves with falsifying threats associated with selection, history, or the like, since the assignment process has controlled for them. Similarly, the closed environment of the laboratory automatically rules out most threats. However, quasi-experimentalists are forced to make explicit and problematic the very threats that other experimentalists do not even have to learn about because their methods and research settings deal with them automatically. It follows from this that the quality of causal inference will generally be lower in quasi-experimental research and that the amount of space devoted to critical examination will be higher. Quasi-experimentation should be characterized by a large number of validity threats that are explicitly formulated and then explicitly tested in attempts to refute their power to explain obtained results. These tests will typically involve recourse to data and circumstances both within a study and across different studies.

The high level of self-criticism that should be found among quasi-experimentalists is not only because of the fewer mechanisms for automatically taking account of threats, but it is also because of the wider range of threats to be dealt with. Few laboratory researchers are concerned with the direct application of their findings, and reports of laboratory research rarely include extended discussion of the range of applicability of results. Yet application and the transfer of knowledge are crucial in quasi-experimental work. Laboratory research concerns the study of processes that bring about a particular outcome, and there is usually less overt concern with what an outcome "stands for," with the utility of concentrating on some outcomes rather than others, or with the utility of concentrating on outcomes rather than micro-level processes that mediate outcomes. Being concerned with a wider range of research questions makes quasi-experimentation seem more problematic than laboratory research. Yet were one to apply the same range of validity concerns, other forms of experimentation would then suddenly seem more problematic. Their clean elegance is in large measure due to prioritizing on a narrow range of all possible research questions.

METHODOLOGY

The Three Mechanisms of Falsification

The probing of hypotheses about causal relationships is achieved by means of three primary mechanisms. The most distinctive is experimental design, and most commentators probably think of quasi-experimentation as an elaborate OXO game. The Os represent observations, and the Xs treatments (or, when there is no X, the absence of a treatment). Other conventions add to the OXO vocabulary — e.g., dotted lines between rows of Os and Xs that represent groups of nonequivalent composition. In general, quasi-experimentalists strive for pretest and posttest measures that are in as long a series as possible, the use of groups that are minimally different from each other (provided that they were not matched on the dependent variable), and the reintroduction or removal of a treatment at different time points. The hope is always to implement a design that, through a combination of the procedures outlined above, will rule out most of the currently identified threats to internal validity.

The second mechanism for ruling out threats involves measurement, often coupled with statistical analysis. If one fears that unexpected historical events could take place between a pretest and posttest and make interpretation more difficult, one can scour archives, hire observers, or interview persons at the research sites in order to discover which historical forces have actually operated and whether they can account for the observed findings. Similarly, when the treatment groups are initially nonequivalent and pretest scores are used as covariates, researchers are doing more than just a statistical test. They are attempting to adjust statistically for a particular pattern of selection-maturation in which the nonequivalent groups are growing apart at a constant rate. Although some commentators feel that a design control for selection-maturation might be more appropriate than a statistical one, the latter is nonetheless possible if one is willing to accept certain assumptions: in this case, assumptions about the form of the (unobserved) selection-maturation pattern and about the absence of bias due to unreliability in the pretest.

The third mechanism for testing whether particular alternative interpretations can be ruled out is critical common sense. We know through a variety of means that not having shoes is hardly plausible as a cause of failure to attend schools in most of the United States, though it may be with some Native American children. Part of our stock of common sense, buttressed by millions of observations, tells us that almost all children in the United States have access to shoes. Critical common sense also tells us that aspirin alleviates headaches. It would therefore be plausible to assume in an experiment on stress reduction that a low level of headaches by arthritis patients may be due, not to drugs designed to reduce stress, but to the aspirins they routinely take to reduce the physical pain of arthritis. Each culture has a stock of wisdom that, upon examination, may prove to be based on social or scientific methods that have winnowed out some of the possible causes of X and have left us with a small edited set of contenders. In other words, critical common sense is one of the means whereby *possible* alternatives are assigned approximate *plausibility* value.

CONCLUSION

Quasi-experimental research is most useful when one wants to answer questions about causal relationships in contexts in which random assignment to treatments is not possible and in which laboratory settings are considered irrelevant to the conceptual issue being probed. Quasi-experimentation is less useful for purposes of prediction, causal explanation (however this is defined), or discovering unimagined causal connections. The premises of quasi-experimentation assume both a greater pessimism about the quality of extant social science theory than is true for methods of causal explanation (i.e., structural equation modeling), and also a greater distrust of correlational data than is the case with scholars interested in prediction. In areas in which substantive theory is weak, or in which the confusion of correlation and causation may have particularly mischievous consequences and independent and dependent variables can be identified in advance, quasi-experimentation is particularly called for.

Utility depends on another issue. Most quasi-experimentalists explicitly or implicitly endorse a manipulability theory of causation. They want to answer the practical question of what happens to Y if X is changed. Quasi-experimentalists might see greater ultimate utility to the scholar's question: What are the determinants of Y? Indeed, like all persons of intellect, they yearn for an answer to the scholar's question, provided that the determinants include manipulable causes and any factors on which such causes directly depend. But yearning is not practical action, and quasi-experimentalists want self-critical, modest knowledge about manipulanda, and they want it soon. They want self-critical knowledge because they realize the difficulty of conceptualizing and ruling out all the plausible (let alone possible) threats to valid inference. They want modest knowledge because their aim is not to "understand" or "predict" all of the variance in the dependent variable — they want only to test whether varying X increases the amount of predicted variance. They want knowledge about manipulanda — things that can be changed — rather than elegant knowledge about structural factors in society or persons that cannot be readily changed. Finally, they want knowledge about manipulanda soon. Some problems of society are too urgent to await the elegant, *well-corroborated* causal modeling that we will eventually attain and for which we quasi-experimentalists, like others, long.

Although quasi-experimentation is largely an OXO framework in search of valid causal inferences about practical manipulanda, it can be modified to meet other research goals. Additions to the sampling and measurement frameworks can, for instance, lead to the structural modeling of presumed explanatory processes, while on-site observational methods can be yoked to the basic design to provide information on a richer array of mediating and outcome variables. Also, the basic designs can be implemented in thought experiments in which critical analysts decide on control groups, pre- and posttest time periods, and then contrast the imagined changes in one set of circumstances with those in another. Quantification is not necessary for quasi-experimental designs to add a critical perspective to causal reasoning about the world. As illustrated above, quasi-experimentation is methodologically flexible, but always within the constraint that it does prioritize on answering causal questions about discrete events, most of which can be deliberately manipulated.

Quasi-experimentalists assume a realist ontology. But the approach does not require this assumption, for one can readily imagine self-critical individuals using (or independently reinventing) quasi-experimental methods to help them analyze the causal forces in their private world which they assume others cannot know. Most quasi-experimentalists also assume a fallibilist epistemology, in which (1) observations of nature are problematic and best based on heterogeneous intersubjective verification, and (2) causal inferences are also problematic because they require ruling out some threats as implausible that, after they have been commented on by later generations with their unique assumptions, may turn out to be "true." Quasi-experimentation therefore has to be modest about its goals and the validity of its achievements. However, it should not lose heart, for many of the dilemmas with which it is beset affect all scholarly research, or all quantitative research, or all cause-probing research. They are problems of knowledge in general and are not specific to the Xs and Os of quasi-experimental design.

About the Author

THOMAS D. COOK

I somehow survived a working-class upbringing in Birkenhead, England, and some disastrous years when I studied German and French at Oxford. I then was nearly sidetracked into becoming a Eurocrat, survived thanks to chance, and came from the University of Saarbrücken to the U.S.A. where I quickly felt quite at home. After gaining a degree in communications from Stanford, I came to Northwestern University, where I have been and been, and been. My research interests are somewhat eclectic, mainly dealing with evaluation and the effects of television.

6

ACTION RESEARCH

A Sociotechnical Systems Perspective

Gerald I. Susman

The Pennsylvania State University

The problems I try to solve either to satisfy my own intellectual curiosity or to perform a professional service for a client have led me to adopt views about the nature of the world and how to learn more about it. These views are the accumulated product of all my past attempts to solve particular kinds of problems under particular sets of conditions. The problems I try to solve take place within organizations, quite often at the level of the work group, where raw materials are converted into products. Most often, I am presented with a problem occurring in an existing concrete setting, rather than a problem raised by theory that then leads me to search for or create a setting within which to understand the problem better. Not only do I desire to solve the problems presented to me; I also desire to do so in a way that the client is as committed as I am to carrying out the solutions.

I come to terms with the conditions described through "action research," a general mode of inquiry that seeks to contribute to the practical concerns of people in a problematic situation *and* to the goals of social science within a mutually acceptable ethical framework (Rapoport, 1970). I come to understand the concrete setting in which there is a problem by making a conceptual representation of it (Lewin, 1938) from which by both observation and reasoning I reach a solution to the problem and test the solution through action. The work of reasoning from the concrete to hypothetical solutions to the problem is carried by a set of interdependent beliefs that are at least provisionally, if not strongly, accepted, so that an inquiry can proceed. These beliefs are the foundation on which new knowledge is created. They are not assumed to correspond in any direct way to any underlying reality. They are only means I use to arrive at testable inferences. Confirmation of these inferences grants them, in Dewey's words, "warranted assertability."

Through action research, problems in concrete settings are re-defined within a framework of concepts and operations that present the problems in a generalized form, thereby permitting action research to contribute jointly to its two goals. Since the solution is tested by acting on it to see whether it produces the consequences it implies, action research unites thinking and doing or theory and practice.

ONTOLOGY AND EPISTEMOLOGY

I believe there is a real world that exists independently of me and of which I will always have imperfect and incomplete knowledge. I come closest to experiencing it directly when I try to minimize inter-preting it and concentrate on nothing but "pure" qualities like colors, sounds, smells, and the like. If I make any pretense to knowing something about that world (e.g., how it works), that knowledge will be limited by the language and conceptual frameworks I have learned as a product of the time and place I occupy historically and culturally. I believe in the independence of such a world because I am continu-ously "bumping up against" it when my expectations and predictions are not realized. Were the world outside of me purely a creation of my imagination, I would expect it to be more compliant to my wishes and provide me with fewer surprises. Although it is not possible to get a direct knowledge of it, I can gain knowledge in an indirect manner by probing the nature and consequences of the beliefs I hold, by asking such questions as: What difference would it make if I acted on these beliefs? Does acting on these beliefs produce consequences that I intend be produced? Can I develop rules for modifying my beliefs to improve their ability to do this and eliminating beliefs that do not?

The Pragmatist Viewpoint

My position is a pragmatist one, and the fundamental epistemolog-ical questions for me are why do I want to know *more* about the world, how should I go about knowing *more* about it, and how can I gain confidence that I have learned *more* about it? I have emphasized the word *more* in these three questions because I believe that no scientific inquiry can begin from scratch. I cannot advance my knowledge of the world except from the vantage point of the knowledge about it I have previously accepted and use as a resource in my subsequent inquiries. I must raise myself to new knowledge by my own bootstraps, so to speak. Since I can never be entirely certain of the knowledge I already accept, any new knowledge I gain may so undermine my world view that it may tumble like a house of cards if the new knowledge seriously challenges what I already accept.

I follow John Dewey (1929) in assuming that knowledge is a human artifact created as a means for coming to terms with the world as well as for creating it. The knowledge we accumulate, our methods for accumulating it, and the criteria by which our methods are con- sidered scientific are all historical products, the result of past attempts for dealing with what Dewey called "problematic situations." The methods used and the criteria for appraising them as scientific are matters of social convention. As situations we consider problematic change, so may our methods for dealing with them and our criteria for judging them as scientific.

Why I want to know more about the world. The pragmatist view- point suggests that I want to know more about the world when I am blocked from, or uncertain about, achieving the outcomes I desire and seek. This occurs because I do not understand the situations in which I want to take action or I am uncertain about what action to take to achieve them. The outcomes may be influenced by any mix of intrinsic or instrumental values. My uncertainty about situations or what action to take in them is what makes them problematic and is the point from which inquiry begins. More precisely, Dewey calls the initially experienced situation "indeterminate" or "unsettled" be- cause the quality of the experience is precognitive and emotional. However, the situation becomes problematic as soon as it is seen as requiring inquiry.

This viewpoint has several implications and advantages. First of all, it should be clear that knowledge is not being created to mirror a reality that is independent of human action and exists in an eternal unchanging state, but to deal with it. Second, starting inquiry from problematic situations reduces the risk that scientific inquiry will degenerate to being merely a scholastic exercise, undertaken not to reduce an inquirer's doubt, but to build a theory for its own sake. Third, this viewpoint increases the likelihood that theory intended for application to practical problems will ultimately serve that purpose.

Theory developed out of attempts to understand concrete situations is more likely to remain applicable to future concrete situations.

How I gain more knowledge about the world. In studying organizations, I start from the assumption that organizations make sense when thought of as systems and draw heavily on theories developed to explain the evolution and maintenance of biological and social systems. This appeals to me since I believe that the world evolves into varying states of organization through processes of mutual adjustment (Wiener, 1954) that are nondeterministic and unfinished. Human ideas play an important role in this process, transforming the natural world through the social systems they create, so much so that humans are partners with nature in the course of evolution. Every social system (shaped by values that create shared definitions of situations) has a technical dimension that is sometimes so well developed that it deserves a label of its own — a technical system. In the modern business organization, the technical system might consist of the movement in time and space of raw materials to be converted by machines or muscles into products; it is organized around instrumental values such as efficiency and effectiveness. Technical systems and social systems coexist and are interdependent (Emery and Trist, 1960). Both are human artifacts, and the values that dominate them influence actions in fundamentally different ways. If the instrumental values of a technical system are allowed to dominate the intrinsic values of a social system, the former will remake the latter in its own image, just as scientific management might do to a workplace and its members. The technical system is then no longer an extension of the social system, to be used to realize the desired outcomes of social system members; rather, it has become an alien object turned back on its creators to oppress them.

I gain knowledge about social and technical systems by assuming first that each is organized into a pattern wherein the parts of each respective system make up a discernible whole. I assume that parts of a technical system were organized to achieve a consciously desired outcome and that my understanding of this system will be hastened by the assumption that the parts have a functional relationship to each other and that some relationships were consciously chosen over others because they improved the efficiency and effectiveness with which the desired outcome can be achieved. This does not preclude me from looking for relationships in the technical system that meet criteria based on intrinsic values or are historical vestiges of earlier technologies. However, I am most likely to do this when parts of the technical system do not fit the pattern that follows from assuming the technical system is dominated by instrumental values.

While knowledge of the technical system is gained primarily through direct observation, knowledge of the social system is gained phenomenologically by "taking the role of the other" (Mead, 1934) in order to understand the shared definitions of system members, with the aid of interviews or by participant observation. The more my definitions of the situation overlap those of social system members, the more will their actions be understood by me. My objective is not complete overlap, because I do not want to live their lives in the existential sense they do. I need a different perspective of the social system as a whole, the values around which it is organized, the functions it performs for its members and for any larger system of which it is a part, and how the parts, especially roles, integrate and maintain this whole. My confidence in the knowledge I have gained increases by following the hermeneutical circle (Gadamer, 1975) or what Kaplan (1964) calls the "circle of interpretation," which takes the form of attempting an initially holistic understanding of a social system and then using this understanding as a basis for interpreting the parts of the system. Knowledge is gained dialectically by proceeding from the whole to its parts and then back again. Each time an incongruence occurs between part and whole, a reconceptualization takes place. The frequency of reconceptualization decreases as the match improves between my conception of the social system and that held by the system's members.

I gain confidence that the sociotechnical systems model on which I draw is adequate for the concrete situations I wish to explain because it performs the functions of the pattern model of explanation (Kaplan, 1964). It provides for predictions (although not necessarily through deduction) by specifying what is needed to fill in the pattern. The pattern does not uniquely determine its parts so that knowledge of the pattern as a whole and of some of its parts does not always enable us to predict the others. The explanation still explains even though it leaves open a range of possibilities so that which possibility is actualized is known only after the fact. The last statement can apply also to the deductive model of explanation because all the factors that would allow a prediction to be uniquely determined are seldom known, permitting us to predict only how likely a particular outcome is.

The pattern model and the deductive model both allow prediction without taking action toward the object of inquiry (other than the act of looking where the model tells us to look to verify the prediction). Yet I do not see myself as a spectator of my world who can stand back from it, make predictions about it, and assume they will be realized if I assiduously avoid interfering in the world once the prediction has been made. The pragmatist criterion of verification requires that we act on our beliefs to see whether they produce consequences that we should expect if our beliefs are warranted. This is the essence of the experimental method, regardless whether I take action on a naturally existing situation or on one constructed so as to test my beliefs. Yet I cannot use prediction in the same way I might for a closed physical system or a simple social system created in the experimental laboratory.

The nature of social systems in and of themselves, as well as their linkage to technical systems, raises practical difficulties in using prediction as a basis for gaining confidence in my knowledge of social systems. The reasons for this were stated in Susman and Evered (1978: 594):

> Unlike deterministic physical systems, the nonrandomness or the structuredness of a social system results from shared codes of conduct or rules of its members. Even if the intended target of an intervention were changing the physical aspects of a [technical] system, e.g., layout, machinery, etc., it still would be mediated by communicating such intentions to members of the social system and gaining the consent of at least its most influential members. Thus, initially, the target of most proposed change efforts concerns the conceptions and ideas of members of the system. If we also consider the personal investments that organizational members have in a particular structure, technology, etc., because of how these arrangements have allowed them to accommodate to conflicts over power, prestige, and attention, we can see that the social system is open ended with respect to the consequences of any proposed change. Acts of communication are unlike actions taken toward physical objects in that acts of communication may simultaneously convey multiple meanings, i.e., manifest and latent content, conscious or unconscious, or they may be subject to different interpretations by sender and receiver. Also, the targets of a proposed change will not know what their reactions will be to a proposed change until they have a chance to contemplate their reactions by mentally rehearsing them or by experiencing the changes first hand.

My criterion for verification when acting on complex social systems of this kind is prediction in a restricted sense. I wish to verify two kinds of belief: (1) An imagined or idealized (Ackoff, 1974) future configuration of a sociotechnical system (i.e., a design) will produce desired outcomes. (2) Certain actions (i.e., a plan) will bring about the design. The first belief is amenable to verification by prediction because I can see whether the design, if realized, produces the desired outcomes (e.g., greater quantity and quality of product at less cost and time, and better quality of working life for all system members). A realized design in this case means that only certain critical structures and processes are within specifications, leaving other, less critical variables to vary or fluctuate more freely (Herbst, 1974).

The second belief is not amenable to verification by prediction because we do not know what actions will bring about the design until we achieve it. The uncertainty arises from the fact that the designers cannot predict beyond a relatively short period (and even within this period sometimes not too well) what the consequences of a planned action will be for the system. Any action taken is likely to set off emergent processes within the system as it seeks to adjust to the disturbance created by the action and to achieve a new steady state. We have some verification that the actions taken were the right ones to take if the design has been realized. Then we can retrospectively reconstruct the plan to see how the system was conceptualized during the stages of its transformation, what intervention decisions this led to, and what consequences followed. Through hindsight, we can affirm or revise our conceptualizations of the system and its stages of transformation and choose the same or different actions if we are faced with similar circumstances. Such retrospective reconstructions provide for learning how to bring about system designs or how to make them happen, not for predicting that a design will be realized by taking certain actions. It is the capability of the planner rather than the validity of the plan that is being improved through this process. The same plan is not likely to be used again (although some of the system conceptualizations will likely prove useful) as no two designs, or the conditions the system faces during its initial and transformation stages, are likely to be the same.

CONDUCT OF THE RESEARCH PROCESS

My conduct of the research process follows the model presented by Susman and Evered (Figure 6.1). It involves a cyclical process with five phases that closely parallel the steps John Dewey (1933) outlined as necessary for reflective thinking. The five phases are *diagnosing, action planning, action taking, evaluating,* and *specifying learning.* The infrastructure of the client's system and the action researcher maintain and regulate some or all of these five phases jointly.

The cycle begins with recognition of a problematic situation, which as Dewey suggests, is a prerequisite for the reflective thinking

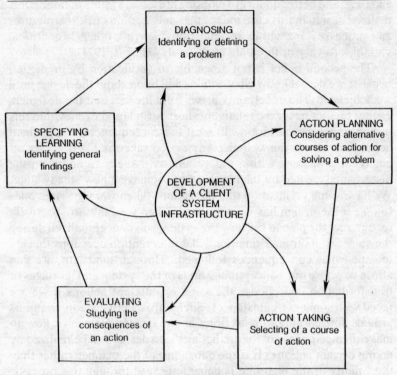

SOURCE: Reprinted from "The Scientific Merits of Action Research" by G. I. Susman and R. Evered published in *Administrative Science Quarterly*, vol. 123, p. 588 by permission of *The Administrative Science Quarterly*. Copyright © 1978 by Cornell University.

Figure 6.1 The Cyclical Process of Action Research

that I am trying to stimulate both for me and for my client. Doubt about how to achieve a desired outcome creates a "snag" in the ongoing stream of un-self-conscious action and leads action, in Dewey's words, "to be turned in upon itself as thought."

Since our discussion is about sociotechnical systems, the desired outcomes are the production of system outputs at acceptable standards and by means that are satisfying to system members. A problematic situation occurs when (1) the system's outputs are not longer being produced at acceptable standards and/or the system's means for producing them are no longer satisfying to members, *and* (2) the system members do not know what actions to take to make the outputs and/or means acceptable or satisfying again. Evidence that system outputs are no longer acceptable might include lower product quantity, poorer quality, slower delivery, or higher costs. Evidence that system means are no longer satisfying might include higher conflict, higher turnover, absenteeism, or poorer coordination. If the client does not already experience a situation as problematic, then I can help sharpen this experience by asking the client to (1) articulate a desired outcome, (2) articulate present outcomes, and (3) compare desired with present outcomes.

I must assume that I could not have proceeded to this point or, at least, could proceed no further unless I have encouraged the client to suspend judgment about what the problem is and to undertake the subsequent phases of the action research model collaboratively with me and with other members of the client's organization making up the client's system's infrastructure shown in Figure 6.1. These system members have been chosen for their representativeness and for the power and influence they can bring to bear to carry out the actions to which they collectively agree. It is no minor task for the consultant to help such a collection of persons to develop into an effective problem-solving group, to reach consensus on how their reality is defined, and to use a process of problem solving to which they may be unaccustomed. Some team building (Dyer, 1977) or process consultation (Schein, 1972) may be required before or while the phases of action research are undertaken.

The Cyclical Phases of Action Research

Diagnosing

Frustration and doubt are likely to accompany the client's experiencing a situation as problematic. Such emotions may not be dysfunctional because they provide the energy the client needs to work on the problem. It is my responsibility, especially if I helped sharpen the experience that makes the situation problematic, to help the client deal with these emotions through developing an intellectual understanding of the situation (Dewey calls this stage "intellectualization"). I do this by presenting the client with a systems framework with which to diagnose the "facts" of the situation. Facts are in quotes because facts are never raw, but are interpreted within the systems framework. The systems framework functions as a "working hypothesis," in Kaplan's (1964) words, by guiding the inquirer toward what facts should be collected. The systems framework, as working hypothesis, guides the collection of facts so that they may be organized into an integrated whole (e.g., systems have boundaries, transform inputs into outputs, achieve steady-states). The sociotechnical systems model makes the following assumptions in diagnosing problematic situations:

(1) A concrete work setting can be conceptualized as two correlated technical and social systems (i.e., a sociotechnical system).

(2) A sociotechnical system produces less than optimal performance when there is a mismatch between the social and technical systems or between the sociotechnical system and its environment.

(3) Only some properties of either system need stay within specifiable limits in order for each to maintain a consistent pattern of relationships within itself and with respect to each other. These characteristics are, for the technical system: (a) location of variances, (b) location of decisions and information, and (c) interdependence between required activities, and for the social system: (a) rewards, (b) values, and (c) roles.

(4) Social system members are guided primarily by instrumental values (rather than by intrinsic values) in selecting efficient and effective means for achieving the desired outcomes of the sociotechnical system.

The client is asked to observe the facts of the problematic situation by using the sociotechnical systems model as a guide. Some of the facts toward which the client is directed include, but by no means exhaust, the following:

(1) *The Technical System*. Identify:

(a) the present *boundaries* of the technical system so that we can determine what is within the system and what is in its environment (this is a tentative identification because we may modify these boundaries later according to criteria to be specified);

(b) the system's *inputs* and *outputs* (How well are their properties understood and how stable are they? When and where do they enter and exit the system?);

(c) the *activities* within the system by which inputs are converted into outputs; and

(d) the *spatiotemporal flow of conversion activities*, the degree of interdependence between them, the location of variances from the planned flow, and the frequency and sequencing of these variances.

(2) *The Social System*. Identify:

(a) the *roles* of social system members (i.e., the activities and decisions formally assigned to them and any informal elaboration beyond what has been assigned);

(b) the *values* of social system members (What goals and objectives and ways of achieving them are considered desirable by social system members?);

(c) *rewards* (Is cooperation or competition rewarded? Is short-term or medium- and long-term performance rewarded? Is the pay differential between members narrow or wide?); and

(d) how much *challenge* and *responsibility* social system members say they want.

(3) Look for mismatches:

    (a) between the technical system and its environment.

        (i) Are boundaries located so that the interdependence between required activities within the system's boundaries is greater than the interdependence of required activities that cross the system's boundaries?

        (ii) Can uncertainty regarding inputs that cross the system's boundaries be reduced by changing inputs? By decisions made by other systems? If not, has adequate decision making been delegated to social system members to deal with it?

    (b) within the social system.

        (i) Is there sufficient consensus within the system on the values that guide member behavior?

        (ii) Is the group sufficiently developed so that it has learned how it will resolve conflicts, make decisions, and choose its leaders?

    (c) between the technical system and social system.

        (i) Do the roles of social system members contain activities that offer as much challenge and responsibility as they say they want?

        (ii) Do the roles of social system members allow early detection and response to variances? Do they include enough decision making and access to information for the social system members to respond alone or in concert with others?

        (iii) Do the values and rewards of the social system encourage the decision making and problem solving that are necessary for the social and technical systems to maintain a steady state?

I encourage clients to use the sociotechnical systems model to explain their problematic situation — why there is a gap between their desired and present outcomes. The key assumption of the model is that the gap results from a mismatch between the two systems. The model is used to observe the facts of the problematic situation, and if one or more answers to the questions asked in section 3 are negative, then we know the reason why the outcomes of the client's system are less than desired. As Dewey (1933: 108) has said: "A question well put is half answered. In fact, we know what the problem *exactly* is simultaneously with finding a way out and getting it resolved. Problem and solution stand out *completely* at the same time."

Action Planning and Action Taking

The sociotechnical system model that defines the problem as a mismatch between two systems leads to solutions that are defined in the same terms. The solution is a better match between the social and technical systems; the two systems will then produce outcomes at improved levels. The concepts of "best match" and "joint optimization" are used in much of the sociotechnical systems literature. The concept of best match does not imply that one and only one design permits the most effective utilization of the technical and social systems. Both systems are open systems, and, consequently, alternative arrangements will yield the same level of performance within the constraints imposed by their most critical requirements. Just as there is no single arrangement that will produce a best match, there is no specific formula that a designer can follow to achieve it. The design process is a search for the best solution to what appears to be a set of conflicting requirements between a social and technical system. The best solution is necessarily an innovation as well as a work of art in the broadest sense of the term. If the solution were obvious it would be merely calculated; there would be no design problem as such.

In practice, design recommendations to bring the two systems into better match follow by reasoning first in terms of one system and then in terms of the other. In this way, we guard against doing violence to the social system by redefining its members and their phenomenal world in technical system terms. We are in danger of reifying or objectifying the social system if we think in terms of finding jointly optimal solutions, because performing such a calculation requires us to define both systems along a common dimensional domain. Yet reasoning about social systems in phenomenological terms and technical systems in physicochemical terms need not imply a Cartesian duality. The differences that appear to exist between the two systems are not due to differences in substance, but to different epistemological assumptions that an inquirer makes in order to gain knowledge about the two systems. Different epistemological assumptions produce knowledge about each system that is not easily translatable or comprehensible to the other.

The *technical system* is represented as a concrete system (Miller, 1965) whose parts are patterned to correspond to the pattern of matter, energy, and information flows identified in the situation being studied. It is assumed to behave in accordance with generalizations and laws found in the body of literature called *general systems theory*. The generalization that it is simpler to regulate systems with greater interdependence within their boundaries than across their boundaries than where the reverse is the case was mathematically demonstrated by Ashby (1956) and Simon (1969) and empirically supported by Miller (1959). The Law of Requisite Variety was derived by Ashby (1956) on assumptions about system disturbances and responses. In Ashby's words, the law states that "only variety in R[esponses] can force down the variety due to D[isturbances]." Thus to maintain a system's steady state in an environment with many disturbances requires an increase in the system's capability to produce appropriate responses.

This generalization and law are among the set of beliefs with which I reason in the problematic situation. If system A behaves according to these generalizations, then system B (which is analogous in relevant respects to system A) will also behave according to them. Accordingly, the following design recommendations can be made about the technical system:

- If the answer to 3a(i) is no, the boundaries of the system should be relocated. This condition is realized by assigning responsibility and authority to contain more interdependence within the system's boundaries.

- If the answer to 3a(ii) is no, decisions made by higher or parallel systems should be delegated to the social system members.

- If the answer to 3c(i) is no, tasks should be redesigned so that they have greater variety, discretion, feedback and control.

- If the answer to 3c(ii) is no, social system members should be trained to be multiskilled in the tasks of many roles and allowed discretion to exchange roles or tasks within roles. Information about variances should be provided to those most likely to be able to respond to it.

The *social system* is represented as a conceptual system (Miller, 1965) whose parts (the behavior of its members) are patterned by (1) shared values that function as "construction principles" (Angyal, 1941) around which behavior is organized, (2) rewards and punishments that system members pursue and avoid if they are rational, (3) constraints of the concrete setting. Because social system members are systems in their own right and act to achieve individual goals and objectives that the social system may not meet, the patterning in the social system is never complete. By reasoning within the terms of the social system, the following recommendations can be made:

- If the answer to 3(i) is no, undertake group discussion and experiential exercises to encourage values such as: trust, acceptance of error, openness, willingness to share information, collaboration with others, and so on.

- If the answer to 3(ii) is no, change the reward structure so that cooperative behavior is rewarded (e.g., common group incentive, reduce or eliminate differentials in pay between different role occupants, reward medium- and long-term performance rather than short-term performance).

The social and technical systems model has permitted us to reason to the set of conditions that should exist if the system is to achieve a higher level of performance. However, taking actions to bring these conditions about is not easy to plan for. Every action that can be taken to move these two systems to a better match may have unintended consequences for reasons stated in the quote from Susman and Evered (1978).

Our reasoned set of conditions are "ideas" (Dewey, 1938), as opposed to facts, because they have not yet been brought into existence. Facts are "generic propositions" about the way in which the problematic situation is presently organized (e.g., X is connected with Y; the proposition states existential conditions). Generic propositions are "material means" for inquiry (Dewey, 1938). Ideas may be stimulated by generic propositions and proceed from them, but they are reached through reasoning or ordered discourse. The "procedural means" for reaching them are "universal propositions" characterized by their if-then form (e.g., If [which makes the proposition conditional or nonexistential] X is connected with Y, then modifying that connection in a particular way implies that Z will result). Ideas remain nonexistential until actions are taken on existing conditions to bring them into existence, in which case they become facts. We also have confirmed by such actions our initial beliefs about the problematic situation and altered it so that it now produces the outcomes we desire. Procedures for confirming such beliefs await the next phase of the action research model.

Evaluating

The following questions may be asked during the evaluating phase of action research:

(1) Did the actions taken bring about the conditions that the sociotechnical model led us to hypothesize will produce the outcomes desired?

(2) If the hypothesized conditions were brought about, were the desired outcomes produced?

(3) If the desired outcomes were produced, how confident are we that it was the hypothesized conditions that produced them?

(4) If the desired outcomes were not produced, what aspects of the sociotechnical model should be reexamined?

Were the hypothesized conditions brought about? Having hypothesized the conditions that will produce the desired outcomes, it is assumed it is feasible to bring them about. In order to bring about the envisioned "best match" between the social and technical systems, actions must be taken toward each system to modify their structures and functioning. It would seem easier to modify the technical system as actions are intended to modify flows of material and information rather than behavior. Yet in both the social and the technical systems, such actions are acts of communication to those members of the client's organization who have the authority to modify either system. If assumption 4 (social system members are guided primarily by instrumental values) holds under the conditions brought about, social system members will agree to accept the new responsibilities given to them and exchange tasks as necessary to maintain the system in steady state. The values and rewards of the social system were modified to encourage such behavior. However, it may be the case that not all social system members have the ability to use the information as intended, nor will they be willing to make appropriate decisions to switch tasks as necessary. The leveling of pay differences may disturb the sense of distributive justice between social system members or between them and members of other systems, thus undermining their willingness to work together as intended. As the sociotechnical system is open, unanticipated events may affect the system's functioning. The consequence of all this is that the hypothesized set of conditions initially envisioned may not be produced. As a result, it is not possible to evaluate the intended hypothesis. The validity of the hypothesis remains untested, but the feasibility of bringing about the intended conditions is seriously questioned (Suchman, 1971).

Were the desired outcomes produced? It may take some time for social system members to learn how to best use the new decisions and information they have been provided. In fact, they may never reach the level of system functioning that is theoretically possible for them to reach. Therefore, the level of performance measured may depend on the time period during which such measurement takes place. The appropriate evaluation question may be "How much improvement is there over time?" Monitoring performance from when system modifications first began through performance plateaus provides an indication of the nature of the social system members' learning curve. Furthermore, changes in the decisions that members make and how they deploy themselves in handling technical system variances may coincide with abrupt shifts in performance. Documentation of such relationships may provide clues as to why there was improvement and how it came about.

Confidence that conditions produced the desired outcomes. If we track the decisions and activities of social system members and correlate any shifts with corresponding shifts in performance, our confidence that the hypothesized conditions produced the desired outcomes will be enhanced. We can gain more confidence, however, by observing such relationships than we can by observing only the hypothesized conditions and the desired outcomes and then trying to increase our confidence by eliminating alternative hypothesized antecedent conditions that might explain the outcomes produced. Eliminating alternative hypotheses is a second choice or "fall-back" strategy that is used when we are ignorant of how the intended hypothesized conditions led to the desired outcomes. Our initial reasoning never led to the assumption that the hypothesized conditions "caused" the desired outcomes; it did lead to the assumption that they provided an opportunity for system members to make decisions and carry out activities in a different manner than they did previously. If our analysis focuses on how this opportunity was used, then we are less likely to fall back on the strategy of eliminating alternative hypotheses. Nevertheless, Cook and Campbell's (1979) lists of threats to internal and external validity can be examined to see whether it is possible to either introduce conditions before any action is taken or collect supplementary data before and/or afterward to see whether any alternative hypotheses can be eliminated. The introduction of any such conditions before taking action should be weighed against their possible effect on the feasibility of creating the conditions initially hypothesized to produce the desired outcomes.

What to reexamine if the desired outcomes are not produced. One explanation for why desired outcomes are not produced has been suggested already. It may not have been feasible to bring about the conditions hypothesized to produce the desired outcomes. However, assuming that the conditions were brought about and all obvious alternative hypotheses have been eliminated, then nonconfirming results can be evaluated against Popper's (1958) falsification doctrine. According to Popper, scientific knowledge is tested by deducing predictions from theory and collecting data to see whether the predictions are confirmed. If they are confirmed, then we gain confidence in the theory, although such confirmations offer no final proof. If unconfirmed, the theory is undermined, but it is seldom that a single falsified prediction would lead to a theory's rejection. However, a failure to confirm that the hypothesized conditions produced the desired outcomes may lead to a serious reexamination of the generalizations on which the tested hypothesis was developed. Any belief may be reformulated to apply only under conditions other than those under which the hypothesis was tested. Some of these beliefs are so central to the conceptual framework, that the theory cannot be maintained without them (e.g., a sociotechnical system produces less than optimal performance when there is a mismatch between the social and technical systems or between the sociotechnical system and its environment). However, the theory may not be totally rejected until the concrete settings studied can be better understood in terms of a different framework. The creation of such an alternative requires a leap of the imagination, a "conjecture" in Popper's terms. The new framework would interpret the facts of the problematic situation in a different way and see different facts than those observed under the old framework.

Specifying Learning

Although this phase of action research is discussed last, one should not infer that learning does not begin until this phase. Learning has been taking place from the moment that the client and I start to make sense of the problematic situation with the sociotechnical systems model. The entire action research effort has been a progressive differentiation of the problematic situation through what Lewin (1935) called a "concrete constructive method." The diagnosing, action planning, action taking, and evaluating phases of action research transform a problematic situation into one that is "settled" (Dewey, 1938). The client does not learn how to achieve such a transformation by simply being taught what the phases of action research are; rather, a capability to do so is developed by actually carrying out an inquiry.

The sociotechnical systems model is applied to a particular kind of setting: a work group in an oil refinery, coal mine, word processing center, and so on. Presumably, by selecting what facts to observe, the model influences our understanding of a specific technology and the manner in which the work group members adapt to it and learn to deal with it. From their observation, recommendations for modifying the technology or undertaking specific training may follow.

The documentation of changes in decisions and corresponding changes in performance can be examined for suggestions as to which decisions new groups should be trained to make effectively. New groups might be trained to carry out those decisions and activities that were shown to be related to improved performance in the groups previously studied without having to repeat all the exploration and learning that those groups experienced.

CONCLUSION

My intention in this chapter has been to demonstrate that action research is a general mode of inquiry that starts and ends in a concrete setting. The manner in which this concrete setting is conceptually represented and the physical and mental operations performed to transform this setting from an "unsettled" situation into a "settled" one demonstrate that action research contributes to a generalized understanding of the situation and, thereby, to the goals of social science. Sociotechnical systems as a conceptual framework was only a secondary consideration in this chapter. It was used as a vehicle for applying action research. Readers are encouraged to try other frameworks that they feel are appropriate to the problematic situations they face.

I have not adequately explored in this chapter how action research is conducted so that a client (an individual or a collectivity) will be committed to actions that can eliminate a problem or so that a client will learn how to deal with similar situations in the future. This was reluctantly intentional because of space limitations and because less has been written on action research as a general mode of inquiry grounded in an articulated set of ontological and epistemological assumptions. As a result, I have spent no time discussing questions such as how to motivate and, if necessary, train clients to collect data for the diagnosing and evaluating phases of action research, or the division of labor between the client and me during these phases. Additionally, some intriguing questions comparing this approach to problem solving with other approaches have not been explored. For example, is this mode of inquiry more useful for problems and solutions that can be defined in rational and instrumental terms than for problems rooted in interest conflicts or in unconscious psychodynamics? Does eliminating problems by modifying existential conditions limit consideration of other ways of eliminating problems such as through therapeutic insight, consciousness raising, redefinition of the situation through dialogue? These are provocative questions that await exploration in a future paper.

About the Author

GERALD I. SUSMAN

One consistent theme in my career has been an interest in helping people solve problems. This theme was manifested early through my bachelor's and master's degrees in psychology, which focused on psychotherapy and counseling. As my interests shifted from the individual to the organization, the helping theme was obscured temporarily. While in the doctoral program at the Graduate School of Management at UCLA in the middle 1960s, I met Eric Trist, who introduced me to the sociotechnical systems framework I used in my dissertation. We worked together four years later on an action research project to introduce autonomous work groups into an underground coal mine. I learned a great deal from him about Kurt Lewin and the applicability of Lewin's work to our project. I began the project believing that what I had learned from descriptive research could be readily applied to our clients' problems. This belief encountered many challenges, not the least of which was convincing the client (and myself) of the applicability of research that was generated through asking different questions than those that concerned the client. This challenge and others stimulated my interest in action research, which Kurt Lewin also pioneered. John Dewey helped deepen my interest in action research by giving a logical justification to what I had come to accept through practical experience.

7

ORGANIZATIONAL LEARNING

Donald A. Schön
Massachusetts Institute of Technology

THE QUESTION

Organizational learning has become an idea in good currency. In organizations as diverse as labor unions, business firms, churches, universities, elementary schools, charitable foundations, social welfare agencies, political parties, and government offices, it has become common for individuals to ask such questions as these: "What have we learned from past experience?" "How can we learn to cope with change?" "Is our learning capacity adequate to the challenges that confront us?" Such questions may originate in a variety of interests. They may reflect a growing recognition of the instability of the environments — social, economic, political, and technological — to which organizations must adapt if they are to survive and flourish. They may indicate a recognition of the need to improve organizational efficiency and productivity, as measured by the "learning curves" familiar in the context of industrial production. Or they may grow out of an awareness of intraorganizational conflicts that express conflicting purposes, interests, or values. For any or all of these reasons, concern with organizational learning has been on the rise.

On the other hand, a moment's reflection on organizational learning is sufficient to produce a sense of confusion. We seem to know what we mean when we say that a child learns to read, a skiier learns to keep his or her weight on the downhill ski, or a traveler learns to plan for contingencies. Difficulties arise, however, when we consider what it means to say that an organization learns. There is a confusion about the normative status of organizational learning and about the kinds of change essential to it. Furthermore, it is unclear what we mean when we treat the term "organization" as the subject of a sentence that has "learning" in its predicate. What is the relationship between "organizational learning" and the learning of individuals who are members of an organization? Is it a sufficient condition for organizational learning, for example, when individual members of the organization learn something important to organizational perform-ance? It is not hard to think of cases in which we would want to say that individuals have learned something that their organization has not (or not yet) learned. What might be meant by "organizational capacity for learning," and what does it mean for an individual to contribute to that capacity?

Questions such as these may be dismissed as "philosophical" so long as organizational learning seems relatively unimportant, or im-portant but unproblematic. When we recognize the importance of organizational learning, however, and are dissatisfied with the extent to which, or the way in which, an organization learns, then such questions become critically important not only to scholars, but to those responsible for organizational performance — and it is espe-cially to those who wish to examine and enhance the learning capacity of their own organizations that I offer the following pages. I shall construct a thought experiment in which to explore the meaning of organizational action, knowledge for action, and learning, and I shall then propose the outline of a method of research on organizational learning.

ORGANIZATIONAL THEORY OF ACTION

Because the idea of individual learning seems, at least initially, to be less confusing than is the idea of organizational learning, let us begin by exploring an activity, first as it might be undertaken by an individual, then by an organization.

Consider a craftsman who earns his living by making and selling wooden shovels. If we were to observe him at work, we would see that he engages in an orderly sequence of tasks: cutting down logs, hauling them to his workshop, shaping them with axe and chisel, storing the shovels, offering them for sale. If we observed him over a period of months, we might be able to describe some of the rules according to which he carries out the system of component tasks called "making and selling wooden shovels."

For example, he might regularly examine the logs he had brought to the shed, selecting only those free of knots and cracks. As he chopped and chiseled, he might continually observe the results of his work, making each cut continue or compensate for the effects of the previous one. When it came to selling, he might price shovels within a certain range, depending on his judgments about the quality of them shovels and the willingness of the buyers to pay.

In short, the craftsman's activity would manifest intelligence. In saying this, we attribute to him certain purposes and ways of achieving them. If he selects logs free of cracks, it is for the sake of making sturdy shovels. He prices his shovels in order to get a profit from his work. The whole sequence of activities can be described as a set of means intelligently adapted to an output, continually changing in response to self-observed performance, materials, tools, and context of operations. For each of a set of qualities — size, shape, sturdiness, smoothness, and the like — shovels fall within an acceptable range. If the shovel is too big, he hacks it down to size. If, in the process, he distorts the shape, he will discard that piece and go on to the next one. The constancy of his product reflects values and norms embedded in his purposes. Smoothness, shape, and size are values; criteria for acceptable smoothness, shape and size are norms that regulate a continual process of error detection and correction.

When we call this behavior intelligent, we attribute to the craftsman norms, strategies of action, and assumptions that make plausible the use of these strategies to maintain these norms; that is, we attribute to him a theory of action (Argyris and Schön, 1974). The craftsman's expectations, the outcomes he treats as "matches" or errors (outcomes mismatched to expectation), the actions by which he corrects his errors — all of these provide the essential data from which we may infer his theory of action.

Paradoxically, the craftsman may be unable to describe the theory of action that informs his behavior or he may attribute to himself a theory incongruent with his actions. He may tell us, for example, that he uses nothing but beechwood, while we observe that, when beech is scarce, he also uses pine. Of course, the craftsman may discover this incongruity for himself by constructing his own theory-in-use from observation of his own behavior.

Now suppose that we observe a small group of craftsmen who have banded together in a shovel-making collective. They will be engaged in a cooperative system, dividing up among themselves elements of the whole task that the individual craftsman carried out by himself (see Barnard, 1967). So we will observe some of them gathering logs, others hacking out the shovels, and others doing the fine chiseling and finishing. Perhaps they will have designated one member to examine the finished shovels for defects. We will observe patterns of interactions among the members, one of whom hands rough-cut shovels to another who fine-chisels them and so on.

Individuals will go about their several tasks much as the craftsman went about his. They will do things in certain regular ways and sequences, and will make, detect and correct errors. But they will, of necessity, communicate with one another concerning their interactive tasks. For example, the fine-chiseller may ask the rough-chopper to slow down because the pile of rough shovels is building up faster than she can manage.

Whereas the individual craftsman controlled the pattern of his own activities, control in the workshop is partly an individual and partly a collective matter. Collective control may be worked out entirely through interaction among workers equal to one another in authority; or, by collective decision, one member may be delegated the task of controlling the work of others. Charged with controlling the day's production, he may ask the others to put in an extra hour of work because they have not met their quota.

Just as we could describe the individual craftsman's activities in terms of a theory of action, so we can do this for the collective. In both cases, there is an overall task system, divided into component tasks governed, in their performance, by norms, strategies, and assumptions. The prevailing norms define what will be taken as an acceptable or unacceptable outcome of action. Errors will be made, detected, and corrected. In the case of the collective, however, the theory of action must include the rules for allocating tasks to individual members and for the mutual adjustment of individual's actions, by which they maintain the cooperation and control on which their organization depends.

For this purpose, each individual must generate an image of the cooperative system on which his or her own performance depends. He or she may make use of organizational artifacts such as maps, programs, and memories. Maps are pictures of the system — organization charts or building plans. Programs describe sequences of organizational action in work-flow diagrams, for example, or in lists of procedures. Memories are reservoirs of information about past organizational experience, for example, price or inventory lists; they may be kept in publicly accessible files or in the head of an "old hand." By reference to such organizational artifacts, which may be idealized and prescriptive, or descriptive of practice, individuals refresh the private images that enable them to adjust their behavior to the behavior of others in the system.

Even with the aid of maps, the construction of organizational theory of action remains incomplete. When a new member of the shovel collective tries to learn the collective's theory-in-use (in order to learn his or her own role), he may observe the patterns of others' behavior, read their diagrams and policy statements, and listen to their stories, but their procedures, advice, and descriptions will not enable him to go all the way to actual task performance. General principles do not decide particular cases. The new worker will still have to complete by his own behavior the incomplete description of task performance that is all the organization can give him.

Moreover, while he or she completes the description of organizational theory of action in one way, others do it in theirs. Their "gap-filling" processes must be continually adjusted, one to the other, in order to produce the concerted activity of a steady-state organization. Organizational activity consists in a continual process of *organizing*. (I am indebted to Tom Burns for this notion). Individuals must continually monitor the clues and exert the influence that allow their performances to remain in concert.

If the members of the collective wish to change their task sytems, they must not only describe the desired change, but make the on-line gap-filling adjustments necessary to its performance as well. Similarly, when an orchestra conductor tells her musicians how to play a passage, she is dependent on their ability to detect and respond to one another's efforts to complete her description.

To sum up, an organization such as the shovel collective *acts* when individual members, functioning as agents of the collectivity, carry out their parts of the larger task system. Like the individual craftsman, the collective has a theory-in-use implicit in the norms, strategies, and assumptions that govern its regular patterns of task performance. As in his case, their theory-in-use may be inferred from the evidence of intelligent action, especially from the detection and correction of errors. But in their case, intelligent action depends on a continuing mutual adjustment of individual behaviors, one to another. Their organizing depends, in turn, on each person's image of the larger system. In this sense, the organization exists in its members' heads. But the members also have access to external maps, memories, and programs, which they must continually complete through mutually adjusted actions.

ORGANIZATIONAL LEARNING

A cooperative system may undergo various changes, some in its theory-in-use. And some of these may be appropriately described as "learning."

Consider, to begin with, the deterioration of organizational theory-in-use. Members of the shovel collective might gradually lose enthusiasm for their work and become sloppy in the performance of their tasks. Two or three persons might leave the collective, taking with them important knowledge about log sorting and seasoning. In order to avoid such "organizational entropy" or loss of organizational memory, members must continually work at the recruitment and instruction of new members, the preservation of organizational maps and memories, and the detection and correction of errors. Gregory Bateson's (1972) observation that maintenance of constancy in any living system depends on continual change also holds true of organizational constancy. Following Bateson, I shall refer to such organizational maintenance as "zero-order learning."

Beyond this, there are levels of learning in which an experience of surprise — a phenomenon, pleasing or unpleasing, that escapes the organization's model of its world — triggers the restructuring of organizational theory, espoused or in use. In the collective, for example, a sudden drop in sales might cause the pricing committee to announce a change in pricing policy. But conversion of a change in policy to a change in theory-in-use requires a change in patterns of behavior within the cooperative system and, therefore, a change in the process of organizing, in individual images, and in public maps, memories, or programs.

The restructuring of organizational theory-in-use may vary in breadth and depth. In this connection, Chris Argyris and I have borrowed Ashby's (1940) distinction between "single-loop" and "double-loop" learning.

In single-loop learning, a single feedback loop connects the learner's detection of error to his or her strategies of action, while norms are held constant. In an organizational context, single-loop learning occurs through the interaction of individuals who occupy different roles in the task system. When production falls off, for example, members may institute a new system of overtime work to bring production back to the desired level.

In double-loop learning, there is a change in the norms built into theory-in-use. A double loop links the detection of error or anomaly both to strategies of action and to the norms by which actions are evaluated; often, there is also a change in the organization's model of its world (Argyris and Schön, 1978).

In the early years, for example, the collective consisted mostly of young craftsmen who had banded together in a rural setting to create a more congenial and collaborative work situation than they had been able to find in the city. They saw profit as a way of securing their enjoyable work environment, and their pricing policies and work schedules reflected in this view.

As time went on, however, some of the younger enthusiasts drifted away. Those who remained began to see the collective as a long-term livelihood. Their families were growing up, and they needed more money. They talked about more businesslike ways of running things, increasing the scales of operations, marketing to shops as well as to roadside stands, emphasizing productivity, concentrating on the more profitable goods. Over a period of months, as they argued the question, factions developed. The profit-minded faction prevailed, its more vigorous opponents left, and the collective started to take on the characteristics of a profit-making business.

Subsequent to this shift in direction, a new issue arose. The members had been used to meeting at regular intervals to discuss questions of policy. They had made it a point to resolve such questions without voting or recourse to formal authority. Under the new mode of operation, however, they found less time for meetings.

Someone suggested that they ought to have a regular manager, a member who had shown him- or herself to be astute in business. This suggestion met resistance from some of the old-timers who still clung to the ideal of collective policymaking. In the following months, however, business declined. Now the question of a manager came up again, this time in the context of concern for survival. A member was elected manager.

In each of these instances, there was a change in norms or the behavior of the cooperative system. In the first case, change was provoked by a perception of changing circumstances that brought to the surface a conflict of organizational values. As some members began to think of the collective less as a short-term escape than as a long-term livelihood, profitability took on a new importance. The measures required to make the business more profitable seemed incompatible with enjoyable work. The conflicting values surfaced in the form of a dispute among individual members, a dispute whose settlement created a new configuration of the values and norms of organizational theory-in-use.

The more businesslike mode of operation, coupled with the perception of a more stringent business environment, led some members to advocate a shift from consensual to managerial decisionmaking. Again, learning took the form of a dispute whose resolution brought about a shift in the values and norms of organizational theory-in-use.

It is important to notice that the first episode of double-loop learning created a context for the second. The collective's perception of incompatible values, expressed through a dispute among individual members, led to changes in organizational theory-in-use and meanings that helped to set the stage for the shift to a more conventional management structure. An episode of organizational learning changed the situation, triggering a new episode of learning, as in a kind of organizational dialectic.

In both single- and double-loop learning, organizational inquiry mediates the shift from an earlier to a later state of organizational theory-in-use. An unexpected outcome of action, a shift in circumstance that reveals and violates (often, at the same time) an earlier, unquestioned assumption, induces individual members to inquire into their situation. Their inquiry takes the form of combined thinking and doing (see Dewey, 1938). They may reflect on previously unquestioned assumptions, gather new information, experiment with new patterns of action, or argue over conflicting interpretations rooted in different values. Their inquiry is organizational in the sense that it restructures organizational theory-in-use, and in the further sense that it is carried out by individuals in interaction with one another.

Organizational inquiry may be centralized or distributed, formal or informal. If centralized, it is initiated and controlled by some individual or group, like the collective's committee, which functions as a center of information gathering, decision making, or action in relation to the rest of the organization, which stands to it as "periphery" (Schön, 1972). If distributed, inquiry is carried out through a number of small-scale interactions among individuals interacting with one another at the periphery, for example, by workers who play out new ways of mutually adjusting behavior in response to shift in the quality of raw materials for manufacture. When organizational inquiry is formal, it is explicitly labeled as such and is initiated, controlled, and terminated by some formally established decision-making process. When it is informal, it occurs through the spontaneous, semiprivate networks of interaction among individuals, for example, in the "schmoosing" that occupies so prominent a place in working life (Schrank, 1978).

Whatever its form may be, organizational inquiry mediates the restructuring of organizational theory-in-use and, as we shall see in the following section, its quality determines the quality of organizational learning.

RESEARCH INTO ORGANIZATIONAL LEARNING

We shall be concerned here with the following research questions:

- Has learning occurred, or is it occurring?
- If so, what kind of learning is involved?
- Is it really organizational?
- What is its quality?

In order to study one or more of these questions in the context of a particular organization like the shovel-making collective, it is necessary, at the very least, to have access to three interrelated phenomena:

Organizational theory-in-use at time t_1	Organizational Inquiry	Organizational theory-in-use at time t_2

In order to tell whether there has been a change in theory-in-use, it is necessary to identify and describe two successive states of the theory-in-use; and, in order to tell whether the change is attributable to learning, it is necessary to study the processes of inquiry that mediate the shift from one state of theory-in-use to the next.

With reference to this very simple schema of organizational learning, we can now ask what we must find out about each element of the schema, and how we can find it out, in order to answer the research questions I have identified.

As a practical matter, a study of organizational learning must begin as a study of organizational learning about something. Otherwise, there is no way of limiting the scope of possibly relevant observation. We might set out, for example, to study the collective's response to the constricting business environment, or we might choose to focus on a particular function, such as quality control in log sorting, tracing the learning, of whatever kind, that occurs in that domain. On the other hand, there is usually no way of being sure, initially, what sort of learning is likely to be of greatest importance to an organization or most rewarding for the organization's future development. Themes of learning may be discovered through exploratory research into organizational practices and individual images of organizational experience. Or a study of learning in one domain may uncover important themes in another domain. For example, a study of quality control in the collective might uncover the prospective shift to businesslike operation.

However we arrive at an initial focus of study, we will need to gather data about the state of organizational theory-in-use relevant to that focus at two or more successive stages in the life of the organization. Suppose we are interested in productivity and product quality. What kinds of information will we need to gather? We will be interested in information about espoused policies, procedures, and programs; in what members of the organization believe to be the norms, strategies, and assumptions that inform organizational behavior; and, most directly and critically, in the actual patterns of practice related to our chosen themes over the duration of the learning process under study.

For example, we will observe how logs are sorted for shovels, which ones are accepted and rejected, the implicit or explicit criteria on which the sorting is done, and how "false sorts" are detected and corrected. We will notice how behavior varies from day to day, or from person to person, insofar as more than one person is involved in the task, and how individuals think about their activities — their images of the task and its place in the larger system — but, in order to get beyond espoused theories, we will probe for the thinking that goes with observed behavior. For example, when a worker examines a log with particular intensity, we may ask, "How are the pieces in this pile similar to and different from those in the other piles?" If we come across sketches, maps, or lists, we will study them and compare them to worker behavior and reports of workers' thinking about their tasks.

As we begin to make sense of our data, we will face the problem of determining whether the patterns of thinking and doing we have observed are truly organizational or peculiar to individuals. These are some of the tests that may be applied:

- Was the practice carried out on one occasion only, or was it regularly repeated?

- Was it limited to one individual or was it present in the behavior of several individuals engaged in performing similar tasks?

- Was the practice incorporated in procedures for decision and control? Was it described in organizational maps, programs, or memories?

- When a new member entered the organization, was he or she instructed in the practice? When an old member left, did his successor continue the practice?

On the basis of such tests, one may decide that a practice is clearly organizational or clearly attributable to individual idiosyncrasy. On the other hand, tests may yield conflicting and ambiguous results that call for additional analysis.

As we turn to the study of organizational inquiry, similar issues arise. Often, individuals inquire into organizational theory of action, singly or in interaction with one another, in ways that are later incorporated into the restructuring of organizational theory-in-use. But there are also kinds of cases in which we would want to say that although an individual has learned, the organization has not. For example,

- A member of the collective invents a better procedure for selecing logs, but treats it as a secret way of reducing his own expenditure of energy. He tells no one else about his invention, and when he leaves the collective, the knowledge leaves with him.

- There has been a problem of cracking that no one has been able to fix. One member notices that the cracked shovels have all been made from a particular species of tree. However, she is afraid of appearing foolish, and keeps her thoughts to herself.

- A member notices that a great deal of work goes into the maintenance of a large inventory of different kinds of shovels. He calculated the savings in labor that could be achieved if the inventory were reduced to a few best-selling items. He presents his case to other members, who pay no attention to him.

In these cases, individuals detect errors in organizational performance, interpret the errors, and imagine new strategies of action that would correct them. But their learning does not become embedded in organizational theory-in-use. What they as individuals know, the organization does not yet know. The individual learning represents an unrealized potential for organizational learning.

Even when inquiry is clearly organizational, in the sense that it leads to a shift in organizational theory-in-use, its quality should be distinguished from the perceived success or failure of the changes that result from it. A good process of inquiry may result in an outcome perceived as bad, and bad inquiry may result in outcomes perceived as good. On what, then, does the determination of quality of inquiry depend?

Argyris and I have proposed that quality of inquiry, in the *interpersonal* context, has to do with the following questions (Argyris and Schön: 1974):

- Are assumptions, especially attributions made to other persons, treated as publicly testable, or are they held in a way that makes them self-sealing?

- Do individuals seek out disconfirmation, as well as confirmation, of the propositions they advocate?
- Do individuals recognize uncertainty, and do they respond to it not only by problem solving but by problem setting?
- Are individuals sensitive to incompatibility and inconsistency in their own theories-in-use, and to incongruity between theory-in-use and espoused theory?
- Do individuals try to bring to the surface their own maps of the problematic situations in which they find themselves, and do they try to share the task of completing and coordinating incomplete and divergent maps?

In the context of *organizational* inquiry, these questions may take the following forms:

- Do members of the collective treat organizational assumptions as testable? And do they search for disconfirming data? Do they, for example, treat as testable their assumption that a tighter and more uniform design of work will increase productivity?
- Are the members of the collective able to integrate workers' pictures of the production process with managers' pictures of the market environment so as to make a single organizational map capable of revealing the interconnections of assumptions and values?
- Do the members of the collective share memories of the collective's past that provide them with a context for the interpretation of present error? Does organizational memory include, for example, the process by which early aspirations of the members shaped the present design of tasks? If not, the collective may continue to respond in single-loop fashion to errors that can yield only to double-loop learning, or they may oscillate for a long time between incompatible values that are horns of a dilemma, without realizing that they are doing so.
- The collective may find that its expectations for level of profit are continually disappointed. There may then be real uncertainty over the proper interpretation of this error. Are the members then able to respond to uncertainty by reflection and by efforts at restructuring their perception of the problem? Are they able to respond, for example, not only by altering work methods and rates of production, but by reconsidering standards for profit with standards for freedom of work?
- Do the members test for congruence of organizational espoused theory with theory-in-use? Do they test for the compatibility of their norms? Do members of the collective test, for example, whether their

values for consensual decision are honored in practice? If so, do they test for their compatibility with the norms of businesslike operations?

- Do the individual members oppose one another without awareness that their opposition represents a conflict of organizational values? If so, one side may win without recognizing the costs to the collective of victory, and without considering a restructuring of the problem that might allow both sets of values to be met.

- Or do members couple advocacy of their own positions with inquiry into the position of others? Do they keep open the possibility that conflicting values could be internalized by the several members rather than distributed among them by polarization?

The quality of organizational inquiry is not a matter of unswerving smoothness of operation and elimination of error. On the contrary, good organizational inquiry depends on making and detecting errors, treating assumptions as testable and designing experiments to test them, recognizing and honoring opposition and conflict. Quality of inquiry derives from the ways in which error is interpreted and corrected, incompatibility and incongruity are engaged, and conflict is converted to productive search, experiment and debate. In all of this, features of good organizational inquiry are interconnected. For example, the search for disconfirming data may reveal errors that lead to the surfacing and restructuring of previously tacit assumptions of organizational theory-in-use. The effort to build a coherent map of the organizational situation may reveal incompatible values that express themselves in a conflict of individuals or groups.

So much for the kinds of information we will gather in order to study organizational learning. How shall we gather it? There are at least three different methods, each with its own costs, benefits, and peculiarities.

The first is the method of *on-line observation*. Here, we put ourselves into a position from which to observe organizational learning as it happens. This has the advantage of increasing the likelihood of direct exposure to relevant patterns of behavior, but one can never be sure beforehand that organizational learning will occur when a researcher positions himself in the collective at a time and place he believes conducive to learning. He may be disappointed. Hence he never knows for certain what kinds of behavior he should exclude. All behavior is potentially suitable for observation. In effect, on-line observation must be linked to on-line interpretation. As the observer begins to suspect that he is in the presence of an unfolding story of organizational learning, he reorients the inquiry so as to trace that story.

In order to be pretty sure of getting access to a case of organizational learning, it is usually necessary to *study the past*. The researcher must attempt to reconstruct an earlier state of organizational theory-in-use, an earlier process of organizational inquiry, and a resulting shift in norms, strategies, and understandings. But writing this sort of organizational history is a difficult business. Most of us are instant historical revisionists. We tend to redescribe the past to suit present interests, sometimes misreading it as essentially similar to the present, sometimes — in the interest of dramatic effect — exaggerating its differences from the present. Moreover, we are often disposed to wipe out of memory the processes by which we got from one stage to another. The task of retrospective research is that of reconstructing from present documents and stories an earlier state of organizational theory-in-use and an earlier process of inquiry, both of which are likely to have faded from memory. Usually, such a reconstruction requires a synthesis of the multiple, divergent, and often conflicting views of the past held by individuals in the organization.

In a third method of study, we try to avoid some of the difficulties described above by *producing the effect we wish to observe*. We initiate a process of organizational learning while at the same time observing and recording it. Members of the shovel-making collective might come together, for example, to explore and work out new understandings and practices concerning the conflicting values of "businesslike management" and "enjoyable work," using that project as an occasion for systematic reflection on organizational learning in the collective.

An advantage of this method is the relatively high likelihood it offers for on-line observation of organizational learning. Its difficulties are the difficulties of action research. In addition to the problem of reflecting systematically on a process in which we are engaged (a problem we may learn to solve through practice), there is also the danger of influencing the phenomena we are observing. This danger is particularly intense when the researcher initiates a learning process, but it is also attendant on studies of the past or participant-observation of the present. Actually, it may be less a "danger" than a fact of life. In the organizational context, the quest for objectivity, in the sense of freedom from influence by the research process, is probably hopeless. A more appropriate kind of objectivity has to do with the researcher's awareness of his or her effect on others. But the researcher cannot learn how he or she affects others unless others are willing and able to tell him or her. They must describe to themselves and discuss with the researcher what they usually treat as indescribable or undiscussable. The researcher must be able to create conditions that increase the likelihood of their doing so.

These three methods of research have been used in practice, sometimes in combination with one another. But, so far as I know, no one has used them to carry out a full research program of the sort described above.

CONCLUSION

I have proposed an operational description of organizational learning as a shift in organizational theory-in-use mediated by organizational inquiry. I have distinguished kinds of organizational learning, offered tests of organizational as distinct from individual learning, and suggested signs of quality in organizational inquiry. In order to do these things, however, I have extracted the process of organizational learning from many critically important aspects of its context. In fact, one never gets to see organizational learning divorced either from the phenomena of a behavioral world in which individuals live with one another or from the political, win/lose games of control, evasion, and dominance in which most organizations abound. These are aspects of organizational learning systems. But in order to study the ways in which organizational learning systems shape organizational learning, we must have a reasonably clear idea of the latter, and this is what I have tried to provide.

About the Author

DONALD A. SCHÖN

I am a transplanted philosopher, brought up on John Dewey's theory of inquiry, tempered by a fifteen-year apprenticeship in organizational consulting and management, and for the past twelve years much influenced by my close collaboration with Chris Argyris on the development of a theory of action approach to organizational learning.

— 8 —

INTERPRETIVE INTERACTIONISM

Norman K. Denzin

University of Illinois

In this chapter I offer the elementary features of an interpretive, phenomenological, symbolic interactionism that may be synthesized or combined with a structuralist approach to the study and analysis of power, knowledge, and control in everyday life (see Mead, 1932, 1934; Husserl, 1960, 1973; Schutz, 1967a, 1967b; Schutz and Luckmann, 1973; Simmel, 1950; Merleau-Ponty, 1973a, 1973b; Denzin and Keller, 1981; Wiley, 1979). After offering a definition of *interpretive interactionism*, I compare and contrast its basic assumptions with those of traditional, positivistic social science. I then turn to its empirical applications, attempting a connection between structural, interactionist, and phenomenological interests. I conclude with proposals for new directions this synthesis might take.

Interpretive interactionism takes as its fundamental subject matter the everyday life world, as that world is taken for granted and made problematic by self-reflective, interacting individuals. The study and imputation of meaning, motive, intention, emotion, and feeling, as these mental and interactive states are experienced and organized by interacting individuals, are of central concern for the interpretivist. The streams of situations which persons construct, give meaning to, and inhabit, are focuses of study. The twin phenomenological and interactional streams of consciousness, which situate the person in the lived life world, are constant objects of

Author's Note: I have benefited greatly from conversation with Joseph B. Hardin on a number of the issues raised in this manuscript. I am grateful for the comments and suggestions of Lawrence Grossberg and Peter K. Manning.

concern (see Denzin, 1980; James, 1890). The intersection between the public and private lives of individuals, groups, and human collectivities must always be addressed in an interpretive report (see Marx, 1963; Sartre, 1976). Qualititative, ethnographic, and thick, fine-grained descriptions of the life world represent the dominant methodological interests in interpretive investigations.

PRELIMINARY CONSIDERATIONS

Interpretive interactionism represents an effort to move beyond the pragmatism of Mead, Dewey, Cooley, Thomas, Blumer, Park, and others into the interpretive and structural realms of post-World War II European social theory and thought. A fundamental thrust of this perspective is on the hermeneutic interpretation of ongoing, lived social experience (Heidegger, 1962). The goal is the presentation and interpretation of a sequence of symbolic interaction.

The interpretivist assumes that interacting individuals approach their life worlds from the standpoint of typified stocks of knowledge that reflect their embodied locations in preexisting and emergent political, economic, ritual, and moral structures of crystallized social experience. These crystallized structures assume taken-for-granted meanings, yet they constrain and control the individual and shape, as well, the ensembles of social relationships that the person inhabits (see Simmel, 1950; Marx, 1963; Schutz and Luckmann, 1973).

This interpretive perspective rejects a decentered, purely structuralist theory of self and society (see Denzin and Keller, 1981). Individuals find location not in exteriorized linguistic, economic, ritual, or mythological codes and structures; their locus, rather, is to be found in their relationship to the everyday life world and in the constitutive practices that make that world meaningful and understandable. Persons, not history and structures or codes, make history and social selves, social relationships, and social structures. However, the histories that individuals make may not always be of their own making, in which case any individual's history becomes the history of other people. Interpretive interactionism attempts to speak to the nuances, realities, and fabrics of these two interpenetrating histories. The ensembles of social relationships that bind these histories together into recurring, structuralized, structurating forms and forces are central to the interpretive enterprise.

Individuals are placed back in history; without living people, there is no history. Interpretive interactionism attempts to study biographies as these articulate a particular historical moment in the life world. Persons, in the here and now, have projects (theirs and others), chosen and coerced ways of thinking and acting that move them toward expressed ends or goals (theirs and others; Sartre, 1976).

The relationships that bind individuals into their historical moments may be characterized as *ensembles* or collective forms that relate individuals to one another. Six types of ensembles may be distinguished. *Series* describe separated individuals who only share a common location in space and time (e.g., persons waiting at a bus stop). A *group* describes a collectivity in a state of reciprocal relationship. A *fused group* is newly formed and opposed to seriality. A *pledged group* develops from a fused group and forms an organized "distribution of rights and duties enforced by a pledge" (Sartre, 1976: 829). An *organized group* transforms a pledged group into action. An *institution* is a group that "develops from a pledged group through the ossification of its structures and the emergence of a sovereignty and seriality within it" (Sartre, 1976: 828). A *class* is the most complicated form of an ensemble. It represents the synthesis or totalization of institutional groups, pledged groups and series. To the above classification may be added (a) *gatherings,* which are series capable of being transformed into groups, and (b) *third parties,* who are individuals capable of unifying a group by observing or commanding it (Sartre, 1976: 830).

An individual's location in the life world at any moment in time is phenomenologically and historically constituted into a body of situated, localized practices (see below) that provide a horizon or frame of experience against which ongoing activity is judged, assembled, and mobilized (Sartre calls this "the practico-inert"). People implement these practices through their projects, and they may do so as solitary individuals or as persons molded together into any of the several forms of ensemble noted above. These practices give the individual a sense of historical continuity in the here and now. When history as past practice is transcended, suspended, or set aside, the individual and the collectivity approach the potential of *totalization.* That is, experience (past and present) is incorporated into future lines of action that place persons in the simultaneous position of making and interpreting their own and others' history (Sartre, 1976: 830).

INTERPRETATION AND SCIENCE

The interpretive perspective is deliberately nonscientific and nonpositivistic. This is so for the following reasons:

(1) Logical positivism and scientific sociology have historically assumed that the language of the natural sciences should and could be

the language of the human sciences. This assumption held that references to the social world that could not be verified under quantifiable, observable, scientifically controlled conditions must — following Wittgenstein's (1922: 151) dictum, be "passed over in silence." Statements regarding human subjectivity, intentionality, and meaning were excluded from the positivist's domain. Interpretive interactionism is founded on the study, expression, and interpretation of subjective human experience.

(2) Positivistic sociology seeks causal explanations of social phenomena. It does so through the use of a variable-analytic language that is largely divorced from the everyday life world. Interpretive interactionism rejects causal modes and methods of analysis. The search for causal "whys," causal paths, causal chains, and causal antecedents is detrimental to the study and understanding of directly lived experience.

(3) The "why" question is replaced by the "how" question. That is, how is social experience, or a sequence of social interaction organized, perceived and constructed by differentially wide-awake, self-reflective, socially constrained, free individuals? How, then, not why.

(4) Positivistic sociology presupposes a theoretic-analytic conceptual framework that stands independent of the life world of interacting individuals. This framework, whether derived from classical or contemporary theory (Marx, Durkheim, Simmel, Weber, Freud, Parsons, Merton, or Homans), assumes that human behavior can be meaningfully categorized and analyzed within the conceptual elements of an abstract, grand, or middle-range theory. Directly lived reality drops out of positivistic sociology to be replaced by such complex variable terms as "base," "superstructure," "division of labor," "bureucracy," "ego-function," "functional prerequisites," or the "latent consequences of purposive action." These second-order concepts divorce human reality from the scientist's scheme of analysis.

(5) Interpretive interactionism aims, as much as possible, for a concept-free mode of discourse and expression. Its mode of expression is locked into the *first-order, primary, lived concepts of everday life*. Following Merleau-Ponty (1973a), descriptive phenomenology attempts to render understandable the "Prose of the Life World." Such a rendering assumes that the streams of situations that make up the life world do not conform to prior conceptualizations. Nor will these streams of experience submit to experimental, statistical, comparative, or causal control and manipulation. Every human situation

is novel, emergent, and filled with multiple, often conflicting, meanings and interpretations. The interpretivist attempts to capture the core of these meanings and contradictions. It is assumed that the language of the life world can be used to explicate its own structures (see the analysis of Raskolnikov's Crime in Denzin, 1981b).

This world does not stand still, nor will it conform to the scientist's logical schemes of analysis. It contains its own dialectic and its own internal logic. This meaning can only be discovered by the observer's participation in the world. The world does not stand independent of perception or observer organization. In these respects, interpretive interactionists find that their own worlds of experience are the proper subject matter of inquiry. Unlike the positivists, who separate themselves from the worlds they study, the interpretivists participate in the life world so as to understand better and express its emergent properties and features.

Interpretive interactionism asserts that meaningful interpretations of human experience can only come from those persons who have thoroughly immersed themselves in the phenomenon they wish to interpret and understand. There is, as Merleau-Ponty (1973a) argued, an inherent indeterminateness in the everyday life world, and systems that attempt to resolve this indeterminateness by going outside the directly experienced realms of everyday life are simply inappropriate for interpretive purposes.

(6) Current social science thought emphasizes the quantifiability of mental and behavioral processes. Such thought treats the human body as if it were a machine that emitted responses and behavior patterns that could be measured and charted in terms of internal and external social, psychological, and biological forces. The interpretive interactionist assumes that: (a) the mind cannot be quantified (Bateson, 1979), and (b) the human body is not a behavioral machine (Merleau-Ponty, 1962). Instead, the body must be viewed as an expressive extension and embodiment of human subjectivity and self-reflexivity. Mind and body are intertwined experiential processes. Each articulates and expresses the other. As intermingling chiasms, they find expressions in the streams of situations that make up the person's life world.

(7) The formulation of causal propositions that can be generalized to nonobserved populations (based on the extensive analysis of randomly selected samples) is a cardinal feature of current social science work. The interpretivist rejects generalization as a goal and never aims to draw randomly selected samples of human experience. For the interpretivist, every instance of social interaction, if thickly de-

scribed (Geertz, 1973), represents a slice from the life world that is proper subject matter for interpretive inquiry.

The slices, sequences, and instances of social interaction that are studied by the interpretivist carry layers of meaning, nuance, substance, and fabric, and these layers come in multiples and are often contradictory. Some flow from other people's histories, and some are of the person's own making. The knowledge and control structures that lie behind these meaning experiences must be hermeneutically uncovered in an interpretive investigation. Every topic of investigation must be seen as carrying its own logic, sense of order, structure, and meaning. Like a novelist or painter, the interpretivist moves the reader back and forth across the text of his or her prose so as to make recognizable as a visible spectacle the fabrics of human experience he has captured (see Sudnow, 1978, 1979).

An understanding and interpretation of the everyday life world must consider the situated, structural, and practical features of that world. It is to these topics that I now turn.

ON SITUATIONS

The everyday world possesses a situated structuredness. The situations of human interaction are phenomenological constructs. They exist only in so far as persons act on them and make them real; yet all experience is situated, in a time-space continuum, for experience occurs in the here and now. Situations envelop, enclose, and capture their participants, yet all situations have emergent, unforeseeable properties and dimensions. All situations contain historical halos, having something in common with other situations that have occurred in the past. Situations are, as Schutz and Luckmann (1973) suggested, historically typified. Situations represent how the person is currently anchored into the life world. Since persons are always anchored in some way in the world at hand, it is impossible to speak of nonsituated experience. Situations, in addition to their enveloping, enclosing, emergent, and historical dimensions, have the following attributes:

(1) They are external to the degree that they are not brought into the person's life world. One person's situation may not be a situation for another.

(2) Situations are internal, phenomenological constructions and may exist only in persons' imaginations.

(3) Situations may be obdurate and unavoidable, in which case their externalities push into the person's phenomenological, internal, situational worlds. (Recent historical examples include Watergate for former President Nixon, and the Vietnam War for former President Johnson.)

(4) Situations have evolving, encompasing depth, as when persons retreat into the worlds of dreams, insanity, play, or intense drama. Such situations cut farther and farther into the person's life world, perhaps eventually shutting out all other situated realms of being and experience (see Sartre's *Nausea* (1939) for one illustration of this aspect of situations).

(5) Situations have structure; that is, they take on recurring, familiarly patterned regularities. These sources may lie outside the person's immediately constructed life world and can be found in the realms of dreams, fantasies, play, science, law, art, theology, language, and morality (see James, 1890, on the several provinces, or worlds of reality, and Schutz and Luckmann, 1973). The structural features of situations are elaborated below.

(6) Projects are realized in situations.

(7) In situations, persons move from seriality to reciprocal relations with one another.

STRUCTURES AS FORMS

Structures are reified, patterned regularities of thought and action that find their realization in the interactional and phenomenological situational streams that bind persons to one another (e.g., their projects and their ensembles). Structures of human experience may be embodied in laws, codes, or the several provinces of reality discussed by James and Schutz. The structures of experience have historical, interactional, and phenomenological elements. Historically, structures precede the lives and interactions of individuals. At some historical point, all structures stand outside of, and are independent of, any specific interactional episode or event. Structures, as patterned regularities, represent potential "could, or would be" yet to be realized interactional events. Like Simmel's (1950: 11, 14, 385, 386) social forms, *structures provide the bare outlines of lived experience; they are forms of interaction,* whose contents must be filled in by the interactions, intentions and experiences of individuals.

If societies exist only in the interactions between persons, as Simmel contended, *then* structures — linguistic, kinship, political, economic, legal, moral, scientific, dramatic, fantastic, or playful — provide the horizons of experience against which the actual contents of human experience are sketched and lived. Experience and interaction filter structure, giving every moment of a reified structure unique meaning and interpretation. In this sense, all structures, if they are to affect the fate and development of individuals, even in unintended, or unanticipated, ways, must be realized interactionally and phenomenologically. However, unlike the world at hand, which is constantly changing, structures "always remain fixed over certain periods of time" (Simmel, 1950: 386). Structures as interactional forms "become crystallized as permanent fields, as autonomous phenomena. As they crystallize, they attain their own existence and their own laws and they may even confront or oppose spontaneous interaction itself" (Simmel, 1950: 10). Gratitude, faithfulness, secrecy, intimacy, marriage, ritual, conflict, freedom, and subordination are also crystallized social forms whose realities subjugate, control, and manipulate spontaneous interactions between persons.

Structures both lag behind and lead in the shaping of inner and outer human experience and consciousness. As Simmel points out, "It is their nature sometimes to be ahead of the inner reality and sometimes to lag behind it. More specifically, when the life, which pulsates beneath outlived forms, breaks these forms, it swings into the opposite extreme, so to speak, and creates forms ahead of itself, forms which are not yet completely filled out by it" (Simmel, 1950: 386).

Structures can be seen (1) as persisting, even after they have been changed (e.g., defined as illegal), (2) as innovative and responsive to change, and (3) as suggestive of change itself. Structures as such may be studied as *synchronic* forms at fixed moments in time and space and as *diachronic* forms as well. Structures studied diachronically will be termed "structures- or "forms-in-use." Structures studied synchronically will be termed "structures to-be-used," or structures that have been used and could be used in the future. The tension between these two structures displays the extent to which a structure has become dislodged from its original formulations and has become an end in and of itself, or has become an archaic, perhaps oppressive, alienating, dominating, historical artifact. Hence, while structures as forms may be studied synchronically and objectively, they are lived and best studied subjectively, in the dynamics of the immediate here and now.

The foregoing suggests that the structures of experience have historical, interactional, and phenomenological elements. Historically, structures, as Schutz and Luckmann (1973: 5) note, come to us as indirect social and cultural pregivens from our predecessors. Interactionally, structures provide the organizing linguistic devices persons utilize when they confront and interact with one another in everyday situations. Historical structures shape interactional structures; this can be observed in matters involving kinship alliances, economic exchanges, ritual ceremonies and political acts of violence, warfare, and conflict (Sartre, 1976).

Phenomenological, historical, and interactional structures flow into the person's inner life, giving it recognizable shape, substance, and content. Stocks of knowledge, vocabularies of motive, and typified structures of experience are all parts of the structure of a person's thinking. Structures, or forms, flow in and out of the person. Their intersection in the chiasms of the lived world constitute paramount reality for the individual. The totalization of these three structures allows the person simultaneously to make and understand history (theirs and others).

Totalization is a constantly developing process of understanding and making history (Sartre: 1976: 830). Persons who live other persons' history lack the ability to accomplish totalization. Structures, as situated forms, then, potentially alientate and dislodge all individuals from their immediate life circumstances.

The diachronic and synchronic study of structures, qua forms, reveals the following:

(1) Structures are differentially hidden from the public's eyes. Some are latent and hidden and understood by small bodies of experts, if understood at all.

(2) Structures have both intended and unintended, apparent and unapparent, consequences for individuals (Merton, 1957).

(3) Structures coerce, control, and manipulate.

(4) Structures assume both ritual and routine features (e.g., the Balinese cockfight as studied by Geertz, 1973).

(5) Structures are both collective and individual in nature. Phenomenological structures are unique to persons. Historical, mythlike structures that pertain to entire nation-states, groups, or primitive societies assume collective proportions (see Lévi-Strauss, 1981; Schutz and Luckmann, 1973).

(6) Structures may be historically specific, in which case they describe over and done practices (see Foucault, 1977, for a discussion of the crime of regicide and its various punishments in seventeenth- and eighteenth-century France.)

(7) Structures as forms find their displays in the localized practices and projects of individuals interacting serially and reciprocally.

(8) The study of structures as localized practices necessarily involves the investigation of power, knowledge, and control in everyday life. It is to these topics that I turn next.

LOCALIZED PRACTICES

A localized practice reifies, often through formally institutionalized techniques and procedures, a specific structural form. Such practices are often staged and executed so as to alter deliberately the fate and development of one ensemble of individuals, often for the benefit (moral, symbolic, economic, political, ritual) of another (see for example, Foucault, 1977: 3). Localized practices include royal weddings, public hangings, political trials, staged degradation ceremonies, sit-ins, cockfights in Bali, public lectures, Christmas parties, basketball playoffs, graduation ceremonies, and political negotiations among others.

Localized practices filter, define, and shape external structural forms into concrete personalized events (see, for example, Sartre's [1976: 351-58] account of the storming of the Bastille in Paris).

Many localized displays of structural forms assume the characteristics of a "celebrative occasion," especially those involving prearranged audiences, performers, expected performances, sponsors, and stages for the occasion.

Some localized practices occur within the phenomenological worlds of the person. Dreams, as recurring phenomenological structures, illustrate this feature of the localized practice. Because they lack the authenticity ordinarily given public practices, their realities are more in doubt. They are subject, as Freud noted, to the vagaries of secondary elaboration.

The lived, phenomenological realness of a dream gives it, however, the features of a turning point event; for having dreamt that dream or sequence of dreams, the person may never be the same again (see Strauss, 1959, on turning point events, and Freud, 1950, on dreams). Phenomenological, localized practices merge personal history with larger biographical structures and they become (retrospectively) celebrative occasions, with both negative and positive interpretations and consequences.

A localized practice involves the exercise of power, influence, and authority, often with physical, emotional, and moral consequences. Localized practices translate power in the abstract into power-in-use. Not only will such practices legitimate the dismembering of a human body, but they will furnish reasons for bringing down a king, killing one's neighbors, or paying to learn how uninformed one is on an intellectual topic. Selves, their lives, their relations with others, even their bodies lie at the core of localized practices.

Structural forms never fully (or seldom) dictate their own practical realization in everyday life. Lecturers miss lines, audiences become rude, a king's pronouncements backfire.

POWER AND KNOWLEDGE ELABORATED

Power's exercise involves the control and manipulation of knowledge and knowledge structures. The local implementation of any structural form quickly translates into those persons who are experts on the form, those who are novices, and those who are, or will be, the victims of another person's stock of knowledge. Structures of knowledge may technically be valid or invalid, but such validity is largely irrelevant, for those in control socially construct their own criteria of truth and adequate knowledge.

Knowledge, here defined as a body of uncontradicted beliefs about a particular segment of reality, is socially and politically constructed. In William James's words: *Any object which remains uncontradicted is ipso facto believed and posited as absolute* (1890: 289). To James's definition, we need only add "not contradicted by a political force with more power than the believer in the belief in question."

The knowledge structures of modern industrialized societies have the following characteristics:

(1) They are centered in modes of scientific discourse.

(2) They are relative and constantly changing.

(3) They are in constant public demand.

(4) They are constantly consumed by ever-larger publics.

(5) They increasingly fall under the control of the universities and centers of higher learning.

(6) They are the sources of constant political debate and social conflict (see Foucault [1980: 151] on these characteristics).

Power does not exist as a solitary entity. It exists only as a process in the dominance relations between persons, groups, and ideals

(Simmel, 1950: 190). There are not bodies of power in a society, only relations or processes of power. As Foucault argues:

> In reality power means relations, a more-or-less organized hierarchical co-ordinated cluster of relations. So the problem in constituting a theory of power . . . is to provide oneself with a grid of analysis which makes possible an analytic of relations of power. . . . Generally speaking I think one needs to look rather at how the great strategies of power encrust themselves and depend for their conditions of exercise on the level of micro-relations of power. . . . It's the characteristic of our Western societies that the language of power is law [1980: 201].

But power is more than a juridicial right, for it translates directly into local practices that may bear little relationship to formal legal codes (e.g., discrimination practices in work settings). Further, power studied as law or as a juridical right leads to an overemphasis on macroconcerns (e.g., the rights of the states, of the president, of Congress with a corresponding deemphasis on the microrelations and practices of dominance in everyday life. Nor can power be translated into materialistic, class relations of dominance, or into the modes of production that characterize a society. Nor is power merely a dependency relationship between two parties where the dependent, or subordinate, person is under the power or influence of another. (Weak, psychologically dependent persons often control the external fates of their so-called controllers.) "The Master is the Slave of His Slaves" (Simmel, 1950: 185; see Simmel, 1950: 274, on the power of Roman slaves under their masters).

Power is force or interpersonal dominance actualized in human relationships through the manipulation, control, and often destruction (both physical and mental) of one human by another human. Power as process serves, manipulates, controls, and destroys humans. Power relationships display shifting contours of dominance and submission, and they reveal underlying hierarchies of prestige, status, and authority. Power relations may exist, as noted above, between persons, groups, or bodies of ideals and codes. Such relations may tend toward equality, and just as one may rule many, many may rule or dominate a few. Power relations are interactive.

> Nobody, in general, wishes that his influence completely determine the other individual. He rather wants this influence, this determination of the other to act back upon him. Even this abstract will-to-dominate, therefore, is a case of interaction [Simmel, 1950: 181].

Power in relationships, as Simmel suggests, assumes a model of minded intentionality; that is, the person who dominates is assumed to do so intentionally, and it is assumed that such dominance will influence or affect the mental states of the person so dominated (e.g., they will be rehabilitated, cured, or justly punished; these effects, in turn, will reflect kindly on the dominant party or body of ideals). Hence, power-in-practice involves a theory of mind in practice. The microrelations of power rest on micro- and macrotheories of mind. Here, local customs, traditions, and cultures find an interplay with larger, historical theories of man, mind, and human intentionality (e.g., man is inherently evil, curable, or good).

Power as process in relationships frees, manipulates, controls, and destroys humans. As process, power is dualistic in nature. It both creates and destroys. It creates and destroys new social relationships, new mental states, new stocks of knowledge, and new ruling powers. Power as process is a liberating force in practice. Power relations are conflictual. Foucault's metaphor of "power is war" is apt, for power is often enforced repression under a reign of both symbolic and real terror. *Yet power as war is only war at the microlevel of everyday practices.* Power in play leaves no one free of its influence (see Merleau-Ponty's [1964b: 147] comments on reactions to the German occupation of France during World War II).

PERSONALIZING STRUCTURE AND PRACTICE

It was noted above that structural forms must be put into practice and that their practical realizations often depart from formal expectations. These departures require discussion, for their deviations are the norm, not the exception. A paradox shared by all structural forms is raised. How can that which is novel, different, and emergent be recognized as a familiar form each time it appears in the interactional world? Such recognitions are possible because the localized display of structural forms are personalized, biographically specific performances, filled with live, interacting individuals, not just shadowy performers, hidden behind roles they are playing on a stage.

Persons personalize structures by bringing their own unique biographies and interpretive practices to bear on the task, event, or interaction at hand. Such structures are uniquely personal ways of being and doing a particular pattern or form of interaction.

These are not structures in the abstract. They exist, are observed, felt, and experienced only in the interactions of persons. Personalized structural practices, if repeated often enough, remove the problematics from problematic situations and hence assume the dimensions of familiar routines and rituals. They become routinized historical, interactional, and phenomenological productions. (Elsewhere [Denzin, 1971, 1978] I have called these forms "behaviorial repertoires.") They assume the following attributes:

(1) They take on fixed times of occurrence (e.g., holidays, deaths, marriages).

(2) They occur in special, often sacred, situations that may be public or private in nature.

(3) They find their expressions in special languages, argots, and dialects.

(4) They call forth special modes of deference, demeanor, and decorum, often requiring special modes of dress and presentation.

(5) They unfold in their presentations and are subject to personal and situational contingencies; hence they are always emergent in tone and flavor.

(6) Situated practices join persons together into celebrative occasions, or joint actions (Blumer, 1969), and they resolve into the actions of persons aligning their selves and bodies with the selves and bodies and practices of other individuals.

(7) Personalized practices draw on local knowledge structures for their organization and validation.

(8) They reflect, directly and indirectly, micro-power relations. These relations of power alter and structure the knowledge base of the localized personal practice.

(9) History, in all its forms — phenomenological, interactional, microlocal, macrostate — finds its expression in these practices.

(10) Power relations are realized in personalized local practices.

The interpretation of interaction and structure involves investigations that report, describe, and reveal the personalized structures that constitute the everyday world as it is lived and experienced. Such investigations must reveal *how* persons assume positions of dominance in their everyday localized practices. Further, such research must reveal the processes by which persons transmit structures of evaluation concerning appropriate and inappropriate local practices. The projects and the ensembles that embody these practices also require research, as do the shifting levels and modes of awareness persons have of their own and other person's practices. (Here shared, public practices are to be compared with clandestine closed, private practices of small bodies of individuals.)

THE LOCALIZED INVESTIGATION
OF STRUCTURAL PRACTICES

The study of these practices must assume two forms. *First,* the directly lived world of the localized practice must be revealed in discursive detail utilizing everyday language in all its confusions and ambiguities. Specimens or slices of interaction (Denzin 1971) from the life world must be reported in actual sequence, reporting the actual words and actions of those studied. These reports, or slices, from the everyday world, must also attempt to capture the interpretations persons give to their practices. These interpretations may be retrospective, as when an investigator asks an individual to report on the text of an interaction sequence, or they may be contained within the text itself, when individuals announce their intentions and feelings as they are acting. The inner phenomenological and outer interactional sides of interaction must be contained in these specimens, or documents. Behavior specimens, interaction slices, introspection, and ethnographic report, if in vivid, lived detail, constitute the canvasses against which interpretations are written.

Such accounts must meet the criteria of *thick* as opposed to *thin description* (Ryle, 1968: 8-9). A *thin description* simply reports a bare fact, independent of any attempt to probe the intentions, motives, meanings, or the circumstances that might surround the fact in question. Ryle (1968: 8-9) offers an example:

You hear someone come out with "today is the 3rd of February." What is he doing? Obviously the thinest possible descriptions of what he is doing, would fit a gramophone equally well, that he was launching this sequence of syllables into the air.

A *thick description* of the speaker's acts would

(1) Describe the speaker's relationship to the recipients of his utterence.

(2) Describe the situation of the speech act (e.g., it was an office, a classroom, a family kitchen, a teller's booth in a bank).

(3) Give the clock time of the utterance.

(4) Situate the utterance vis-à-vis an ongoing activity (e.g., "Today is the 3rd of February and we are going to lecture on speech acts.").

(5) Describe the speaker in some detail, perhaps giving a short biography relevant to the activity at hand.

(6) State that the speaker probably assumed that he was giving someone the date and not another date and indicate that the recipient of the information probably assumed that it was correct (e.g., the speaker was not trying to deceive her).

A thick description reveals or permits the uncovering of underlying knowledge and relational structures that the persons observed may or may not understand yet are acting in terms of at the moment. A thick description goes beyond fact to detail, context, emotion, and web of affiliation and micropower.

Thick descriptions go beyond the mere accounting (or presentation) of the rules or principles that underlly a sequence of interaction (e.g., the rules of conversational turn taking, topic switching, power avoidance, table etiquette, altercasting, emotional display). The actual interactions, action, exchanges, and conversations that accompany and embody such rules must be presented.

When the researcher does focus on rules, it is necessary to maintain a distinction between an interactant's abstract knowledge of a set of rules and their actual in-use familiarity with the rules(s) in practice (see Ryle, 1971: 212-225, for an elaboration of this distinction, e.g., *knowing how* versus *knowing*).

In the social sciences today thin descriptions abound and find their expression in correlation coefficients, path diagrams, F ratios, dummy variables, structural equations, and social indicators. Thick descriptions are relatively rare, yet they constitute the stuff of interpretation. If, to paraphrase Geertz paraphrasing Simmel and Weber, "*Man is caught in webs of significance, feeling, influence and power that he has woven, then the interpretive task is one of unraveling and revealing the meanings persons give to their webs.*" Goffman (1967) has stated that the study of social life involves the analysis of "moments and their men." The present discussion reverses that directive.

The *second* form of any investigation of structural practices must present materials on the structural and interactional regularities evident in the everyday practices under study. Cavan's (1974) study of the social structure of a rural hippie settlement in the coastal valleys of the California redwood forest in the early 1970s provides an illustration.

Employing guidelines suggested by the Royal Anthropological Institution (1951), Cavan focused on the following structural regularities at the level of local hippie settlements.

(1) *Life cycle:* birth, death, naming, tending, weaning, contraception, marriage, bethrothal, dowries.

(2) *Household habits:* food, sleep, elimination.

(3) *Everyday round:* division of social labor, language.

(4) *Leisure forms:* pastimes, decorative art, architectural art, music.

(5) *Material culture:* styles of dress, kind of dwelling unit, cultivation.

(6) *Politics:* type of collectively, method of governance, figurehead.

(7) *Economics:* sources of income, method of production, division of economic labor.

In addition to reporting regularities under each of these structural categories, Cavan reported the time tables of interaction, the pathways of travel, the routine activities, the felt (and unfelt) authority structures, and the language and meaning structures evident in the hippie settlements. Her research offers one model (others can be found in the classic works of Malinowski, Radcliffe-Brown, Mead, and Bateson) for interpretive structural study. The sights, sounds, and smells of the hippie settlements are partially brought to life in her report.

The interpretivist attempts to bring the life world alive in full, vivid detail. The networks of social relationships, as ensembles that connect interactants into webs of meaningful experience and actualized structural practices, must be captured. The microrelations of power and knowledge that dominate and structure these practices also require presentation. Lacking these dimensions of thick description, the investigator's report assumes, to quote Cavan (1974: 346) a "static, lifeless character." It becomes just another structural account of everyday social life, lacking the meaning, substance, and fabric of real people living out real lives (in their everyday worlds).

There is more to an interpretive investigation than just the doing of fieldwork, the establishing of rapport with informants, the selecting of observational sites, the collecting of documents, the forming and testing of hypotheses, or the revamping of existing theory. Interpretation, the rendering of a body or sequence of experience understandable from the standpoint of everyday language users, requires, to repeat, the presentation of thickly contextualized meaning structures.

About the Author

NORMAN K. DENZIN

Norman K. Denzin is Professor of Sociology and Humanities at the University of Illinois, Urbana. He received his Ph.D. in sociology from the University of Iowa in 1966. He is the author of *The Research Act* (1978) and *Childhood Socialization* (1977) and editor of *Studies in Symbolic Interaction: An Annual Compilation of Research.* He has recently completed a monograph on emotion, entitled *Reflections on Emotion: A Social, Phenomenological, and Interactionist Inquiry* (1983) and is at work on a series of studies that will be gathered together under the title *The Structures of Interpretation.*

9

LIFE HISTORY METHODOLOGY

Gareth R. Jones
Texas A&M University

The purpose of this chapter is to argue that a qualitative approach to social analysis based on the life history methodology should be regarded as a unique tool through which to examine and analyze the subjective experience of individuals and their constructions of the social world. Of all research methods, it perhaps comes closest to allowing the researcher access to how individuals create and portray the social world surrounding them. The life history methodology offers an interpretive framework through which the meaning of human experience is revealed in personal accounts, in a way that gives priority to individual explanations of actions rather than to methods that filter and sort responses into predetermined conceptual categories.

SOCIAL REALITY AND SUBJECTIVE MEANING

Our humanness, and the relationship between social reality and subjective meaning, are embedded in the tension between two counterposing tendencies. On the one hand, human beings desire and attempt to express their humanness through their actions on the world. On the other, the world presents itself as an already constituted reality that must be understood and mastered if the potentialities of consciousness are to emerge and develop. In the dialectical relationship between these two processes, which we shall characterize as the "expressive" and "rational" dimensions of human action, we find the basis of our nature as human beings and of the culture or social reality that expresses that nature.

The situation is clearly illustrated in the case of Helen Keller, whose autobiography, *The Story of My Life*, presents a vivid example of the quest for humanness and of the processes through which humans structure and understand their world. Completely deaf and blind from early childhood, and hence without the usual taken-for-granted cues and props of sight and sound, her life is a remarkable illustration of the life history methodology's potential for revealing the basic structure of human life.

Helen Keller's story is one of a struggle for expression and of the importance of shared symbols, language, labels, and definitions of reality as both resource and constraint on the development of express-ive activity. It shows how human nature and culture can be seen as a developing reflection of the depth of meaning people find in their actions or projects, and how this in turn is a function of the socially constructed schemes of experience through which humans make sense of their actions. It shows in short, the extent to which human-ness is learned, and how once learned, it can be used expressively to shape and change one's understanding of the world. Human beings impose themselves on, and create, their world, yet they do so through a network of typifications that endow a particular culture with a coherent "rationality" as a system of shared meaning.

Helen Keller's life history reflects two distinct stages of develop-ment, divided by the event of her learning to communicate through language, which allowed her to enter the social world and use it as a resource. Prior to this her life was characterized by the intensity of her internal struggle for expression. She was unable to make herself known to her family and could only understand them in terms of such physical sensations as pleasure or pain. Her actions were uncontrol-lable and the taken-for-granted patterns of family and social life had no meaning for her because there was no way in which she could internalize them. As she herself describes it:

> Have you ever been at sea in a dense fog, when it seemed as if a tangible white darkness shut you in, and the great ship, tense and anxious, groped her way towards the shore with plummet and sounding line and you waited with beating heart for something to happen? I was like that ship before my education began, only I was without compass and sounding line and had no way of knowing how near the harbour was [Keller, 1954: 35].

She could not forge or create a shared reality because she lacked all the conceptual means necessary to build or to interact with that reality. As a result, her actions afforded her little satisfaction for she could not endow them with meaning and the reaction of others to her behavior mystified her, for she could not understand the effects of her actions on them. Her ability to break free from this situation rested on her capacity to create and use those typifications or "frames" of interpretation through which humans make sense of their situations, and which for most individuals are so quickly learned and taken for granted. As she reports, in contrast to children who hear and acquire language without any particular effort:

> The little deaf-child must trap [words] by a slow and often painful process. But whatever the process the result is wonderful. At first . . . my ideas were vague, and my vocabulary was inadequate, but as my knowledge of things grew and I learned more and more words, my field of inquiry broadened. . . . The beautiful truth burst upon my mind — I felt that there were invisible lines stretched between my spirit and the spirits of others [Keller, 1954: 39-40].

Helen Keller's struggle for full humanness illustrates the key dimensions through which we all construct our world. Her life history provides a direct and vivid illustration of what ethnomethodologists and other phenomenological sociologists try to demonstrate in their attempts to reveal the structure of the everyday social world by creating situations that question, disrupt, or destroy the interpretive schemes normally taken for granted (Garfinkel, 1967). Helen Keller shows us how human action manifests a tension between expressive and rational elements of experience, and how an understanding, or entering into the world of the latter, is a condition for full development of the former. As human beings, we must learn how to negotiate the social world before we can impose ourselves on it.

EPISTEMOLOGY AND QUALITATIVE METHODOLOGY

It follows directly from the ontological position described above that knowledge is grounded in the everyday, common-sense world, and in the constructions and explanations members of that world use to describe their reality and actions. This is because the structure of the social world, and its "organized" nature, emerge out of the typical patterns of interaction that derive from the typifications in use in a social context (Douglas, 1970; Bittner, 1965). Only through the analysis of the processes through which individuals enact and create social reality can subjective meaning be grasped. This calls for an epistemological position that is interpretive rather than normative, being concerned with elucidating meaning rather than with determining causality (Berger and Luckmann, 1966; Glaser and Strauss, 1967).

From this interpretive perspective, knowledge and understanding are context bound, and the theories advanced to account for the form of the social world and nature of human action are directly linked to the questions asked, and ultimately, to the historical and social context in which they are asked. Interpretive research seeks to address such questions from "within" social phenomena by bringing to the surface the essential dimensions of a social process or social context. By contrast, the normative style of inquiry seeks to study phenomena from "without." As a result, it is inclined to impose a definition on the subject of inquiry and to postulate relationships of a hypothetical kind. In so doing, it defines the problem of study at an ontological level at which the researcher is in control. Such a perspective suggests that the possibility of obtaining knowledge hinges on the adequacy of theory and method rather than on the intrinsic nature of the phenomenon being studied.

The interpretive position suggests that this epistemological stance is inadequate in that empirical techniques involve a way of looking at the world and of judging everyday experience that is divorced from the reality they study. In other words, the techniques or theories that are used achieve epistemological priority over the actual ways in which members create social reality. The rationale given for the use of such methodologies is that they offer a more scientific, verifiable account of the way in which the world is constructed, but as Popper (1968: 107) comments: "Observations and even more, observation statements and statements of experimental results, are always interpretations of the facts observed; they are interpretations in the light of theories." Theories and research methods structure and explain the world according to their own internal logic, for they impose their own definition on the situation and also constitute what is to be considered scientific explanation. Epistemologically, the kind of understanding or knowledge arrived at may thus be no more than an artifact of the theory or research method, and unrelated to the reality being observed. This dilemma is, of course, part and parcel of all theory development, including the interpretive, though the latter, in using the meaning structure of individuals as the research base, attempts to do less harm to the facts observed. It also recognizes that facts are "theory laden" in that members who talk about their realities or projects implicitly or explicitly offer the rationale behind their action. The social world is not seen as a "neutral" testing ground against which theory can somehow be examined, but as containing its own rationale and constituted logic. Responses and statements are not sterile facts to be fitted into some predetermined conceptual framework; they carry as much epistemological priority as the researcher's constructions.

From this interpretive perspective, concepts and theories become essentially exploratory instruments that have no epistemological priority over the phenomena of the social world. As Phillipson (1972) has noted, it is the researcher's job to reconstruct the social world in terms of formalized constructs that capture the contingencies of the situation and the manner in which reality is created. Often this will involve a reconstitution of the logic in use or rationality of the actor's definition of the situation, so the researcher must adopt a suitable methodology to avoid damaging the actor's explanation. The task is to demonstrate that analysis is congruent with the interpretive schemes used by those studied, while recognizing the researcher's own influence on the situation. The researcher's involvement in a situation, as interviewer or participant, for example, influences the definition of the situation because the researcher brings theories and interpretive schemes both as scientist and member to that situation. Over time, the typifications used by social scientists become a part of the typifications used by members of a culture as illustrated, for example, in the way psychoanalytic and sociological terminology has entered into the discourse of everyday life. Thus just as the rationale behind the actor's account becomes a part of the analysis, so the rules, standards, and concepts used by the researcher, both as participant and scientist, need to be brought to the surface and made an integral part of the analysis itself (Cicourel, 1972).

The status of the truth or understanding aimed at in qualitative methodology is thus a product of the stance taken toward the relationship between theory and data, data and the real world, and theory and the real world, and of the complex process of verification that proceeds between different forms of knowing and interpretation of the social world. Ultimately, the adequacy or validity of a theory can only be judged in relation to the facts of its realm of discourse or in relation to theories that pertain to explain the same phenomena. Theories may only have the status of "better than" rather than "proven" (Feyerabend, 1975; Popper, 1968; Campbell, 1979).

THE METHODOLOGY OF THE LIFE HISTORY TECHNIQUE

When the research problem involves an investigation of the ways in which individuals account for their actions, the life history methodology offers itself as an appropriate technique. It is a technique that explicitly recognizes the collusion of the researcher in the research process and allows the researcher access to the processes involved in meaning construction. It recognizes that each person has an implicit theory to account for action, and it also recognizes that the researcher brings implicit or explicit theories to the research situation. In this regard, the methodology struggles to find a balance between the theory in the real world and the theory in the researcher's head, the research material modifying and developing the theory, and the theory interpreting, condensing, and transforming the themes that emerge from the material. Validity is established by demonstrating that sociological explanation is congruent with the meanings through which members construct their realities and accomplish their everyday practical activities (Phillipson, 1972: 92). Both the research material generated and the form of analysis to which that material is subjected expose the processes through which the social world becomes meaningful for the members of a culture and the purposive and expressive acts that underlie the typifications used to express reality and segments of reality.

As the name implies, the technique takes as its research data the accounts of individuals about their lives or about specific segments of their social world. These accounts document the relationship between an individual and his or her social reality; they describe the ways individuals interpret and define the contexts in which their lives have been acted out and the meaning their participation had for them. There are two basic forms of account that are suitable for life history analysis. The first are those already available to the researcher in the form of autobiographies, diaries, records, and correspondence, and the second are those the researcher generates through in-depth interviewing (Filstead, 1970; Bogdan, 1974). A third form of account that is essentially an amalgamation of these two forms is found in the material contained in anthologies in which researchers have collected multiple individual accounts of some segment of social reality, for example, of work experiences (Terkel, 1974; Fraser, 1969).

To ensure that the interpretive power of the technique is used to its fullest extent, it is necessary to set out some criteria for judging the descriptive adequacy of the researcher's analysis and the material generated. To some extent, these criteria can only be framed with the research question in mind, for interpretation is in part constrained by the concepts and constructions drawn from the field of study itself. It is the researcher's task to develop constructs that best interpret the material, and so criteria become context bound. However, it is possible to set out certain issues that must be addressed if the researcher is to use the life history methodology appropriately. The criteria presented below have been developed from a phenomenological, social interactionist persepctive along dimensions suggested by Dollard (1944).

Criterion 1: The person must be viewed as a member of a culture. The first criterion recognizes that an individual enters a cultural milieu from the moment of birth. Also, that the world and segments of social reality have a present, past, and future which is embodied in interpretive schemes the individual grasps as common-sense knowledge. The life history technique must describe and interpret the actor's account of his or her development in the common-sense world, or in relevant segments of social reality (e.g., organizations) and the ways in which he or she comes to possess the stocks of knowledge peculiar to those realities.

Criterion 2: The role of significant others in transmitting culture must be recognized. Criterion 2 directly relates to the first since it emphasizes the role of the family group, peers, leaders, and others in transmitting socially defined stocks of knowledge. More generally, in phenomenological terms the most important relationship is that of the "we relationship" (Schutz, 1967b). Here, the actor is confronted by the directly experienced other in the vivid present and brings to this encounter a whole stock of previously constituted knowledge. This includes both general and specific knowledge of the other person's interpretive schemes, their habits and their language. From the "we relationship" stems all possibility of knowing the social world and the interpretive schemes and stocks of knowledge peculiar to segments of the social world. The person builds up knowledge of the world and this knowledge serves as the basis for subsequent encounters with the world. Thus the life history technique attempts to describe the typifications that arise from the "we relationship" and how they become interpretive schemes.

Criterion 3: The nature of social action and the basis of social reality and culture must be specified. The life history technique must specify the meaning systems or modes of action at work in a particular context or culture and show how the person's actions become oriented to that situation. In this connection the analysis of the "background expectancies" (Cicourel, 1967) or taken-for-granted assumptions present in the context should be described as should the rules, codes, or standards routinely invoked by members to accomplish their activities. Similarly, the expressive beliefs about the basis of social reality contained in myths, rituals, and in language itself should be explored and analyzed (Pondy et al., 1983). Such material should be thematically organized by the researcher in order to expose the underlying rationality of the typifications used to describe the social context.

Criterion 4: The continuous, related character of experience over time must be a focus of analysis. Criterion 4 seeks to ensure that the processual development of the person is adequately described by the life history technique. The significance of events in life history material and the attributions members currently make concerning those events should be examined to understand how they are constituted from a historical sequence of events. The degree to which definitions of reality change over time and the themes that connect otherwise disparate events is a major focus of the life history technique.

Criterion 5: The social context must be continually associated with the action of the person. This criterion complements the above for it emphasizes that the action of the person cannot be divorced from the context in which it occurs, and conversely, that the nature of the social context must be specified if such action is to be understood. The life history technique assumes that, just as the typifications used by the individual change over time, so may the typifications used to define the context. Beyond the analysis of the bases of social reality, the relationship between subprovinces of meaning must be examined, for example, the relationship between work and nonwork, in order to understand the transformation of one context into another.

Thus these criteria are interrelated; each accentuates one aspect of the relationship between social reality and subjective meaning. They also provide guidelines for doing life history research, for obtaining and analyzing material to ensure that theory is grounded in members' accounts of their action.

ORGANIZATIONAL ANALYSIS AND THE LIFE HISTORY APPROACH

The world of formal organization can be viewed as a network of typifications, as a particular form of language that has been produced historically through the rational and expressive acts of its population. This language is constituted in three main ways. First, organizations possess constitutive rules that reflect the form of rationality embodied in the wider milieu or environment to which it belongs. These rules constitute a basic grammar of organization; in the case of economic enterprise, for example, this grammar is represented in the language of finance, profit, loss, or turnover that determines the basis of its continued existence. Second, the language of any given organization is constituted historically as a collective memory of associations, events, and recipes for action expressed through the organization's structure, technology, rules, procedures, myths, and stories. Third, organizational language is constituted contemporaneously by organizational members on the basis of their shared and competing interpretations of that language. When there is tension between the various elements involved in this process, the organizational language changes. For example, when changes in the organization's context give rise to new constitutive rules that cannot be handled within existing meaning structures, the organizational grammar changes. The introduction of new technology or changing views about the nature of the social responsibility of business may lead to the reappraisal of the organization's means of control, for example. Also, members may attempt to redefine the culture of the organization by introducing new typifications or action strategies into the organizational language, for example, by changing the criteria for organizational success or reward.

In using the life history methodology to approach such issues the researcher's aim is to uncover the grammar of an organization's language, to expose the ways in which the typifications offered by a particular organizational language condition the experience and action of organization members, and to understand how members themselves account for the premises contained in the organizational language. The methodology can be used to generate and analyze life history accounts of organizational members in a variety of ways.

For example, suppose that the researcher is interested in the study of organizational socialization or career development and the ways in which dominant organizational members seek to impose their definitions of the situation on others. One form of account immediately available is that contained in the autobiographies, diaries, and correspondence of prominent entrepreneurs, philanthropists, and politicians. Here the criteria described in the last section would be used to analyze these accounts in order to expose the manner in which entrepreneurs or founders transmit to the organization its values, rationality, and ethos. For example, values may be transmitted by personifying a certain managerial style or image. On the other hand, the researcher may choose in-depth interviewing as the research strategy. The aim of the methodology in this case would be to generate accounts that reveal the rational and expressive typifications that underlie the everyday experience and meaning of organizational socialization. The role of the organization's socialization practices and its "rules for inclusion" in shaping the individual's interpretation of the situation would be an important focus of analysis here (Van Maanen and Schein, 1979). In this sense, the progress of a career would be examined in terms of the member's understanding and use of the typifications offered by the organizational language. For example, promotion, transfer, changes in managerial style or organizational structure all affect the process of socialization for they continually affect the definition of the situation and the member's orientation toward the organization. Also, by comparing and contrasting the individual's experience of socialization in different segments of social reality, for example in work or nonwork or across different organizations (as well as the same organization historically) the meaning of socialization will emerge. The analysis of Helen Keller's autobiography described earlier suggests the way in which members' accounts would be approached.

However, the process of reaching this level of understanding may present certain problems, for in everyday terms the experience of socialization in organizational life is frequently taken for granted. Members may be unable to articulate the rules and interpretive schemes they follow even though their behavior is in accordance with those rules (Winch 1958; Garfinkel, 1967). It is in this situation that the advantages of the life history technique are realized, for the researcher is able to set up a series of oppositions in order to gain access to the ways in which socialization is manifest in an organization's language. The oppositions are created in the following order: first, oppositions within members' accounts, second, between members' accounts and third, between members' accounts and the researcher's constructions of the situation.

In order to generate oppositions within members' accounts, the researcher must first obtain the members' taken-for-granted accounts of organizational socialization as reflected, for example, in views of supervision, work practices, or managerial style. The next step is to obtain the significant events and critical incidents that vividly portray how socialization occurs in the organization and then to examine these against the backdrop of taken-for-granted assumptions. In this way, the member's unreflective stance toward the organization is ruptured and the rationale behind forms of managerial succession or stories of organizational entry or exit is exposed. Similarly, the process of leading members through their organizational careers and asking them to chart out the significant events in that passage leads them to adopt the role of the autobiographer when describing the way they have controlled and been controlled by the organization's typifications. In the second stage of the research process, the researcher sets up oppositions between members' accounts. This is achieved in the case of socialization by interviewing both those responsible for socializing newcomers and the newcomers themselves. In this way, different interpretations of the process of socialization are obtained, depending on the person's understanding of the meaning of the organizational language. The effect of the newcomers' previous experiences on their subsequent orientation to the organization is an important issue here.

When this material has been obtained and provisionally analyzed in terms of the categories and dimensions that have emerged from the material itself, the third opposition is set up.

Here, the object is to create an opposition between the members' accounts and the researcher's constructions of the situation in order to avoid a premature collapse of the material into descriptive categories. This is achieved in the following manner. First, the researcher analyzes the material obtained from members' accounts in terms of a chosen theoretical orientation. The theoretical potency of the members' accounts is ignored. The material is synthesized in terms of the researcher's theoretical framework. For example, in the analysis of Helen Keller, the concepts of rational and expressive action were developed in order to explain the way in which she came to understand the social world. Her own explanation of events was provisionally ignored. The researcher's stance toward members' accounts then changes. The theoretical potency of the members' accounts (i.e., their definition of the situation) is admitted, but now the researcher "confronts" the members' explanations of events with the explanation produced by the theoretical framework. One acts either on the assumption that the member's explanation is the "true" one and the researcher's "false," or vice versa, in order to find the balance between the theory contained in the member's construction of events and that in the researcher's. In Mead's terms, the researcher takes the "role of the other" while simultaneously being in the role of researcher (Mead, 1934). Through the opposition thus created, the researcher attempts to expose the themes and processes that encapsulate and explain the research material parsimoniously, while preserving the internal logic of the material itself. In essence, the researcher attempts to formalize the "unsaid" or ambiguous portion of the accounts in a theoretical framework that exposes the nature of the typifications that lie behind the process of organizational socialization and career development.

At a theoretical level, the researcher faces the problem of accounting for the form of members' constructions and the way these change and develop over time. How, for example, do different forms of socialization relate to differences in managerial values or to position in the organizational hierarchy? Here, the longitudinal dimension of the life history approach gives the researcher the opportunity to examine how a member's construction of events leads him or her to act in a certain way. For example, by using such incidents as the effect of a change in lifestyle or organization as anchoring points, it becomes possible to generate accounts describing the typifications or attributions members use to describe their changing involvement in the organization. Any written correspondence or records accompanying such changes could also provide a useful conceptual input into the analysis, for such material also suggests the typifications at work in a particular context.

If the aim of organizational analysis is to expose the rationality behind organizational action, to account for the ways in which organizations and people interact with and define one another, and to understand the processes by which they orient their action to the future, an understanding of the meaning they attribute to the past is a necessity. The life history approach provides a useful method for doing this by listening to the stories that organization members can tell and exploring the collective memory of ideas, associations, events, enactments, and recipes for action and prejudices that lend organization its detailed character. Familiar topics of research focusing on the study of organizational climate, control, and the general enactment of relationships within and between organization and environment all lend themselves to analysis in these terms.

About the Author

GARETH R. JONES

My interest in the life history methodology began during my doctoral work at the University of Lancaster. I was faced with the problem of how to examine the validity of a set of theoretical propositions I had developed to account for the way in which people differentiate between, and give meaning to, classes of experience such as work and nonwork. In the course of this research I first used survey instruments and then interviewing techniques to examine my propositions. But I was soon presented with two problems. First, people found it difficult to conceptualize and explain their experiences and to go beyond taken-for-granted assumptions when explaining their behavior. Second, my findings were as much as function of the structure I imposed on the data as of anything intrinsic to the material I was collecting. Although these problems arise with the use of any form of methodology, for my research they were particularly disturbing since I needed to reach a level of explanation, which, while incorporating people's accounts, exposed the cognitive structure behind those accounts. It was a solution to this problem that lead to me use the life history methodology.

10

STUDYING ORGANIZATIONS AS CULTURES

Linda Smircich
University of Massachusetts

ORGANIZATION AS A NETWORK OF MEANING

The essence of the social world rests in those patterns of meaning that shape and sustain human action and interaction. When we talk of a social reality, or of the reality of an individual or group, we refer to the meaningful experiencing of events. People forge their experience of the world through actions that become meaningful in a wider social context. This process can be best understood through what the gestalt psychologists have conceptualized as a relationship between figure and ground. Meaningful action and shared social realities depend, to a great extent, on the nature and development of a figure/ground relationship in which elements in a potentially vast perceptual field are differentiated from their wider context and interpreted through a frame of reference that provides the basis for a coherent organization of perception and experience. The emergence of social organization depends on the emergence of shared interpretive schemes, expressed in language and other symbolic constructions that develop through social interaction. Such schemes provide the basis for shared systems of meaning that allow day-to-day activities to become routinized or taken for granted.

The stability of such modes of organization depends on the continuing existence of common modes of interpretation and understanding. Novel situations must be interpreted within the context of accepted frameworks of meaning, or else new interpretations must be constructed to sustain organized activity. The process of negotiating meanings for such experiences is crucial for understanding the way organization evolves in the midst of events that upset formerly taken-for-granted meanings and ways of life. The processes through which a group of individuals negotiate and interpret their experience are thus central for understanding the way patterns of shared meaning sustain organized activity.

This view emphasizes that people enact their reality either individually or in concert with others. They are not merely bystanders, but active participants in the making of experience. They impose themselves on, and thus make, their world through intentional action that assumes its meaning and significance within the context of interpretive schemes embodying a particular pattern of purpose, value, and meaning. It is through such action and interpretation that human actors construct and give meaning to their external world and also give form to their evolving nature as human beings. Human actors do not know or perceive *the* world, but know and perceive *their* world, through the medium of culturally specific frames of reference (Hallowell, 1955). All forms of human organization, though apparently concrete and real, are in actuality constantly being enacted and made meaningful by their membership in this way.

The enactment of reality may, of course, be influenced by some form of power relationship. Those who seek to lead organized activity, for example, often seek to enact a particular form of organizational experience for others (Smircich and Morgan, 1982). They may attempt to define interpretations and meanings that can become widely understood and shared by organization members so that actions are guided by a common definition of the situation. Those with power are able to influence the course of organizational development through control over valued resources and through use of symbols by which organization members mediate their experience. Widely shared interpretations of an organization's history, traditions, or goals and values, for example, may be used to provide a source of coherence to experience that allows a sense of identification to develop, thus binding individual and group. The unique set of meanings that a group develops portrays its ethos or distinctive character, which is sustained and elaborated through symbolic forms such as language, rituals, ideologies, and myths (Pondy et al., 1983).

The achievement of shared meaning in many areas of organizational life may be problematic since organizational leaders have no monopoly on the development of meaning. All members engage in this process, shaping organizational life through the interpretations and meanings they attach to everyday experience. Thus the organizational strategy favored by a dominant coalition may be countered by rival frames of reference and poorly implemented by accident or design. Disjuncture in systems of meaning, a case of different realities, may account for what is commonly referred to as a "communications breakdown." These and related considerations raise many intriguing questions for organization theorists to explore such as: What holds a group of people together as an organization? Through what processes do they change? How much disjuncture in systems of meaning can there be before an organization suffers disintegration? In order to understand organizational life in these terms, we must be concerned with discerning the operative structures of meaning, socially established and sustained, through which people engage and experience their organizational world.

STUDYING NETWORKS OF MEANING

We may borrow the concept of culture from anthropology as an epistemological device to help frame and guide the study of organizations from this point of view. Those anthropologists who treat cultures as systems of shared meanings, such as Hallowell (1955) and Geertz (1973), provide models that emphasize the importance of context in attempting to understand the patterns of action that are meaningful to others.

Turner (1971) also uses this approach, suggesting that since an organizational culture rests in a commonly held fabric of meanings, these meanings should be sought by analyzing the knowledge that individuals possess about their situations and by examining the understandings that the individual has of him- or herself, the boss, colleagues, subordinates, and the wider context within which the organization operates. By gaining this understanding, the researcher will discover the explanations, rationales, anecdotes, normative views, myths, and mysteries of that part of the culture that the individual occupies.

An analysis of an organization as a culture must go beyond any single individual's understanding of the situation, however. It must be concerned with knowledge of the whole, and the multiple meaning systems or "counterrealities" that may be in competition with one another.

The researcher can use several kinds of evidence to piece together a multifaceted and complex picture of the meaning system in use. In general, three forms of evidence may be used: observation, reports from informants, and the researcher's participation in the setting. The analysis may proceed through the activities of observing and listening, and the making and testing of inferences, which, over time, can lead to an appraisal of the meaning existing for the people involved in the situation, including the researcher.

Through such analysis a detailed description of the various kinds of symbol systems and associated meanings can be developed. However, an additional step, necessary to a cultural analysis, is the articulation of the recurrent themes that show how the symbols are linked into meaningful relationships and how they are related to the activities of the people in the setting. Themes present the patterns in symbolic discourse. They draw the relationships among symbols in use; they provide the context against which symbols have meaning; they specify the links between values, beliefs, and action. As such they form the basis of the world view or ethos expressed in various symbolic modes and represent the heart of any analysis of an organization as a culture.

What are the consequences of this view for epistemology?

The primary consequence is that, at first, the type of knowledge generated from this form of inquiry must be what Polanyi (1958) refers to as "personal knowledge." It is a form of knowledge in which the subject/object relations that characterize positivist science give way to subject/subject relations with a focus on intersubjective meanings. This form of knowledge is not universal in form, but specific to people in particular relationships. It presupposes the uniqueness of persons and recognizes that knowledge is not independent of the knower. It is existential and deals with the quality of *being in relation*. It is concerned with understanding relationships within their specific context.

Therefore, the purpose of this approach to the study of people who are organized is diagnostic — to get at how organization works (or more precisely, what it means to be organized) in particular and in general. This orientation is actually highly congruent with the interest of those researchers who attempt to study how "organizations" interact with their "environments," and the ways in which they appear to follow particular courses of action. Researchers who are concerned with such issues as: What do top managers know about their environment (their world)? How do they perceive their world? What do they want from their world? are really asking questions of existence and choice which fall within the domain of personal knowledge.

When we discover and reveal the meanings underlying social action in organized situations we learn about groups in particular circumstances. The knowledge is thus about specific relationships. But at the same time it may be possible to build an understanding of the more general shared structures of meaning that extend beyond the specific situation and are found in other complex organized settings. This wider form of knowledge can be used to contribute to a broader understanding of, for example, the dynamics of corporate cultures and subcultures in general.

A second consequence of this view for epistemology is that the analysis of an organization as a culture is an interpretive endeavor. This does not set the researcher apart from those who pursue other forms of organizational inquiry as might first be suspected. Because, in fact, all researchers engage in interpretive acts in the translation of data into meaningful forms. All data, whether verbal, statistical, or pictoral, are meaningless when abstracted from context. Data only become significant when they are made sensible and coherent through the mediation of human meaning. Thus all scientific knowledge suffers the fate of what Cassirer (1946) called the "curse of mediacy."

There can be no one-to-one mapping of the "real" organizational reality onto the pages of an academic journal. The interpretive researcher recognizes this and aims to see the world as the organization's members see it, to learn the meaning of actions and events for the organization members, and to portray these accurately. To do this requires an appreciation of, and reflection on, the wider context of experience. In providing interpretations of the processes of organizing in corporate settings, or in any setting for that matter, we are not concerned with specifying cause-and-effect relationships. Organizational life is a pattern or "stream of evolving relationships" (Burns, 1978: 439) between symbolic forms. This makes labeling discrete cause-and-effect relationships inappropriate and impossible. What we are after, instead, is an understanding and an elaboration of the wider context of social action.

The researcher studying an organizational culture tries to uncover the structures of meaning in use in the setting and to synthesize an image of that group's reality and make it available for consideration and reflection. Within a particular setting, the analysis of the organization as a culture may serve the same purpose as that served by therapy for an individual. The researcher reflects back to a group a many-sided image of the systems of meaning in use. Through the process of guided self-reflection, a deeper understanding of the dynamics of behavior can be gained. The increased awareness may spark insights that lead to change. The activities of the researcher often result in consciousness raising, facilitating and guiding a process of self-exploration on the part of a group with the potential for change. The research process generates information that may challenge the image held by organization members; it is not a neutral process. This is also true when a researcher sends a group a report of "research findings" or when the researcher conducts an interactive feedback session to discuss the data collected. Some researchers have been more conscious of this than others, including it as an explicit aspect of their model of research. (The chapter by Susman in this volume on the action research perspective provides such an example). An awareness of the role of the researcher as someone who may influence the system of meaning being studied serves to highlight the role of all researchers as potential agents of change.

Thus the grounds for evaluation of research espoused by the postivist tradition are not appropriate to organizational inquiry. Networks of shared meaning do not lend themselves to study by methods of detachment and objectivity. Instead, the researcher is "scientific" in that the collection and reporting of data are done systematically, with care and discipline. Evaluation rests not on criteria of objectivity or coherence, but on the integrity, the soundness, of the analysis. How well does it capture the experience of that group? How well does it allow others to know the meanings for social action held by the people in that setting? How well is our understanding of social life beyond this particular setting enhanced? These questions provide the important reference points against which the utility of the research is to be judged.

IMPLICATIONS FOR THE CONDUCT OF RESEARCH

The researcher studying organizations as cultures is concerned with *learning* the consensual meanings ascribed by a group of people to their experience and *articulating* the thematic relationships expressed in this meaning system. This orientation has several practical consequences for the conduct of research that differentiate it from other approaches to the study of organizations:

(1) *In the field the researcher's role is that of learner; there are certain skills appropriate to that role.* Meanings do not exist in objects or activities; they are assigned to events by people who perceive and interpret their context. Therefore, because the researcher's concern is with meanings, and not with facts that lie outside human actions, the researcher needs to be close to, not detached from, those social interactions in which meanings are rooted and elaborated. The researcher of an organizational culture generally makes a commitment to spend a significant period of time in the setting observing and interacting in order to learn directly from the organization members.

To do this, the researcher needs to establish a relationship conducive to learning, one that is nonthreatening to the people in the setting. Fundamentally, this means establishing rapport and building a climate of trust, acceptance, and openness so that the researcher will be invited by people to see the world from their point of view. To do this the researcher needs to convey respect and care for the individuals from whom she or he hopes to learn.

In the realm of social interaction, there is no single, objective answer to such questions as: What is happening here? What does this mean? The researcher needs to be sensitive to the variety of perspectives that may be part of any situation. The researcher studying an organizational culture is in a sense aiming to do an "empathic ethnography." The quality of empathy implies being able to "stand in the shoes of the other" and to see how the world looks to him or her. In the same way that therapists strive for empathic understanding in client-centered therapy, organization researchers can strive to achieve empathic understanding of the meanings present for the members of a group in order to explore the realms of intersubjective meanings that give them a sense of unity and identity.

There are two particular interpersonal skills — reflective listening and free floating attention — both drawn from the psychotherapy literature, that are useful for learning and understanding the perspectives of others. Reflective or active listening is an energetic effort to receive fully the message being communicated by another through verbal and nonverbal means. It involves attending to the words and feelings being expressed explicitly or implicitly and encouraging the speaker to continue to elaborate. Encouragement to continue can be given through a range of means, from nonverbal (head nods, silence) and minimal encouragers ("I see," "hm hmmm"), through reflective statements ("It sounds like you're saying . . . "). An account of how this skill can be used in ethnographic research can be found in Spradley (1979).

Along with taking the care to build relationships conducive to learning, the researcher has to be able to tolerate a high degree of ambiguity, for learning about and understanding the world of others takes time. At first, and perhaps even for a long while, the data the researcher acquires will seem unclear, unrelated, and probably overwhelming. The researcher who attempts to short circuit the process and responds to pressure for immediate answers operates on her or his own needs at the expense of staying within and understanding the world of the people in the setting. The researcher should attempt to avoid this and to maintain free-floating attention, so that he or she is responding to what is actually present in the situation.

There are some very real obstacles to implementing this approach to the study of organizations. The first is the issue of entry, and how to gain agreement from key individuals to allow the presence of an inquisitive outsider. This seems especially difficult in business organizations in which the norms around productivity and proprietary information may make the presence of an outsider even less acceptable. The researcher may be seen as disruptive and as someone who will interfere with the work getting done. He or she may be seen as threatening or as someone who will disclose company secrets to others. There are probably not very many organizations like the insurance company that gave the researcher her own office space, allowed her to be an observer of the top management group in all their various activities and to conduct multiple interviews, and did not request feedback of any kind. Most organizations would expect to receive something in return for their cooperation. That such an open and free arrangement was acceptable to the insurance company was itself an interesting piece of data about the culture of the group. The president was happy with such a relationship because it was quite consistent with his style of management and the overall mode of interpersonal action, which was oriented to maintaining an atmosphere of calm and order. To have requested feedback from the researcher or to have participated in a joint exploration of their culture would have meant opening up the situation for potential change. What may have at first appeared as an open culture based on the ease of access for the researcher was in fact one quite carefully oriented toward maintaining a facade of harmony, agreement, and the status quo, which avoided any conflict and disagreement.

A second obstacle to studying organizations as cultures revolves around maintaining the role of learner. One of the challenges to people with education in management who want to do ethnographic work in corporations is that people will expect them to play the role of "management expert" because of their prior experience with outside consultants who do just that. They often want to know the researcher's views, opinions, and evaluations. Although one cannot deny one's training in management and organizational behavior, it is important that researchers studying organizations as cultures clarify their roles and reassert their desire to learn about the organization from the people in the setting, rather than be seen as having the answers to organizational problems.

(2) *An iterative approach to the analysis of data is used.* Researchers of organizations as cultures do not usually start with a set of a priori hypotheses to test in the field. Instead, they learn about the meanings of social action through the course of their interaction with

people in a particular setting. Their work proceeds in a way that allows the themes present in the setting to emerge and to be explored in cycles of data collection and analysis (see for example, Bogdan and Taylor, 1975; Spradley, 1979; Schwartz and Jacobs, 1979).

Overall, the researcher is striving to present a holistic view of the shared meanings, or images of organization, that the members hold. The holistic view usually gets built up very slowly from multiple sources of data. The researcher may feel a good deal of anxiety and worry that there will be no sense to the data or that important things are being missed. But worry and anxiety, although natural enough feelings for the individual doing his or her first field study, are blocks to the maintenance of free-floating attention. To the greatest extent possible, the researcher must strive to be relaxed and maintain a "taking in" posture in order to remain sensitive to what is happening in the setting.

After I had spent several weeks in the insurance company referred to above, certain issues emerged from the observations and from direct interaction with the staff members. For example, I had heard the phrase "teamwork" used many times and wanted to know more about what it meant to the staff. I had also observed the weekly staff meetings and seen how differently the staff members behaved when they were in that setting from how they behaved in individual interaction with me. An interview was designed in order to learn more about the staff's views on these issues.

One concern frequently raised regarding this approach to inquiry is the possibility of deception. It is of course true that people may purposely deceive or avoid certain issues, but these possibilities are even greater with quantitative techniques that do not involve face-to-face interaction. With face-to-face interaction, formal and informal over time in the setting, the researcher gets a great deal of feedback and observes the person frequently, gaining insight from nonverbal cues as well as from words, all of which provide information for evaluation.

The participant observer has the important advantage of her or his own experience in the setting to complement the other sources of data. Thus, for example, I could see for myself during our interviews that Mr. Hall, the president of the insurance company, did not like to deal with difficult issues. His discomfort was conveyed verbally and nonverbally so that I began to feel discomfort and thought maybe the questions were too "sensitive," despite the fact that I did not have this kind of reaction with any of the other executives. Thus the comments by the staff members that Mr. Hall liked to play things "cool" and that the group did not deal with problems but instead "buried them" were confirmed by my own interactions with the president and by my observations of the group in action.

The heart of the analysis of an organization as a culture is the elaboration of key themes that are built up from multiple sources of data. At the end of my stay with the insurance company, the data consisted of daily field notes, the interview tapes, documents, and my own experiences of being in the organization. At that point I had impressions of themes; the most forceful ones involved the inauthentic mode of interpersonal relating the executive group displayed and a pervasive air of dissatisfaction with the performance of the president. Both of these themes were eventually combined into a paper, "The Management of Meaning" (Smircich and Morgan, 1982), which was built up around a description of a key event, Operation June 30th, that occurred during my field work. Through a discussion of the meanings assigned to that event, we attempted to convey a holistic image of the sense that the executive staff made of their experience in the insurance company. We also attempted to show how the process of leadership was itself a form of symbolic discourse open to interpretation.

In another study in a design and development corporation, field work extended over several years and was much broader in scope. The theme that lay beneath individual organization members' explanations for their current state of affairs was the lack of consensus on organization identity and the various reactions to that situation. While the insurance company was characterized by the suppression of feelings, the design and development company was characterized by expression of feelings of pressure, stress, and even despair. These feelings prevailed throughout the organization and were linked to a change in strategic direction that plunged the firm into a sharply different environment, one that required operating at a much greater level of complexity and uncertainty. The top management group sought to pursue a strategy of growth and risk, but they sensed that a group of long-term professional employees, who represented a critical resource due to their knowledge and personal contacts with customers, were resisting this direction. At the same time, many people below the top levels of management expressed the belief that the company did not have the capability to operate successfully in the new domain. The lack of convergence on a collective self-image was played out on the individual level by confusion and disagreement about roles and responsibilities; it was further demonstrated in the decline in financial performance after the change in strategy. The underlying pattern of conflict regarding the image of the organization in its world was a unifying framework for understanding life in this organization.

(3) _The focus of attention is on symbols_. When individuals come together, they communicate through a world of symbolic relationships. Because of this shared symbolic system, a sense of commonality develops so that interaction takes place without continual negotiation of interpretations. Much of this commonality is developed through and sustained by such processes as rituals, slogans, myths, ideologies, stories, and specialized vocabularies. The observer of an organization as a culture seeks to study those forms of symbolic discourse because they are the mode of interpretation through which patterns of meaningful action are enacted. The researcher aims first to understand the meaning of particular symbols in use by a group and then to build a holistic view of how the meanings of the symbols interrelate with social action to express the group's image or world view.

Often the most accessible symbol system is language. By attending to what people say, we can learn how they make sense of their experiences. There are a number of techniques from linguistic analysis to literary criticism that are useful in gaining insight into the ways in which groups of people organize their perceptions. For example, the insurance company study included an analysis of the executive's use of imagery — the verbal comparison of an object, idea, or emotional state with something else. The images present in everyday language are indicators of the meanings and attitudes that give form and coherence to the speaker's experience. For the insurance group the most imagic language was found in the descriptions of their interpersonal relationships. They drew contrasts between two opposite ways of interacting (e.g., brutally, as in "a jungle," or loyally, to "a team"). Most executives believed their group was perched precariously in the middle — not a team and dangerously close to degenerating into junglelike behavior. There was a high degree of overlap in the imagery used by these executives to describe the way they dealt with one another, indicating a similar method for interpreting their experience. There was also a high degree of convergence between the way the executives described their interaction patterns and the way they were observed behaving in the group.

In building a cultural analysis there is a danger in exclusive reliance on verbal data collected via interviews because the researcher may lose sight of the broader view of the context within which to interpret the words of the speaker. Additionally, sole reliance on verbal data collected through interviews assumes that the researcher can automatically ask the appropriate questions, those that are most relevant for tapping the experience of a particular group, in most cases an assumption with very little support.

For these reasons, participant observation for significant time periods with interviews conducted after some time in the setting is the favored strategy for data gathering. In this way there can be attention to nonverbal or behavioral symbolic action, as well as to the verbal or cognitive, and there is greater likelihood that the questions ultimately asked in an interview will be relevant because they have emerged from interaction in the setting.

While the analysis of language is important and represents an almost untapped area of investigation for the field of organization studies, it represents only one form of symbolic analysis. There are nonverbal forms of symbolic discourse such as rituals and complex forms (e.g., the practice of leadership, which has verbal and behavioral components), that are rich in meaning. Again, drawing from the insurance company study for an example, the Monday morning staff meeting was a ritual in that it was formalized and stylized behavior repeated in that form. For the staff members it was symbolic of the way their president wanted business to be conducted: calmly, cooly, harmoniously with no conflict or controversy, but also with an air of unreality. They interpreted their behavior in that setting as a guide for when they were outside of the watchful eye of the president. Thus the meaning of the social action of the staff meeting became applied in a rulelike manner to the other forms of interaction among the staff.

CONCLUSION

In these ways the researcher can understand organizations as cultures. The approach stresses the very active role people play in enacting their organizational reality and in developing shared interpretations for their experience. The researcher studying organizations in this way makes a commitment to learning about how a group makes sense of its experience, which, as has been shown, implies methodological practices that require empathy and involvement and the use of the self as an instrument of research. The outcome of such an approach is greater information about and understanding of the dynamics of group activities that lead them to emerge as "organized."

About the Author

LINDA SMIRCICH

I remember that when I was younger, before I really knew what the word anthropology meant, I wanted to be Margaret Mead. That interest has stayed with me, although my work takes place in corporate boardrooms rather than among primitive civilizations.

The foundations for my thinking about organizations were set by undergraduate study in anthropology, sociology, and phenomenological psychology. Added to that was four years experience in that exemplar bureaucracy, the telephone company, followed by graduate work at humanistically oriented Syracuse University and participation in group relations training programs at the National Training Laboratory at Bethel, Maine.

The critical incident that has led me to formulate the position articulated in this chapter was a summer-long observational field study of the executive committee of an insurance company. That experience enabled me to see organizations as systems of shared meanings, or cultures, held together by social interaction patterns of the members and to ask the question, How does a group of people maintain a sense of organization?

— 11 —

UNCOVERING COGNITIVE MAPS

The Self-Q Technique

Michel G. Bougon

The Pennsylvania State University

I am interested in how people pattern their experience into knowledge and utilize this knowledge to organize themselves and others. To research these interests, I develop nonreactive methods of mapping the knowledge of participants in organized settings. To understand these methods and the paradigm underlying their development, we must examine the nature of experience, knowledge, and organization themselves.

FROM EXPERIENCE TO KNOWLEDGE

To me, "experience" denotes raw experience, intimate phenomenological experience, energy flowing through the skin. It can be light energy falling on the retina, sound energy impinging on the eardrum, mechanical energy impacting tactile corpuscles, or any other sensory excitation singly or in combination. This raw experience constitutes the ontological stratum upon which we erect our perceptions, knowledge, and epistemological systems.

Schemas, Perception, and Epistemology

To me, the basic epistemological question is: How does this flow of energy across the skin become knowledge about ourselves and our physical and social surroundings? The answer on which I base my research is that the process transforming raw experience into knowledge relies on cortical schemas, and particularly on the interplay between raw experience, schemas, patterns, perception, and knowledge. For perceiving patterns into one's raw experience (i.e., for acquiring knowledge), one needs schemas. For organizing and retaining that knowledge, one needs further schemas. Schemas, perception, and knowledge are intimately interrelated, and one cannot be isolated from the others.

The cortical schemas that interest me are not the schemas usually presented in current cognitive psychology textbooks, which have more in common with computer architecture than they do with the cortex. Rather, they are those flexible, proactive patterning processors identified in primitive form by Ward (1886), Binet (1894), and Bergson (1896) and given a cortical basis by Head (1920), who first clinically demonstrated that they originate from particular arrangements of neurons in the cortex. Bartlett (1932), acquainted with Ward and Head, first introduced English readers to the notion under the names of "scheme" and "schema." Since that time, many researchers have adopted the concept of schema, notably Piaget (1936), Merleau-Ponty (1962), Cicourel (1969), Goffman (1974), Norman (1976), Neisser (1976), and Weick (1978).

For these and other researchers, schemas are involved in numerous conative, emotive, and cognitive behaviors. Extending the work of these researchers, I propose that cortical schemas possess an additional property that has not been discussed before: Schemas have the property of handling the energy flow across the skin *as a whole*. Therefore, schemas empower us with such feats as recognizing patterns at a glance. For example, when you meet a person, you are often able to recognize that person at a glance by the *whole* pattern of face, look, demeanor, intonation, scent, mannerism, and so on. Similarly, chessmasters recognize patterns at a glance on a chessboard occupied by two dozen or so pieces, and using these patterns they are able to reconstruct such chessboard layout "from memory" after seeing it for only a few seconds — a feat unachievable by the non-master-level player because he or she has not yet acquired schemas for these patterns (DeGroot, 1965). A similar process occurs when we identify a pattern in a mosaic. If one examines the details, one cannot construct the whole from the parts. The parts are just bits of ceramic of uniform color. However, looking at the whole, one sees the pattern intended by the artist (and sometimes, unintended ones).

The phrase that captures this process of pattern perception at a glance is "identification without examination." This brings to mind gestalt perception, but schematic perception is more than gestalt perception because schemas constitute a mechanism through which gestalt perception can be accomplished (Bougon, 1980: 32-114). Thus, while Gestalt perception remains phenomenological, schematic perception accounts for the phenomenon and explains its occurrence. In addition, schemas account for a person's capacity for perceiving, conceptualizing, and acting in terms of wholes. In their operation, schemas encompass processes that begin with a person's raw experience, proceed with processing the neural signals, and culminate in perceiving, conceptualizing, learning, remembering, and acting on the basis of wholes.

We treat a pattern that we know as one unit, as one whole, as one idea, as one concept. It is because we have the capacity to treat a pattern as one unit that we can attach such a unit to another. For example, we attach names to faces or melodies with which we are acquainted, although these names are incapable of communicating the underlying pattern to a noninitiated person. Thus a name tags a concept and a concept tags a pattern and forms a cognitive unit that arises and grows from raw experience and that is handled as one unit in perception, thought, or memory. Further, in contrast to its companion pattern, this cognitive unit — this "intellectual element" (Bergson, 1902) — is typically an abstract, "imageless," and "wordless [. . .] element of thought," as reported by Galton (1907: 58, 60, 78) and Binet (1903), who stressed the general incompatibility of thinking and imaging. For example, when I think "I'll go home," I know quite well what I mean and what is involved without any accompanying images of myself, my bicycle, the streets, or the house.

Thus a pattern is associated with a concept (and vice versa), and in the cortex, "schema neurons" are associated with one or few "concept neurons" (and vice versa). In his studies of speech perception, Liberman found such a connection between abstract "non-sonic" concepts and patterns. Liberman (1970) observed that nonvowel phonemes such as /d/ are heard as /d/ only within speech. If you isolate the sound patterns corresponding to /d/ and listen to them, you may hear an upgoing glissando on high pitches or a downgoing glissando on low pitches. But, as Liberman found, "when we present and perceive these exactly same stimuli as speech, we cannot hear anything like a glissando, no matter how hard we try. What we hear . . . is speech, not sound; our perception . . . yields at the lowest conscious level an irreducible linguistic segment called /d/." I find that the observation by Liberman of the relation between the abstract, abruptly discrete, unitary, nonsonic concept /d/ and its corresponding sonic pattern constitutes the prototype of the relation between a dimensionless, "punctiform" (i.e., point-sized) concept and its corresponding pattern (in the context of a larger pattern, such as speech). Similarly, while operating on the cortex, Penfield (1968) observed a connection between patterns and points. Penfield observed that touching specific points of the temporal cortex with a needle electrode elicited specific "recalling of the stream of a man's awareness in full detail." As he reports,

> When the electrode is applied, the patient may exclaim in surprise, as the young secretary MM did: "Oh, I had a very, very familiar memory, in an office somewhere. I could see the desks. I was there and someone was calling to me, a man leaning on a desk with a pencil in his hand." In general, these examples of recall of experience were strongly visual or auditory or both. A good many patients were caused to hear music. Each of them seemed to be present while listening to orchestra or voice or choir. The same piece of music could be recalled by the electrode after a short interval and the subject, if asked to do so, could hum along, accompanying the piece that he or she was hearing.

So we see again the familiar association between a point (such as one or a few "concept neurons") and a pattern (such as an image or a "piece of music").

Thus the strength of my schema approach to epistemology is that it allows me to treat a pattern (and thus a whole) as one unit denoted by a companion concept, and the strength of my raw experience approach to ontology is that a person's holistic raw experience is matched by his or her holistic perception of patterns into it.

FROM KNOWLEDGE TO ITS MAPPING

The old question, "What does it take to know or understand a person and his or her behavior?" has received a variety of answers. In my approach, a person's perception, conceptualization, and behavior arise from an interaction of his or her experience with his or her schemas. In addition, the schema approach indicates that knowing a person would entail knowing his or her whole schema-structure. Clearly, that is not possible as schemas can be known only by their results, and a brain dissection to map the neural nets embodying the schemas, if possible, would be fatal.

Yet there exists an approximation to that unattainable knowledge. Remember that every schema is associated with a concept. Consider also that concepts are the notions behind words, and that a schema can reconstruct the pattern of concepts that it recorded. Therefore, to the extent that concepts in the concept-structure of a person are tagged by words, we can explore that concept-structure.

The concept-structure incorporates verbal and nonverbal concepts. The verbal concepts, by definition, will always be expressible, but many nonverbal concepts will not until a socializing experience attaches intersubjective verbal tags to them. Thus, getting to know a person is possible within the approximation. Utilizing Korzybski's (1941) metaphor, I shall designate a person's concept-structure the territory to be explored, and the recording of that exploration a cognitive map.

A concept-structure can be mapped in several ways. Informally, a person can collect bits and hints and piece them together. We shall not discuss this method here. Formally, a researcher may set up special nondirective interviews such as the "Self-Q" interview presented later in this chapter. Certainly, the maps thus collected are not the same thing as the territory. Yet that may not always be a weakness since for understanding a territory a map is often more useful than is the territory itself.

Cognitive Maps and Cause Maps

In discussing schema-concept pairs, we noted that on the one hand the pair's concept is dimensionless and thus compatible with verbal expression, and on the other hand, the pair's schema is spatial, capturing wholes and patterns, and thus inherently nonverbal. Hence, the contents of a concept reside in the pattern recorded in its associated schema. Since the recorded pattern will often be a pattern of concepts, the contents, or the meaning of a concept, will often reside in a pattern of relations among concepts. When I consider all possible types of relations occurring in patterns of concepts (e.g., contiguity, proximity, continuity, resemblance, implication, causality, and their derivative verbs), and when I map a schema registering such relations, then I call such an exhaustive mapping a *cognitive map*. If I limit myself to mapping causality relations, then I call the mapping of the schema a *cause map*. In Figure 11.1, I present a cause map. The concepts mentioned by the musicians of the Utrecht Jazz Orchestra in analyzing their view of the orchestra are arranged in a polygon. Between the concepts, forming the central web, are the cause/effect relations mentioned by the musicians, such as the one between "quality of own performance" and "number of criticisms received" (Bougon, Weick, and Binkhorst, 1977: 610).

Because the contents and meaning of a concept reside in the pattern recorded in its associated schema, by mapping the schema- or concept-structure of an actor in a social entity, we map what that entity and his or her experience of that enity means to him or her. To study cognitive maps is to study meaning as a relational phenomenon, as expressed, for instance, in Berkeley's analysis (1709/1910), in James's model of memory (1890: 1: 586), and in Titchener's saying that "the gist of [meaning] is that it takes at least two sensations [i.e., perceptions] to make a meaning" (1910: 368). To Titchener, "meaning is always context" (1910: 367). To Bartlett (1932: 20, 229), meaning arises from "connecting" sensory data to a schema. Boring (1954: 577) sums up the essence of these views by pointing out that without a relatum a datum has no meaning. Thus, by uncovering cognitive maps, we reveal the meaning of social territories in a manner consistent with the concern for contexts of these and other social theorists.

Cognitive Maps and Enacted Environments

By mapping a person's schema and concept-structure, we map his or her enacted environment, which is an intense abstraction from his or her experience (Weick, 1977). By doing so, we map also his or her "enacted self," that is, his or her perception of self that — like his or her enacted environment — he or she has constructed from an attentive and active interaction between his or her schemas and his or her raw experience. Hence a cognitive map contains the enacted self and the enacted environment of a social actor, as well as the pattern of their relationship. Thus a cognitive map approach to the analysis of social action does not draw lines and boundaries (like skins and walls) between person and group and between group and environment. For example, examination of the cognitive map of the Utrecht Jazz Orchestra musicians (Figure 11.1) shows concepts that one may declare either remote, external, and environmental (such as "availability of own new numbers"), or near, internal, and personal (such as "quality

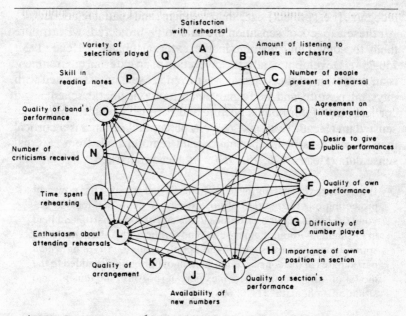

NOTE: Significance is p < 0.07 and is defined as follows: If 12 people say two variables are related, at least 9/12 must give the identical sign (+ or −) to the relationship; if 13 or 14 say the variables are related, 10 must give the identical sign; if 15 say the variables are related, 11 must give the identical sign; and if 16 to 19 say the variables are related, 12 must give the identical sign. The only significant negative relationships are P → N, F → N, B → N.

SOURCE: Reprinted from "Cognition in Organizations" by M. Bougon, K. Weick, and D. Binkhors published in *Administrative Science Quarterly*, Vol. 22, p. 610 by permission of *The Administrative Science Quarterly*. Copyright © 1977 by Cornell University.

Figure 11.1 Cause Relationships Mentioned by a Significant Number of Orchestra Members

of performance"), as well as concepts that one may not assign comfortably to these categories (such as "agreement on interpretation").

We must therefore be careful in drawing distinctions between internal and external components — between enacted self and enacted environment components — of what may be called "enacted life." For as Head (1920) and others have shown, our understanding of the external world is an externalization or projection that Weick (1977) has named "efferent sensemaking." For example, Head has shown from experiments conducted on brain-injured people that we "project" our world, and "removal of the cortical factors in sensation reduces to elementary proportions the power of projection." His experiments show that under such conditions "it is not possible to

recognize [i.e., project] size, shape, weight, and spatial relations. . . .
All these aspects of sensation are said to be projected; we attribute
them to something inherent in the external object" (Head, 1920:
750-754). Developmentally, the projection of an external environment
is an extension of the schemas built from sense data associated with
physical posture and body movement. A kinesthetic schema is a
cortical map of our body's posture and periphery built from internal
sense data (Head, 1920: 607, 669). A perceptual schema is a cortical
map of our externality, peripheral and remote, built from external
sense data (Head, 1920: 751, 754). As Head remarked,

> It is to the existence of these "schemas" that we owe the power of
> projecting our recognition of posture, movement, and locality be-
> yond the limits of our own bodies to the end of some instrument held
> in the hand. Without them we could not probe with a stick, nor use a
> spoon unless our eyes were fixed upon the plate. Anything which
> participates in the conscious movement of our bodies is added to the
> model of ourselves and becomes part of [posture, movement, and
> situation] schemata" [1920: 606].

This developmental progression from the kinesthetic and postural
to the environmental and conceptual is a view shared also by Titchener, Bartlett, and Piaget. Titchener (1910: 367) wrote "originally,
meaning is kinaesthesis." Bartlett (1932: 229) relied on this insight by
Titchener for his theory of schemas. And Piaget wrote: "Action
schemas constitute the principal source of concepts" (1961: 385) as
well as "at the level of behaviors, a schema never has an absolute
beginning but always derives, by successive differentiations, from
previous schemas that go back progessively to reflexes or spontaneous initial movements" (1967: 18).

Pursuing this line of thought, I propose that the projection of a
social environment is a generalization of the projection of a physical
environment. Just as extension of kinesthetic schemas permits projection of a physical externality, extension of complex schemas em-
bedding conative, affective, and cognitive schemas permits projection of a social externality. Thus we can project charisma and leadership on a person. We can project a classroom, church, or mob on a
gathering of people. Or we can project tenseness or playfulness on a
meeting. Thus when analyzing an organizational situation in terms of
schemas, an analyst's attention is directed to projected aspects of
participants' externalities. But when he or she analyzes it in terms of
the traditional "discovery of *the* environment," his or her attention is

directed to internalized representations of "the discovered environment." An implication of treating environments as enacted or projected is that "unless something is attended to, it does not exist"
(Weick, 1979: 28), and that unless we possess a perceptual schema for
that something, "it" does not exist.

Cause Maps as Maps of Motivation Structure

A cause map of a person's concept-structure can be interpreted as
a map of his or her motivation structure, as it displays that person's
ends, means, conflicts, and contexts for sensemaking. For example,
in the Utrecht Jazz Orchestra, "quality of band performance" and
"satisfaction with rehearsals" were among the ends variables in the
musicians' map (Bougon et al., 1977: 614). A cause map displays
means/ends beliefs necessary to the construction of plans and the
initiation of behaviors directed to desired endstates (March and Simon, 1958: 31; Axelrod, 1976). Conflicts between the desired states of
the variables and their probable states given the patterns of means
indicates potential sources of frustration or anxiety that may spur
constructive, destructive, or withdrawal activity. Finally, in contrast
to languages' lineal statements, a cause map constitutes a self-
contained "cybernetic statement" summarizing one's sense-making
activities. This summary of sense-making activities is chiefly reflected in the *pattern* of those variables forming essential states
(Ashby 1952) or ends that a person strives to achieve or maintain
(Porac, 1981). In turn, this summary of sense making becomes the
context within which one's activities make sense. This circular situation reminds us that cognitive structures are noted for their self-
sealing, self-fulfilling tendencies (Berger and Luckmann, 1966: 23;
Pfeffer and Salancik, 1978: 81).

An observer watching a person's activities without knowing their
context, as displayed by that person's cause map, may well endow
these activities with a meaning different from the one that person
attaches to them. This was the basis of Weber's (1947) distinction
between *verstehen* and *erklären* in his analysis of social phenomena.
He illustrated the distinction with the example of a woodcutter: "We
understand the chopping of wood . . . in terms of motives [verste-
hen], in addition to direct observational knowledge [erklären], if we
know whether the woodchopper is working for a wage or . . . 'work-

ing off" a fit of rage" (1947: 95). Understanding a woodcutter's cause map is a new and explicit way of conducting Weberian *verstehen* analyses.

Finally, in the tradition of Hume (1748/1967: 86), we must understand that causality relations projected by actors on their enacted environment are arbitrary but plausible. For instance, arbitrariness restrained by plausibility in making cause/effect connections was observed in perceptions of equity (Weick et al., 1976).

THE SELF-Q TECHNIQUE

Cognitive maps will enrich our understanding of social territories only if we can access these maps. The access problem is a difficult one, for cognitive maps are reports from inaccessible cortical schemas. Moreover, there is a threat of bias as a researcher may influence the process of uncovering the maps.

To obtain cognitive maps, a researcher is required to uncover the subjective knowledge of another. To create a situation in which cognitive maps can emerge as fully as possible with a minimum of researcher's influence, I have developed a self-questioning interview technique ("Self-Q"). The technique is nondirective and nonreactive and greatly frees the interviewer from initiating and steering the interview. The gist of the technique rests in transfering most of the initiating, steering, and validating problems to the interviewee. To that end, I use four successive interviews.

In the first interview, I collect concepts nondirectively. In the second interview, I verify the concepts and notions collected in the first interview. I also obtain their sorting in different classes as well as their ranking by importance. In the third interview, I obtain causality relations among the concepts in the cause map. And in the fourth interview, I verify that cause maps make sense to the respondents themselves.

The first interview. The objective of the first interview is to obtain concepts from the interviewee without the interviewer himself mentioning any concept, lest they might become "planted" in the interviewee's mind. Further, these concepts must scatter broadly over the social territory covered by the study.

Since these interviews are, by design, uncooperative on the interviewer's side, it is important to establish a good rapport between interviewer and interviewee from the start. The walk-in small-talk on the way to the interview room is designed to allay fears or anxieties.

At the very least, the walk-in reduces anxiety until experience and evidence indicate to the respondent that he or she can lay his or her apprehension aside. In addition, since the interviews are oriented to identification of important personal and idiosyncratic beliefs, the formal introduction is designed to leave a respondent convinced that his or her privacy will be utterly respected and protected.

To initiate the process of self-questioning, I typically set the scene with statements of the following kind:

> I would like to interview you about _____ (for example, "your view of the 999 organization"). It is evident that you are the expert on *your own view* of _____. Therefore, what I would like to do is have you ask yourself questions about _____. Please do not answer these questions. While you are asking yourself these questions, I will be writing them down verbatim. If at any time you feel that you want to review what I have written, feel free to do so. . . . Please, let's begin by you asking yourself an easy question.

The method works easily: After the first few minutes (when there may be some spluttering and pausing), there are few, if any, long silences and the whole interview is typically very productive. One may see that the introductory phase and the establishment of good rapport are important since much good will and dedication are demanded from the respondent who strives to find, without actual help, what he or she should talk about.

Sometimes, the respondent stalls. I have developed graphics for suggesting to the respondent alternative ways of asking questions (Figure 11.2). These are useful as they give the self-interviewer a chance to start afresh if he or she feels he or she is running out of questions. For example, I draw on a pad, in front of the person, an ellipse and say: "This represents the 999 organization"; then I draw another ellipse around it and say: "This represents the larger context in which you consider 999. Now, let's pretend that these three small circles in 999 represent respectively you ('I'), you looking at yourself ('me'), and others in 999 ('they')." I continue: "Here is 999, yourself, and the larger context. I would like you (pointing to the 'I' circle) to ask yourself some questions about you (pointing to the 'me' circle), 999 (pointing to the inner ellipse), and its context (pointing to the outer ellipse)." After some clarification and hesitation, the respondent proceeds to raise from 10 to over 100 questions.

To illustrate, the following questions were generated by students in relation to their class: "I wonder how much effort I should put into this class?" "How does 999 give me information about administering a museum?" "Why am I lax about readings?" "Why do I talk to

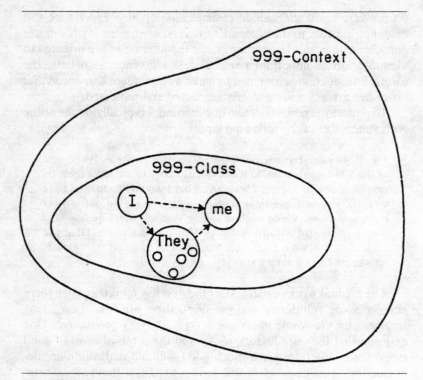

Figure 11.2 The Context and Perspectives Used in Self-Questioning

people after the class?" "How does 999 prevent me from enjoying cultural events?" "How does the 999 instructor perceive the class?" "Why don't I participate more in 999?" "What motivates me to come to class?" "Why do I keep my social life separate from my academic life?" "What do I want to get out of 999?" "How do I react to your lecture style?" "Why do I stereotype people in the class?" "What am I going to be when I get out of school?" When the raising of questions falters, I point back to Figure 11.2 and its components — "I," "me," and "they" — and say, for example: "How about trying out this way: Suppose that you (pointing to 'I') ask questions about people in the class (pointing to 'they')." When this falters, I may turn to saying: "You are the 'me' (pointing to the 'me' circle) in the 999 class (pointing to the inner ellipse); now, you (pointing to the 'I')ask questions about 'me,' that is, yourself." With difficult respondents, I may rely on several variations. Typically, each variation elicits from two to twelve questions. After fifty minutes, I end up with anywhere from two dozen to two hundred useful independent concepts to be employed in the second interview.

I walk the respondent out of the interview room. This provides him or her with an informal means for clarifying and bringing closure to questions and issues that may bother him or her. For the interviewer, it is a chance to understand and validate some important areas of what has been learned. This constitutes the first built-in validity check of the procedure.

It is important to note that contrary to a TAT or Rorschach interview, we do not ask the person to tell us stories that different images bring to mind. We ask for specific questions about a social territory. A factor that facilitates disclosure rests in pointing out to the respondent that there are no right or wrong questions because we are seeking his or her personal and unique *knowledge* of a social territory. Such a knowledge either exists or it does not, and whether it does is not a matter of right or wrong. Another facilitating factor rests in bringing to the respondent's attention that there is no desirable answer because we do not seek answers to his or her questions.

The second interview. The second interview verifies the concepts collected in the first and sorts and ranks them by importance. To conduct this interview, each concept elicited in the previous interview is written as notions on a card. With few exceptions, all the concepts are written in the definite mode, such as *"my* grade in *999,"* or *"my* hours in the job at *the X YZ newspaper,"* or *my* chance of getting a *job in Arts,"* or *"my* balancing *homework* and *dating,"* or *"my* prestige with *my friends."* We present these cards to the respondent and ask him or her: Do you recognize your idea? Does the card capture what you had in mind? Shall we alter it? Should we split one into two? Any card that was the result of a misunderstanding by the interviewer stands a good chance of being found meaningless or inappropriate as he or she tries to build a network of meaning around it. For example, in presenting the card "becoming a housewife," I found that the respondent froze and became angry. I suggested tamely that the phrase had come up in the previous interview, to learn that she had said (or meant) "becoming a mother." This constitutes the second built-in validity check, what Black and Metzger call "validation as part of the eliciting process" (1965: 159).

I ask also if the cards suggest any overlooked notions that should be added. This process rarely results in new suggestions for enlarging the set of notions already on the table, consistent with Ware's (1978) finding that persistent and elaborate requests for new notions suggested by the ones the respondent is attending to remain fruitless. The material verified and ranked in interview 2 provides the basis for the third interview.

The third interview. The third interview is designed to collect the causality relations among the concepts in the cause map. The interview has two parts. In the first part, I explain to the respondent the special questionnaire that he or she will complete alone. The questionnaire has a page for each concept in the map. On each page, the respondent provides the magnitude of the causality relations (from "absent" to "strong") and the sign of the influences ("increasing" or "decreasing"). Before he or she goes home, I ask the respondent to practice on a special trial page. I answer his or her questions and diplomatically correct his or her errors.

In the second part, the respondent completes the special questionnaire at home. He or she returns it in an envelope sealed and addressed to me to reaffirm the confidentiality of the interviews.

The fourth interview. In the fourth interview, I present the respondent with various graphical displays of his or her cause map and I ask if they make sense to him or her. This constitutes the final global validity check. This is in line with Filstead's remark that "it is crucial for validity . . . to try to picture the empirical world as it actually exists to those under investigation, rather than as the researcher imagines it to be" (1970: 4).

CONCLUSION

Nobel physicist Paul Dirac's (1930) view that beyond our experience and its interpretation lies "a substratum of which we cannot form a mental picture without introducing irrelevancies" expresses an ontology comparable to mine since we both say that we never talk about *the* world — social or physical — only about our construction of it. In 1789, Chemist Antoine Lavoisier observed that "the impossibility to dissociate language from science and science from language persists because every natural science always involves three things: the sequence of phenomena whose study identify that science; the concepts by which we remember these phenomena; and the words in which we express these concepts. The word must call forth the concept; the concept must portray the phenomenon. All three mirror the same essence." Lavoisier's observation expresses an epistemology comparable to mine since we both say that when talking (using words) or thinking (using concepts) about a phenomenon (such as our experience), we must rely on a precarious pyramiding of words upon concepts, of concepts and patterns upon phenomena, and of phenomena on substratum.

The perspective I have developed *combines* a reductionist ontology based on definite concepts and words, and a phenomenalist ontology based on indefinite and irreducible patterns and schemas. Such an integration combines the strengths of what are typically viewed as two polar ontologies in a way that puts the alleged structuralist-interpretivist schism into perspective. The perspective also integrates the notions of meaning and knowledge. Knowledge-by-acquaintance *(connaitre, erklären)* is about concepts, thus patterns. Meaning and knowledge-by-understanding *(savoir, verstehen)* are about patterns of concepts, hence patterns of patterns. In the perspective offered here, pattern is knowledge or meaning; knowledge and meaning are patterns.

To apply this perspective and collect the pattern of concepts that organization participants use to remember their organization-phenomena (to use Lavoisier's phrase), I developed the Self-Q interviews. These interviews can also be applied to investigating people's cognitions and attitudes, to revealing individuals' construction of situations, or even to developing survey questions that are relevant to the surveyed.

The Self-Q technique illustrates the invention of a general research method by theoretical considerations for theoretical considerations. The manner in which I conceived the phenomenon that I wanted to study required and led to a method consistent with that conception: Some ammunition for the cause of those who believe that method exists only in the context of an ontology, epistemology, and theory, which when left implicit often makes methods perfidious.

About the Author

MICHEL G. BOUGON

My intellectual life began when I decided that I would not let any thought enter my mind without prior examination. I was then in high school. I feared that if my mental foundations were not laid intelligently, the edifice I might build would skew or perhaps collapse; at any rate, it would not be the reliable instrument for the perception and understanding that I desired. From then on, although teachers dictated lecture-notes, I recomposed them in my mind before writing them down in a personal version that was coherent across all fields.

During and after my years in a Grande Ecole, I concentrated on understanding things rather than minds. Following the Grande Ecole, I worked in two laboratories.

I gained some of the understanding I sought. One result was that my work was successful — perhaps too successful, because as people found out that the equipment I built worked without my babysitting it, they made me join a thousand others they laid off during the 1970 recession.

I decided it was time to understand minds and behavior in organizations as well as perhaps position myself to be the one doing the layoffs next time. I went to a business school. There I heard Jeff Pfeffer say the truth aloud with impunity; I decided I wanted academic freedom for myself too. I saw Gerry Salancik devise clever experiments and expose peoples cognitive malleability; I thought they reinforced other clever cognitive experiments by Piaget, whom I liked. When Jeff left for Berkeley, I became Karl Weick's research assistant. I found that Karl's ideas on cause maps, organization, and evolution resonated with what I knew of Piaget's psychology. I wondered if somebody had related the two. It soon dawned on me that if I wanted to read on this topic, I would have to write it myself. The Utrecht Jazz Orchestra article was my first attempt at it. My dissertation was a second attempt. My third attempt is this chapter.

12

STUDYING ORGANIZATION THROUGH LEVI-STRAUSS'S STRUCTURALISM

Stephen Turner
University of South Florida

The structuralist anthropology of Lévi-Strauss is guided by a provocative hypothesis: that various sets of cultural phenomena have a hidden structure, and that these structures are members of a limited class of formal possibilities (Lévi-Strauss, 1963c: 160, and developed through 1963a, 1963b, 1966, 1969, 1973). Related strategies of inquiry based on similar hypotheses have been seriously pursued both in linguistics and literary criticism, and there seems to be no reason, at least in principle, why these strategies could not be extended to the study of other varieties of customs and practices.

The potential importance of such inquiries may be readily grasped. If we think of the inquiries in terms of analogy with Chomskian linguistics, we can see that as linguistic structures serve to circumscribe the formal possibilities of certain aspects of speaking (Chomsky, 1968), so could the possibilities of other kinds of activities be circumscribed. If we think of them in terms of analogy with literary criticism and Jacques Derrida's (1970), work we come to see traditional philosophical terms like "fundamental" and "inherent" (Rorty, 1978) in a different light. Such terms become recognizable as a kind of special plea for particular orderings: When one says that some way of describing the world captures its inherent or fundamental

Material in this chapter excerpted from Stephen Turner, "Complex Organizations as Savage Tribes," *Journal for the Theory of Social Behavior,* Vol. 7, No. 1 (April 1977), pp. 99-104 reprinted by permission.

nature or describes what is "really there," one is selecting a particualr way of describing from many. Derrida objects to this. He suggests that the various ways of describing or ordering (or, put a little differently, of generating "readings") are not arrayed in any mysterious hierarchy signifying which are more or less fundamental or inherent. Each reading is just another mode of organizing goings-on. To say that one reading identifies the "inherent" order is to provide a particular ordering of the orderings — for which there are also alternatives! We simply do not arrive at the last ordering, the one true ordering for which there are no alternatives. Lévi-Strauss speaks in a way that is congenial to this second reading when he calls what he does in analyzing myths "the myth of myths," and when he characterizes myth analysis as interminable. (The problem of what Pierre Bourdieu calls Lévi-Strauss's "objectivist approach to practices" [1977: 19-28], particularly the idea, which also appears in Chomsky, that one reaches the single, basic "structure" of a kinship system [or syntactical system], is taken up critically by Derrida [1970], and Hoy [1978: 77-92]. In his later work, especially in the volumes on Myth, Lévi-Strauss seems to abandon "objectivism," as the self-characterization of his work as the myth of myth suggests).

In this chapter, I will contrast some of the traditional theoretical and methodological strategies of the sociological study of complex organizations with the strategy that the Lévi-Straussian hypothesis suggests, particularly in terms of the Derridadist interpretation. My remarks are designed to serve two general purposes: (1) to inculcate some unease about the way in which certain theoretical and methodolgical problems in the sociology of complex organizations have traditionally been approached, especially with respect to common assumptions about "what an organization really is," and (2) to show how a Lévi-Straussian reading of organizational goings-on is done. The discussion will take this form. I shall first show how standard strategies in the sociology of complex organizations might deflect us from a recognition of alternative readings. I shall then present an example of an analysis or reading of a structural pattern in organizational life. Finally, I shall make some general remarks on the explanatory import of such analyses, and on their "ontology" and "epistemology."

GETTING BEYOND THE LEVEL OF APPEARANCES

The methodological distinctiveness of the Lévi-Straussian approach lies, in large part, in its formulation of the problem of generating alternative readings of social life. We may gain some appreciation of this by comparing the views of Lévi-Strauss with the classical sociological formulation of the problem in Durkheim's *The Rules of Sociological Method* (1964).

Durkheim points out that when we study a class of phenomena scientifically for the first time, we already have some definite but rudimentary concepts of the phenomena. These concepts typically have previously regulated our behavior as it related to these phenomena, and they therefore have a certain psychological hold on us, the hold of ingrained habit. He offers an explanation of the nature of this hold and gives a reason for its special power in the study of social phenomena. The mind, he says, is "overrun . . . by the details of social life. . . . Unable to perceive the relations which would properly organize these details," we revert to organizing the data with "the superficial concepts we employ in ordinary life," thus aggravating our disability (1964: 18). He uses this characterization to establish the first corollary to his first methodological rule: All preconceptions must be eradicated (1964: 31).

To this point in the formulation, Durkheim and Lévi-Strauss are as one. It is at the point of Durkheim's suggestions for overcoming the effects of these intellectual habits that they part company. The dissimilarities between their notions of "the relations that would properly organize" the data are the source of this divergence. For Durkheim, writing under the influence of the nineteenth-century scientific world view, the proper relations are those governed by laws of cause and effect. Since some social facts "lend themselves more readily to objective representation" than do others (1964: 44), the causal laws connecting these facts are more accessible to the observer: It is on these laws that Durkheim advises sociologists to concentrate their attention (1964: 46). Lévi-Strauss's conception of "the appropriate organizing relations" precludes this strategy.

Lévi-Strauss replaces the "causal law" explanatory conception with a very different view. This conception, and its peculiar epistemological imperatives, may be preliminarily characterized in this way: To explain is to discover an order of relations that turns a set of bits, which have limited significance of their own, into an intelligible whole. This order may be termed the "structure." It is only when considered as a whole that the structure is intelligible; so there is no question of revealing it piecemeal, by establishing the accessible connections first, á la Durkheim. Lévi-Strauss's remarks on the kind of strategy Durkheim advises are acerbic. "For fear of being misled," he says, the sociologist is "compelled in advance to leave out of consideration all . . . nuances, details, and even values" (1967: 43).

The "overly subjective" aspects of social life are evaporated off by the sociologist, leaving an apparently manageable residue. But the appearance of manageability is deceiving. On the Lévi-Straussian view, it is like excluding pieces of a child's picture puzzle: By giving the child only some of the pieces of the puzzle, we do not simplify his or her task, but make it impossible. Thus the Lévi-Straussian methodological animus is directed against the *preselection* of what is to count as significant.

These divergences are reflected in the alternative way in which Lévi-Strauss describes the problem of "getting beyond." This manner of description deserves a more detailed examination. Lévi-Strauss points out that the "preconceptions" of which Durkheim speaks are fundamentally of the same character as scientific models: they are means of ordering, techniques of description. The difference between these indigenous conceptions or "conscious models" and the models Lévi-Strauss seeks to construct — and the difference that makes these "conscious models" or preconceptions obstacles to inquiry — is to be found in the purpose they serve. The purpose of the indigenous models is not to explain human customs, but to perpetuate them: They are constructed to facilitate the acceptance of the customs of a social order, not to facilitate the analysis of the customs. He points out that it would be our natural expectation that models constructed for the purpose of facilitating acceptance would order the phenomena in a misleading, and particularly an oversimple, fashion, just as the moral rules one teaches a child, such as "never lie," are oversimple. In societies like our own, these "indigenous models" present special difficulties. We have no means of putting any distance between ourselves and these ways of ordering. They are so familiar to us that we do not see them as "ways of ordering" at all. Instead, we see them as "the order which is in the phenomena." In societies radically unlike our own, societies in which one is exposed to "buffetings and denials which are directed at one's most cherished ideas and habits by other ideas and habits which must needs contradict them to the highest degree" (1967: 43), this disability is forcibly removed. The Lévi-Straussian methodological strategy is to exploit this — to pursue our inquiries in societies in which we can recognize "preconceptions" for what they are, and see "ways of ordering" for what they are.

There is, to be sure, no guarantee that we will transcend our own culture's blinders even in the study of these societies, and this Lévi-Strauss readily concedes. It may be that our knowledge of these distant societies will "remain as bizarre and inadequate as that which an exotic visitor would have of our own society" (Lévi-Strauss, 1967: 44). He gives the example of the Kwakiutl Indian whom the anthropologist Franz Boas invited to New York and who reserved all his intellectual curiosity for such things as the brass balls that decorated staircase banisters and the bearded ladies then exhibited in Times Square. Indeed, the problem of totemism seems to be a case of the same kind. It is "set-up" for us, and not a problem "in itself."

It is Lévi-Strauss's hope that there are problems that are not "set-ups" but are problems "in themselves." Derrida would reject the distinction. But he would perhaps agree with Lévi-Strauss that an ethnographic outsider, no longer in the cultural context where his or her intellectual standards can be made to apply, is at a special advantage in constructing new models, new readings of social life. All this may be summarized by saying that the Lévi-Straussian strives to avoid being trapped by preselection of what is and what is not significant, whether this preselection is done on the basis of methodological preconceptions like Durkheim's (as to the lineaments of "the real"), or on the basis of largely unconscious cultural preconceptions (whose possibility is not acknowledged), such as we are likely to bring to the social goings-on of our own society. One point about preselection should be especially stressed: Preselecting the class of legitimate descriptions so that "values" or "valuative" descriptions are excluded is equally otiose. What makes this otiose is not the mere fact that they are preselections, however, but the idea that this "preselection" selects what is "really there." Put differently, we must understand *each* reading as a preselection, conscious or unconscious. So a consciously value-free reading of organizational goings-on is acceptable as long as we do not pretend that this has any special claim on reality.

IMPLICATIONS FOR THE STUDY OF COMPLEX ORGANIZATIONS

This strategy and its justification reflect oddly on the sociology of complex organizations. There is the clear implication that sociologists of complex organizations are victims of their familiarity with the phenomena they study, disabled by the grip of "preconceptions" or "conscious models" they have acquired in the course of growing up in a society set about with complex organizations. This implication gives rise to several questions.

Lacking our indigenous conceptions of complex organizations, what order might an outsider find in organizational life? And what might sociologists have been led, by their intimate connection, to misperceive? The latter question turns on another: What are the principal "ways of ordering" or "indigenous theories" that facilitate the acceptance of the customs of organizational life and confound its analysis?

The third question may be approached first. The most obvious instance of a "way of ordering" or "indigenous theory" in organizational life is the "formal structure" of the organization. Consider what the formal structure is made up of: a set of norms or rules that the participants are aware of and use in explaining one another's behavior in certain contexts. We can immediately recognize a resemblance between this body of consciously grasped rules and "indigenous theories" (see Scheffler, 1970: 58f.). Both facilitate the learning and acceptance of the customs of group life, and neither may be expected to give an accurate account of these customs. Distortions arise in the same way. Even the most "simple" natural language, like the most "simple" actual social structure, is an extremely complex system. The speaker's account of his or her linguistic system or social structure is sure to be a grossly simplified and partial one.

For example, in giving an account of language rules, we may hit on some device for expressing a rule (like the spelling device "i before e, except after c"). The device may not be accurate, yet may assume considerable popularity because of the way it simplifies a complex process in terms of an elementary formulation. In a similar way, accounts of social arrangements, such as the structure of an organization, may be taken by organizational members as a model of organizational reality. Such accounts, as expressed in an organization chart, are, in effect, literary constructions, governed by literary conventions. Although often used by organizational researchers as representations of a basic organizational reality, they should be called into question, just as indigenous pictures of social arrangements and social behavior would be called into question by a social anthropologist studying a primitive society.

The structuralist following Lévi-Strauss would emphasize that there is an enormous amount of other patterned social relationships that are intertwined with the pattern that the "formal structure" pictures. There is a danger in adopting the distinctions that organizational actors make in order to define the organization or its problems because there is nothing to assure us that any given element of the participant's conscious models of the organization does not hide from our view connections that are part of the underlying order of the phenomena. Return to the analogy of the child's puzzle. There is nothing to assure us that leaving these patterns out of account will not have the same effect as discarding pieces of the puzzle.

It is obvious that formal structure — job descriptions, formal responsibilities, and so forth — does not exhaust the order of values, sentiment, fears, and identities in the organization. These structures never simply coincide with the self-defined boundaries, aims, and character of "the organization." It might be, for example, that a model of certain crucial parts of the structure would include patterns in the lives of the members and clients of the organization, or in the lives of members of the organization "outside" of the organization, such as their self-definitions as human beings, or exclude patterns that we have ordinarily thought of as within the organization's boundaries, or in some other sense as "part" of the organization. In many offices and elementary schools, for example, there are elaborate customs — noticeable to me, as a male, perhaps because these are activities engaged in by women — governing birthdays, ritualized gift giving (operating under rules sufficiently complex to make Boas's Kwakiutl feel quite at home), food exchanges requiring enormous effort and bearing on participants' self-conceptions, and so on. In sheer quantitative terms, these activities often involve much more time than do such organizational tasks as performance evaluation or goal setting, and they often are a much larger part of the employees' awareness of the organization. Few employees in a grade school can identify the formal structure in any detail. Many can recall who brought the zucchini salad to the reading specialists' breakfast for the teachers (and for that matter, these events may be the only rituals by which persons and categories are publically identified).

If organizational self-definitions are viewed as potentially misleading fragments or preselecting devices (just as we have suggested the "formal structure" should be viewed), the quantitative study of correlations between structural features of organization begins to look as if it is the study of accidental consequences of the literary conventions that govern the way in which organizational fictions are contrived. A term like the "office" or "at work" may be the boundary mark relevant to the explanation of particular patterns of practice or action, while the "organization" is little more than an accountant's and lawyer's retrospective interpretation, with no greater claim to reality than any other myth.

AN EXAMPLE OF ORGANIZATIONAL CONFLICT

In order to illustrate how structuralist analysis can be applied to the study of organization, it will be convenient to focus on a brief example. The organization from which our example is drawn is a firm that services electric motors. The firm is a small one, with thirty-six employees, including three managers, nine driver/salespersons, and four repair units, each with one foreman and five workers. The four repair units specialize according to size of motors. The sales unit takes orders, picks up motors to be repaired, and returns them to customers. The same unit serves all four repair units.

The four repair units face slightly different work demands. For the units working on the larger motors, the main managerial problems are internal, and the time spent on jobs is for the most part dependent on events in the shop. For the small motors unit, there are more uncertainties in the process. Jobs are smaller, and the flow of jobs into the workshop has a great impact on operations. Sometimes the shop is idle because of insufficient work; at other times it is overloaded, with a lot of small jobs calling for urgent attention at the same time.

The foreman of the small motors repair unit is a first-rate specialist, but constantly criticizes the drivers for being lazy, for not doing their jobs, and for anything else he can think of. For him, the drivers are to blame for problems in his workshop. If the drivers do not pick up enough small motors, the shop is idle, and in the foreman's opinion, this makes him and the shop look bad. If they pick up a lot of motors, and the customers expect them back quickly, it also makes the shop look bad, because the work cannot be done on time. The foreman is generally concerned with the relatively poor image of his unit compared with the others.

Constant criticism and back-biting is thus a major feature of the organization. The managers "read" the problem in vaguely military terms, as one involving "morale," and are inclined to rationalize what is happening in terms of a personality conflict between the foreman of the small motors unit and the drivers. The one thing they want most is for the foreman to stop criticizing. They think that he is doing a good job. The drivers get along with all the other units, and the managers think that they also do a good job. So the managers do not accept the foreman's descriptions of the drivers. The drivers are annoyed about the criticisms, but feel that there is nothing they can do about them. Their description is that the foreman is a "jerk," and even suspect that he is fouling up their orders on purpose, failing to have jobs completed when they have promised them to customers.

The drivers either pretend there is not a problem and try to be nice, or at least civil, because to get their job done they need the repair work done in a predictable, timely way. They are furious about the unfair criticism, but they do not want an open fight because they cannot see any satisfactory solution. They feel that they can do nothing to make the small motors foreman stop feeling as he does, even if some manager makes him stop talking.

The foreman, the drivers, and the managers have different "readings" or "myths" for interpreting the situation. These readings or myths attempt, in effect, to "patch up" deficiencies in what may be described as the "formal structure myth." The various organizational members are required by their job descriptions to do certain activities. But they cannot, because, in their respective readings, various factors prevent them from doing so. The various readings of the situation guide the actions of the people involved, in a way that serves to perpetuate the situation. Indeed, we can see that the readings, as actors' accounts, are central to the very construction of the situation. They provide shorthand explanations and justifications for, and guide, the actions.

The situation can also be read in another way, using a structural analysis emphasizing the importance of balance, in a manner similar to the general analysis of reciprocity offered by Mauss (1967). Balance or reciprocity is a basic structure that appears to run throughout social life. Gifts call for some return; what is owed must be paid; evil must be balanced by punishment. If we read an organization as a set of ritualized activities that produce "balance" or "fairness," we can see how various rituals serve to enact a balance. "Formal structure," in these terms, is just a name for certain rituals of deference for which there are probably balancing rituals outside the formal structure (e.g., flowers for secretaries during National Secretary's Week). We can read the situation in the case under discussion in terms of such "balancing rituals."

The foreman's criticisms of the drivers can be interpreted as a balancing ritual. In effect, the drivers are seen by the foreman as evil doers, and evil doers must be punished, for balance. Criticism is a punishment ritual. Punishment makes the balance. The elaborate explanations and justifications of the criticisms are, like any other myth, attached to a ritual. The "ritual" can be read as a fragment of the larger structure it signifies. Structuralist analysis attempts to arrive at readings of situations that locate the elements within the whole. In the case under consideration, the structure of the situation conceived in terms of balance provides a framework for interpreting the significance of the myths and rituals that provide the case with a detailed content, i.e., with specific organizational characteristics.

READING ORGANIZATION

The temptation in response to this kind of analysis is to say, "Of course, organizations aren't really about rituals and fairness; they are goal-seeking systems of imperative coordination." And one can justify this sort of claim by saying that "the existence of the organization, after all, is a matter of its functioning as a goal-seeking system — if it doesn't succeed, it dies." But the Lévi-Straussian riposte is that this is just to accept the managers' myth, or a fragment of the managers' myth, about the organization. "Survival" is a consideration that recapitulates this myth.

I recently encountered a striking example of this myth in an insurance company that motivated its salespeople around the theme, "it's a jungle out there," issuing styrofoam pith helmets to the salespeople and putting posters of tigers in a jungle on the office walls. How is the "reality" of the world to be separated from this ritual enactment? Why isn't the "reality" real enough without the enactment? The answer is that the "reality" cannot be separated from the enactment. One can read the world as a jungle, and to perform an activity as brutal as selling life insurance it may be necessary to think of the world in this way. Similarly, to run a company it may be necessary to perform rituals — giving reports, for example — that enact and thereby intellectually order the activities of the company in a particular way.

The mistake is to take any given one of these enactments as the true and definitive one, and to say that "this is what the organization is *really* about." "Survival of the organization as a system" is one reading, one myth, and only a partial one. Other readings may be just as crucial, even for the manager. Indeed, an organization may not survive unless such things as rituals of balance are preserved, anymore than the Kwakiutl potlatches Mauss describes would survive. One might point to the long-running labor troubles of certain airlines as an instance of this: the employees, so to speak, stopped bringing their share of effort to the potlatch, and felt perfectly justified in this according to their view of what was fair. In some of these cases the organization did not survive.

The "ontology" of structuralism, on the literary criticism interpretation, is that all ontology is myth. There is no one right myth: No single reading has separated the real from the not-real. Thus the epistemological problem of generating these readings is not a matter of determining what is real and the relation between theory and reality. Each reading involves a particular way of selecting evidence and a way of counting something as evidence: "Counting as" and interpreting go together — there are no data free of interpretation.

The explanatory force of a reading rests on fitting an anomalous fact into a larger structure, in terms of which it becomes intelligible. In reading the foreman's complaints as a balancing ritual, we "generated" it from a structure, but only after we knew what we were trying to generate. The "ontology" of this approach is a philosophy of mind that says that minds have particular capacities, the existence of which is shown by the possibility of constructing generative models that produce things, such as sentences, that correspond to what the speakers of language produce in speech.

The research implications of the approach are difficult to specify in detailed terms in so short an essay, except to say that all the techniques of interpretive research have roles to play. The primary implication is this: Organizational episodes, such as the conflict described in our case, are often not readable in the organization's own terms, yet can be read in other ways (see, for example, Turner and Weed, 1983). Long-term organizational arrangements may also have a readable order.

The most "readable" things about this order are the rituals of the organization: the ceremonial aspects of different kinds of meetings, from the body language of board members when a subordinate makes a presentation, to the revivalist style of union strike meetings; the rituals of dress (see Turner, 1977), in which only certain persons are permitted particular distinctions of dress, and categories of persons are marked by different, but sharply limited, ranges of permissible styles; the rituals of speech, such as use of language style to mark rank (the boss, for example, may purposely speak in a conspicuously ungrammatical or coarse way to the subordinate, to say, implicitly, "I can be familiar and vulgar to you, but you can't be that way to me"); and the folklore, especially the narrative structure of such things as stories about the rise and fall of executives or about the history of a company (these stories, indeed, sometimes have the deep ethnographic significance, as well as the drama, of such things as the Icelandic sagas or *Beowulf*).

These may be "read" in ways familiar to us from the study of primitive societies. Our problem is not so much *how* to read them — each of these things had numerous analogues in other social orders — as it is simply to notice them in the first place. The stories that are told about why an executive was a success or a failure, for example, because they are so familiar to us, are difficult to recognize as a form of epic, but for organizational participants, they serve many of the purposes that epic poetry did — such as supplying a framework for evaluating one's future career or expectations about the aims and ambitions of others. Once we do recognize them as epics we can see them as a mode of intellectual organization — one of several modes found in the social life of any given organization.

Relatively little research has been done on these topics, although, with the rise of interest in Japanese-style management, there is a great deal more interest in the study of organizational culture. Of course, in looking at Japanese organizations one is immediately struck by the peculiarity of their rituals, as well as by the centrality of these rituals to their style of management. But we must realize that we have our own rituals, equally "peculiar" and equally central to our way of organizational life. A tribal chief would feel quite at home in the kind of corporate atmosphere in which titles and perks have an elaborate structure and great personal significance to participants. These matters, which may strike one as so much mumbo jumbo when they occur in the far reaches of the Amazon, are characteristic of large bureaucracies the world over.

Metatheoretically, structuralism is quite different from other approaches. "Comprehensiveness" is not a virtue for a reading, nor does a reading ever purport to be uniquely valid. Readings do not cumulate in any additive sense. But we do get better at giving readings and talking about ordering principles, once we have seen more of them. If Lévi-Strauss's experience is correct, patterns come to seem quite repetitive in the sense that the same kinds of ordering principles work in one place after another. Interpreted in a Chomskian fashion, this suggests the existence of a deep underlying structure built into the ordering capacities of the mind and that it is in these capacities that the "psychic unity of mankind" consists. Interpreted in a Derridadist fashion, giving the readings is its own end, and the value of the readings is in the act of reading, not in the promise of some sort of ultimate grounding in the "capacities of the human mind." All other approaches are acceptable and valid for the structuralist — including the managers' myths, the idea that the organization is "real," that it is an open system, an organic being, or whatever, so long as it is understood that each approach is merely another reading or ordering, another myth.

About the Author

STEPHEN TURNER

Sociological theory was my earliest serious academic interest, and it came early enough that I could outgrow it. I did so by examining the basic intellectual adequacy of the sorts of things given as theories. Sociological theory, particularly the study of complex organizations, struck me as particularly inadequate and misguided. Yet it also struck me that occasionally social science ideas did illuminate features of complex organizations, and I persisted, explaining its relevance, as in my paper "Complex Organizations as Savage Tribes" (1977). Shortly after writing this I became involved in the more practical world of an organizational development consulting group, and began to think seriously about what value organizational theory might have when understood not as a feeble imitation of Newton, but as a source of a vocabulary that seemed to have some value in coping with particular organizational problems in a practical way. In the hands of these consultants it did have this value. My chapter is an attempt to adapt some Lévi-Straussian ideas to this use, and more generally, to consider how some views of this type of social science bear on the whole question of alternative theoretical vocabularies. A more elaborate and practically oriented discussion of similar material may be found in *Conflict in Organizations,* co-authored with Frank J. Weed (1983).

13

THE OTHER

A Model of Human Structuring

Robert Cooper
The University of Lancaster

The self is a function of the other.
— *G. H. Mead*

Everyone is the other, and no one is himself.
— *M. Heidegger*

Man's desire is the desire of the Other.
— *J. Lacan*

The logic of Otherness is immanent in social structure. Structure is always relationship between "others."

The Greek myth of Echo and Narcissus allegorizes the significance of the Other as human ontology. Narcissus was the solipsist who rejected the affections of the nymph Echo, who eventually wasted away until only her voice remained. As punishment for his inability to love others, the gods made Narcissus fall in love with his own reflection, which paradoxically he both possessed and yet could not possess. Finally, he thrust a dagger into his heart. The myth's meaning lies in the necessarily illfated attempt by Narcissus to live through himself alone and to reject the live-giving structure of the outside society, mediated by other people. We know ourselves only through the echo of the Other.

In everyday thought, the Other is that which is separate in the sense of not being *this* but *that;* it is disjunctive, alternating between the either . . . or. Its deeper ontological meaning reaches down to the ancient Greek sense of a condition that uniquely characterizes human experience and which the Greeks enshrined in their term for man, *anthropos,* whose root *anthr* later gave the German *andere(r),* meaning "other" or "different." As ontology, the Other is that which includes disjunction *and* conjunction. It is like the rim of a glass, which while separating inside from outside at the same time brings them together, or the edge of a coin, which separates as well as joins the obverse and the reverse.

In our own time, it has been Heidegger's special task to recover this original but lost meaning of the Other as the "original unifying unity of what tends apart." In *Being and Time,* Heidegger thought of the Other as an "in-one-anotherness." In later works, the concept is analyzed in terms of *difference* – from the Greek *diaphora,* which means a double crossing or reversing. Difference is that which mediates between two and, in so doing, holds apart while holding together. We talk of the turning of the year or the turning of a page, by which we actually mean a crossing. It is impossible to think of the action of crossing without the action of reversing, for one crosses from A to B and only knows that one has reached B by returning, in the mind at least, to A. In the progress of the year, Otherness emerges through the reversal (the point of difference) of spring and summer into autumn and winter. It would be appropriate to say that the seasons are in-one-another through a process of mutual reflection or reversal much as you see yourself *in* a mirror, which is equivalent to saying that the mirror returns you to yourself. In the turning of a page we reverse one side into the other and the point of difference or in-one-anotherness is the edge of the page that both divides *and* joins.

The humble screw and nut are further everyday reminders of the Other inasmuch as a screw is a nut without a hole just as a nut is a screw with a hole. We may say that screw and nut complete each other through the mediation of lacks and fills, for a screw is the fill of a nut that lacks and, conversely, a nut is the fill of a screw that lacks. In this way, screw and nut are in-one-another, reflectively returning.

Such a conception of Otherness informs Merleau-Ponty's ontology, in which reflexiveness and reversibility become the essential means by which the human being knows his or her world. In various works, Merleau-Ponty (1964a, 1969) pursued and elaborated this definitive feature of his proprioceptive phenomenology, namely, that the body knows itself only through taking the position of another through which it comes back to itself. "Vision is not a certain mode of thought or presence to self; it is the means given me for being absent from myself, for being present at the fission of Being from the inside — the fission at whose termination, and not before, I come back to myself" (Merleau-Ponty, 1964a: 186). Here, the fission is the point of difference, of disjunction/conjunction. Kant's gloves can be understood in this way. The left and right gloves, as mirror images of each other, represent reversal in one dimension and, in that *dimension,* are not interchangeable and so must remain different. But one glove, say the left, can be turned inside out (i.e., reversed) to become the same as the other (right) glove. In this second step, the "termination of the fission" is represented by the finger tips of the glove, the points at which inside becomes outside, left becomes right. For Merleau-Ponty, the ontological significance of the point of difference lies in its pivotal or axial function; it is the point at which things turn round each other. The Other is no longer simple reflection but a structure in which actions take place in one another.

THE SOCIAL OTHER

We know that Freud recognized the pervasiveness of Otherness in the structure of human activity, especially the work of reversibility as a characteristic of unconscious and primitive formations. To indicate the primary role of reversibility in human experience, Freud (1957) draws our attention to the philologist Karl Abel's analysis of the "antithetical meanings" behind "primal words." In the most ancient languages, contraries such as "strong/weak," "light/dark," "big/small" were expressed by the same verbal roots. In Ancient Egyptian, *ken* represented "strong" *and* "weak." In Latin, *altus* means "high" *and* "deep"; *sacer,* "sacred" *and* "accursed." An additional mark in the form of intonation, gesture, or other device was normally associated with the concept in order to give it an unambiguous meaning; for instance, by a picture of a man, limply squatting or sitting erect, according to whether the ambiguous hierograph *ken* was to mean "weak" or "strong." The determining mark essentially transformed a reversible process into an irreversible state. Such reversible structures are seen in Freud's dream work, especially in the more elaborate form of "overdetermination," and also characterize social relationships from the process of primary socialization to the joke.

Complex reversible or circular structures, called "overdetermined" in psychoanalysis, emerge as "total social facts" in the ethnology of social structure. A social fact "totalizes" in the sense that it condenses within itself, like a symbol, a multitude of social dimensions and meanings. Despite its complexity it is reducible to the concept of reversibility, and for Lévi-Strauss is epitomized by the gift.

Now the essence of the gift is that it must be *returned* in some form; it sets up an obligation or claim. Despite their structuralist provenance, both Mauss (1967) and Lévi-Strauss (1969), and perhaps especially the latter, limit their interpretation of gift exchange to its essentially bonding nature. Yet in the data they both present, there are at least hints that the structure of gift giving is somewhat more than they indicate. At the level of the obvious, we can easily see that gifts are accompanied by a sort of rule of return. A bit of thought is required to realize that the gift, to quote Merleau-Ponty (1964a) in a related context, implies for the giver a "double reference to himself and the other person," and since every receiver is also a giver, the double reference is also mirrored in the other.

It is precisely this point that Mead (1934) assumes to be basic to the social process and indeed to the development of mind: "Reflexiveness . . . is the essential condition, within the social process, for the development of mind." (Mead, 1934: 134). Mead tells us that reflexiveness means the *turning back* of the individual's experience on him- or herself, which suggests that his ontology is similar to that of Heidegger and Merleau-Ponty.

For Mead, the "double reference" occurs in the "conversation of gestures," the building block of communication, in which A's stimulus calls out B's response, and B's response returns as the stimulus for A's response, and so on. B is the other for A, and A is the other for B. Here, as elsewhere, Otherness does not reside in any one term but lies between terms, as it were.

In Mead's conception of the process of human communication, the "I" is spoken by the "generalized other," which is a pooling of the attitudes of others. Specifically, others' attitudes are pooled into the "me," which is a mean or average of the positions of "I" and "Others." The "me," therefore, functions as a medium or central axis that enables a social structure to be. In this context, we can speak of any single term's meaning as being "authored" by the "other," and it is no accident that these two latter terms are lexically so alike.

The special character of the medium or mean may be better understood through Merleau-Ponty's (1964a) suggestion that reversibility is analogous to the linguist's "zero phoneme," a kind of imaginary plane that has no value in itself but serves to bring out values in others such as we see in Helson's (1964) conception of the "mean" as a functional zero in psychophysical judgments. Given a range of stimulus values to identify, the human subject can only respond by first locating their mean or average value, from which he or she is then able to estimate the remaining values as "deviations" or "differences." In effect, the mean is that which divides the total range of values into two subranges that are understood as mirror images or "returns" of each other.

In analyzing the social structure of a South American people, the Bororo, Lévi-Strauss (1963a) reveals the workings of a similar process in suggesting that the mute role of a certain institutional axis was to "give meaning" to the social structure as a whole. Ostensibly, the Bororo village is organized on an exogamous East-West axis that is crossed perpendicularly by a North-South axis whose function is not empirically clear but which appears to serve as the sole unifying device in the Bororo social structure, joining together otherwise disparate elements. In itself, the second axis has no value and exists simply for the benefit of other terms in the structure. For this reason, Lévi-Strauss ascribes to it a *Zero-Value* (whose structural resemblance to Helson's *functional zero* may be noted in passing). Yet this second axis, like the determinative added to the ambiguity of primal expressions, serves to signify inasmuch as it creates conditions for two otherwise separate moieties to exist in one another. In other words, this axis creates the "double reference."

Both Parsons (Parsons and Bales 1955) and Lacan (1977) have dealt, in their different ways, with the double reference. In his analysis of family structure and socialization, Parsons relies on logic and psychoanalysis to argue the fundamental role that the double reference plays in structure, especially social structure. His conception of the double reference is presented in terms of disjunction and conjunction which he equates with the individual and social dimensions of social structure, respectively. Parson's originality lies in refusing to see the individual-disjunctive and social-conjunctive as separate features of structure. For him, they are complementary facets of the same structure.

It is necessary to remind ourselves exactly what Parsons means by the logic of disjunction and conjunction. Both processes are regarded as fundamental to human thinking and occur simultaneously in any act of thought. In adding together four different things — say, apple, orange, pear, banana — we reason by conjunction: $1 + 1 + 1 + 1 = 4$. At the same time, we reason by disjunction because each one of these different things is made the *same* in the sense that it becomes simply one more thing to be added up.

In this sense, being "individual" means that you and me are "undivided" symbols of the concept "human being." Any one of us taken separately makes up a whole human being. Following Parsons, we can say that you *or* me is a human being, but we are not allowed to say that you *and* me is a human being for this involves at least two human beings. So we are "disjointed." But in conjunction we are "divided" and we become "undivided" by joining together in the same group. Mother, father, daughter, and son added together make up the family group. We cannot say that mother *or* father is the family, for the family is a conjunction of these individuals.

Basing his analysis of the socialization process on Freud and (to a lesser extent) Mead, Parsons views the first stage of this process, the mother/child identity, as conjunctive since it is structured in terms of absolute identification of mother and child who are joined as one; at this stage, disjunction has not appeared. Disjunction or individual identity is realized through the Oedipus phase, where the father intervenes to break up the absolute relationship between mother and child and places himself between them as a third term. In so doing he creates a double reference that integrates the conjunctive and the disjunctive.

A similar analysis constitutes the theory of human development in Lacan's psychoanalysis, especially in the so-called Imaginary and Symbolic orders. In the Imaginary, there is no distinction, only a perpetual merging of terms into each other; no "I," no "you," no "me," to speak of. The Imaginary is the order of the conjunctive. In the Symbolic, a sense of the individual who is also part of a structure is introduced through the process of naming, which ascribes a fixed position in the social structure. The Symbolic is the order of the conjunctive/disjunctive.

In Lacan's *mirror stage* the child identifies itself with and through the image of the "other" — the mother, other children; there is no understanding of itself as a separate "I"; it imagines itself as the "other." In the particular case of the mother/male child relationship, the child fuses with the mother in a process of imaginary mutual appropriation in which each lives through the other. This moment of continuity is suppressed by *the Name-of-the-Father,* when the father imposes constraint by naming the specific roles in the family structure. The function of the name is to constrain, and constraint is the source of pattern. (The etymology of "father" as *pater* reflects that of "pattern"). At this magical point the social becomes individual and the individual becomes social.

In small group studies of social structure, especially studies based on factor analysis, two dimensions — individuality and sociability — are consistently reported. But a defect of much of this work is that these factors are interpreted as being separate. Yet they are clearly equivalent to the individual (disjunctive) and social (conjunctive) facets of social structure noted by Parsons, whose special merit in the present context was to view them as mutually defining. It is this fact of interdependence or coupling between individual and social that is of high significance in understanding Otherness as the basis of social structure, for, among other things, it implies recursiveness or circularity, which is merely another way of saying in-one-anotherness.

A METHODOLOGY OF THE OTHER

The mathematical logic of circular order has been worked out by Guttman (1954) in his concept of the *circumplex*. Guttman has shown that when you intercorrelate measurements of polarized variables (i.e., which have both negative and positive values), the latent structure that emerges is of a circular order. Circular structure has been demonstrated in regard to human intelligence, attitudes, and so on.

Perhaps the most systematic empirical studies of circular structure have been carried out by social psychologists in the field of interpersonal behavior. Foa (1961), in a neglected but important paper, has discussed much of the background literature and has presented a mathematically based case for circular structure, much of it coming from Guttman's model.

To demonstrate the methodology of the circular model, let us take one study, reported by the psychologist Timothy Leary (1957), of the personality structures of psychiatric patients. Leary describes the circular organization of sixteen behavioral variables around two orthogonal axes: dominance/submission and hostility/affection, the former representing the individual facet of structure, the latter, the social facet.

It is worth noting that Leary justifies his circular rationale by discussing similar methodologies put forward by various scholars including Parsons and Freud, who, in particular, considered Lichtenberg's "compass of motives" as a model especially appropriate to the circular structures latent in human action.

Leary's main types of behavior were:

(1) Managerial-Autocratic

(2) Competitive-Narcissistic

(3) Aggressive-Sadistic

(4) Rebellious-Distrustful

(5) Self-Effacing-Masochistic

(6) Docile-Dependent

(7) Cooperative-Overconventional

(8) Responsible-Hypernormal

He reports that the quantitative relationships (expressed in terms of correlation coefficients) between these behavioral characteristics are arranged in a circular order and that the "average size of the correlation coefficients decreases systematically as the intervariable distance on the circular arrangement increases."

Foa's fuller demonstration of the circular logic behind Leary's findings depends on a reanalysis of the latter's concepts in terms of three facets: the *content* of the action (rejection or acceptance), the *object* of the action (self or other), and the *psychological mode* of the action (emotional or social) which yields eight profiles:

(A) rejection of self, emotional

(B) rejection of self, social

(C) rejection of other, social

(D) rejection of other, emotional

(E) acceptance of self, emotional

(F) acceptance of self, social

(G) acceptance of other, social

(H) acceptance of other, emotional

The circular structure of the profiles, when viewed as a system, is more easily seen in Figure 13.1.

We can now apply Foa's scheme to understand more precisely the nature of the circularity in Leary's original data. In Figure 13.2, A through H represent Foa's eight profiles (see above), while plus and minus signs represent the presence or absence, respectively, of a particular profile.

From the table, we see that Leary's Managerial-Autocratic type is interpreted in Foa's scheme as a mix of social and emotional rejection of other and social and emotional acceptance of self. The rest of the types can be interpreted in the same way. But the real point of the exercise is to indicate that these various types of psychiatric behavior may only be understood in terms of their interrelationships. In other words, meaning derives from the types *turning round each other,* and Figure 13.2 suggests how this may occur.

First, let us make explicit the circular structure of Figure 13.2 by looping type 8 (Responsible-Hypernormal) back to connect with type 1 (Managerial-Autocratic). When this is done, we find that those types that are farthest from each other on the circular structure are also diametrically opposed in terms of their constituent variables. Type 1 (Managerial-Autocratic) is the exact opposite of type 5 (Self-Effacing-Masochistic), that is types 1 and 5 are *inverted reflections of*

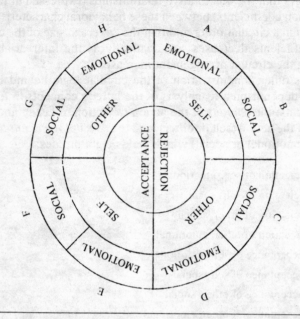

Figure 13.1   The Circular Logic of Leary's Analysis Behavioral Types

		A	B	C	D	E	F	G	H
(1)	Managerial — Autocratic	–	–	+	+	+	+	–	–
(2)	Competitive — Narcissistic	–	+	+	+	+	–	–	–
(3)	Aggressive — Sadistic	+	+	+	+	–	–	–	–
(4)	Rebellious — Distrustful	+	+	+	–	–	–	–	+
(5)	Self-Effacing — Masochistic	+	+	–	–	–	–	+	+
(6)	Docile — Dependent	+	–	–	–	–	+	+	+
(7)	Cooperative — Overcontentional	–	–	–	–	+	+	+	+
(8)	Responsible — Hypernormal	–	–	–	+	+	+	+	–

Figure 13.2   Foa's Eight Profiles / Leary's Behavior Types

each other. Likewise, types 4 and 8 invert each other. By the same logic we find that the nearer to each other the types are *on the circular order,* the more similar they are in character. The movements of this structure bear a remarkable similarity to the movement of time throughout a 24-hour period. We might characterize this movement as a cycle of progression-regression, in which the crepuscular light of dawn gradually turns into the brighter light of midday, thereafter falling away to dusk and finally reaching its darkest period at midnight, at which point the cycle begins again. The points of extreme inversion return to each other, as it were, through a logical and stepwise process that can be observed in the Foa-Leary space by taking A and looping it around to meet H. This enables one to see the continuous, step-by-step movement of the elements around the circle so constituted.

However, the circularity of this space moves in two directions at the same time. As well as the A-H loop, there is also, as we noted earlier, the loop made by connecting Leary's types 1 and 8. It is of interest to note that we cannot create this double circularity by shaping the actual page on which the data are presented. We can do this in one dimension only if we rely on the page — if we turn the page round so that A meets H, it becomes impossible to do the same with types 1 and 8 *at the same time*. In order to think of such double circularity, a torus structure is required.

The two-directional nature of the structure involves a continuous turning round each other of types and profiles in the sense that the rows (types) of the table connect horizontally and the columns (profiles) connect vertically. There is also a horizontal/vertical interaction that reveals itself by analyzing neighboring rows and columns — each row and column moves, as it were, into its neighbor by means of a single discrete change of position of sign (+, −), thus giving to the whole structure a spiral movement in two planes at the same time.

Combinations of signs (types, profiles) represent the logic of conjunction; the differences between them, the disjunctive. But the above analysis suggests that this structure corresponds to an in-one-anotherness in which conjunction and disjunction combine and define each other. It seems that conjunctive and disjunctive processes each occur within a frame defined by the other.

In this connection, the Foa-Leary space has the character of a Möbius strip, a ring-shaped band having two separate surfaces, one inside and one outside, but twisted at one point so that the two surfaces become one to symbolize a divided whole. Now the point of twist is equivalent to the point of reversal, which in its turn is a point of lack since it is neither one thing nor the other, neither this side of the Möbius strip nor the other side. Lack, as neither one thing nor the other, lies *between* terms; in other words, it is Heidegger's concept of "difference" (i.e., "that which mediates between two and in so doing holds apart while holding together"). A lack is therefore a medium. In the Foa-Leary space, lack as mediation has a clearly defined character. If, as before, we take types 1 and 5 as examples of binary oppositions or inversions of each other (i.e., their constituent variables are diametrically opposed), type 3 occupies the role of medium in that it shares exactly and in a lawful way the variables that make up types 1 and 5. Also types 1 and 5 are media for other types. We thus see that the medium is that which *lacks* the clear and unmistakable characteristics of the terms it mediates. In other words, a special feature of the medium is that it is ambiguous in relation to the terms it mediates, for the property of combining within itself the differences of its mediated terms means that the medium negates such differences and makes them, in some sense, the same.

It is possible to see this feature of medium as equivalent to measurement, which itself is a necessary step in the institution of human structuring. The essence of measurement is that it enables comparison by making differences the same through the use of symmetrical or equal units; and what is the same is also timeless (i.e., permanent and indestructible). These characteristics of medium explain its function of "returning" or "reversing" inasmuch as one returns to that necessary and fundamental operation of symmetrizing, which gives meaning to all differences, whether temporal or spatial. Differences have no separate, individual meanings and may be understood only in terms of each other, which is simply another way of saying mediation. We echo here a basic principle of information theory where information emerges only from a *set of equally likely possibilities* – randomness, if you like — without which no form or structure is possible. In other words, information or structure is not a property of individuals but of, let us say, otherness. In terms of the Foa-Leary space, each personality type possesses a "double reference": As a disjunction, it is paired with another type in a binary opposition, and, as a conjunction, it is a third term, a medium, which gives both measure and meaning to the other oppositions in its space. It is essentially a matter of parts being shared among a whole. The parts or disjunctions share the "whole" of the medium, while the medium, in a reverse action, unifies the parts. This double role entails a continuous oscillation, a kind of alternating current, between medium and mediated, which Derrida (1978) recognizes in his concept of *différance* as a process that continuously defers the return to the same. As we have noted, the medium symmetrizes or homogenizes the field of experience. Carried to the extreme, this would mean the loss of the medium itself since it can be known only through the terms it mediates. Hence the necessity to postpone the lack or loss of distinction brought about by mediation; yet distinctions, in their turn, must refer or return to a center or medium by means of which they can be compared and thus evaluated.

SOCIAL ORGANIZATION AND THE OTHER

The Other is a structure — not simply another person or thing — that characterizes social organization. The essence of structure or organization is that of two terms mediated by a third, the relationship between the three terms being characterized by a process that alternates between division and combination. In the social sciences it is usual to think of social organization in terms of the "individual" and the "social." In the present context, the social is simply the process of otherness or mediation that occurs (minimally) between two individuals, the nature of this process being expressed as the *combination* of the two parts into the one of a larger whole and the *division* of the larger one into two smaller parts. This draws attention to a paradoxical feature of otherness, namely, that unity or wholeness can emerge only through division or difference.

> For nothing can be sole or whole
> That has not been rent [Yeats, 1933: 294].

This principle lies at the heart of social organization, which, because of it, is fated to perpetual division and to mourn the loss of a supposed anterior unity.

We can picture the medium as a center or nucleus with properties that make it, as we have already suggested, analogous to measurement, the essence of which is reference to a standard. But the standard has to be understood as being more than a point of reference and more like a dynamic constraint on variation and difference. A tension, of the order of a compulsion, operates in which the medium exerts a centripetal effect on its differences. This is, again, the point at which things turn round each other — the rim of a glass, the edge of a coin, the finger tips of Kant's gloves. It is at this point of meeting that the differences become symmetrical, equal, where they share the same measure (more precisely, they are the same) and thus, of course, do not differ. At this primal point, this origin, everything condenses into a unity, which we can only know indirectly, by inference and deferment, i.e., through difference, as a *lost* whole. (In the language of information theory, the "lost whole" can be recognized in the concepts of variety and constraint [Ashby, 1956]. "Wholeness" occurs when all elements in a given set can vary independently of each other, thus giving absolute freedom. The idea of a medium's "symmetry" means that all its elements are "equally possible" as parts of a larger set from which the differences are taken. But wholeness in this sense is a form of randomness and so has to be constrained. Constraint therefore reduces the freedom intrinsic to the whole, and "loss" is the loss of possibilities or freedom that constraint brings about, which, paradoxically, can only be understood as loss through the imposition of constraint.) However, to know something by inference and deferment is to know something that is not irrevocably lost but merely held in suspension, placed in limbo. This is exactly the timeless quality of the medium as measure, which, since it is permanent and indestructible, is resistant to all change. The whole or unitary character of the medium is therefore essentially *indivisible* and resists differentiation. This means that a principle of symmetry operates in human structures so that differences are understood fundamentally as inversions of each other and thus are seen as necessarily equivalent. It suggests that symmetry acts as a loadstone to draw all differences back to a common source where, and only where, they can be understood — compared, evaluated — in terms of each other. The implications for social organization are especially significant, for the essential indivisibility of symmetry means that it refuses to accept the absolute dominion of asymmetry or differentiation that characterizes the "division of labor" in social existence, and in fact *it seeks to reverse such division*.

In his analysis of social power, Canetti (1962) has caught the essence of this reversal of social division in his concept of the "sting." Power, it seems, is the expression of order via command. A command consists of *momentum* and *sting*. The momentum is the force on the person to act, while the sting, invisible and mute, remains behind after every command is obeyed. The sting is indestructible and waits, often for years, for the chance to avenge itself by reversing the original command. "What spurs men on to achievement is the deep urge to be rid of the commands once laid on them" (Canetti, 1962: 306). The sting is therefore a device whose goal is to free the command's recipient of a "deference order" and thereby make the relationship "whole." (Elsewhere Canetti [1974] has demonstrated the significant role of the sting in Kafka's social relationships). The sting is yet another way of expressing the idea of return or otherness as an a priori structure governing social organization. Hughes's (1951) account of the relationship between the Chicago apartment house janitor and his tenants, focusing on the garbage that serves as a medium between the two, vividly illustrates the workings of the sting. It is apparently not the garbage per se that is troublesome to the janitor, but the perception that it reflects the tenants' low valuation of him. But as a true medium, the garbage can be turned against the tenant: bits of torn-up letter paper in the waste inform the janitor about hidden love affairs, unopened letters tell him of impending financial disaster or of financial tall talk. "The garbage gives the janitor the makings of a kind of magical power over that pretentious villain, the tenant" (Hughes, 1951: 320).

When Mauss (1967) examined the functions of gifts in ancient societies, he emphasized the obligatoriness of giving *and* receiving them. That is, gifts, far from being voluntarily exchanged, symbolize an instinctive and impulsive form of action over which we have no control. It is important to understand that the gift is not the result of an act of kindness. In fact, Mauss's evidence is that it is an act that is intended to place the other *in debt* so that the return of the gift serves to free the recipient from the state of "deference" created by the "kindness" of another. The form instituted by the gift is that of the medium, which here very clearly functions as a measure that evaluates the "division of labor" according to a preexisting and sacred symmetry. To accept a gift without returning it is to disequilibrate a relationship and do violence to the concept of measure itself.

Both in the sting and in the gift we observe what appears to be a basic social force in which symmetry or wholeness continually tries to reconstitute itself against an equally continuous force of differentiation. More simply, we might say that symmetry resists being shared, and this resistance constitutes an ineffable core that is beyond rational, conscious management.

Information theory, it is worth noting, is based on the idea of binary division but this is invariably limited to choice between objects or events viewed from the position of an *individual* decision maker. It seems not to occur to the information theorist to reverse his or her customary usage of the binary idea by asking what happens when a single object or event is chosen by two people. If he or she were to do this, he or she would reveal the operation of two desires competing for the same object. The essence of desire in social organization is that it is *shared* (i.e., divided) among people *and* objects. Its etymology also reflects this — "desire" is cognate with the French *déchirer,* to tear or rend, and with the Latin *desiderium,* a longing for that which is lost. What is rent and lost is the idea of the whole.

It is precisely this sense of loss that defines the human condition. To be human is to enter the social structure as a duality and not as a unity. Mead's (1934) model of human interaction is a formalization of this insight, and the whole of psychoanalysis rests on it. Social organization is a system of information exchange whose function, as we have said, is to defer the loss of itself. The actors in the social structure thus represent themselves to each other as lacks of a larger whole. Desire is the presence of a lack or loss that is represented to us by another, whose desire is the reflection of our own lack. It underlines the ontological, as opposed to the instrumental, basis of knowledge, that is, lack is information that is missing to being.

For Hegel (1931), desire is the desire for *recognition* (i.e., to be valued by the other). In other words, desire is the desire to be desired, to be wanted; since a want is a lack, when you want me, you fill my lack.

A's lack is expressed, through language, as a call to B to fill the former's lack. B, as the other, is the sign of A's lack as A is the sign of B's lack. The call is of one desire to another desire. It is not the call to fill in a biological need such as hunger but *an appeal for valuation,* which is why Hegel says that desire is the desire for recognition. Value, as the complement of desire, seeks to fill the lost whole of the lack.

All this comes down to saying that B's response to A's call is essentially a token or sign of the latter's lack, and this is equivalent to saying that it valorizes or fills the lack. This is why lack has the character of mediation, for , as we have already noted, a medium (such as the spoken or written word) provides information that is missing to being; i.e., it fills a hole and thereby makes a whole. (In this connection, we may note that "word" is etymologically related to "worth" [i.e., value] and that the latter derives from Old English *weorthan,* to become [to which the modern German *werden,* to become, is related]).

We can now perhaps see that sting, gift, and desire are different ways of expressing the mediating function of the Other in social organization, for they are all premised on the paradoxical principle of sharing an essentially indivisible and permanent whole. Sharing or division is the potential destruction of the whole, but nothing must be allowed to destroy that which is the very source of division itself; hence the force that lies behind sting, gift, and desire is the force that seeks to preserve the whole. The central role of this force in social process is recognized by Mauss (1967) in his discussion of modern formal organizations. Despite their much-flaunted rationality, formal organizations are ruled by an essentially intractable structure — the Other — which is the nucleus of all social organization. In *Finnegans Wake,* James Joyce encapsulated the intractability of social relationship in the covert notion of symmetrical human bondage, thus: "His producers are they not his consumers?" This symmetry of reversed opposition represents the obduracy of the Other, and the desire to actualize it is a fundamental compulsion in social life, which Mauss (1967: 75) expressed in the following words: "The producer-exchanger feels now as he has always felt — but this time he feels it more acutely — that he is giving something of himself, his time and his life. Thus he wants recompense . . . for this gift." The giving of time, of effort, of a significant portion of a life, is seen as a call that demands an adequate and just response from the other since only this form of reciprocation can give individual actions both measure and meaning. It seems that this is what Goffman had in mind when he depicted formal organization as a superstructure imposed on a more primitive social core:

> In our society . . . a formal instrumental organization does not merely use the activity of its members. The organization also delineates what are considered to be officially appropriate standards of welfare, joint values, incentives, and penalties. These conceptions expand a mere participation contract into a definition of the participant's nature of social being. These implicit images form an important element of the values which every organization sustains, regardless of the degree of its efficiency or impersonality. Built right into the social arrangements of an organization, then, is a thoroughly embracing conception of the member — and not merely a conception of him *qua* member, but, behind this a conception of him *qua* human being" [1968: 164].

The significance of Goffman's quotation is contained in the idea that formal organization is at bottom social organization that defines "social being" and not "organizational membership." It is the social measure, the symmetrically bonded relationship with the other, that above everything else constitutes the nub of formal organization. In a footnote, Goffman alludes to Gouldner's (1955) analysis of the "indulgency pattern" of management that informally underpinned the bureaucratic organization of the General Gypsum Company to support the priority of "social being" over the "organizational member." In this still-classic study, pervaded by a sensitive sociology of the human condition, Gouldner reveals the central issue of all formal organization when he questions Weber's treatment of the concept of rational-legal authority. "For Weber, authority was given consent *because* it was legitimate, rather than being legitimate *because* it evoked consent" (1955: 223) — so that consent, for Weber, was taken for granted and therefore unproblematical. However, if one takes the concept of otherness as the central problematic of social organization, consent as the expression of "social being" and the satisfaction of social demand becomes the source of rational-legal authority. We may understand this connection through the original meaning of "rational," which, rather than the idea of "instrumental efficiency," refers to an equitable sharing or "rationing" of the goods and bads that characterize all other-centered activity. Consent is given to another on the understanding that what is given is returned in some way. The idea of equivalence, one thing for another, is implied. Hence the concept of consent is bound up with the idea of symmetry or return, which Gouldner (1973) elsewhere calls the "norm of reciprocity."

Formal organization, like all conscious and rational social arrangements, entails the differentiation of people and objects in time and space. In contrast, the Other, especially in its function of mediation, draws differences back to a supposed prior state of wholeness unconstrained by time and space in which there are gaps, no discrepancies, where everything is full and equal. Despite the Other being a "perfect" form that can exist only in certain privileged states of suspension (such as the mathematically pure world of measurement and the condition of the "sacred" in religion), the fact that it is ever present as a desired yet impossible absence in social relationships suggests that what ultimately organizes the social world is not the tangible and immediate reality of people and things but the structural presence of a metalogical absence.

About the Author

ROBERT COOPER

My youthful intellectual interests were centered on thinkers and writers who addressed themselves to what I saw as critical issues in the study of the "human condition." Freud, for example, was (and still is) a big influence on me. I went into undergraduate study in psychology (Reading University) with the naive expectation of satisfying my untutored desire to answer the question posed to Oedipus by the Sphinx. Still expecting, I moved on to a sociology department (Liverpool University) with the twin aims of broadening my education in social science and obtaining a Ph.D. Despite having two degrees, I am largely "self-taught" in the social sciences; i.e., the knowledge I value most has come not from my institutional training but from a long process of posing and answering my own questions. In this process I have learned that social science is not the study of social action per se, but the study of *method;* i.e., method is our language for engaging reality. In other words, *we become the methods* we use to understand what is "out there." This seems to me to be the central problem of the social sciences in that their subject matter has the same form as that of those who study it, so that social scientists are *already included* in the very methods of their discipline. This is by no means a novel observation. Eddington saw it in modern physics. The rise of hermeneutics in recent times is based on the mutually defining relationship between the interpreter and what he or she interprets. Hence, I regard social science as primarily a self-reflective activity in which the *structure* of method is the major means for understanding the social world, and most of my current writing has to do with this issue in one way or another.

14

DRAMATISM AND THE THEATRICAL METAPHOR

Iain L. Mangham

University of Bath

Michael A. Overington

St. Mary's University

Opposite the cars the platform was flanked by a row of barracks where bundles destined for immediate shipping were piled. These barracks . . . faced the platforms with a long wooden wall. On this wall Lalka had *trompe l' oeil* doors and windows painted, in gay and pleasing colors. . . . Each door was given a special name, stencilled at eye level: "Station Master," "Toilet," "Infirmary.". . . To the left of the barracks two doors were cut into the barbed wire. The first bearing a wooden arrow on which "Wolkowysk" was painted. The second . . . said "Bialystok.". . . In the Sibylline language of Treblinka, "Wolkowysk" meant the bullet in the back of the neck or the injection. "Bialystok" meant the gas chamber [Steiner, 1967: 162-165].

At its simplest, dramatism is a method of examining and analyzing social action *and* people's explanations of social actions. The method understands five elements — the "pentad" — to be basic in explaining all social action; in Kenneth Burke's rendition, "any complete statement about motives will offer some kind of answers to these five questions: what was done (act), when or where it was done (scene), who did it (agent), how he did it (agency), and why (purpose)" (1969a: vx). Mystification occurs when only one or two of these five elements — act or scene or agent — are presented as the explanation for what is, or will be, taking place, and participants in or observers of some activity are persuaded by the parsimonious lure of such explanations to formulate the other elements as consistent. This concern for mystification (which has tenuous links to Marxist thought) is an emblem in all Burke's work that is reflected most faithfully in the writings of Hugh Dalziel Duncan (especially 1962, 1968, 1969). Yet any dramatistic analysis is inherently critical and demystifying in examining *all* elements of social action, in inquiring as to the priority attached to one or another aspect of the pentad, and in trying to "round out" accounts of social action so as to give due weight to all five elements and their relative consistency.

Few stages have such final exits as those on Treblinka "station." There, the impression of a stop on the way to some resettlement in the East was a mystification of Scene that kept the transported Jews under the thralldom of symbols that offered them hope as one condition of their seeming Agency — the choice of a door. But that was mercilessly demystified by the whips that lashed them the last few yards to the gas chambers. The disproportion between the evil mystifications of the Nazis and the organizational contexts in which we work as dramatistic analysts is immense. But it is surely a disproportion that we must recall and even celebrate in our practice, no matter how innocuous are organizational mystifications. It could all be so much different, and the ubiquity of power — in the persons of those who cannot be required to explain themselves — is a constant reminder as to the instrumentality through which such differences are achieved. Whether of Scene or Act, of Agent or Agency, the *terminus ad quem* of all mystification in our century is these very chambers of death in the extermination camps.

DRAMATISM

In the twentieth century, Kenneth Burke has been the great source of dramatism, and although his more important thinking is contained in perhaps four volumes (1965, 1968, 1969a, 1969b), the bibliography of his writing in Frank and Frank (1969) does run some seventeen pages. Despite the extensive secondary analysis of his work (especially Rueckert, 1969; Duncan, 1962; and self-interestedly, Overington, 1977a, 1977b), we still have no definitive account of his intellectual influence. However, it is plain that from Mills's (1963) classic essay, which introduced his ideas to social scientists, to volumes like White (1978), which constitutes a development and extension of Burkean notions to the whole textual enterprises of the human sciences, Kenneth Burke has never been less than a central figure in efforts to understand language and action. Sometimes this centrality is acknowledged; more often it is not because his work has been marginal to most of the interested disciplines. It may be paradoxical, but as Peter Manning (1980) notes, the crux of many disciplines today now rests at the margins. It is there that Burke will grow in importance.

For Burke and for ourselves, working and writing in a dramatistic key, people are actors who *play* characters; they are works of dramatic art. The notion of persons as mere theatrical performers is an unfortunate narrowing of his views that has characterized much work employing a theatrical metaphor at the same time as it has played false with the actuality of the theatrical experience. It is through language that we become self-conscious, capable of playing a number of characters to varying audiences and yet still retaining a grasp of an acting self. In this notion of the distinction between ourselves and our roles — a theatrical consciousness, if you will — exist the links between dramatism and the tradition of symbolic interactionism that stretches from the work of James, Cooley, and Mead to the present.

However, it would be no more than a mystification of Agency for us to claim that language is all when it comes to understanding selves and society — the human capacity for action is much more than a talent for conversation. We paint buildings and portraits, build bridges and sets, make shoes and love, play cards and flutes; we work and disport ourselves in myriad ways, but it is language that introduces into life a sense of negation — a separation of those things that should be done from those that should not. Society can be regarded as composed of persons making and breaking the regulations and expectations of their living, honoring and dishonoring the authorities that are presented as the license for such patterns of life. It is we, after all, who make the rules and not they us. Conduct, therefore, is a drama of met and failed expectations, a morality play with consequences for the actors that has a parallel motivational commentary that both actors and critics may and do use to justify, explain, exculpate, license, excuse, and in general account for the drama and their part in it.

Society, then, is composed of all the diversity of human action conceived of as a drama of moral order that catches up our material existence within a motivational gossamer of symbols. Social scientists have been fated to add their voices to this shimmering array of explanations. Thus people may experience their existence as part of a class struggle; as bound up with the loss of freedom to impersonal, legalistic bureaucracies; as a neurotic conflict with a parental image;

and so on, all by virtue of our motive mongering. What kind of knowledge do these traditions constitute? Surely this will depend on whom you ask; but from our viewpoint, at best, they help demystify the conditions of human life by featuring forgotten elements; at worst, they add further oppressive weight to one or another single-factor mystification of human conduct.

And so, if social scientific knowledge is to be treated as one among many forms of motive mongering, is dramatism any different? What would recommend it as a way of knowing, as a kind of knowledge? Clearly, we would not want to advocate this kind of knowledge because it is true and others false, or because we are singularly exempted from motive mongering on the grounds of our ability to attribute this activity to other social scientists. Dramatism gives one no criteria for such smug demarcations of one's own virtues and the vices of all others. Indeed, we could rest our case quite well on the tacit rationale presented in the horrifying vignette of the mystification of Treblinka "station" and the interest Dramatism has in the examination and critique of processes making such moments possible, even as barely imaginable endpoints. But there is more to be said. We are not talking about some simplistic notion of demystification as an unmasking, a revelation of the truth; rather, we are offering dramatism as a technique of analysis of human interaction and also as a method for assessing social theories of human conduct. The demystification of action that can be achieved by reclaiming neglected pentadic elements has its counterpart in the critique of theories of action that similarly neglect elements of the pentad (for example, Zollschan and Overington, 1976). And here, unlike other theories of action, dramatism provides the method for demystifying and criticizing itself. It is possible, therefore, to produce a dramatistic account of some situation, and, without shifting one's ground, equally possible to analyze that account.

It is plain, however, that understanding dramatistic principles (as the Nazis so obviously did) is no indicator of how that knowledge will be used. Practically, these principles are used more often to mystify than to demystify; it is only in the social scientific use of dramatism— seeking to give due weight to all elements of the pentad in the explanation of human conduct — that we can find an implicit commitment to the demystification of any single-minded explanatory scenario. For this reason, the theater (both as performance and social organization), devoted as it most commonly is to the creation of staged naturalness (to the mystification of "acting"), has served as the major source of conceptual invention for the dramatistic theorist and researcher. Therefore, while dramatism in Kenneth Burke's formulation serves as our methodological framework (a social psychological aesthetic), writers have used theatrical metaphor (see, for example, Biddle, 1979; Brown, 1978; Goffman, 1959; Harré, 1979; Heilman, 1976; Klapp, 1962; McCall and Simmons, 1978; Mangham, 1978; Manning, 1979) as a resource for thinking creatively and consistently within this framework (for applying and developing the aesthetic).

Recourse to such notions as role, scripts, settings, costumes, masks, presentation of self, altercasting, stage fright, and so forth (readers are spared a further display of our bibliographic talents) have become commonplace among social scientists. What is much less common is the acceptance and consistent use of this metaphor as a "way of seeing" (and hence not-seeing) and the recognition that theater itself can be both a mystifying and a demystifying activity, offering both an escape and an invitation to action. In this brief space, we shall first indicate how theater is an essential site of mystification wherein Brecht proposed the construction of a theatrical strategy of demystification; second, we shall present a case study of analysis and demystification in a large manufacturing organization; finally, we shall say something about research strategies and draw some conclusions.

THEATER AS MYSTIFICATION AND DEMYSTIFICATION

Theatrical performances achieve their effect through emphasis on the Act such that conventions of acting provide for easily grasped consistencies between Acts and Scenes, Agents, Agencies, and Purposes, and audiences are seduced into a theatrical consciousness that allows them to enter into and become part of the world presented on the stage. Goffman (1959) and others have noted that in social life, as in the theater, there is a form of "willing suspension of disbelief"; we each perform the function of the charitable audience to the other and are expected to do so if the very fabric of social life itself is not to be reduced to shreds. Lasky (1980: 81) claims somewhat more forcefully that human society is characterized by what he terms "the will to be deceived": "Our species loves the specious. Dark corners of the psyche long for the fraudulent. Bamboozlement is part of *la condition humaine*." Which may be overstating things a little — hypocrisy may be a much more common lubricant of social life than is bamboozlement — but it nevertheless serves well enough, if true, to illustrate why it is that the theatrical metaphor is so readily applicable to normal social interactions.

The possibility of the theater becoming a demystifying agent was promulgated in this century by Berthold Brecht, a German playwright and director. He proposed that a distinction be drawn between the traditional, Aristotelian theater and that which he termed "epic theater." The former demands the "identification" of the spectators with the play; they are supposed to show empathy if not sympathy with the characters and the circumstances portrayed for their entertainment. The Aristotelian theater, Brecht claimed, shows the structure of society (represented on the stage) as incapable of being influenced by society (in the auditorium). Life and Art are therefore seen as distinct, and Art is only in its own service. The play refers to itself, and the elements of performance (setting, actors, and so forth) operate through conventions that direct the attention of the audience solely to the action. In the epic theater, the

> spectator is not made the victim, so to speak, of a hypnotic experience in the theater. In fact, it has a purpose — the teaching of the spectator a certain quite practical attitude; we have to make it possible for him to take a critical attitude while he is in the theater (as opposed to a subjective attitude of becoming "entangled" on what is going on) [Brecht, 1964: 78].

Aristotelian theater is, of course, mystification. The answer for Brecht and his disciples was to manipulate elements of the pentad such that the audience would find it difficult to submit unthinkingly to what was presented to them. For example, his decision to make visible the lighting apparatus was a means of challenging one element of theatrical mystification. "If," he wrote "we light the actors and their performance in such a way that the lights themselves are within the spectator's field of vision. . . he sees that arrangements have been made to show something; something is being repeated under special conditions" (Brecht, 1964: 141). For the most part, he concentrated on the Agent (actors) as the key to this desired state of alienation. Through the actors' calculated lack of involvement with their characters, the audience was to be released so as that which hitherto had been taken as "natural" had the force of that which is startling. The *verfremdungseffekt:*

> consists of taking the object or relationship of which one is to be made aware . . . from something ordinary, familiar, immediately accessible, into something peculiar, striking and unexpected. What

> is obvious is in a certain sense made incomprehensible but this is
> only in order that it may then be made all the easier to comprehend.
> Before familiarity can turn into awareness, the familiar must be
> stripped of its naturalness, we must give up assuming that the object
> in question needs no explanation. However frequently recurrent,
> modest, vulgar it may be it will now be labelled as something
> unusual [1964: 143-144].

Actors who stand in free and direct relationships with their part (as
opposed to those who are their characters) are able to allow their
characters to speak, and more, they are free to "present or report."
Such a presentation encourages the members of the audience to
"alienate" themselves from a naive involvement in their part as
audience (no longer to be located as an undifferentiated mass but as
individuals capable of reflection and action) and allows them to grasp
the theatrical mystifications that have hitherto induced their identification with the actors and the acting; it demystifies the theater.

Such ideas can be of considerable utility in studying and working
with members of organizations. Many institutions in whole or in part
are marked by mystifications of one form or another. Churches and
universities display myths of Purpose: preparation of the elect in one
form or another. Industry occasionally mystifies the Agent: Salvation
lies in the hands of the engineers or accountants, exporters, or whatever; or claims that some Agency making money, for instance, justifies everything else. Very occasionally, the Act, doing something,
anything, is held to be the explanation for all else.

Over the past several years, a number of studies conducted
through the Centre for the Study of Organizational Change and Development at the University of Bath, England (generally supervised
by Mangham), have produced a body of material that is typified in the
following report, in terms of both the experience reported and the
richness of information encountered in organizations. In this report, it
is the Scene (or setting) that constitutes the explanation for all else,
and its demystification, the purpose of dramatistic consultancy.

A DRAMATISTIC CASE STUDY:
THE BEAGLE OF THE HESELTINES

Analysis

The firm concerned employed some 15,000 people at a number of
locations and was divided into three manufacturing divisions, each

presided over by a production director who — together with directors of finance/personnel, purchasing, administration, new products, and marketing — constituted the senior team. This group, as did two other firms, reported through the managing director to a holding company. The dramatistic researcher (in this case, Mangham) agreed to work with the senior team, which appeared willing to allow him free access to themselves, their meetings, and their weekly management sessions with the managing director. They permitted him to tape individual conversations with them as well as many of the weekly sessions.

According to the managing director, the purpose of the Monday sessions was "to advise me as Chief Executive on the decisions I need to make, to help make better decisions by criticizing and commenting upon proposals enabling me to hear the likely effect on different parts of the company as to what the proposed decisions will have." Moreover, he believed that his senior team understood that their function was "to agree overall policy and be committed to it," since he had reminded them that they were "directors of the company and therefore . . . [had] a collective responsibility for the running of the company as well as their own individual part of it." Yet in the sessions, there was little advice, few comments, and virtually no criticism except insofar as a proposal affected a particular function. There was no apparent commitment to overall policy, nor any attempt at it. There was virtually no conflict. A number of issues, apparently of considerable importance to the company, were repeatedly raised over the period of six months that the researcher sat in with the group and were repeatedly left unresolved. Other issues, perhaps of greater urgency, were not resolved in the meeting but disappeared from the agenda and, occasionally, from the records of the meeting.

To the researcher, the conduct of the actors in the situation appeared to be inconsistent with a commitment to work together for the corporate good, the declared and apparently agreed purpose of these sessions. This problem of dramatistic inconsistency, of course, arises because the researcher had yet to grasp the nature of the purpose for *these actors,* and his puzzlement was a reflection of his own (or his acceptance of the managing director's) formulation of their purpose. An explanation of the apparent inconsistencies could be available to him only through talking to each of the actors individually and discovering, as he did, that each of them was operating within what may be termed a "mystification" of the Scene or setting. For virtually all of them, explanations of their own conduct and that of their peers were couched in terms of the overwhelming impact operating within a "family owned, family dominated" firm had on them. The setting for each (except for the managing director and others who were members of the family) was one in which the most senior positions traditionally had been held by family and, more important, one in which the family policy had been to keep all decision making to themselves. The senior managers' purposes were consistent with this Scene:

> The Heseltines practise management by gossip. . . . promotion and performance appraisal [are] done by members of the family. . . . They seem to decide everything ultimately on a Saturday morning in the privacy of their own homes.

Managers act as individuals since it is widely regarded that this is what the Heseltines *really* desire:

> If you take the three major divisions, the Heseltines run us like a troika. As coachman, John (the Managing Director) climbs up and tries to hold us together but occasionally throws a firecracker down on us just for the hell of trying to hold in three mad horses careering in separate directions.

The family was seen as always having followed a policy of divide and rule, whatever current protestations to the contrary:

> There's no real criticism. You don't rock each other's boats. You hesitate to criticise in front of an employer called Heseltine.

The family set the tone of individual hard work and lack of pretension that has important implications for the conduct of the managers, however senior:

> The family is not recognized as being very people minded. I think they have a Quaker lack of pretension and stuffiness, and as you'd expect, they don't live the high life. . . . They're all shy, diffident, or eccentric in their own way. They don't appear to have . . . the kind of humour where you can laugh easily with them about things. No disrespect intended, but they're as starched and stiff as their Quaker forefathers.

In short, the researcher could see that the managers were able to explain all conduct with reference to the Scene or setting as constituted by the family. The Purpose of the company (from their perspective) was simply to maintain the family in the style to which they had become accustomed; the Acts of the managers (not rocking the boat, sticking to their own patches) were justifiable given that the family really did not desire help, no matter how much individual members might protest to the contrary; the Agency, the group meeting, served only as "a charade, a farce, a pretence at integration" and was treated as such; and the Agents — the managers — performed in line with what they took to be the expectations of important members of the family, though some were very aware of their own parts in sustaining such expectations.

Demystification: A Drama of Consultancy

Continuing with the theatrical metaphor, the conduct of the researcher may itself be characterized as a five-stage process in which he or she acts successively as audience, critic, dramatic coach, dramaturge, and casting director to the enterprise with which he or she is working. To this point in the case study, he or she has acted as audience to the senior managers' performances. Now, as critic, he or she must present an analysis of the scenic mystification that has concealed alternative modes of action in the authoritative consistency it afforded to all explanations and conduct at this senior level. Naturally, this critical analysis implies that there are alternatives for explanation *and* conduct, and willy-nilly the researcher finds him- or herself auditioning for the more or less combined parts of dramatic coach, dramaturge, and casting director. If successful in this audition (and many are not, for success depends as much on a convincing performance as on a credible analysis), dramatistic initiative passes into the researcher's hands. He or she can then test out the cast to find out what kind of dramatic range they have, work up new scripts with them, coach them in their parts (suggesting casting problems and new actors as necessary), and finally cast and coach an internal dramaturge in order to provide the enterprise with some institutionalized protection against new mystifications and him- or herself with a cover for that final exit from this stage.

Demystification, for the Brechtian, it will be recalled, consists of giving the "natural" the force of the "startling," alienating performers from their performances in order that they can view them as something peculiar, striking, and unexpected. Dramatistically, the technique is used to allow the repressed elements of the pentad to return to consciousness.

The researcher attempted to achieve something of the same effect for this group of performers (which included members of the Heseltine family) by convening a two-day meeting, during which time they would be invited to adopt a critical stance to themselves as a group, their purposes, the scene within which they found themselves, and the consequences it had for their actions. Here, the researcher auditioned through his critical comment by presenting his observations, playing extracts on tape of their meetings, and quoting without attribution from the conversations he had held with each of the cast. Gradually, through a process of examination, discussion, argument, and negotiation too complex to document in the space available here, it was acknowledged that there was not a monolithic "family," but rather a collection of agents capable, as was John — the managing director — of acting out a variety of scripts. Consequently, they, as managers, were able to explore the formation of their conduct consistent with the possibilities of their revised conception of the "family" as a collectivity of diverse agents.

As a result of this two-day meeting, the researcher was hired as a coach, dramaturge, and casting director. With a new explanation for the "family" and a consequent agreement on the importance of the weekly managerial sessions, it became possible to work up new scripts, to extend the dramatic range and performances of the managers within them, and to recast those unable to give persuasive life to their new characters. Of course, all this took much time and effort for all concerned; but gradually the old mystification lost its authority and the full range of pentadic explanations and the actions they license was opened to the senior management. The final act of this drama of consultancy — the casting and coaching of an internal dramaturge so as to institutionalize the process of demystification — was not played out, with the researcher leaving the stage prematurely to resist being altercast for the part by the managing director.

RESEARCH APPROACH

This little "report" glosses the process of research: It gives an illustration of how dramatistic researchers work and what they expect to find without going much into detail of research techniques. In a strong sense, this displays a fundamental conviction that human action can be understood without recourse to complex techniques of investigation, much as most theatrical performances make sense to audiences without them doing much more than being attentive. Yet there are more or less experienced theatergoers, more or less competent students of drama and the theater; indeed, there are even persons who combine all these virtues with some guiding aesthetic principle in order to offer critical appreciations. Dramatistic researchers are much like these critics. For our techniques of inquiry (watching, listening, questioning, and so on), we draw on the competences available to any member of human audiences, but we use these as practiced devices to be guided by our understanding of dramatistic principles and the analytic interests stirred up by the theatrical analogy.

How, then, do dramatistic researchers observe? Our primary interest is in interactions, and our first concern here is for language. In other words, our basic data are speaking and not speaking, the way in which such speech and silence are presented, the characters that are and are not constructed in this talk, the time and place of that speaking, and the timings and placements to which it refers. Transcripts, therefore, were prepared from the tapes of the weekly managerial sessions, and these served as the kind of texts that researchers study while developing an understanding of interactions. The notes on performances made by dramatistic researchers are what guide such studies. Of course, these will vary in rigor and insight from researcher to researcher, but it would be a mistake to suggest that just anyone could learn to take helpful, important notes. In addition to experience and dramatistic sensibility, good notes on such performances require critical flair, and that cannot be learned no matter how long the training. Obviously, we cannot all be good theatrical directors or critics. Likewise, we all know that good social science is done by good social scientists: The democracy of science depends on a franchise that is restricted to the able.

Yet, as you will recall in our case study, the researcher was puzzled in his initial efforts to grasp the character of these interactions by the inconsistencies between the stated purposes of the meetings and the kinds of acts and agents it contained. It was this dramatistic puzzle that guided the conversations that took place between meetings, where those who played characters could be encountered as actors and asked for some account of their performances. In these conversations with individual managers, one can discern a process of mutual education where the researcher and the various managers explore what is happening in these senior levels of management and try to work out possible answers to their own and the researcher's puzzlements about the enterprise. From such conversations dramatistic researchers develop confidence in their eventual conclusions and their application to events and situations far beyond observations, or even in their capacity and willingness to observe. The ultimate root of this confidence — our belief that the constellation of data will be a trustworthy resource in which to develop an account of managerial conduct — is in the venturesome character of these interactions and conversations. There are real consequences here for us

all, participants and researchers alike, and little else in life goes so
credibly together as do consequences and truth.

All this, however, says little about the techniques of data analysis
used by dramatistic scholars. Essentially, they are not far removed
from techniques of literary criticism. Critics operate on texts and
performances in order to produce a credible account of the material
that is guided by more or less consistent aesthetic principles. For the
dramatistic theorist, these principles are those of the pentad and the
consistencies that exist among the five elements. It is in seeking to
locate Scenes, Acts, Purposes, and so on, in finding out what links
them, that one is able to present a plausible understanding of the
material; and *plausibility* is the crux of this or any other social scientific analysis. The key issue, here, is for whom the understanding is
meant to be plausible. In our case study, the production of evidence
and the conclusions drawn from that had to be rigorous enough to
evoke belief in an audience composed of the managerial interactants
themselves. This audience offers problems and suggests techniques
of analysis and presentation quite different from the problems and
techniques relevant to an audience of social scientists. Readers will
recall that the researcher staged a dramatic demystification for his
managerial audience wherein he auditioned for dramatistic initiative
with a crafted presentation of self and analysis in which the performance and the evidence were mutually supporting. To present an
analysis of the same material to an audience of social scientists would
require an equally careful assessment of that audience's expectations
and the form in which rigor was to be communicated (see Overington,
1977a, for a treatment of dramatism as a "rigorous" social scientific
method).

But for all that, there must be a question as to how far one goes to
mold one's work and its presentation to an audience. We are aware
that our choice of vocabulary to describe techniques of dramatistic
analysis is bereft of the kinds of words — "sampling," "reliability,"
"validity," "interview," "generalization," and so on — that are more
customary for social scientists. We could have used such words; there
is an audience for such "scientific" performances, but that was not
our purpose. We think it unlikely that most of those who respond
favorably to the conventional melodramas of scientific presentations
will have or want to develop a taste for the Brechtian drama and
Burkean language that constitute our mode for "seeing" organizational conduct. Rather, we have to summon, to invite an audience for
our kind of performance, our kind of language, so that it can become
another kind of scientific presentation.

CONCLUSION

And so we end with talk — and the social sciences are nothing if they are not a form of discourse — about our vocabulary and our sense of audience. Beginnings and ends are important moments for dramatistic analysis, and these concluding remarks are a brief reflection of an essay framed between a vignette of the extermination camps and a display of our commitment to a way of speaking scientifically that celebrates the kinds of relationships we seek, and often find, in our research. "Conversations" are not "interviews," and conversationalists can expect to give and receive a kind and quality of information unknown to interviewers. In this chapter the talk has been about demystification as a process that can be pursued with people in organizations against our sense of the Nazi state as some kind of ultimate form of organizational evil.

We have advocated dramatism as a method of social analysis that allows its practitioners to tell stories about organizational mystifications, and in the process, teach their audiences both how to locate mystifications and to relate persuasive accounts of them. We have expressed our conviction that this works without techniques for collecting information more specialized than those used by competent members of theatrical audiences — that the demystification of organizational life can be achieved by those who live it, given contact with experienced dramatistic analysts. We have argued that confidence in the process is secured by the kind of information that only consequential relationships provide for analysts with sufficient talent — that no technical training can substitute for such analytic flair. Finally, we have adopted a pragmatic criterion of plausibility for judging the merit of dramatistic analysis, insisting on the rights and obligations of specific audiences to establish what should be taken as plausible.

Dramatism is no self-indulgent stance toward the social world: There is little chance to luxuriate in the superiority of one's analytic posture and the revelations it offers. The only mystification Burke and Brecht allow is that of the *necessity* of self-reflective action; we cannot avoid such an unexamined assumption about human action. Without it, to talk of "mystification" or "demystification" would be meaningless: Without it, the Nazis would be incapable of "evil." We would not live in that world.

About the Authors

IAIN L. MANGHAM

I was released from grammar school at the age of sixteen to push a handcart for my father (a house painter). After National Service, I trained as a teacher at an Arts college, Bretton Hall, and discovered Artaud, Evreinoff, Beckett, and Brecht. I studied for an external degree of London University early mornings and late nights and introduced myself to Weber, Simmel, G. H. Mead, Erving Goffman, and the like. I completed a part-time Ph. D. in psychology at Leeds utilizing a dramaturgical perspective to look at interaction in groups; I worked for an American pharmaceutical giant in Italy; I came to the University of Bath in 1973.

I am interested in creativity and the factors that inhibit it within organizations. I remain essentially an Arts man, deeply suspicious of those who claim to advance "scientific" theories of human behavior.

MICHAEL A. OVERINGTON

When I was an undergraduate my teacher, Charles Estus, first introduced me to some of the work of G. H. Mead and Kenneth Burke. I was fascinated, and when I went off to do graduate work in Madison, I took along all of their books that I could lay hands on. During the next five years, in among the various seductions of main-line sociology, I was able to find the time and support to read my Mead and Burke. In particular, I remember one long, midwest summer that was given extravagantly over to a careful reading of Mead and later, during a time that was meant to have been spent on a dissertation about Hugh Duncan, six months luxuriantly devoted to writing a chapter on Kenneth Burke. When I look back on what I have been doing since that time in graduate school nine years ago, I find that my writing has been in two areas that are linked in my understanding by concerns that Burke expresses. One line of work has been to talk about the moral character of scientific communities through a concern for the rhetorical form of their practice. The other has been directly interested in exploring a dramaturgical approach to social life. This chapter is one product of a collaboration that is trying to take seriously all that the theater can offer as a realm of conceptual invention.

15

CRITICAL THEORY AND ORGANIZATIONAL ANALYSIS

John Forester
Cornell University

Critical theory provides an empirically based, practically interpretive, and ethically illuminating account of social and political life. In this chapter, I discuss the assumptions on which critical theory is based and focus on the analysis of organizations as structures of communicative interaction. In order to illustrate the theoretical and practical import of this perspective, I examine how a critical theory of organization might help social actors to anticipate and counter systematic obstacles to their achievement of personal autonomy, social cooperation, and democratic political discourse and influence.

THE ONTOLOGICAL AND EPISTEMOLOGICAL ASSUMPTIONS OF CRITICAL THEORY

At the heart of critical theory is the assumption that human beings can recognize one another as such and shape the course of human affairs as a result of a special inheritance: the capacity of being social or, what investigators like Habermas (1971, 1973, 1975, 1979) analyze and refer to as intersubjective, communicative competence. Only

Author's Note: I would like to thank Dudley Burton, Cathy Campbell, Kieran Donaghy, Ralph Hummel, and John O'Neill for their helpful comments on an earlier draft of this chapter.

because human beings share a repertoire of skills of communicative interaction (language seen as shared practice, following the later Wittgenstein) can they make sense together, whether they then cooperate or fight with, care for or objectify, nurture or exploit one another.

Habermas uses the concept of "communication" to link specific actions (promises, threats, orders, offers, reports, questions, requests, approvals, denials, agreements or disagreements, and so forth) to the structural settings in which those actions take place and are understood by participants to make sense. Communication occurs between particular actors, but in historical contexts that they inherit, yet may also seek to change. The analysis of communication logically requires attention not only to individual speakers and listeners (i.e., the interactors), but also to the structural settings of power, status, and possible domination in which any interaction takes place and has its actual, situated, practical meaning. Critical theory seeks to show the practical, moral, and political significance of particular communicative actions, speech acts (Austin, 1961; Searle, 1969), and nonverbal communications more generally. It also investigates how a given social structure may itself be a structure of systematically distorted communicative actions that practically and subtly shape its members lives.

Critical theory can thus be seen as a structural phenomenology. It is a phenomenology because it attends to the skilled and contingent social construction and negotiation of intersubjective meanings. It is structural because it attends to the historical stage on which social actors meet, speak, conflict, listen, or engage with one another. Ontologically, it marries subjectivist and objectivist positions. Human actors make sense of daily life subjectively, through communicative interaction, but "sense" depends on context or setting — the objective social structure in which those actors work and live. A patient finds a doctor's diagnosis subjectively credible in part because of the objective structure of doctor/patient relations in our society. The same diagnosis offered by a butcher, grocer, lawyer, or passerby on the street would have quite a different subjective meaning because of the objective, social, and political structure of the communicative situation.

Through the analysis of situated communicative actions, critical theory can thus call attention to political and moral aspects of the skilled performances of actors shaping one anothers' lives, and of the institutions and organized settings in which those interactions are framed. By linking understanding of "micro" social actions and practices with a "macro" understanding of settings, critical theory avoids presenting either a structural account of social life lacking concrete social actors, or a methodologically individualist account of social action neglecting the structural settings in which any action makes sense. In this way the critical theorist is able, as Schroyer (1973) has observed, to reformulate the classical Marxist critique of ideology in terms of critique of systematically distorted communication.

Critical theory articulates an ontology and epistemology of historically shaped human beings whose concrete structural and organizational relations work in each instance either to distort or to emancipate citizens' lives. The theory thus provides a foundation for (1) the empirical analysis of communicative interaction and structural settings, (2) the interpretive analysis of meaning, and (3) the normative analysis of systematic distortions and violations of the free discourse of human beings implicit in the most ordinary communication, i.e., in what O'Neill (1974) describes as our most essential "making sense together."

COMMUNICATIVE INTERACTION: SHAPING BELIEF, CONSENT, TRUST, AND ATTENTION

Communicative interaction lies at the heart of social action. More lonely or strategic actions, such as reading a report or competing in a card game with an opponent, or institutionally bound actions such as judicial sentencing or applying an organizational rule, are derivative cases: They rely on prior communicative actions and conventions for their sense, propriety, and identification. Here we will focus on the analysis of communicative interaction as the fundamental type of social action.

The reconstruction of ordinary language use shows that speakers and listeners make and recognize four claims to the validity of what they say and hear. In both the simplest uses of speech ("When's the meeting?") and the more complicated ones ("What right did they have to do that?"), listeners evaluate these four claims:

(1) a *truth claim* referring to the existence of some state of affairs (e.g., the time of day, another's action, someone's presence, and so on);

(2) a *legitimacy claim* to be "appropriately in context," because the same words mean different things in different situations;

(3) a *sincerity claim* that the speaker really means and intends to say what is being said; and

(4) a *comprehensibility* or *clarity claim* that what is said has an ordinarily clear and coherent meaning (when this claim is in doubt we ask, "What do you mean? Would you say that again?").

These four claims derive from what is described as the "double structure of speech," in that communicative interaction involves both *content* and *relationship*. Claims regarding "truth" and "clarity" relate to content, and those regarding "legitimacy" and "sincerity," to relationship of speaker and listener. The distinction emphasizes that human agents are not only intentional in the monological, Husserlian sense (that consciousness is consciousness *of*), but are attentional as well (we are concerned *with*, engaged *with*). Even seemingly innocuous instrumental acts conveying contents, call and direct practical attention as well — they "metacommunicate" politically and morally.

When claims to truth, legitimacy, sincerity, and clarity are ordinarily accepted, they produce specific pragmatic effects. The pragmatic effect of the accepted truth claim is to shape the listener's *beliefs*. The pragmatic effect of the accepted legitimacy claim is to gain the listener's *consent*. Similarly, the effects of accepted sincerity and clarity claims are to shape the listener's *trust* and *attention* (or focus). In simple communicative acts (questions, promises, offers, statements, threats) speakers thus not only utter words; they also shape the beliefs, consent, trust, and attention of those with whom they speak.

This is innocuous enough in many situations. Consider ordering a cup of coffee in a restaurant. We assume, when the waiter or waitress asks, "Do you want some coffee?" that there truly is some coffee to be had, that saying "yes (please)" will legitimately count as a request for it, that we have been asked sincerely, and that we know clearly what the question means. We do not need critical theory to order a cup of coffee. However, in other instances the process may have moral and political significance, because communicative claims are often distorted. Misrepresentation of facts may betray truth claims (e.g., false advertising may be used to shape belief). Abuse of expertise may betray legitimacy claims (e.g., laypersons' consent may be manipulated). Lies may use a sincerity claim in an ironic fashion. Jargon may mystify, not because of the length of the words employed, but because it betrays the implicit clarity claim of ordinary speech, so listeners stand confused wondering, "This is clear? What does this mean?" Cooperation and communication free from domination may be implicit in the most simple acts of speech, yet they are never guaranteed.

Consider, for example, the moral and political significance of a president's vow to remedy inflation by cutting back federal spending for social programs while retaining a "safety net" for the "truly needy." How are we to evaluate and respond to a local official's reiteration and affirmation of such claims? Only the most cynical and politically irresponsible citizen can simply ignore such a question altogether. Here we have political and administrative claims made about (1) the true workings of inflation, (2) the proper and decent, the right ways to respond to these "economic problems," (3) the good faith and sincerity of established leaders, and (4) the clarity of "the problems" to begin with. Clearly, each of these claims might be contested, and each claim pulls in a different direction. There is far more to political rhetoric than words (see, for example, Edelman, 1971, 1977).

At stake here is the pragmatic molding and reproduction of the citizenry's social and political identities, beliefs and knowledge, consent and deference, trust and confidence, attention and sensibility. Ordering coffee may be simple enough; evaluating political, administrative, and professional promises, statements, decrees, warnings, threats, and problem definitions is another matter. Here critical theory may help quite a bit, for it exposes the political and structural production, and the vulnerability, of citizens' (subordinates', workers', womens', students', clients') beliefs, consent, trust, and attention. Revealing the structure of communicative action, critical theory alerts us to the subtle and possibly systematic ways in which social action, and social actors, may be deceived, mislead, manipulated, or mystified. In this way it shows how structures of organized action may function to make legitimate, uncoered political consensus or political discourse difficult to achieve. In addition, the analysis of systematic violations of ordinary claims of communicative interaction points to an important use of power in social organization.

COMMUNICATIVE ETHICS AND THE CONTINGENT RECOURSE TO DISCOURSE

Critical theory suggests that communicative action always involves the anticipation, in principle, of an ideal of uncoered consensus and of nonmanipulated understanding and agreement. As McCarthy (in Habermas, 1975) has noted, this is central to the meaning of speech itself. As he writes,

The very act of participating in a discourse, of attempting to come to an agreement about the truth of a problematic statement or the correctness of a problematic norm, carries with it the supposition that a genuine agreement is possible. If we did not suppose that a justified consensus were possible and could in some way be distinguished from a false consensus, then the very meaning of discourse, indeed of speech, would be called into question.

Speakers and listeners ordinarily presume that the validity claims made in speech can, in principle, be checked. For example, when we doubt that a factual claim is true, we assume that we can, in principle, find out what is true. When we doubt a legitimacy claim, we assume that we *might* justify another position as actually legitimate. We assume when we doubt another's sincerity that we can know in general what sincerity is indeed, and when we are puzzled at another's clarity, we assume, if what is being said makes any sense at all, that clarification is possible. Technically, this means that as listeners we *presume the possibility* (but not the fact) of participating in discourses — social and communicative processes — that might reestablish accepted claims to truth, rightness, sincerity, and clarity, claims on which we could then act.

When communication breaks down, or when we reject a particular claim, we can go on — to the extent that the communication or claim interests us — through discourses that allow us to check the claims that are in question. Habermas argues that our ordinary presumption of discourse is a normative anticipation of a situation we rarely achieve: an ideal speech situation in which all the evidence might be considered, in which all the conflicting rightness claims might be debated without compulsion, a situation in which checking or justification could really be carried out without manipulation. This simply is what we claim when we argue that a statement is (really) true, or that a position is (really) right. We do not mean that listeners can be manipulated to agree that the statement is true or that the position is right. We mean just the opposite: that without manipulation and with the consideration of the evidence and the proper justifications, others could accept without domination (i.e., freely), as social and rational beings, the truth of the statements or the legitimacy of the positions that we claim to be true or right.

This line of argument is of great significance for organizational analysis because it leads us to examine the social structuring of actors' recourse to discourse. When organizations or polities are structured so that their members have no protected recourse to checking the truth, legitimacy, sincerity, or clarity claims made on them by established structures of authority and production, we may find conditions of dogmatism rather than of social learning, tyranny rather than authority, manipulation rather than cooperation, and distraction rather than sensitivity. In this way critical theory points to the importance of understanding practically and normatively *how* access to, and participation in, discourses, both theoretical and practical, is systematically structured.

In addition to studying the systematic distortion of communication and the use of power that this entails, critical theory offers an approach to understanding the structure of organizations. Such an approach would investigate the process by which a particular mode of organization shapes, offers, encourages, blocks, or makes credible criticism and learning (possible forms of discourse) regarding the fundamental communicative claims (truth, rightness, sincerity, clarity of meaning) that constitute its very identity. I have attempted to carry out such a structural phenomenological analysis in several other papers (see, for example, Forester, 1980, 1982a, 1982b). Figure 15.1 draws on this work to illustrate some of the concrete ways that decision making, agenda setting, and felt need shaping are used in the realm of public policy matters to manage comprehension, trust, consent, and knowledge.

When discourse is blocked, the very intersubjectivity and sociality of human beings is threatened: Cooperation is endangered, belief can no longer be grounded, consent cannot be justified, and attention is distracted. As discourse is denied to participants, they are likely to be rendered dependent, powerless, ignorant, and mystified. An understanding of the way an organization helps or hinders access to discourse is of great social and political import, for as Freire has suggested, "Any situation in which some men prevent others from engaging in the process of inquiry is one of violence" (1970: 33).

UNNECESSARY AND ILLEGITIMATE DISTORTIONS

The critical theory of communicative interaction thus has important implications for organizational analysis. If action is understood to be communicative, organizations can be recognized as systematic structures of communicative interaction. Phenomenologically, organizations can be seen as complex, self-reproducing, claims-making structures. If we see that all communicative interaction is constituted by reciprocal claims regarding truth, rightness, sincerity, and clarity, we can also see that organizations not only produce goods and services, but also produce and reproduce their members' knowledge and beliefs, their deference and consent to organizational authority, their trust in limited spheres of social coop-

The Exercise of Power	Effects of Misinformation			
	Comprehension (Confusion/Distraction)	Trust (False Assurance)	Consent (Illegitimacy)	Knowledge (Misrepresentation)
Decisions	Resolutions passed with deliberate ambiguity; confusing rhetoric (e.g., regarding the "truly needy").	"Symbolic" decisions (false promises).	Decisions reached without legitimate representation of public interests but appealing to public consent as if this were not the case.	Decision that misrepresent to the public actual possibilities (e.g., deciding to dispose of nuclear wastes "safely").
Agenda setting	Obfuscating issues through jargon or quantity of "information."	Marshaling respectable personages to gain trust (independent of substance).	Arguing that a political issue is actually a technical issue best left to experts.	Before decisions are made, misrepresenting costs, benefits, risks, true options in the planning process.
Felt needs shaping	Diagnosis, problem definition, or solution definition.	Ritualistic appeals to "openness," "the public interest," and "responsiveness"; the encouragement of dependency upon benign, apolitical others.	Appeals to the adequacy and efficacy of formal "participatory" processes or market mechanisms without addressing their systematic failures.	Ideological or deceptive presentation of needs, requirements, or sources of satisfaction (false advertising, "analysis for hire").

SOURCE: Forester (1982a: 73). Reprinted by permission of the *Journal of the American Planning Association*, Vol. 48, 1982, p. 73.

Figure 15.1 Power, Information, and Misinformation: The Management of Comprehension, Trust, Consent, and Knowledge

eration, and their attention to a selective range of organizational problems and tasks. Organizations produce "results," to be sure, but they also, and more subtly, reproduce the beliefs, consent, trust, and attention of their members and those with whom they interact. They produce and reproduce structures of power, language, and work. This is no less true of a firm that markets products commercially than it is of a hospital or city government administration. The services produced vary enormously, but these organizations nevertheless share a communicative and reproductive structure of social relations that constitutes the basis of their social and political relations of production. Even the most instrumental, apparently neutral, means/ends-oriented action is politically significant, as attention is shaped to necessity and possibility, and hence to hope, cynicism, passivity, and committment.

Thus organizations may do more than simply structure practical communicative claims. They may systematically distort those pragmatic claims on their members' attention. They may misrepresent facts or falsely advertise. They may claim expertise, rights, or authoritative precedent where they have none. They may mislead their clients to protect organizational prerogatives or mislead the public to protect or enhance private gain. As human service organizations, they may distract attention from basic social needs and restrict public agendas to much narrower issues. Medical care institutions, for example, may ironically distract public attention from vital forms of community preventive care. And these organizational distortions may not be deliberate and calculated, but rather an ongoing inheritance, the consequence of a structuring of attention inherent in a given organization's structure. For each of the practical communicative claims made by organizational actors, then, listeners may be subject not only to accidental or naturally necessary distortions or to willful and calculated distortions, but more subtly and politically significant, to socially unnecessary, structurally systematic distortions.

Accidental distortions may be by definition unforeseeable, socially unpreventable, and therefore necessary. Cognitive limits on memory, translation, and precision may produce naturally necessary distortions that are not the result or embodiment of political domination (except where these limits are historically political products resulting, for example, from forced deprivation; then these limits are political products, rather than a reflection of the natural endowment of the human species). Also, a socially cooperative division of labor may produce socially legitimated and perhaps necessary communicative distortions (experts may know more about clients' problems than

Contingency of Distortion	Autonomy of the Source of Distortion	
	Socially Ad-Hoc	*Socially Systematic/Structural*
	I	II
	• idiosyncratic personal traits affecting communication	• information inequalities due to legitimated division of labor
Inevitable Distortions	• random noise	• transmission/content losses across organizational boundaries
	(cognitive limits)	(division of labor)
	III	IV
	• willful unresponsiveness	• monopolistic distortions of exchange
Socially Unnecessary Distortions	• interpersonal deception	• monopolistic creation of needs
	• interpersonal bargaining behavior (e.g., bluffing)	• ideological rationalization of class or power structure
	(interpersonal manipulation)	(structural legitimation)

SOURCE: Forester (1982a: 72). Reprinted by permission of the *Journal of the American Planning Association*, Vol. 48, 1982, p. 72.

Figure 15.2 Bounded Rationality: A Critical-Theoretic Reformulation Distinguishing Types of Misinformation or Communicative Distortion (Bounds on the Rationality of Action)

the clients, e.g., problems of hormonal disorders), but here, social relations are nevertheless domination free because communicative inequalities have been legitimated by all affected. The especially crucial task for a critical social theory is not to assess these types of communicative distortions but rather to assess a remaining type: distortions that are in no sense natural to the species or socially necessary (as a division of labor might be), but that are instead unnecessary fetters to social cooperation and democratic discourse, fetters that perpetuate themselves through the systematic suppression of discourses in which generalizable interests could be freely represented and discussed.

Figure 15.2 provides a framework with which we can analyze the various forms of distortion encountered in organizational settings. For example, as I have suggested in relation to the process of urban planning (Forester, 1982a), all four types are evident in everyday decision making. Figure 15.2 illustrates some of the detailed modes of distortion encountered in urban planning. Analysis of communicative interaction in these terms raises many intriguing questions regarding the way that organizational rationality is, in Simon's (1947) phrase, a "bounded rationality." A careful analysis of the ways that organizational communication may constrain rationality reveals that rationality is indeed bounded, but in ways that are often far from necessary. Some of the constraints on action are often deliberately created as such, or they may be unintended consequences of custom, status, or power relations that are neither inevitable or immutable. This analysis reveals that while certain bounds on rationality stem from factors in Quadrants I and II of Figure 15.2 and are probably unavoidable, other bounds falling within Quadrants III and IV are contingent and mutable, thoroughly social or political. This analysis illustrates the rich potential of a critical organization theory concerned with investigating and revealing the unnecessary constraints distorting rational action with a view to altering them in an emancipatory, democratizing manner.

The critical theoretic analysis of the possible distortions of practical communication is grounded then, not simply and grossly in "the needs of" capitalism or of socialism. The analysis is grounded, more profoundly, and more concretely, in the historical contingency of ordinary human intersubjectivity and understanding. Mediated by language and communication, organizationally structured ideological distortions block citizens' recourse to discourse and cripple political action because they distort citizens' basic abilities to make sense of the situations they face. These practical distortions are disabling, obscuring what is the case, subverting cooperative and reciprocal social relations, claiming legitimacy for the illegitimate, deceiving actors about the truth of events no less than about the truth of what they may do, or whom they become. Because critical theory provides a means of examining how such systematic *institutional* distortions of communication may undermine and threaten our most ordinary sense of what seems to be the case, it provides a provocative, politically and morally illuminating structural phenomenology for examining the nature and consequences of various modes of human organization.

A NOTE ON METHOD

Critical analysis of organization does not call for radically new methods of investigation and research. As is clear from the preceding discussion, the research strategy requires an approach that is both phenomenological and structural. Phenomenological research methods that allow us to be sensitive to the lived experience, interpretations, and understandings of organizational members are central for discerning the way social practices are constructed on an ongoing basis. Structural modes of analysis that allow us to discern the economic, political, and social contexts in which such actions take place are also necessary. The basic stance with regard to both process and context must be interpretive in nature, in that the main objective is to construct the sense of situations from personal and institutional standpoints, through participation, observation, and analysis of contextual data.

In relation to the analysis of decision-making situations for example, files will need to be studied, meetings attended, participants (old and new) interviewed, records checked, and conflicts assessed. The researcher will need to "learn the language" with its range of ordinary nuance and constructions underlying particular modes of verbal and nonverbal expression. As Lukes (1974) and Crenson (1971) have shown, for example, even empirically absent "nondecisions" can be assessed, understood, and explained as a result of particular prior empirical conditions (for example, threats, deference, resistance met with overwhelming power and continually leading to failure; perpetually defeated efforts of particular types; and so on). In addition to many papers in the present volume, the works of Geertz (1973) and Vickers (1965) provide many insights into the nature of the interpretive style required. Giddens (1977, 1979) offers insights into the analysis of "structuration." O'Neill (1972) addresses the issues involved in combining phenomenology with structural analysis, and Dallmayr and McCarthy (1977) survey problems in the use of phenomenological methods in this style of research.

Together these works provide the methodological guidance necessary to engage in a critical style of research that integrates empirical consideration of communicative interaction, practical attention to structured situations of action, and normative attention to the conditions under which actors are able socially and politically to construct their worlds together. As has been shown, while human beings anticipate in everyday speech the potential for cooperative action and democratic discourse free from domination, these goals are by no means guaranteed. The realization of communicative action free from domination is contingent on social and political conditions (e.g., possible tyranny; severe structural inequalities along economic, racial, or sexual lines; a class structure systematically reproducing poverty and exploitation) that may work to suppress, though unnecessarily, those possibilities of cooperation, moral community, and responsible political life that we do actually share as human beings.

Critical theory may help us to recognize, anticipate, and counter those systematic, socially unnecessary distortions of communicative interaction that reproduce domination and so hold us subtly captive. In so doing, it may provide us with an empirically based, interpretively sensitive, and ethically illuminating research program that in turn may deliver to its students the promise of any critical sociological imagination: pragmatics with vision. Where there is no pragmatic analysis, there may be no effective and ethical practice, no improvement. And as Scripture warns, where there is no vision, the people perish.

About the Author

JOHN FORESTER

I write, caught between a rock and a hard place. The laws of history seem to be producing little emancipation; voluntarism and liberalism more generally seem recipes for despair that culminate in victim blaming.

Our traditions, cultures, genders, classes, races, and institutional settings provide deeply taken for granted stages on which we act and make whatever sense we make together. Yet it is we who act toward and with one another: kindly or callously, sensitively or cruelly, forgivingly or unforgivingly. We are practical phenomenologists whether we like it or not. With every utterance we create meaning, in every act of listening we interpret, seek to understand, bring to bear a skilled hermeneutic attentiveness.

So settings make sense of us, and we of them. Understanding *how* this is so seems to be as difficult as it is obvious *that* it is so, and I find the problem abides. It is central to Marx, to Durkheim, to Weber, to Heidegger and Wittgenstein, to Buber — and more recently to Habermas, whose work, I find, insistently charts the common ground, the vision of sociality, of history, and of action, to be found and cultivated here. Through temptation and incentive, vocation and invective, the world makes us; yet we have a little something literally to say ourselves. Perhaps we have only the fragile possibilities of organizing together, addressing injustice; through our daily attention and neglect we reproduce our world, for better or worse.

Actors shaping others' expectations, we are all planners of sorts. Stephen Blum of U.C. Berkeley teaches the most important thing I know about planning: "planning is the organization of hope." It is incumbent upon us all that our planning not be the diffusion, the isolation, the individualization, the disorganization of hope. This is what I try to write about.

16

ANTI-METHOD AS A COUNTERSTRUCTURE IN SOCIAL RESEARCH PRACTICE

H. T. Wilson
York University

In what follows, I propose an alternative way of looking at social science research practices. Instead of viewing these efforts exclusively or mainly as a *means* of acquiring knowledge about social structure and social interaction, I treat these activities and protocols as a *form* of social interaction expressive of certain structural and normative properties endemic to advanced industrial societies.

My inspiration for this point of view is to be found in the phenomenological sociology of Alfred Schutz, in particular in his discussion of the "postulate of adequacy" in an essay titled "The Problem of Rationality in the Social World," originally published in 1943:

> Each term used in a scientific system referring to human action must be so constructed that a human act performed in the life-world by an individual actor in the way indicated by the typical construction would be reasonable and understandable for the actor himself, as well as for his fellow man [Schutz, 1967a: I: 85].

What I propose to do is to *radicalize* or *politicize* this postulate, so that it functions as an alternative mode of *action* for social scientists and their subjects as objects, rather than simply as an epistemological complaint. Thus the emphasis on radicalization. What makes such an effort unavoidably political is the way it mobilizes the observed actors not simply as people who must find type constructions of their action "reasonable and understandable" (following Schutz), but who must *agree* with the social scientific rendition as well, or further dialogue between researchers and subjects must take place.

CONTEMPORARY SOCIAL SCIENCE AS A MODE OF RATIONAL DOMINATION

Social research nowadays is best understood as part of the bureaucratic-meritocratic mode of domination so characteristic of contemporary social life. Whereas in the past rationality and domination could be seen as distinct, if not opposing, notions (see Weber's notion of substantive rationality [1947: 184-186, 211-218], Wilson [1976b, 1981a, 1981b], and Knight [1960]), modern bureaucracy and meritocracy attempt to fuse them. The process of rationalization and world deenchantment of the major religions, as observed by Weber, has increasingly provided a bureaucratic prototype for economic, political, and administrative structures. Indeed, in contemporary social life we are forced, like Weber, to confront the issue of rational domination as a *primary* mode of organization. The celebration of neutrality and objectivity, qualities that are perceived to stem from the posture of the disciplined observer who is somehow not part of what is being studied, provides the basis for the design and occupancy of positions in a stratified social order that displaces earlier forms of social organization reflecting ascriptive criteria like birth, class, ethnicity, and gender (Weber, 1946: 196-244, 1947: 324-353). Bureaucratic values displace traditional values as the foundation of a new order in which certain elements of a society dominate others in and through their control of operative definitions of rationality and normalcy.

Modern social science reflects this wider structure of rational domination in at least three ways. First, and perhaps most obvious, it is based in a rationalized division of labor that draws clear distinctions between lay and professional. Social scientists are professionals within a meritocratic order of stratification and typically hold their position on the basis of technical qualifications that ostensibly reflect their ability to speak authoritatively in relation to an area of knowledge (Collins, 1979; Wilson, 1977: chap. 9). The twin bases on which their prestige, power, and influence are premised are professionalism and scientism. Both are ideologies of expertise based on public deference to the esoteric character of professional (e.g., legal, medical) and scientific knowledge (Wilensky, 1964; Gilb, 1966; Haug and Sussman, 1969). This division of labor institutionalizes a social pattern in which certain individuals are perceived to possess or have access to reason and knowledge while others are presumed ignorant or inferior in this regard.

Related to this point is a second: that modern approaches to social research presume and institutionalize a dependency relationship in which the researcher adopts an exploitative or caretaking attitude toward the subjects of research. Professionalism and scientism, no less than bureaucratic rationality itself, favor an approach to action and decision premised on detachment, distance, and neutrality. These are acknowledged to be the absolutely indispensable bases for relating to subjects, clients, patients, recipients of service and welfare, and so on if the interests of rationality are to be served (Parsons, 1951: 58-67). Combined with this is the seemingly irresistible claim that such postures and protocols are the best guarantee of a high quality of professional competence and service. Here the ideology of professionalism can be seen to merge with scientism, since it is to detachment, distance, and neutrality that we allegedly look for the promise of an objective knowledge of the lawlike behavior of organic and inorganic nature from scientists. Social scientism combines both professional and scientific ideals in its endorsement of *disciplined observation* as the sine qua non without which the production of needed social scientific knowledge is inconceivable. The net effect of this is to turn those being researched into "objects" or "raw material" for an investigation whose main function is to confirm, and occasionally to disconfirm, social scientific hypotheses about them (Marcuse, 1964: 144-169; Leiss, 1974; Wilson, 1977: chap. 3). Even in phenomenological research, where the concern is with studying situations from the member's point of view, the member may still be reduced to an object for research — a *means* of getting to some other end.

Social scientists thus operationalize rational domination by reference to both a scientistic approach based on the idea of a "domination of nature" where nature is passive potentiality, mere raw material, and to a professionalistic approach based on caretaking and a dependent clientele image. In both cases the relation is one of asymmetrical dependence rather than of interdependence. They do not interact as equals. The caretaking role is of particular interest in this regard because the concern for "client" or "subject" may disguise the way that presumed expertise or superior knowledge on the part of the researcher provides the basis for a generalized asymmetry. There may be no attempt on the part of researchers and subjects, for example, to restrict the asymmetry to the issues about which the professional clearly possesses superior knowledge, skill, and experience. To do so, of course, might jeopardize the substantive content of meritocracy itself. Instead of continually assessing individuals in given positions to see whether they ought still to occupy these positions, they are presumed to possess the requisite capacities *because they occupy the positions*. This point is now quite well recognized in terms of the "Peter Principle" (Peter, 1969). In this sense it is apt to characterize many or most meritocratic structures in social science as *formally* rather than substantively rational in the Weberian usage (see Young, 1958, on the problems that arise in trying to honor the *substantive* ideal of meritocracy).

This brings us to our third point: that as a form of social interaction, social science clearly reflects and reproduces the wider social structure in which it is set. Advanced industrial societies produce and sustain the social sciences as activities that they need, and as is apparent from the discussion above, the structure of social scientific activity reflects the wider bureaucratic/meritocratic structure. The processes, practices, and protocols by which the social scientists' own knowledge is acquired are central rather than peripheral to the social, economic, and political reality in which they and their subjects as objects find themselves. The asymmetrical power relationship between social scientist and subject that characterizes the research process is but one aspect of the wider social division of labor. There has been a distinct failure on the part of social scientists to update Durkheim's initial support for a "moral code" among sociologists in favor of normalizing an abnormal (anomic) division of labor in and through established hierarchical channels (see Durkheim, 1952, particularly the preface to the second edition of 1902 and the concluding sections).

The bureaucratic structure of social science appears in modern society as the prototypical ordering structure reconciling authority and knowledge (domination and rationality) in and through the aegis of a full-time salaried career divorced from both legal ownership and any right to appropriate one's position. Meritocracy, the public administrative ideal that supplanted amateurism (England), traditionalism (Canada), or spoils (the United States), underwrites bureaucracy's ascendancy in social science as a key element of the social division of labor in these societies.

Objective knowledge, both esoteric and relevant, is equated with the possession of professional qualifications, particularly where these capabilities are understood to possess a scientific pedigree. Location in some bureaucratic structure has become synonymous with upper-middle- to high-caste status in an order in which work and career values are increasingly the unchallenged basis for asserting and sustaining one's claim to individuality and personhood (Wilson, 1977: chap. 8). Rational domination, however undesirable it may be in substantive terms, quickly becomes little more than a formal requirement once the class- and status-based consequences of the demand for "objective knowledge" make themselves apparent.

Given this state of affairs, it is hardly surprising that modern social science contributes little to the possibility of radical social change. As has been observed elsewhere (e.g., Baritz, 1960; Marcuse, 1964; Wilson, 1973), social science for the most part serves and reinforces the needs of those in power and hence the status quo. The *anti-method* I propose here seeks deliberately to subvert established professional practices in order to respond to the reality of political apathy and collective frustration over austerity and diminished expectations with positive suggestions that will merge nonviolent and incremental processes of interaction with the possibility of significant society-wide impact.

TOWARD A COUNTERSTRUCTURE FOR SOCIAL RESEARCH

Radicalizing the postulate of adequacy begins by underscoring the fact that reason is a property *of being human* and that any professional or scientific training is superstructural relative to this well-distributed human capacity. The fact that actors' *knowledge of the world* and capacity for reason is as much a datum and resource for the social scientist as are their actions is nicely underscored by one of Schutz's corollaries to the postulate of adequacy: "What makes it possible for a social science to refer at all to events in the life-world is the fact that the interpretation of any human act by the social scientist *might* be the same as that by the actor or by his partner" (Schutz, 1967a: I: 85-86; see also Garfinkel, 1967: 262-283). What could better draw attention to the ultimate significance of common-sense capacities for thinking, speaking and reasoning relative to institutional modes of training and certification, than this? From this it follows that the professional/lay distinction only has reference to an asymmetrical surplus of power and status if the professional is able and willing to make his or her social scientific claims comprehensible to the subjects who are the empirical basis for what is claimed. This idea provides the foundation for the counterstructure proposed here.

The task of implementing this proposal is not simply a question of being sure that subjects know what precisely they are being asked to do as respondents, participants, and so on. This is simply normal social scientific practice and has always been taken seriously by competent social researchers because of the obvious "payoff" such an effort promises.

What is at stake here is a second requirement with two parts, namely, that, subjects must (a) understand what social researchers have produced about them in the form of descriptions, explanations, predictions, and so on, but in addition must (b) concur in the results once the social scientist has made clear to them exactly what the results are and what they mean. Thus the research findings must be at the very least acceptable to them as a rendition of the way they are or were behaving, thinking, believing, or feeling.

If these findings are *not* acceptable once subjects have come to understand what descriptions, explanations, and/or predictions have been produced out of their labor as behaving, thinking, believing, or feeling respondents, participants, and so on, then a continuation of the dialogue already begun in (a) must take place. What appears to be a mere means to the appropriation and accumulation of social scientific knowledge virtually (or totally) independent from the research situation becomes a central part of the activity itself. Dialogue has to take place at at least one stage after completion of conventional research efforts.

This is the case even if it turns out that subjects agree with, or find acceptable, the social scientific rendition of their behavior, thoughts, beliefs, or feelings. The reason for this must be clear. Responding and/or participating subjects cannot know whether they agree with the social scientific rendition or find it acceptable until they understand what has been produced out of their labor as respondents and/or participants.

Even if it is discovered that subjects do, after all, understand and thereafter agree with what has been produced about them, this can only be known as a consequence of the dialogue that follows completion and production of the research by social scientists. Every study becomes a panel study, however truncated, as a result of this two-part requirement, and no subject need remain anonymous unless they choose to do so.

This requirement of dialogue and process would not, it is hoped, come to function as a mere "cooling-out" technique or procedure perfected by investigators and "applied" to the research subjects (see Goffman, 1952). To this end, the scales would have to be balanced by giving subjects the right not only to resist descriptions or explanations of them produced by social scientists, but also to write counter-descriptions or explanations of their own wherever they found it impossible to accept the social scientist's rendition.

This "counterstructure" should be published alongside the professional version and accorded the same status and recognition in every other way. These suggestions, I believe, should become a formal requirement of social, behavioral, and administrative research, and ideally should be ensconced in professional codes of ethics, in order to help realize an updated version of Durkheim's (1952: 32-38) desire for sociology as the moral science of society.

The usual problem of enforcement here would, it is hoped, be less problematic because of the awareness of subjects that such formal requirements existed. The ironic upshot is that human subjects might as a result receive treatment on a par with that received by nonhuman research subjects. More significantly, this alternative would overcome the means/end split as it has been institutionalized in the practices and protocols of professional social science. This, as noted, is to a large extent the result of social scientific invocation of both a scientistic and a professionalistic ethos for legitimating their esoteric and more activist concerns and interests.

Instead of taking the form of a detached and neutral study of the way subjects as objects think, feel, believe, and behave, an emancipatory social science like I am proposing would mobilize the research situation as a central element of the society it is determined to investigate and "know," rather than treat it as a mere means to eventual top-down intervention. It would become a central manifestation of an in-process critique that would overcome the spatiotemporal distinction between thought, communication, and change ordained by causilinear reasoning and the disciplined observer.

Perhaps most significantly, it would speak to the limits of meritocracy and legal-rational authority, as they take ideological shape in professionalism and scientism, in the name of common-sense capacities as a *human* resource that is surprisingly well distributed across classes, ethnic and language groups, genders, and cultures. These capacities are thus not simply the logical basis for superstructural modes of knowledge and knowing such as scientific and professional activities, but remain their *phenomenological* basis as well. There is an ongoing *dynamic* relationship between the professional/scientistic superstructure and the common-sense substructure, in the sense that the first presumes and takes for granted human and specific cultural "membership," while the second is continually subject to new "sedimentations" produced by these superstructural institutions (see Wilson, 1982; Freire, 1970).

What makes this proposal clearly and unambiguously subversive is precisely the way its operation undercuts the idea that the manifest function of social research is (or should be) self-justifying in the form of the accumulation of expert and "objective" knowledge. In so doing it points to what only appears to be a preliminary requirement, but in fact constitutes its latent function — communicative equality and reciprocity through the interaction of researchers and subjects.

It is this latter function that could become a key element in any effort at societal reconstruction per se, if only because the research situation already constitutes the basis for new processes and practices aimed at generating expert knowledge through communication. In effect, real process would annihilate the distinction between communication and change altogether because reciprocity would effectively be guaranteed by the formal requirements and stipulations I have suggested.

Such an effort to overcome the sort of distorted communication virtually endemic to the professional/lay distinction as it takes shape in social research operations clearly seeks, as noted, to update Durkheim's now tame demand for a professional "moral code" among sociologists. Whereas Durkheim saw salvation in the very existence of social scientists committed to "normalization" through incremental intervention and reform, I find the stated objectives of "organic" (industrial and civil) solidarity more a *problem* for collective life in the advanced societies than a "solution." Social scientists, in short, have too vested an interest in meritocracy as the basis of a formally rational system of domination.

By refusing to accept the deification of *society* as a synonym for collective life in the way Durkheim did, I unavoidably take issue with the entire normalization project he authorized because its origin really is its goal (society). That this goal *begins in* the commitment to the objective authority of specialists, and professionals in the societal division of labor should serve to underscore the way that intervention and reform can function as a professional, scientific, and bureaucratic *control* on change (see Wilson, 1977: chaps. 1, 2, 5, and 10).

The key to the success of this entire enterprise is to understand the way that a spatiotemporal bias in favor of division of labor presently serves to justify both the professional/lay distinction and a causilinear view that distends communication from change and sustains meritocracy as a form of rational domination whose organizational embodiment is bureaucracy, whose occupational ideal is professionalism, and whose intellectual model is (natural) science.

The formal requirements for carrying out social research stipulated above cannot help but bring many presumptions about superiority and subordination out into the open, if only because social researchers will really have to learn what they might later claim to know "objectively" at first hand. How can social researchers possibly stand in support of undistorted (or less distorted) communication when they rely on deference to professional and scientistic trappings in order to get so much of their "normal" work done?

Without unqualifiedly dismissing participant observation per se, it must be clear from my proposal that the idea of carrying out this and similar types of research without informing the relevant population or universe being researched in advance would violate its commitment to openness, no matter what the researchers' reasons might be. Indeed, anything that compromised the central role of the research situation as an open-ended process in its own right would have to be anathema to my proposal, *no matter from which "side" of the dialogue it emanated*. Thus studies like Garfinkel (1967) and Milgram (1965), as well as more conventional approaches, would be brought into question on this score.

A final point must be mentioned, even though it would clearly water down the impact of the proposal wherever it was implemented. Individuals and groups must be allowed the opportunity to *waive* the conditions set forth in this proposal if they desire to participate asymmetrically as research subjects in ways of which this proposal is on the whole critical. Even if this might eventually result in a microcosmic version of the apathy so central to politics in the "civic culture," where the supreme right *in practice* appears to be the right *not* to vote and participate in political life, a true commitment to openness demands that we acknowledge such an "opting out" procedure and make sure that individuals are aware that it exists.

Indeed, I would argue that it is in this particular decision that free choice as a necessary prerequisite to reciprocity and researcher/subject equality must begin. We must, in other words, not take advantage of any of the already existing asymmetries and inequalities in our zeal to repair them in and through this proposal. This would be tantamount in the final analysis to a new form of caretaking, and has an all too poignant precedent in Lenin's (1916) system of postrevolutionary organization (see also Wolin, 1960: chap. 10).

CONCLUSION

I must now turn to the possibilities for implementing this proposal and the problems that will invariably be associated with such an effort. Taken as it stands, adherence to the postulate of adequacy, and its consequent radicalization in the ways suggested would doubtless put the brakes on much of what passes for sociological research at the present time. As such, it will require from social scientists a significant commitment to the idea of a social science that seeks to free itself from the repressive and distorted communication that underwrites contemporary practices. If I believed that every social scientist were truly committed to a narrowly professional and scientistic approach to their work, I would not hold much hope regarding the possibility of implementation. It is because I believe that progressive humanization is important relative to professionalism and careerism for many social, behavioral, and administrative scientists that I make the proposal and seek in what follows to address what appear to be the key problems in implementing it.

In terms of practical difficulties, there are those that stem from:

(1) *Indifference* on the part of the researched subjects as to what is said about them or what generalizations are reached on the basis of information about them. This might lead them to give their consent pro forma or waive it without thinking.

(2) *Hostility* on the part of subjects that might lead them to deny consent, or to give their consent, only to sabotage the research efforts.

(3) *Ignorance* or *social pressures* on the part of subjects about the nature and purposes of research that would prevent them from engaging in an interactive relation with the researcher or that would lead them to agree to research even when contrary to their interests.

(4) *Hostility* or *indifference* on the part of the dominant "rational" institutions that provide funding, access, and other kinds of institutional support.

(5) *Hostility* or *social pressures* from other researchers or from those who control careers and publishing opportunities.

These factors present real barriers to the achievement of a research practice free from the usual communicative distortions. However, with appropriate support from social researchers who value the objectives the proposal is concerned with achieving, they are by no means insurmountable. By giving due consideration to the issue of developing a "moral code" that systematically attempts to counter repressive and distorted research practice, and with support from the mass media, particularly broadcasting, much could be done to explore the possibilities of establishing many elements of the counterstructure.

The alternative is not an encouraging one, since it involves continued adherence to the reality principle of collective life in the advanced societies, where a generalized sociological rationality is threatening thought and reflexivity with annihilation while seeking to reconstitute practice and discourse in its own image. Too long have we tolerated as acceptable research styles that approach the top-down asymmetry of either dependent factory (and other) employees, as in the human relations movement, or dependent marginals and deviants receiving social assistance or variously suffering under incarceration or constraint (see Marcuse, 1964: 108-114; Jowell, 1975; Wilson, 1973, 1981a, 1981b).

It is the denial of the *priority* of substantive or common-sense capacities for thinking, speaking, and reasoning found in the ongoing procedures and practices of society's dominant institutions that has motivated my attempt to revive the sociological imagination (Mills, 1959) through this critique of, and alternative to, normal "methodical practices" (Becker, 1975) in the social sciences and related disciplines. The idea that reason can be comprehended as a relatively undistributed individual possession of societal members is what makes me feel the need to turn the social research situation to the task of disproving this fact, ideally in the hope that such a dialogical approach might thereafter become an important fact of life in society's dominant institutions as well.

It is the commitment to merging revolutionary with piecemeal efforts by giving scope to the latent as well as the manifest functions of social research that clearly marks out this proposal. I want to begin "locally," taking the established structure of the advanced societies as a working given, while encouraging both general and specific critiques even though I "understand" that it is precisely the real relation between the social sciences and society that necessitates "normal" social research and compels us to acknowledge its central role.

I believe that this proposal could make it possible for us to realize the "openness" so often professed to be an ideal of the social sciences (e.g., Popper, 1945, 1957). The basic principles of inquiry and research on which the methodical practices of the social sciences are presently premised clearly violate this ideal. Popper's understanding of the nature of an "open society," for example, is transparently two-faced because of its closed, even repressive, attitude toward thought and thinking about social matters. The view of social science as social technology that pervades Popper's work merely reflects dominant ideology and institutional practice (see also Knight, 1960; Wilson, 1976b, 1977, 1979, 1981b).

It seems to me that the refusal of social scientists to take this proposal seriously would only serve to draw attention to the hollowness and hypocrisy of their alleged concern for improved practice in the advanced societies. Such demurrals would allow "institutional complexity" to front for vested interests, thereby becoming a permanent barrier to new beginnings like the one suggested here, and would aid and abet the problematic trends already alluded to.

Any conclusion to such an analysis and proposal needs to reaffirm the fact that we have here the possibility of a significant new beginning in the attempt to confront seriously our shibboleths regarding dialogue, reciprocity, rationality, and openness as ideals in general. If we are serious as social scientists about what we claim we care about regarding the matters under consideration here, then the idea that these disciplines can continue in their professional and scientistic postures as handmaidens of established institutions and authorities must be brought into question. After all, what is the point in accumulating such knowledge at all if its accumulation is seen to be a function of attitudes and orientations that deny or render nugatory the very goals allegedly valued by those who engage in the effort?

About the Author

H. T. WILSON

Though trained in political science and constitutional law, I quickly left these fields on arriving in Canada from the United States in 1967. In one sense I had left behind me my dissertation on American broadcast regulation. In another sense, however, I was only moving to more theoretical concerns that had always been of interest to me even in my most "practical" moments.

Since 1970 I have sought to carry our research in the spirit of Max Weber, with his commitment to analysis of the three key institutions of modern Western civilization — capitalism, experimental science and science-based technology, and the rule of law and modern bureaucracy. In addition, however, I have sought to extend, both affirmatively and critically, Weber's theory of social science, with his conern for concepts, frameworks and methods. Until recently this took the form of applications of the thinking of first-generation critical theorists, particularly Adorno and Marcuse. These concerns have been complemented since 1977 by an effort to integrate the work of Wittgenstein into an analysis of the relation between tradition and innovation.

During the past year, I have concentrated increasingly on political science and political analysis, in particular, an attempt to bring to public notice the changing nature of the newly emerging public sphere in advanced industrial societies. The present essay points to the social scientific research situation as a form of social interation rather than a neutral means for studying it at a distance. As such, it constitutes one significant, if unexpected, opportunity to extend and reformulate our conception of a possible public sphere in these societies.

17

SYNTHESISM

A Case of Feminist Methodology

Lynda M. Glennon
Rollins College

Among the many issues feminism is said to address, I would place "dualism" as central (Glennon, 1979). At base a socially constructed categorization that has come to be considered "lawlike," this dualism has many variations, both philosophical and practical. These include: head/heart, reason/emotion, fact/value, mind/body, public/private, self/other, objective/subjective, individual/collective, work/play, industry/domesticity, left-brained/right-brained, and normal/paranormal, to name just a few. The culturally specific connotations of "masculine/feminine" as opposite categories is, then, but one more variation on the dualism that pervades everyday life and thought.

In confronting the issue of male and female roles, therefore, feminism takes on all the dualistic presuppositions that underlie social life. The woman question goes beyond such strictly gender-based concerns as sexism and male supremacy to the center of what many consider to be a major crisis of modernity: the all-pervasive dualism of thought and action that splits our rational and emotional selves and demands that our public and private lives be kept strictly separate.

It appears to me that there are four different foci within the feminist movement, and although all four confront dualism either explicitly or implicitly, each does so in a singularly different way. Each is founded on a cluster of assumptions about humanity and society that hold together as a package. I consider these clusters "ideal types" in the Weberian sense in that they are composites of qualities extracted from concrete feminists' writings and conversations, yet they are not meant to correspond exactly with any one given person or group. I have named the four Instrumentalism, Expressivism, Synthesism, and Polarism (Glennon, 1979). These names have been selected instead of the more commonly recognizable ones of Masculinism, Femininism, Androgynism, and Anatomism in order to try to break apart the automatic linkage of "masculine" with rational ("instrumental") and "feminine" with emotional ("expressive") categories, since I see the habit of linking gender with behavioral oppositions as a symptom of the problem with which feminism is concerned. For this reason, "Synthesism" makes more sense than "Androgyny" (itself derived from Greek roots for "male" and "female") even though the two are both concerned with the fusion of oppositions.

In the sections that follow I will discuss aspects of dualism, describe the four feminisms just mentioned, and then focus more sharply on Synthesism as the feminist type that has the most radical solution in transforming dualistic into dialectical social organization. All of this will serve as the prelude to a discussion of Synthesism's program for research methodology and the study of social organization.

DUALISM: THE HEAD/HEART ISSUE

Almost all descriptions of modernity share the view that a dominant trait of our social life is the split between the emotional and the rational and between our public and private selves (Berger et al., 1973; Brittan, 1978). The fact that we are seldom the same people at home as we are at work has been noticed by most social commentators, if not by most people who declare "I'm not really me" when at work or the "real me" can be found at home relaxing. Such bromides as, "Don't mix business with pleasure," and "When you work, work: when you play, play," abound. Home and work life are separated, and the line between fun and seriousness clearly drawn. We have all absorbed folk wisdom that ranges from "Surgeons cannot operate on members of their own families," to "Husbands should not try to teach their wives how to drive," all intended to prove that only bad can come of mixing the rational and the emotional. Teachers, nurses, and social workers are warned to avoid emotional involvement with their charges. The mass media are pervaded by the assumption that family life and work are incompatible. Television provides example after example of this dualism, particularly as a form of sex ideology in commercials, dramatic series, and situation comedies. Proverbs, poetry, philosophy, cartoons, and jokes do the same. Females are portrayed as emotional, passionate, and intuitive, yet illogical and fickle. Males are said to be rational: analytical and productive but also insensitive and impersonal.

While everyone seems to agree that both the rational and the emotional aspects of life are needed if we are to survive, throughout history philosophers have puzzled over their relationship. Some propose that the relationship between head and heart is a dialectical one, with the two bound together in a unity, each acting back on the other. Others propose a dualistic relationship: an either/or state of affairs wherein if one comes into play, the other vanishes. In much social research, the dualistic vision dominates. Taking their cue from Parsons (1951), sociologists often propose that expressive (emotional) and instrumental (rational) activities fall along a polar axis. It is argued, for example, that in small groups these two functions need to be performed by separate individuals who work in sequence in their separate specialties to keep the group moving ahead with tasks and to maintain a sense of solidarity and good will (Parsons et al., 1953). It is also argued (Parsons and Bales, 1955) that families require similar role specialization in order to remain in equilibrium. Since the mother has a prebirth connection with the child, she is viewed as taking up expressive leadership, with the father, almost by default, being left to take up the instrumental requirements. This structural basis (not biological principle), which Parsons considers socially necessary, is his foundation for sex role duality. Socialization cements the outcome in that children generalize to all females and males the expressive and instrumental specializations they experience with their own parents.

If established sociologists proclaim it inevitable that reason and emotion be dualized and that it is structurally impossible for a family to endure without a male/female dichotomy, can there be in fact any escape from dualized sex roles? According to Parsons and colleagues, no, but according to feminists, yes. As a point of critique, I have selected Parsons's very terminology in naming two of the feminist types found in my research in order to question the foundation of dualism in Parsons's own terms.

Feminists believe that sociologists who take dualism as a given are simply drawing on their own experience in the everyday world, where most of the reality we experience (or observe) has reason and emotions theoretically and practically in opposition and dualized into either/or compartments. In effect, they are taking a specific, historically relative condition — dualism, which probably evolved along with the structures of Calvinism and capitalism—and proclaiming it a *law* of human nature and social structure. These proclamations in themselves help perpetuate the very reality of dualism and give further weight to the status quo. If we go on describing in lawlike terms what we find in the social world (the relative "is"), say feminist critics, we, in fact, will have soon *created a law* (the inevitable absolute) by removing from our consciousness any possibilities for considering alternatives.

The four types of feminism I found in the feminist movement all address the questions "Who am I?" "What does it mean to be human?" and "What is the good society?" These are, of course, questions that plague everyone in modern society, and so these "ideal types" are generalizable to those other people and groups who are challenging the dualistic status quo.

THE FOUR TYPES OF FEMINISM

Instrumentalism. In addressing these larger questions of world view and meaning, Instrumentalism posits that humans are most authentic when rational, productive, and individualistic. It solves the marginality problem of being caught between opposing demands to be both rational and emotional by eliminating the expressive, private sphere altogether. Dualism will be replaced by an instrumental "monism."

Expressivism. Here, the assumption is that the only path to happiness lies in one's emotional life. The exact opposite to Instrumentalism, Expressivism posits that communal, spontaneous relationships are the only legitimate ones; the ideal human is warm, supportive, and nonmanipulative. This ideal type would change the formula that equates present female expressivity with inferiority and make it the superior orientation. It would "expressivize" all people, males included. In other words, females are not to adjust to the dominant instrumentality at all. On the contrary, males are to change into expressive beings and, having no more carriers, instrumentality will thus eventually wither away. A mirror image of Instrumentalism, this second ideal type would destroy dualism and its attendant marginality by completely eliminating the undesirable orientation.

Synthesism. This ideal type rests on assumptions that the ideal human is a dialectical fusion of reason and emotion and that any division of self into roles is dehumanizing. It advocates the total reorganization of society to eliminate division of labor as we know it, requiring change of both females and males, each having to integrate within the orientation that was thought of as the preserve of the "opposite" sex. The private/public dualism will disappear in the utopia envisaged.

Polarism. The fourth ideal type posits an essential difference (for some biological, others ontological) between females and males. Some polarists maintain that the true female and male "principles" have yet to be discovered and given concrete form in any given society. Polarism does away with the marginality struggle by eliminating the caught-betweenness felt by women who have no clear-cut, liberated definition of what it means to be female. Polarism keeps the notion of duality intact — instrumentality and expressivity are still irreconcilable — but it proclaims that both females and males must find their true gender essence and leave behind the caricatured roles that pass for femaleness and maleness in sexist society.

The first two of these "feminisms" reflect the society-wide tendency toward the one-dimensional solution wherein one of the oppositions overwhelms the other in zero-sum fashion. Polarism's conservative solution seeks a more clear-cut dualism than is experienced presently. It is Synthesism alone that has the genuine "radical" solution, proposing alternatives not yet thematized in present-day society but in sync with some of the society-wide searchings for the "new paradigm" (Ferguson, 1980; Talbot, 1981; Watts, 1975). All four of the ideal types described can and do exist in cognitive tension in any one person or group, over time or at the same time. Thus any given feminist is likely to exhibit aspects of the synthesist type, now to be described in fuller detail.

SYNTHESISM IN THE EVERYDAY WORLD

Well-roundedness, ambivalence, and marginality are not the same things as Synthesism because they rest on either/or ideas about the rational and the emotional. Synthesism stands in complete opposition to this duality of head and heart. But how can instrumentality and expressivity be experienced at the same time when all our observation seems to indicate that the two are inherently incompatible? The Synthesist reply is that the two may be blended in a dialectical union whereby each infuses and transforms the other. Instrumentality gives a hardness and a crispness to expressivity, which in turn gives a softness and resilience to instrumentality. The reciprocal acting back on each other is carried on in a continual process of dialectical becomingness. The kind of person Synthesism considers ideal is one whose warmth infuses her or his drive and whose strength gives substance to her or his gentleness. She or he reconciles the two opposites in such a way as to inspire *and* soothe at the same time all those interacting. The extremes of instrumentality and expressivity are abolished; hardness and softness transcend one another, creating an entirely new unity.

Although few people can be found who are in this kind of synthesis, we see examples of this scattered here and there in our social world. Synthesist feminists refer to the many preliterate hunter-and-gatherer tribal societies (for example the Tasaday people of the Philippine rain forests) that have no way of linguistically distinguishing between work and play to show that it cannot be a law of human or social nature to dualize the public and private. Others point to traditional societies as examples of the lack of a gulf between work and home life. Even in present-day society, they find models that challenge the taken-for-grantedness of dualism. For example, in crisis, powers of compassion and productivity may reciprocally infuse one another, giving a unity never dreamed possible (witness the remarkable feats where mothers are able to lift automobiles to free their children). Some find such a fusion possible in those transcendental experiences in individual or group athletic activities in which the mind/body, self/other, and rational/emotional dichotomies are abolished. Others find a fusion possible in sexual love, which at its best moments obliterates the distinction between self and other. Some find still other examples of a fusion of the rational and emotional in collective work — political, religious, or communal — where the individual/group goals are united and the public-me and private-me distinction is overcome, and in charismatic leadership — the teacher who is loved by students and so manages to help them bring forth their most creative work, the doctor whose devotion to patients' emotional needs gives fullness to necessary medical skills, the boss who inspires employees to go all out because of the emotional tie between them, and the lawyer whose personal involvement with clients and issues enhances legal skills.

To give further evidence that synthesism is plausible, feminists of this type cite the Black woman and the single parent as concrete models of an expressive/instrumental union. The Black woman for the worst possible reasons was forced to develop her instrumentality while holding onto her expressivity. Single parents of all races find that role specialization is impossible since there is only one person to take on the two leadership roles. Until quite recently, the sociological establishment diagnosed both Black and single-parent families as being dysfunctional — they could not dualize instrumental and expressive orientations in two parents the way the model of the nuclear family required. In the last few years this indictment has been challenged and the Black family and single-parent family are looked at not as deviants but as models for change. Some Black women and single parents do keep the two orientations separated in dualistic fashion, some feeling well-rounded, others feeling nearly frantic. But some such parents do manage to approach synthesis, emerging with a stamina that infuses gentleness, a spine that gives shape to resilience, and a sensuousness that softens efficiency.

At bottom, synthesism sees in human nature a dialectical unity that transcends the distinction between male and female, since both sexes share the same existential conditions. Simone de Beauvoir captures this essential unity in the following terms:

> The fact that we are human beings is infinitely more important than all the peculiarities that distinguish human beings from one another. . . . In both sexes is played out the same drama of the flesh and the spirit, of finitude and transcendance; both are gnawed away by time and laid in wait for by death, they have the same essential need for one another; and they gain from their liberty the same glory [1961: 685-686].

The male/female duality violates the wholeness of human nature, splitting us into either/or half-people. Society does not allow us to express our total humanity, so we end up trying to experience vicariously our lost selves through the "opposite" sex. The following scenario embodies the logic that unity must be sought in ourselves, not in an opposite:

> He is playing masculine. She is playing feminine. He is playing masculine *because* she is playing feminine. She is playing feminine *because* he is playing masculine.
>
> If he were not playing masculine, he might well be more feminine than she is — except when she is playing very feminine. If she were not playing feminine, she might well be more masculine than he is — except when he is playing very masculine.
>
> So he plays harder. And she plays — softer. . . .
>
> He desires her for her femininity which is *his* femininity, but which he can never lay claim to. She admires him for his masculinity which is *her* masculinity, but which she can never lay claim to. Since he may only love his own femininity in her, he envies her her femininity. Since she may only love her own masculinity in him, she envies him his masculinity.

The envy poisons their love.

He, coveting her unattainable femininity, decides to punish her. She, coveting his unattainable masculinity, decides to punish him. He denigrates her femininity — which he is supposed to desire and which he really envies — and becomes more aggressively masculine. She feigns disgust at his masculinity — which she is supposed to admire and which she really envies — and becomes more fastidiously feminine. He is becoming less and less what he wants to be. She is becoming less and less what she wants to be. But now he is more manly than ever, and she is more womanly than ever. . . .

So far, it has all been very symmetrical. But we have left one thing out. The world belongs to what his masculinity has become. The reward for what his masculinity has become is power. The reward for what her femininity has become is only the security which his power can bestow upon her. . . .

She is stifling under the triviality of her femininity. The world is groaning beneath the terrors of his masculinity [Roszak and Roszak, 1969: vii-viii].

Polarization, envy, resentment, denigration, further polarization, and absolute power imbalances are the results of sex role duality; this is the sequence that follows on the heels of sexual duality. Our essential unity violated, we try to recover our lost half by bonding with the opposite sex but end up fearing and hating our opposites, resentful that they can be what we cannot. As de Beauvoir (1961: 685) has noted, the war of the sexes is really a war within the self.

Synthesist feminists say that sexual dualism brutalizes both males and females, but that women suffer more as the powerless, trivialized bottom of the hierarchy. Males have to put up with alienation from self and from the opposite sex, just as females do. But females, treated in a subservient way, are made to feel inferior. In addition to the scorn females receive for embodying that part of human nature that males are not allowed and by which they feel simultaneously attracted and repulsed, females are further vilified because they encapsulate the dreaded expressivity the whole society considers inferior. Women truly then become "other" and not just "opposite." Intent on maintaining the "macho" image, the male pretends and asks the female in turn to pretend that he is the "ideal" male:

Man is concerned with the effort to appear male, important, superior; he pretends so as to get pretense in return; he, too, is aggressive, uneasy; he feels hostility for women because he is afraid of the personage, the image with which he identifies himself. What time and strength he squanders in liquidating, sublimating, transferring complexes in talking about women, in seducing them, in fearing them! He would be liberated himself in their liberation. But this is precisely what he dreads. And so he obstinately persists in the mystifications intended to keep woman in her chains [de Beauvoir, 1961: 677].

Males need liberation, too, say Synthesist feminists, but their power and privilege mystify their oppression and keep them from seeking that change in the status quo, to release them from pretense and hostility and give them back to themselves.

SYNTHESISM AND RESEARCH STRATEGY

In the conduct of social research, Synthesism questions the dominant positivist paradigm, which is founded on dualistic presuppositions. Gone is the exclusive emphasis on the instrumental/rational ethos reflected in such patterns as the strict separation of fact and value and the detachment of researcher from subject and context (value neutrality). Gone is the exclusive use of measurement by quantitative instruments that serve the canons of operational validity and replicability in the interest of prediction and control, as well as the emphasis on linear, analytical logical style (left-brained thinking). The hierarchy of knowers that dichotomizes layperson and expert disappears, along with all modes of interacting in the research setting that foster such a hierarchy — no hidden agenda or secret research purposes are allowed, no distinction between scientific and everyday language.

These patterns, however, do not entirely disappear. To achieve such a goal would be the Expressivist solution to the confusions of dualistic caught-betweenness. Synthesism instead brings these patterns together with their oppositions and in so doing, creates new forms of investigation. Synthesist methods would include passion, affection, advocacy, experiential embeddedness, intuition, diffuse process, communalism, consensual procedures, cooperative interaction, and emulative communication (wherein one reflects, supports, and extends the content of the other's communication instead of criticizing, analyzing or judging it; see Bernard, 1981; Miller, 1976; Schaef, 1981). Synthesism is founded on dialectical premises that reject "the law of the excluded middle" in positivism's Aristotelian logical base. Thus the idea that a thing can be either A or non-A, which leads to the whole dualizing tradition, is replaced in Synthesist logic with Hegelian-based notions of both/and possibilities. In the words of Lefebvre, dialectical logic presupposes that "there is something more in every idea. Nothing is wholly or indisputably true; nothing is absolutely absurd or false. Each thesis is false in what it asserts absolutely but true in what it asserts relatively; and it is true in what it denies relatively (its well-founded criticism of the other thesis) and false in what it denies absolutely" (Lefebvre, 1968).

Synthesist research attempts to redress the imbalance reflected in contemporary positivism. As Bardwick (1974: 62) has noted:

> There is developing a realization that we have accepted, institutionalized, indeed, deified a mode of analyzing, thinking, and perceiving that distinguished between the conscious and the unconscious, mind and body, rational and emotional. We pay homage only to the conscious rational mind. That is personally costly and a terrible distortion of reality. The cry within the sciences to open up what one can see by admitting as data that which one feels, to place emphasis on the whole of the experience instead of the measurable parts is a rejection of the limitations of a scientific, masculine reality and an acceptance of the need for the addition of the holistic feminine.

Grafted together in a holistic unity (a task by no means easy or immediately realizable), these oppositions would transform one another. The closest research practice that incorporates both extremes is that of "participant observation," which combines the polarities of knower and known in a possible simultaneous transcendence. As Campbell (1982: 23) has noted, this provides the basis for a cooperative, consensual, equalitarian mode of feminist scholarship that creates an alternative way of knowing the world insofar as it unites woman as object of study with woman as subject of study. "It rises up against the norm of pseudo-objectivity which precludes knowledge through experience and insists that we can be at once knower and known. . . . Feminist scholarship makes a whole of emotionality and rationality. It is holistic." Research in this mode is collaborative, with the researcher and those being researched joining together in the enterprise, both learning from and sharing with each other (see Cook, 1980; Easterday et al., 1977; Eichler, 1980; Gould, 1980; Millman and Kanter, 1975; Smith, 1981, for further methodological guidance). This kind of research often emerges when female researchers interview mothers and housewives about matters that are personally troublesome (e.g., social isolation, child-rearing practices). Oakley (1981) describes in some detail the dilemmas she encountered in the practice of social research, particularly in one-to-one interview situations, until she realized that her own personal involvement was indeed central, productive, and to be thematized throughout all of social research. Thus a Synthesist approach would encourage the asking of questions by the interviewee of the interviewer such as "What would you do in my situation?" at the very least. In the more utopian version, there would be no dichotomization of interviewer/interviewee roles.

Because all feminists, no matter which of the four ideal types is involved, share certain base assumptions in seeing present-day gender arrangements as detrimental to women who must struggle together to change things, certain advocacy stances are likely for all four types. Smith (1979), for example, stresses the need to develop a sociology *for* women that would have as its primary concern the exposure of conditions that are harmful to women's full self-development as perceived by the feminist scholar-participant. Smith (1981) also proposes, in Synthesist style, the development of the method of "Institutional Ethnography," which stems from the ways in which women come to understand the world. This method unites the experiential level of understanding of life in the everyday world with large-scale social structures, thus combining micro- and macro-levels of analysis. She uses the example of how walking one's dog, being careful to control its meandering, can lead to a grasp of the notion of private property rights, capitalist social formation, and similar macrostructures.

In similar fashion, a Synthesist feminist would be acutely aware of the interplay of macro- and microstructures, seeing the two in an interpenetrating unity. In this way, face-to-face situations create and sustain large-scale social arrangements. In an organizational setting this means that one would be sensitive to the ways in which, for example, social class structures are reproduced in terms of linguistics, demeanor, tastes in leisure and food, and so on. One would also be observant of how, say, the instrumentalization of structures in the public realm is a reciprocal of how people arrange their personal, everyday lives. Thus the orderly, taxonomic styles in bureaucratic structures (Berger et al., 1973) can be found in one's own bathroom medicine cabinet, kitchen recipe holders, and spice racks, to name but a few instances. Those who decry systems "out there" must begin to see that they hold in place because of the reality "in here."

Given full rein, Synthesism would restructure the world of work so that the instrumental-rationalistic goals would be joined with the expressive patterns mentioned previously: communalistic, cooperative, emulative, nonhierarchical, personalized ways of interacting. The fusion of these two oppositional modes would result in a new kind of structure that abolishes strict division of labor and does more than add separate stroking activities such as company picnics, human potential training, psychotherapeutic services, and office joke contests to existing arrangements. The slogan "business is business" would be rendered meaningless. The image of "me at work" (productive and instrumental) and "me at home" (relaxed, expressive) would fuse into an undivided "me." There would be no parceling of oneself into this or that specialized role because there would be no specialized roles (whether occupational, gender-based, age-graded, ethnic, racial, religious, and so on).

Synthesism believes that expressivized productivity will be created by, and will in turn create, a nonspecialized, unplanned, organic process. All of life will be a continual, becoming, unfolding dialectical process. Work will be integrated with laughter, anger, joking, and inspiration in a flowing ongoingness without having specialized roles emerge for worker, joker, stroker, or executive. For this feminist ideal type — "the personal is political" — is a truly revolutionary call for the end of dualism.

About the Author

LYNDA M. GLENNON

I was raised in a blue-collar Irish neighborhood in New Haven, Connecticut. A series of encounters between town and gown (Yale University, that is) quickened my interest in the social differences that separate people. In junior high I became the leader of the Black Rebellion Girl's Club, modeled after Marlon Brando's gang in *The Wild Ones,* but by my senior year in high school I was both captain of the cheerleaders and class salutatorian. At the promptings of my teachers I applied to college, where I majored in sociology to try to begin to make sense out of the apparently permanent social marginality in which I found myself located. After a career there that alternated between being president of the debate club and the reigning Bohemian of the college, I entered graduate school and stopped after earning my Master's in sociology to teach for several years, convinced that the predominant quantitative emphasis in sociology ruled out my interest in doctoral studies. In the late sixties I discovered a different kind of sociology at the New School for Social Research, and to this time I have been interested in attempts to synthesize the two paradigms represented there: phenomenological and critical studies. This concern has figured in several contexts. I have been examining the perceived dualities of instrumental (rational) and expressive (emotional) orientations as they appear in social thought and social arrangements in family, sex roles, media, popular culture and paranormal studies. I have also been searching out paradigmatic alternatives to dualism in Western and Eastern social thought.

— 18 —

INITIATING COLLABORATIVE INQUIRY

William R. Torbert

Boston College

This chapter documents and discusses the first eighteen months of an institutional self-study within a school of management. It begins with a description of the notions about human being, human doing, and human knowing that underlie self-study. As a whole, the chapter is intended to serve as an invitation to the reader to consider bringing this process of self-study to his or her own life and institutional setting.

The general claims the chapter makes are: (1) any administrator optimally exercises and balances four kinds of leadership, of which one kind is encouraging a continuing institutional self-study process; (2) continuing self-study is necessary if any institution is to become increasingly effective over the long run (7 to 21 years); but (3) current models of personal learning, institutional effectiveness, and scientific methodology obscure rather than illuminate the self-study process described here.

Author's Note: I deeply appreciate the critical receptivity of members of the Boston College School of Management faculty who are participating in the exploratory phases of the research reported in this paper. I wish to thank particularly Professors Aragon, Bartunek, Bowditch, Fisher, Keyes, Kugel, Murphy, Neuhauser, Van Tassel, and Viscione for their varied kinds of help in conceptualizing, organizing, conducting, and criticizing the research activities reported here. I also wish to thank all of them, and Keith Merron as well, for their comments on an earlier draft of this chapter. A more detailed version of the findings reported here can be found in "Initiating an Institutional Self-Study," a Boston College School of Management working paper.

At the same time, positive notions of administrative leadership, organizational effectiveness, and scientific research presented below begin to address the following general, interrelated dilemmas:

(1) Is there a kind of self-knowledge (either on the individual or the organizational scale) that is objective rather than merely subjective, that illuminates previously hidden core assumptions rather than merely multiplying the amount of superficial information to be digested, and that facilitates increasingly effective action rather than generating self-consciousness, unproductive conflict, depression, and paralysis?

(2) Is there a kind of social science that relates directly to the requirements for synthesis, timing, and commitment inherent in intentional action; or is social science necessarily restricted to the values of analysis, timeless theory, and detachment?

(3) Is there a viable, nonviolent process of individual, organizational, and social change from the inside out; or is external change agentry (whether we speak of consultants, market pressures, media exposes, law enforcement, or revolutions) the only realistic vehicle of social change?

(4) Is there a general way of defining, measuring, and increasing individual or organizational effectiveness that works in such a way as to expose, test, and resolve tensions about what constitutes genuine effectiveness; or are different criteria of effectiveness necessarily hostile to one another, necessarily the "property" of different constituencies, and necessarily local rather than general in applicability?

(5) Can schools of management become leading-edge models of organizational effectiveness and of social scientific inquiry, simultaneously influencing the worlds of business, education, and science, such that the field of management becomes a "major" profession like law or medicine; or is management merely an art and its related disciplines merely unsystematic applications of purer sciences?

HUMAN BEING

The predominant organizational context of our age, whether we are speaking of capitalist, socialist, or Communist countries, is bureaucracy. Bureaucratic theory is based on the assumption that human beings possess "limited rationality" and are capable of making instrumental, "satisficing" choices among a few concrete alternatives, but are not capable of constituting the universe of choices to begin with or of arranging outcomes to maximize values (March and Simon, 1958). The hidden elitism of the theory reveals itself when one recognizes that the theory is itself an instance of constitutive thinking. Bureaucratic theory prescribes role definitions for organizational members that limit their concern to issues of efficient implementation of purposes taken as givens. By so restricting members from the regular practice of constitutive thinking, of experimenting with their own behavior, and of attending to possible incongruities among intuition, theory, practice, and effects, bureaucratic organizing creates a self-fulfilling prophecy, tending to make the proposition about persons' limited rationality statistically true even if it is not true in principle.

Existing research shows that bureaucratic organizing is both ineffective at translating abstract purposes into outcomes (Warner and Havens, 1968) and inefficient (Argyris, 1957; Gouldner, 1959; Merton, 1957). At the same time, the turbulent conditions of the cybernetic-electronic age themselves work against the bureaucratic perspective. Reorganizations (e.g., acquisitions, product diversification), technological change, radical shifts in the political-economic environment, and fads, facts, theories, and paradigms that succeed one another with ever-increasing rapidity in the information environment all threaten existing personal and organizational self-definitions and explications of purpose that may have been timely only a year or two previously. Consequently, there is considerable "real-world," "objective" reason for hoping that human being is not, by and large, limited to instrumental, "satisficing" rationality and action. But is there any "real-world," "objective" basis for believing that human being is self-transformable into something more than satisficing being?

The cognitive developmental tradition in psychology (Kegan, 1981; Kohlberg, 1972; Loevinger, 1976; Piaget, 1936) is one source of theoretical and empirical support for the notion that human beings can repeatedly reconstitute themselves and the world about them throughout their lifetimes. But the still more challenging question is whether human beings can develop an attention capable of intentionally increasing personal or institutional effectiveness. To do so, one's attention must become capable simultaneously of: (1) spanning the realms of intuition, theory, practice, and effects (at the personal scale) or the realms of purpose, structure, operations, and outcomes (at the institutional scale); (2) locating (rather than blinding oneself to) incongruities among these qualities of experience; and (3) intervening in one's own thought or practice (or in the institution's structure or operations) to correct incongruities. Any form of attention less inclusive, less sharp, or less effectual might simply be solving the wrong problems at the wrong times and then ignoring the relevant negative feedback. But is this kind of attention attainable? Is this kind of attention in fact the birthright of human beings? This question leads us directly into brief considerations of human doing and human knowing.

HUMAN DOING

The foregoing question already offers the outlines of the model of managerial and institutional effectiveness from which the institutional self-study to be described in this chapter begins.

The model of effectiveness takes the real-time perspective of a manager who is faced with multiple demands on his or her time and attention without a clear-cut and complete definition of personal or organizational purposes and priorities at the outset. He or she will certainly *not* be effective if he or she puts attention only on immediate demands without clarifying priorities and purposes, and he or she will also certainly *not* be effective if he or she puts attention only on clarifying priorities and purposes. Some kind of balancing and interplay between these two movements ("doing what's in front of one" and "wondering what to do") — some way of resolving these apparent opposites into one harmonious movement — must be achieved if the manager is to be effective.

In this model of effectiveness an organization is viewed as engaged in a task structurally analogous to that of the manager: Namely, at any given time it faces multiple environmental demands and constraints without clear-cut, complete, agreed-on organizational purposes and priorities. If it is to be effective, the organization, like the manager, must develop activities that permit and encourage fundamental questioning of purposes simultaneous with accomplishment of specific tasks.

In order to operate effectively, both an individual manager and a social institution must generate activities that continually ask and respond to four fundamental dilemmas: (1) how to determine purposes worthy of pursuit, (2) how to produce the outcomes desired, (3) how to learn whether the outcomes are in fact congruent with purposes, and (4) how to balance appropriately (through plans, agendas, task structures, interventions, rewards, and controls) activities relating to the three foregoing questions, as they are interrupted by one another or by apparently extraneous matters.

This manner of approaching the question of managerial and organizational effectiveness permits the formulation of a general definition of organizational effectiveness that neither posits in general nor excludes any particular criteria of effectiveness. *Effectiveness can be defined as congruence between purposes and outcomes* (all outcomes, intended and unintended, human and material).

This definition of effectiveness implies a metasystem — or, in other words, an institutional self-study process — through which any organization can explicate and renew its dedication to its increasingly particular purposes, determine its particular criteria of effectiveness, and develop increasing congruity between these particular purposes (and effectiveness criteria) and outcomes.

HUMAN KNOWING

The challenging question remains: Can human doing in fact achieve the kind of effectiveness described in the abstract above? Can human being in fact develop an attention so active that it simultaneously illuminates one's own intuitive purposes, strategies, actions, and effects in the outside world? The model of collaborative inquiry proposed here and elsewhere (Torbert, 1973, 1976a) suggests that disciplined personal and institutional self-study, which focuses on four territories of human experience and explores their relationships to one another *as one acts, is* possible. The four territories are: (1) the visible, outside world, (2) one's own action as sensed by oneself in the process of acting, (3) the mapping process itself, the world of thinking, and (4) the attention that can focus on any of the other three territories, or encompass all, including itself, at once (see Figure 18.1).

On the other hand, a variety of other research traditions have concerned themselves with the two neglected territories of action and intention as self-experienced. For example, Ignatian prayer, Buddhist *vispasana* meditation, Hindu raja yoga, and Freudian and Jungian dream analysis exemplify research disciplines that explore the territory of attention, intention, and purpose at the individual scale. Certain theater exercises (Schechner, 1973), the Eastern martial arts (notably tai chi), traditional instruction in crafts, and the Gurdjieffian sacred dances cultivate a sensual knowledge of one's own practice.

Two of the territories open to research in a community of inquiry — one's own action as experienced from within and the dynamics of attention as experienced by the attending being — are disregarded in

Collaborative Inquiry Model	In Science Hypothetico-Deductive model	In Systems Theory	In Planning	In Organizations	In Society	In Terms of Human Attention
Empirical data	Data (or *capta*)	(Outside world)	(Outside world)	Product or Service	Historical events	Focal object
Sensual awareness	Data-gathering instrument	Goal-directed feedback	Tactics Goals	Craft Skills	Roles	Focal awareness
Reflexive, dialectical thinking	Logical theory	Structural feedback	Strategies Objectives	Formal and informal structures, processes	Norms	Subsidiary awareness/ground
Intentional, observing attention	Intuitive model (Kuhn, 1970)	Consciousness (Deutsch, 1963)	Objectives Ideals (Texas Instruments) (Ackoff and Emery, 1972)	Policy	Values, myths (Parsons, 1960)	Thread of intentionality/region (Heidegger, 1966; Husserl, 1962, Perls et al., 1951; Polanyi, 1958)

Figure 18.1 The Four "Territories" Open to Research in a Community of Inquiry (as denoted in different languages)

the conventional hypothetico-deductive approach to knowledge. The Cartesian model of reality on which the hypothetico-deductive approach is based divides the world in two — into thought and matter, theory and fact, map and territory, reflection and action, science and politics. As a result, the hypothetico-deductive approach treats thought itself as reified theory rather than as a territory in which dynamic action occurs and rarely inquires into its own presuppositions and actions (Mitroff, 1974, is an exception). Indeed, the hypothetico-deductive approach tends to regard itself as neutral, disembodied, value-free intellection rather than as profoundly normative religious/political action that includes the world in the course of study.

According to the model of reality that articulates all four territories of experience, the normative aim, both for a social scientist interested in valid knowledge and for a social agent interested in effective action, is to create a real-time community of inquiry that focuses on and integrates these different realms of experience. Such a community would be characterized by some specific product(s) or service(s) and by a continuing inquiry into purposes, strategies, one's own practices, and outcomes, assessing their relative congruity or incongruity. Its highest value and aim would be the cultivation of a reflexive, self-overcoming, timely inquiry, integrating empirical, sensual, dialectical, and spiritual kinds of knowledge in action. Elsewhere the author has tried to show that if this kind of inquiry is treated as the primary political value, it would permit the realization of the three great traditional political values: (nonexclusive) fraternity, (nonexploitative) liberty, and (nonconformist) equality (Torbert, 1974, 1976b).

INITIATING COLLABORATIVE INQUIRY IN AN ADMINISTRATIVE ROLE

I entered my current institutional role as Associate Dean responsible for the Graduate Division of the Boston College School of Management after eighteen years of research and practice relating to personal and institutional self-study, and after having developed the general models of effectiveness and inquiry already briefly sketched in this chapter. Deeply committed to this inquiry process on the basis of my experience, I was prepared to make a major commitment to personal and institutional self-study as a valuable activity for the school, in terms of both its teaching and its research functions. At the same time, I was well aware that the notion and practice of self-study can be introduced only gradually and allowed to "prove" (or "disprove") itself in the context of other people's ongoing experience. Different people will want to test the value of this model of inquiry in different ways (What is its effect on the institution's budget, on morale, on the quality of products or services, and so forth?). The same will be true for readers of this chapter. Although the foregoing introduction elaborates the underlying assumptions of this model of inquiry, it hardly proves them true. The challenging question remains: Can human beings in concert develop an attention so active that it simultaneously listens back toward its own origin, sees through the ironies of thought's metaphors, tastes its embodiment, and recognizes the aesthetic effects of its lifetime in the externally visible world? It would be a particularly blatant incongruity to claim that a self-study process — an inquiry intended to become increasingly collaborative — was based on anything other than a question.

My view of the place that institutional self-study takes in an overall conception of administrative leadership offers one way of understanding the relationship of self-study to other life activities. My overall conception of administrative leadership is that it consists of four distinct kinds of activities (see Figure 18.2), addressing four different spans of time and derived from the four distinct territories of experience discussed earlier.

I name the four kinds of leadership activities: (1) Responding to External Opportunities (which may arise unexpectedly at any moment); (2) Accomplishing Role-Defined Tasks (which tend to arise and be completed within a one-week to one-year time frame); (3) Defining and Implementing a Major Initiative (which requires on the order of three to five years); and (4) Encouraging Institutional Self-Study (which is best imagined as requiring 7 to 21 years, or a generation, for the reasons already suggested and also because it is the background from which truly timely and appropriate new major initiatives can come into focus).

Because these four time spans interpenetrate one another and influence one another, effective management over any extended period of time requires juggling and balancing all four kinds of leadership all the time. Indeed, on closer observation, each of the four kinds of leadership has both long- and short-term qualities (e.g., there will be occasions when the success of the longest-term aims depends on one's immediate response to an unexpected opportunity). Because tasks relating to the two short-term kinds of leadership are more "externally" determined at any given time, while the two long-term kinds of leadership are more "internally" determined (if they are

Theories of Study and Activity	Encouraging Institutional Self-Study (7-21 yrs)	Defining and Implementing a Major Initiative (3-5 yrs)	Accomplishing Role-Defined Tasks (1 wk — 1 yr)	Responding to External Opportunities (unexpected)
Purpose*	To generate continuing self-study based on model of collaborative inquiry.	To generate new Model MBA dedicated to effective, responsible practice.	To demonstrate commitment to quality and to responsive action	To develop linkages to leading edge managerial practice.
Strategy*	Develop familiarity with model first, then explore incongruities among territories, then focus on precision of data.	Major changes in core curriculum.	In general, bureaucratize; in particular, respond to stage of individual or group.	Relate to creative sectors of economy: (a) small business, (b) high-tech companies.
		Development of interdepartmental faculty team to plan and implement changes (2/79).	Additional rewards for student high achievement; tying research support for faculty to creativity, productivity.	Journeys off-campus.
Practice**	(See remainder of chapter)	Unanimous faculty vote in favor of 13 curricular changes (9/79).	Perception of office as responsive in everyday terms (?).	Federal and state funding for Small Business Development Center, 1/81; On-site part-time MBA section at high tech company, 1/81; IBM grant for restructured curriculum, faculty summer research, and self-study process, 9/80.
Outcomes**	(See remainder of chapter)	Implementation of restructured curriculum (9/80).		

*The specific purposes and strategies outlined here are the purposes and strategies that the author developed during his first year at Boston College.
**See text of Torbert (1980) for more extended examples of practices and outcomes in regard to each kind of administrative leadership.

Figure 18.2 Kinds of Administrative Leadership

being exercised at all), demands relating to the different kinds of leadership can be in considerable tension with one another. If a leader is at all passive in structuring time, the more immediate, more external demands will gain preeminence. On the other hand, if over time a leader actively juggles and balances the four kinds of leadership, one would expect the demands of each time span increasingly to complement and support activities relating to the other three.

If an administrator fails to perform effectively in regard to the two shorter-term time spans, he or she comes to be regarded as unhelpful and unrealistic ("incredible"). If an administrator fails to perform effectively in regard to the two longer-term time spans, the organization does not redesign or restructure itself to meet new environmental contingencies or to more nearly achieve its foundational purposes. Any given Major Initiative involves restructuring a specific part of an institution, while the self-study process involves a continuing testing for possible incongruities among purposes, structures, practices, and outcomes that may suggest areas requiring restructuring.

Because I believe that today's institutions increasingly require a self-restructuring capacity given the turbulent political and economic environments, and because I believe that schools of management can powerfully support students' development of self-restructuring, personal learning strategies only if the schools themselves exemplify the plausibility and efficacy of self-restructuring processes, I wished at this stage in my career to join a school open to such developments.

In choosing my current position, I evaluated the institution in terms of its current posture with regard to each of the four kinds of activity described above. The three most important "facts" that emerged for me were: (1) the graduate school of management was on the brink of a major restructuring of its MBA core curriculum with the dean's support; (2) the university as a whole, founded and still led by the Jesuit Order, recognized, by intuition and experience, the possibility and desirability of relating knowledge to action through a morally consequential communal self-study; and (3) the dean himself, my immediate superior, seemed open, not in a rhetorical sense, but in a behavioral sense, to collaborative inquiry.

BEGINNINGS OF THE INSTITUTIONAL SELF-STUDY PROCESS

Once one begins with the notion of social science as including personal, institutional, and cultural self-study on the part of actors in the midst of everyday lives full of other priorities besides self-study, a series of questions arise as to how and why persons might choose to become engaged in such a study and what relationship such a study would take to their other real-time obligations. If the process is to be truly one of self-study, we can imagine that different people will initially be attracted to, or repelled by, it for a variety of reasons. Next, they will either test self-study directly or else observe others testing it in their "neighborhood." This step may lead them to reevaluate the desirability of self-study and to increase or decrease their investment in the process. In other words, any self-study process that is more than a fad will begin as a very partial commitment and will assume a more central role in a person's or institution's life only gradually as its risks and potentials are explored.

Events, Findings, and Effects During the First Year of Explicit Self-Study

I formally introduced the notion of studying our own managerial and organizational effectiveness to the school's faculty at a series of three informal research seminars in June of 1979, seven months after entering the administrative role. Some 25 of 60 full-time faculty members attended one or more of these seminars.

The three initial faculty research seminars introduced the models of inquiry and effectiveness presented earlier in this chapter. In addition to *theoretical* discussion, the seminars also included activities relating to each of the other three kinds of research — *empirical*, *sensual*, and *attentional*. These were (1) the chance to critique the "effectiveness" interview schedule later used to interview two-thirds of the full-time faculty with regard to validity and reliability issues; (2) a tai chi dance exemplifying research on one's own practice; and (3) a meditation exemplifying the process of inverting and widening one's attention to include simultaneous inquiry into purposes, strategies, one's own practice, and the outside world.

The faculty members present at the seminars raised many questions: (1) Is the model of inquiry a mechanism for self-deception? (2) Can awareness of personal or institutional incongruities across the domains of purposes, strategies, practices, and effects generate a demoralizing, paralyzing self-consciousness? (3) Won't people's short-term concerns and conflicting self-interests prevent the development of shared purposes? (4) To explore these kinds of issues requires a fundamentally different kind of faculty meeting from our present ones: How can one imagine that happening here? (5) Is effectiveness really an issue that faculty members care about in their roles as academics?

The alert, confronting nature of the questions could itself be taken as a clue about whether this model of inquiry generates a self-satisfied self-deception. Similarly, the unusual nature of the three research meetings themselves exemplified a new kind of faculty meeting.

The self-study process may have had its first significant impact on the school's overall effectiveness during these meetings. One meeting turned to a discussion of the likelihood that the school's faculty would act favorably on the major institutional initiative being developed at that time — a thorough-going revision of the MBA core curriculum. There was great pessimism that the faculty would reject the initiative, no matter how cogent, because of a history of low trust during the previous administration. The public acknowledgment of this block and of the hopelessness it had generated over the past years, as well as the discussion of the collaborative, consultative process through which the initiative would pass on the way to the faculty vote, seemed to generate renewed energy to support the initiative among those present (who were among the most active in school affairs). Even though several of those present were still unconvinced that the initiative would pass a faculty vote, the formal faculty meeting was in fact characterized by thoughtful, constructive questions and a unanimous vote in favor of all thirteen proposed revisions.

During the six weeks following the initial research meetings, eleven faculty who had been present at the final meeting participated in the "effectiveness" interview and a further research meeting to discuss the results of the interviews. The interview questions were mostly open ended, in order to: (1) determine how different faculty members constructed standards of effectiveness for their own professional conduct, for the school, and from the point of view of their academic field; (2) test each respondent's willingness to engage in on-line inquiry by rethinking toward the end of the interview how his or her different approaches to effectiveness related to one another; and (3) give the respondents the opportunity to become committed to the study to the point of eventually developing roles as researchers, as well as respondents.

Because the object of collaborative inquiry is personal and institutional self-study in action, all stages of data collection are viewed not just as formal procedures for yielding valid empirical results, but equally as actions that in their overall structure and moment-to-moment conduct either enhance or inhibit commitment to continued inquiry.

The peculiar twists given to the issue of validity in collaborative inquiry include the fact that the primary criterion of validity is not the generalizability of findings to other settings, but rather their pertinence to future effective action of the social system studied, and the fact that the primary critical public for the study is not the journal referees in one's scholarly field, but rather, one's colleagues in the social system studied.

Given the small proportion of faculty participating in this pilot set of interviews, the results permitted no defensible generalizations to the school as a whole. However, one specific finding generated considerable discussion at the feedback meeting and influenced the actions of the dean and myself during the following year. This finding was the factor most often mentioned (by nine of the eleven respondents) as inhibiting the school's effectiveness. The following comments are all direct quotes from the interviews, in the format in which they were presented at the feedback session:

Factors Inhibiting Greater Effectiveness of the
School of Management
(in order of frequency of mention)

1. Climate of not doing much: a vicious circle.

   - A lot of things (e.g., Educational Policy Committee meetings) feel basically dead.

   - I don't sense that a large number of faculty want to move ahead.

   - We're not all saying we want to do it.

   - People have to want to be great, be willing to pay the price.

   - Pervasive sense of mediocrity, general discouragement.

   - Negative self-concept about research production.

   - People here put themselves down; we have an organizational inferiority complex.

   - Negative attitude that says you give up once you get here.

During the year following this feedback session, the school's faculty approved not only the revised MBA core curriculum, but also two other significant innovations in the internal structure of the school. In addition, three new interinstitutional programs that relate the school more closely to the small business and high-technology environment in the Boston area were developed. These opportunities would almost certainly not have developed had not the dean and I been willing to devote considerable attention to them. And we, in turn, might well *not* have been willing to devote our attention to these possibilities had we not been concerned about how to replace a "climate of not doing much" with more positive activity cycles. Thus, as incomplete as the pilot set of interviews were, the data from them had a powerful impact, through the school's administrative leadership, on the school's relationship to its environment during the ensuing year, and the new levels of internal and interinstitutional initiative may have, at least temporarily, supplanted an institutional sense of "not doing much" with a sense of positive accomplishment.

This interpretation is supported by two sets of data: (1) In a second round of interviews with 25 additional faculty members six months after the pilot interviews, the school was rated as significantly more effective than it was in the first round, and no factor like "a climate of not doing much" was mentioned as inhibiting the school's effectiveness. (2) When the eleven faculty originally interviewed in July 1979 were asked in July 1980 whether they viewed the school as more or less effective than it was a year earlier, none viewed it as less effective, two viewed it as essentially unchanged, and the other nine viewed it as more effective (average 3.97, where 3 = "same," 4 = "marginally more effective," and 5 = "markedly more effective"). All who viewed the school as more effective expressed qualifications, the most prominent of which were: (1) the innovations had yet to be proven; (2) although there is more activity, objectives are still not clear and shared; and (3) they might be confounding their own personal sense of having had a better year than the previous one with an institutional change.

I was initially concerned about the validity of the data I would collect on this question in brief phone or face-to-face interviews, especially given that I, as one of the school's administrators, presumably hoped to hear that the school was viewed as more effective this year than it was last year. I therefore mentioned this concern in a number of cases when I asked the question as one way of exorcising this possible course of contamination. Since faculty members responded to the question with the hesitation and qualifications suggested above, I have some confidence in the fact that their responses *did* represent genuine reflections and not merely "socially desirable" comments. Afterwards, I realized that there was an additional reason for my confidence in the validity of this data. I asked myself how many of these ten persons had criticized or opposed initiatives of mine in the year between the two sets of questions about the school's effectiveness and found that six of the ten did disagree with and confront me on at least one issue.

The findings of the second round of "effectiveness" interviews were sent to the entire faculty on March 24, 1980, along with a memo inviting faculty to discuss the findings at small group meetings scheduled in April. Altogether, twenty faculty members attended two such small group meetings. One characteristic shared by both of these meetings, as well as the feedback meeting after the pilot interviews, was the tendency for faculty questioning and commentary to focus on *institutional issues related to effectiveness* rather than on personal effectiveness or on theoretical or methodological issues in defining and measuring effectiveness.

Not surprisingly, the most sensitive issue discussed at each meeting arose at the very end of each meeting. Both groups raised the same issue: Namely, how to develop and support the research capabilities of the faculty. Interestingly, this issue would seem to lie right at the crossroads of institutional, personal, and scientific issues relating to effectiveness. At each meeting, one faculty member identified him- or herself as an example of someone in midcareer who needed to rediscover a connection to original research, but had doubts and uncertainties about how to do so. Each meeting discussed two recent examples of research projects in which senior faculty members with excellent field contacts teamed up with junior, more research-oriented faculty members.

In this regard, the self-study process described here can potentially have a direct impact on the school's effectiveness. Because the ideal of collaborative inquiry weds valid research to effective practice, more members of our faculty who have been relatively inactive in terms of research productivity may find themselves attracted to this kind of research than would be attracted to the hypothetico-deductive approach. For example, over the past year, eight other faculty members from five of the seven departments in the school have shared responsibility for the development and conduct of one or another of the research activities described here. Of these eight, only three are currently conducting and publishing new research in their field. Some among the other five may find this study itself a vehicle for reentering the arena of original research and publication. Clearly, however, it is much too early to assess whether the institution as a whole will find this kind of research worthy of sustained attention.

The Second Year of Self-Study

The second year of the self-study process seems to be characterized by an intensified inquiry process among four different subgroups at the school, with no school-wide self-study functions whatsoever. The largest subgroup is the MBA core curriculum faculty team and the entering MBA students participating in the new program. Two different kinds of research and feedback cycles are occurring in this arena: research on the student and faculty responses to the implementation of the curriculum, and research on student and faculty constitutive assumptions about, and actual practices in, the social world. Data from the first type of research have been fed back to faculty and students twice this year with subsequent discussion and changes in practice, illustrating the risks and benefits of participating in an organization willing to study its own effectiveness.

Data from the second type of research will eventually help to determine whether the MBA program influences participants' constitutive assumptions and action effectiveness. For example, one of the measures to be administered, both to students and to faculty willing to participate, is Loevinger's Sentence Completion Test, from which it is possible for trained judges to make clinical inferences, with excellent reliability, about a person's stage of ego development. Because changes in ego state are structural, second-order changes in the way a person relates to the world — self-restructuring changes — and because research on educational institutions so far indicates that they do *not* influence students' ego development systematically (Loevinger, personal communication, 1980), Loevinger's Sentence Completion Test seems a particularly challenging and apt measure with which to gauge whether the revised MBA curriculum at Boston College has a unique impact.

A second subgroup engaged in a self-study process is a year-long seminar composed of some two dozen faculty and business people, half from the School of Management, half from other Boston area universities and businesses. The aim of the seminar is to study and publish an edited book on the theory and practice of "responsible self-regulation" as a guide for the conduct of one's professional role, of institutions, and of the political economy.

A third subgroup of a half-dozen members of the school meets weekly to engage in attention exercises related to "tracking" all four "levels of experience" in one's everyday work and leisure.

A fourth subgroup does not meet at all, but rather consists of another half-dozen members of the school who are finding individual reasons for questioning their basic assumptions about personal and social reality because of initially non-work-related traumatic experiences they are suffering. For these persons the question of how to conduct a self-study process that results in more effective action is no mere formal possibility, but a felt, existential need that is bringing them into a new relationship to the notion of self-study.

Describing these second-year self-study initiatives is beyond the scope of this chapter, but the mere listing of them suggests some of the unexpected sources and directions of an institutional self-study process.

CONCLUSION

This chapter really arrives at no conclusions. It ends as it began, with an invitation to others to join in the personal, institutional, and epistemological process of self-study in action with others.

According to the model of administrative leadership presented at the outset of this chapter, the self-study process is rightly conceived as a very long term process. As the initiating researcher, I was frankly surprised that after only one year the self-study process at the Boston College School of Management apparently had had some impact on the institution. Certainly, though, the self-study process cannot yet be said to have "taken root" at the school as a widely valued activity. And, of course, there is no evidence whatsoever yet that other institutions will explore this process. Nevertheless, the foregoing story of a year in the life of an institution permits certain points to be made on an illustrative basis.

First, the reader will have noted the fear, expressed not just once but in most of the meetings relating to the research, that "purpose talk" would lead nowhere and that research findings could result in a paralyzing self-consciousness. These fears are common at the outset of a self-study process and tend to be fed, rather than calmed, by argument. What can save the self-study process from these negative outcomes is the interplay between the self-study activity and other shorter-term administrative activities, where the insights from self-study can be "put to work" in a variety of ways. Initially, there is a strong temptation to establish new programmatic directions at self-study meetings in order to establish their usefulness, but it is best to resist this temptation because:

(1) discussion of new programmatic directions can divert the group from self-study;

(2) agreement about new programmatic directions would reduce the group to an "interest" group, and disagreement about new programmatic directions would probably further divert the group from self-study;

(3) the relationship between insight and truly corrective action is deeply mysterious and can perhaps best be discovered by observing the patterns of self-study participants' organizational actions over time, without attempting initially to prechoreograph them; and

(4) the relationship between a genuinely motivating and unifying sense of institutional purpose and words that express such a purpose is also deeply mysterious; any verbal answer offered early in the self-study process to the question of personal or institutional purpose risks becoming mere propaganda on behalf of particular programmatic directions.

Second, while fear of the uselessness of institutional self-study is most prominently illustrated by the foregoing story, unexpectedly useful and positive consequences of institutional self-study are also illustrated. The exploration about whether the school's faculty could have "good meetings" just before it did have an unusually unified meeting, voting in favor of the revised MBA curriculum, is one such illustration. The exploration into the "climate of not doing much" at the school, which played a role in generating a number of new developments over the following months, is another illustration. Both illustrations show that the process of institutional self-study can influence an institution in positive ways well in advance of achieving statistically significant conclusions about the matters of concern. Indeed, as both examples illustrate, the process of institutional self-study can result in action that *in*validates the original findings.

However obvious it may be in analytical terms that the whole point of negative feedback is to correct the course or structure of the system receiving the feedback, an institutional process that reliably receives, interprets, and corrects for negative feedback is remarkably rare. The purpose of engaging in institutional self-study, according to the models of organizational effectiveness and social science presented here, is to generate increasingly intelligent, self-corrective action.

Finally, the foregoing review of early institutional self-study activities at the Boston College School of Management indicates movement through three phases of development, which may be generalizable to other institutional self-study projects (Torbert, 1980). Because the entire paradigm of collaborative inquiry is generally unfamiliar, institutional members must:

(1) first develop an initial familiarity with, and willingness to explore further, the overall model of inquiry and effectiveness, in this case,

through activities such as the initial research seminars and feed-back sessions of the first year;

(2) then develop a "taste" for, and skills at, identifying and correcting major unclarities about, and incongruities among, purposes, strategies, operations, and outcomes in this case, through activities like the seminar on Responsible Self-Regulation and the implementation of the revised core curriculum with feedback from the research on student outcomes; and

(3) only as a final phase develop the skill and commitment to seek moment-to-moment and word-to-word precision and high-quality outcomes in terms of analytic validity, aesthetic appropriateness, and political timeliness, in this case, through an activity like the more carefully controlled and precise empirical research using the ego-stage measure.

In any given institution, one can imagine a widening series of such cycles, beginning with a few people motivated to become a self-study group, then widening to include one or more task-related subgroups at the institution (e.g., a particular department or committee in a university setting). Thus the process through which institutional self-study comes to embrace more participants within any one institution, or more institutions, is an oscillation between invitations to new groups to join in self-study and periods of concentration wherein committed participants seek to institutionalize the self-study process within their own activities and reflections. At each new phase the question is confronted as to whether participants in the self-study process have developed only a new rhetoric or actually a new and more effective mode of practice. If only a new rhetoric about "collaborative inquiry" has developed, then one can predict that (1) the self-study process will encounter serious resistance in the next phase and (2) self-study participants are unlikely to succeed in practice in addressing this resistance in such a way as to expand and intensify the self-study process.

Even if participants significantly increase the timeliness, appropriateness, and validity of their action-inquiry process and thus also increase their effectiveness, they may very well still encounter serious resistance in the next phase. This resistance may arise for one, or a combination, of four reasons: (1) the self-study process threatens the personal defenses of potential individual participants; (2) the self-study process threatens political interests of groups; (3) the self-study process raises the level of acknowledged tension between ideals and actualities to an unaccustomedly high level; or (4) the self-study process is itself initially interpreted as representing a narrow interest.

As suggested by the illustrations on previous pages, an essential aspect of collaborative inquiry is addressing such resistance in ways that intensify and expand the inquiry.

About the Author

WILLIAM R. TORBERT

The first major influence on my intellectual development was my father's career as a Foreign Service Officer, which exposed me to four different languages by the time I was ten.

As an undergraduate and graduate student at Yale in the 1960s, I was fortunate to meet a number of gifted teachers — Paul D'Entreves, who quoted in all four of those languages and more in the course of any one of his lectures on political philosophy; Chris Argyris, with his uniquely probing concern for the relationship between words and deeds in professional life; Bill Coffin, with his uniquely spirited blend of epigrammatic humor, Christian gratitude, and political effrontery; Lord Pentland, with his uniquely active and enduring, yet unostentatious, exercise of self-study in action. All of these teachers addressed the gap, the common incongruities, and the possible interplay between value and fact, between ideal and actual, in one's personal, professional, and political life with others.

In my reading, the works of Arendt, Bateson, Churchman, Erikson, Gurdjieff, Jung, Kegan, Mailer, Marcuse, Mitroff, Nietzsche, Ouspensky, Plato, Tillich, and Wittgenstein seem to me most nearly to address the challenge of discovering, formulating, and enacting the psychological, political, and epistemological conditions for integrating inquiry and authority.

During my twenties and thirties, my experiences in administrative roles, in dance, theater, and the martial arts, and with friends of different races, nationalities, sexes, and religious disciplines have repeatedly emphasized for me the great distances and gaps among intuition, theory, action, and outcome, as well as the diversity of approaches to bridging one or more of these gaps. The search for theory that reawakens me and other practitioners to these existential gaps, and to what can bridge these gaps, continues to motivate my research, my teaching, and my administrative work.

19

TRANSFORMATIONAL THEORY AND ORGANIZATIONAL ANALYSIS

Orion F. White, Jr.

Virginia Polytechnic Institute and State University

Cynthia J. McSwain

University of Southern California

The approach to social analysis we call "transformational" is linked to the strong humanist mood that moved into the field of public administration in the 1960s and draws inspiration and specific concepts from such diverse sources as process philosophy, gestalt psychology, transactional analysis, intepretive sociology, and radical political science. Its main or summary emphasis, however, is taken from the work of Jung (1966, 1968) and analytical psychology — specifically, those aspects of analytical psychology that have implications for understanding social dynamics.

ONTOLOGICAL ASSUMPTIONS

Transformational theory builds on a view of social reality that gives equal and valid ontological status to individuals, interaction, and institutional aspects of social reality. Specifically, its assumptions can be represented with the aid of Figure 19.1, which, following Kirkhart and White (1977), recognizes four levels of organizational reality.

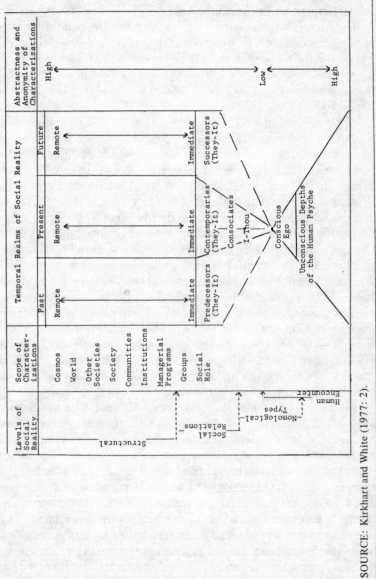

SOURCE: Kirkhart and White (1977: 2).

Figure 19.1 A Transformational Approach to the Analysis of Social Reality

The *structural level* refers to institutional arrangements embodied in patterns of expectation and social contract that define social structure with varying degrees of abstraction and anonymity (Schutz, 1967b). These patterns can be construed as a residual phenomenon that define the limits of human consciousness of members of the social order. (Berger and Luckmann, 1966).

The *social relations level* refers to the realm of social consciousness or life world, in which individuals negotiate and renegotiate with others. It is the world of directly lived experience in which individuals engage and interact with others through conversation and other modes of discourse. This level provides the focal point of action in organizational life.

The *nomological level* refers to the realm of individual consciousness. This realm contains many types of consciousness through which individuals experience and construe reality in different ways, as exemplified in Jung's (1968) four functions of the psyche (see also, Edinger, 1973; Neumann 1969; Progoff, 1973; Whitmont, 1969), in the distinction between left- and right-brain activities, and in the characterizations of consciousness offered by Bateson (1972). These different modes of consciousness reflect preferences or styles of coping with the outside world. In these different kinds of conscious attitudes, psychic energy assimilates and integrates information from experience in different ways, and the possibility arises for what Martin Buber (1970) has called "I — Thou" relationships, which convey an intuitive appreciation of the mystery of one's own and another's uniqueness. Conversation in the "I — Thou" relationship (in contrast to the "I — It" or "I — They" statements that characterize the social relations level) contains many first-person statements; the basic quandry for each person in conversation is how to allow themselves to be fully present.

The *human-encounter level* involves a dialogue with the deepest levels of the human psyche. This process is activated by energy from the depths of the psyche, flowing through the medium of symbols into the conscious ego and the external world. This unconscious energy exerts a major impact on thought and action in the world, whether this is directly recognized or not. The action of the unconscious is projected outside the individual, and attributed to the environment, and its effects on ego and personality are often poorly appreciated.

These four levels of social reality are linked by transformational processes that convert unconscious energy to form the human ego (at the nomological level), social relations, and social structure. We can begin to understand these relations by appreciating how a particular human individual is centered in the physical body, which is real in the sense that it has an automonous dynamic of its own. While it is true that each body is unique and autonomous, it is concomitantly true that human bodies are similar in basic form and process. They are all generically human bodies and are at once general and specific.

Each human being in his or her physical reality is also a representation of the realm of the psychological — that is to say, the unconscious. It is the status accorded the unconscious that is perhaps most distinctive to the transformational perspective. The unconscious is seen as being an objective reality analogous to that of the body, in that it is as highly structured and as lawlike in its processes as is the body — and just as autonomous. The unconscious is also collective and individual; like the body, it exists in conjunction with other separate entities to form an objective whole. Just as bodies are connected through the seamless web of human ecology (such that our using an aerosol spray today affects the probability of a person in China getting skin cancer tomorrow), so the unconscious is similarly structured, in that individual psychological events affect the psychology of others. Thus interest in achieving female liberation in the West correlates with stirrings in the protected environments of the Middle Eastern harem halfway around the world. The unconscious as a collective whole, however, can be manifested only in the particular individual, just as the human form can only be observed in the particular body.

The conscious aspect of the individual consists of transformed unconscious energy. This energy has, through the process of maturation, come under the direction of the individual rather than been expressed autonomously through him or her. Consciousness is an aspect of the ego, which itself is necessarily differentiated from the unconscious. Consciousness is like the palm tree on the island of the ego sitting in the sea of the unconscious. As such, the conscious attitude can be aware of and thereby transcend the ego (in the sense that the palm tree rises above the island), but it is nonetheless dependent on it. The project of human life is seen as the development of an appropriate relationship to the unconscious such that unconscious energy is transformed or made available to consciousness.

Transformation occurs as energy moves from the unconscious side of the person over to the conscious side. This energy is channeled from the unconscious by symbols through their evocative power. Symbols are essentially mysterious and ineffable (as, of course, is the unconscious) and are represented indirectly through "analogues" (i.e., physical or operational representations of the psychic realm). Since the process of transformation is dynamic, such that the person and the unconscious are constantly in a state of evolution, analogues can be appropriate for evoking or blocking energy, or for drawing it off too rapidly in an eruption. The "evidence" of what is being discussed here is directly apprehendable: The "energy" is what one feels full of when one is enthusiastic. Consciousness is congruent with the idea of maturity — a word generally taken to have direct empirical referents in behavior and an ostensible meaning. The unconscious is known through awareness of our own occasional strangeness — in moods that unaccountably come over us at times, and through dreams, of major and minor import, that occur as we sleep. The individual is always to some degree in a state of unconsciousness.

What this transformational perspective yields is a picture of social process that is centered in the individual, where the flow of energy from its source in the unconscious, through consciousness, into social relations and activity, is the central focus. Social relations are based on projection: The unconscious projects images into the external world that are then perceived as reality, and the objective of social relations is the mutual resolution of these projections. All things outside the individual, especially aspects of social life, act as analogues for the unconscious. This means that we can see a direct and real connection between the individual, the "other," and the social order. Other people, indeed society, represent the collective or personal unconscious, analogically. Hence for all intents and purposes, the project of individual consciousness, society, and social relations is the realization of the unconscious.

Another way of appreciating the significance of this process and the importance of the unconscious in social life stems from the realization that transformation lies at the basis of meaningful action. As Kirkhart and White (1977) have suggested, meaningful experience involves the discovery of capacities and potentials in self and situations that have previously remained hidden. Such experience provides the basis for reconstruction of self and situation and for further reconstructions in the light of experiences thus generated. Such transformational capacities have their roots in the unconscious, for the necessary reconstruction usually hinges on the realization in consciousness, of something that has been suppressed. The feeling of "aha" or "sinking in" that often accompanies such realization expresses the process linking unconscious and conscious experience that is involved here. As is well known, such reformulation often mobilizes energy that was previously trapped, facilitating a level of action considerably greater than that which had existed before. This is precisely what happens when we have a "meaningful experience" — we are energized in some positive way that usually provides a basis for action. Following Kirkhart and White (1977), it is also easy to see that the only true problems of human existence rest on the stopping or diversion of this process. We encounter problems when the flow of energy from the unconscious becomes "blocked," creating immobility and consternation, or when it is directed in destructive ways.

Viewed from the perspective of transformational analysis, we are encouraged to see the world of formal organization as an expression of the human psyche. The pattern of activity may express or hinder the nature of human being. Transformational organization theory offers a means of understanding organization and of changing organization in ways that express and enhance the capacities of its human agents. The perspective emphasizes that everything, most of all people, exists only in relationship — not relationship as social interaction, but relationship through direct and real flow of human energy from its collective source through the person into activity and interaction, much as water moves from sea to sky to raindrop or snowflake to stream to river to sea. Each element has a discrete identity that is made discrete through its relationship to the whole process of which it is a part.

EPISTEMOLOGICAL IMPLICATIONS

This analysis suggests that an understanding of the world hinges on understanding the way unconscious energy mobilizes a relationship between self and situation. Human knowledge is a direct product of the process through which humans engage and act in their world; it expresses a relationship between internal and external, subjective and objective. Traditionally, social science has sought for a knowledge emphasizing one or another extreme in this relationship. The realists, for example, have tended to reify the social world in the search for an objective, external form of knowledge, treating the individual as a social artifact — the sum of whatever set of institutional or organizational vectors bear on him or her at a given moment. The idealists have tended to reify social process, finding the locus of human existence and knowledge in conversation and in other subjective modes of social construction. The transformational perspective suggests that it is necessary to bridge the gap between these extremes and ground knowledge in an understanding of the way the internal world of ideas and ideals (or in the jargon of analytical psychology, of archetypes) is linked to the external world of matter. Both are treated as equally real and important in human affairs. Pursuit of truth in either realm is seen as missing the point in that neither realm can ever be known completely to consciousness because the two realms are inextricably connected. Consciousness can only know, can only operate properly, in relationship to the two realms.

The problem of the social researcher is thus one of finding an appropriate means of linking one's self to the situation being researched. The transformational perspective emphasizes that our capacity as human beings, and hence as social researchers, is basically one of acting *in relation to* situations. The "in relation to" is all-important for the way we make sense of the situations being studied, and it defines the basis of transformational epistemology. The "in relation to" defines a praxis that links theory to action in a particular kind of involvement in the world. The important point from the transformational perspective is that this involvement be reflexive and acknowledge the essential mysteriousness of the realm of ideals by holding to the view that knowledge of the material world must always, and can only, be tentative and incomplete.

All this boils down to an epistemological position that is essentially based on *human interest: Something is true to the extent that it is interesting.* So also is it good. As Arendt pointed out that evil is banal, we point out that banality is evil. Valid knowledge is knowledge that is interesting — in that it acts as an effective analogue in drawing out the energy of the person viewing it. While it must be disciplined to the point of having the power to command attention and focus concentration and dialogue, it must never be so complete as to overwhelm its recipients. The knowledge presentation that is so comprehensive, "slick," complete, and conclusive that it leaves its audience completely speechless, or alternatively, is so poorly executed that it leaves its audience totally dismayed, are the two types that are unhelpful for the construction or discovery of truth. For a research statement to have truth means that it possesses evocative power.

RESEARCH PROCESS AND METHOD

As is evident from the above discussion, transformational research basically involves an orientation and posture that is practical in intent and reflexive in nature. It attempts to generate the sort of understanding that will, to somewhat oversimplify the matter, facilitate the relationship of the conscious attitude to the collective unconscious of the social order by increasing the reflexivity of the way in which the conscious attitude regards and "deals with" the unconscious. In this sense, all transformational research is action research, though the research itself can take a variety of forms. Since truth is found in the continuing emergence of energy from the unconscious as it flows into action through effective symbolic analogues, it is neither discovered nor even created; it must constantly be *re-created*.

Consistent with this view, transformational research brings an affirmative bias toward all research contributions, since in the final analysis, all research is a manifestation of the unconscious and hence, *to some extent,* is true. No contribution, no statement in scientific dialogue, is ever to be discounted completely. (This attitude is what led Jung to be able to make sense out of the babblings of asylum inmates, and by understanding them, gain insights into their "cases.") Critique has a role to play as an analogue generating dialogue and debate in a way that draws out and clarifies *interest,* the benchmark of truth.

All human phenomena are of potential or real interest to transformational theory and can be studied in many ways. Hence the research agenda is, simply, everything. If it is necessary to prioritize efforts, attention should perhaps be turned to areas of paradox, irony, or puzzlement in social life and to the social dynamics of energy transformation, rather than toward "social problems" or theoretical or empirical anomalies that are problematic in a strictly intellectual sense.

All methods of study are eligible, for all dimensions of research practice are themselves analogic representations of the unconscious and thus an aspect of what is to be studied. Different researchers favor different types of research studies because of their unconscious nomological preferences. What is important is that the researcher adopt a reflexive stance toward the research process, so that it can evolve in an open-ended manner. To say that some research methods are unacceptable, or to shy away from one's favored perspective, would alienate one from the unconscious, which these methods express. The point is that the researcher should deal with their existence, through disciplined reflexive involvement (such as that found in archery, fencing, flower arranging), which is intended to evoke the mysterious "it" that lies at the source of nature and human action. As the researcher practices the discipline toward the ultimately mysterious objective, the discipline itself will become transformed, both in content and method, in much the same way that Kuhn (1970b) describes the development of scientific revolutions.

The specific methods of experimental, case, historical, interpretive, and critical analysis, and any others offered by various social science disciplines, are thus all appropriate for transformational research. However, their use and nature would be modified through the research process itself, incrementally and serendipitously, in the manner described above. The only specific methodological requirement is that the researcher(s) should append to each study a "methodological appendix," a statement of their personal experience in conceiving, designing, carrying out, and writing the research study. The point of this is to indicate, through personal evidence, the possible symbolic meanings of the research effort. This would provide some extra indication as to how the unconscious of the researcher is connected to the collective unconscious, and how both of these, indirectly and directly, underlie the genesis of the research.

Since transformational research is always intended to be a reflexive, symbolic analogue, the design would always be considered to be emergent and the process participative and as open as possible. The dictates of rigor would be kept through careful objective and subjective documentation of the entire process. An illustration of the required stance is found in what occurred at the NTL Institute in Bethel, Maine, when the "T-Group" (a significant new symbolic analogue in that day) was invented. It was through a participative process that involved the radical posture of listening to, and acting on, the suggestion of one of the participants in the sessions that Kurt Lewin hit on the concept of feedback and learning through the processing of experiential feedback. This idea held great "truth," that is, reflexive, symbolic power.

To illustrate further, let us consider some studies that might be carried out under the transformational approach.

(1) Case studies. The two authors of this essay are currently conducting a study of the phenomenon often referred to as "whistle blowing" in government administration. We are reviewing and developing case study materials of numerous incidents in which employees of government agencies have made public inside "goings on" they considered to be unethical. What we wish to explain is how it is that these people, who are acting in the name of the generally held, dominant, and official moral norms of administration, are so frequently and severely punished for their acts. Our hypothesis is that such acts are experienced by those around the whistleblower as acts of hubris or ego inflation to which the appropriate response, at the personal or human level, is some form of ostracism or rejection — so as to impose an opportunity for humility on the part of the whistleblower. It is our view, though, that this takes place at a highly implicit or unconscious level. This research fits well into the body of literature concerned with ethical issues in administration.

(2) *Historical studies*. Conventional historical description can be quite valuable in documenting how it is that the general relationship of whole societies to their collective unconscious leads to the emergence of major symbolic analogues that either threaten or enhance social life. A model for the type of historical work we have in mind includes Burke's (1980) studies of the history of technology. By tracing linkages between the development of analogues, we can see more clearly how the unconscious expresses itself and thereby has an impact on macro-level social events — such that, as in one of Burke's stories, we see how the development of the "touchstone" founded the reliable use of gold as money, leading through myriad connections to the development of nuclear energy, and, extending his example, to the Three Mile Island nuclear reactor crisis. We use this example because the modern nuclear reactor, even in the way it looks and certainly in the danger it poses, is a virtually perfect analogue to how the collective unconscious reacts to an unreflexive relationship on the part of consciousness. By overasserting the conscious attitude in modern technology, we have, through conscious manipulations, amassed and now attempt to direct huge amounts of energy. It is becoming increasingly clear, however, that conscious processes have serious difficulties in maintaining adequately controlled expression of this energy. As a consequence it regresses (as the nuclear core melts and sinks the way it would in a reactor catastrophe) and then erupts with devastating force (as the core would when it reached the water table underlying the reactor). We find similar ideas in the literature on administration in such work as White's (1958) historical studies of the "principles" guiding various phases of U.S. presidential administration.

Other historical work could attempt to describe the unconscious, mythic underpinnings of major "soft" and "hard" analogues (that is, social and technical processes) that characterize a society. We suggest that it might well be interesting to engage in more heterodox historical studies that describe directly the events of the collective unconscious of a group of people, for example, by gathering data about dream patterns of a particular population over time. (This indeed is what Jung did in explaining the emergence of Nazism in Germany — though his data base was limited to the dreams of his own German patients.)

(3) *Interpretive studies*. We mean by interpretive studies those research works of phenomenological inspiration that attempt to describe the subjective meanings of social events from the point of view of the actors involved. Of particular import here are people involved in current social issues of both broad and narrow interest. In those

who publicly espouse highly ideological positions we can find aspects of the unconscious directly embodied as analogues. This affords a unique opportunity to find out "what is going on," so to speak, in the unconscious. Intriguing illustrations are found in the statements of individuals and groups who have recently made apologies and pleas for understanding rapists, and of those who have argued the positive benefits for children who are victims of incest and sexual abuse by older members of their families. Such events are direct testimony to how the unconscious reacts to the conscious attitude, how it reminds unconsciousness that what it (consciousness) must do is transform and integrate the elements of the unconscious — elements that in their primitive form are often expressed through the analogues of evil and destructive acts.

Research is needed to promote understanding of these elements in society and appreciation of how the conscious forms through which society is given its structure and pattern tend to lead to the alienation of elements in the unconscious. These then erupt into antisocial patterns of behavior. At present most of this work is done by journalists and other writers. It is consistent, however, with those forms of social science interested in the interpretation of marginal groups.

(4) Social criticism. Related to this point is the idea that, in our view, research that pursues a project of social criticism is perfectly appropriate to, and needed in, the transformational approach. Just as we noted above that the villains of social problems need to be researched so as to bring about their transformation, so must we do the social critique that brings to light the problems in which they are involved and that are beneath our consciousness at any given time. Our version of social criticism, however, would not be based on the presumption that it could move society toward a given design or pattern considered good or ideal. The transformational view, it should be clear by now, rejects the idea of progress. It is, rather, oriented to the notion that all social action is simply in the direction of bettering the degree of reflexivity that holds in social relationships. This is a continuing, indeed permanent, task, and it is a task that must proceed from the assumption of the basic humanness of all people. Such a presumption demands that the principle of acceptance underpin all human action. This means that we would need to develop a form of social critique avoiding the "good guys"/"bad guys" format, one that does not play a role of rescuing the victim and punishing the victim's persecutor. All this, which is our tradition of social critique, is simply a game that works to avoid the issues we want to address.

The reader might have noted that we have discussed the research process in generic terms rather than in terms of organizational research specifically. This is intentional in that we see all social phenomena as relevant to the understanding of events in organizations. Organizations simply hold the broader events of society in microcosm and vice versa. It would be difficult to distinguish research topics or approaches distinctive to organization studies from those one would use in social science generally. The same holds for research findings. This is why organization theory is eclectic in its orientation, and why we would have it continue to be so, though there are in fact number of works that adopt a transformational approach to organization theory (see, for example, Ingalls, 1976).

Let us, for the sake of space, stop this inventory here, reemphasizing that the methodology we prescribe for transformational theory is the same as that in current practice. We only wish to add a provision for participation or openness in the process, so that the research format remains emergent as the research process proceeds. A reflexive relation to the unconscious begins from the point of taking things from where they are. Innovations are to be achieved not through prescription but through acting reflexively in the research process itself.

The "purpose" of studies is to document, to make more sensible to our presently rationalistic minds, the reality of the unconscious and how it operates in social as well as in personal life. This purpose is suited to the present relation of the conscious attitude — highly overassertive and dominant — toward the unconscious.

CONCLUSION

In the remarks presented above we have had two basic objectives: (1) to set out an ontological and epistemological position that is truly humanist in its commitment and that founds the social science research process in an appreciation of the human unconscious; and (2) to validate, as a consequence, most of what we are presently doing in the social science disciplines as we study organizations and other social phenomena.

In pursuing these objectives we have found ourselves stating a position about our basic assumptions that seems so heterodox as to be eccentric. Our feeling about this is that the position we state regarding the unconscious as the centerpiece of social science is at least a step in the right direction. We are somewhat awed by some of the implications of this position and have a concern that the more graphic and startling implications may be symptoms of some degree of intellectual hubris. It is undeniably a hazardous business to speak so directly of the unconscious and its dynamics as we have here. Our preventive against these dangers is to state explicitly that we are aware of this and humbly solicit reactions from those engaged by this point of view. Our project, to be consistent with its own tenets, must be carried forward reflexively, and part of its meaning is that it must be done on a broadly collaborative basis through a process of action, reaction, and re-creation. Our hope, at this point, is that we will be able to engage others in the process of building a transformational approach to social analysis.

The essence of our project insofar as a transformational organization theory is concerned is to base organization studies in a humanist commitment. It has long been of concern to us that organization theory, especially in public administration, has pursued humanist ideals in only a secondary or superficial manner. Caught up as we have been in the liberal visions of progress, we have lost sight of the reality, preeminent in the humanist viewpoint, that human life must be lived wholly, through pain as well as joy, and that this will always be true. Jung said at one point, "All neurosis is always an avoidance of legitimate suffering." In a way, by focusing our attention on the one problem of how to achieve "progress," we are avoiding the more important, real, and truly difficult matter of how to live with each other well *now*. The belief of the transformational view is that by letting go of the idea of progress and focusing our attention on the question of relating to the unconscious appropriately, the matter of how things turn out in the long run will take care of itself.

Philosophically, then, the position we are taking is a form of conservative anarchism, in that we start from an acceptance of things as they are and move slowly, by replacing structures with carefully wrought human processes, to a condition in which we rely on human relationship as the basis for social order. Along with this goes the whole-hearted posture of *human acceptance* that is characteristic of the anarchist position. Our view is that a social science, especially one that puts its attention on the intimate world of organizational life, must be *integrative* in emphasis. It is a science that must comprehend and build on folk wisdom, religious and mystical knowledge, and immediate experience, as much as it does on the abstractions of the thinking process. It must see social matters in terms other than those that create images of wrong doers, good doers, and victims; otherwise, it falls into the trap of being part of the problem by victimizing through the process of analysis.

We want to say simply that transformational theory wishes to make organizational analysis friendly and enthusiastic. Our view is that a science of the social, which is to say, the *human,* world, must in the end be a practical, playful, and healing art.

About the Authors

ORION F. WHITE, Jr.

I entered my academic career with the political commitments typical of a member of the liberal wing of the U.S. Democratic party. This carried over into my work as a concern with developing ways of understanding how to relieve some of the oppressions created by rigid and overwhelming bureaucracies. Then, as the sixties and seventies unfolded, I experienced, along with many others, a rather severe disillusionment with the myth of social progress achieved through government programs that has traditionally been the inspiration of people working in my field: public administration. This social and cultural crisis was accompanied by the development of a critical literature in the field of political science and the social sciences generally that attacked — effectively, it seemed to me — welfare liberalism, the classical liberalism of the American Constitution, empiricism, technicism, progress, American pluralism, organization, and administration, and a few other of the underpinnings of my sense of social justice and how to achieve it. Hence, I was driven, in my concern with human emancipation, toward deeper and deeper levels of analysis (i.e., levels more and more intimate to the human person), until I arrived at where I am now, in the realm of human development at the intrapsychic level. Hence I have gone from conventional political concerns with social justice through government programs, to being concerned with organizations as oppressive structures, to a concern with oppression at the interface between people in roles within organizations, finally to the radical humanist concern with achieving liberation from the psychic prisons that we construct around ourselves in organizations.

In short, a combination of critique driving me away from my prior views and my encounter with Jungian psychology and social analysis has enabled me to see an alternative approach to the problem of freedom at the personal level of analysis.

CYNTHIA J. McSWAIN

My interest has been always in the mysterious and the ineffable. As a child I lived close to a religious, symbolic side of life through my minister father's connection to the church. My natural introversion heightened my fascination with the mystical and the transcendent.

As an adult I have continued to explore the unseen world of the unconscious, which for me is the source of our conscious actions and energies. I am attached to a Jungian outlook as it offers the richest appreciation of the unconscious as an objective reality with an archetypal structure and a process of individual development.

I have worked in local governments in Texas and North Carolina and in the federal government in Washington, D.C., always captivated by how individuals and societies change. Now I teach public administration and focus my attention on public organizations and their management. I see these as immediate, contemporary analogues for the unconscious and thus as critical to understanding individual and collective development.

20

ORGANIZATION AND PRAXIS

Wolf V. Heydebrand
New York University

PRAXIS AND INNOVATION

In this chapter, I want to consider organization as a form of praxis. This perspective suggests a conception of organization as a more or less continuous process of organizing, to be distinguished from an organization as a structured, more or less stable outcome of the organizing activity. In addition, the concept of organizational praxis needs to be distinguished from organizational practices, organizational action, and organizational behavior. Organizational behavior refers to objective causal sequences in the movements and responses of organizations under the impact of external forces and determinants. Organizational action refers to the relatively more subjective, goal-directed activity of an organization vis-à-vis other organizations in its environment. Such action tends to be oriented toward problem-solving processes and the transformation of the environment (e.g., reduction of uncertainty or of dependence). When such goal-directed problem-solving activities are institutionalized and become habitual, one may speak of organizational practices. By contrast, organizational praxis refers not only to the technical transformation of the environment and to the solution of practical problems, but also to the conscious self-transformation of collective actors. This requires a high level of understanding and insight into the motivational and causal links among actors, social structures, and history. Thus organizing activity, cooperation, undistorted communication, and domination-free interaction are central to the concept of organizational praxis.

Following these distinctions between behavior, action, and praxis, we may further distinguish between three different types of innovations. Organizational innovations may be imposed or adopted as a result of a process of interaction between organization and environment. Such behavioral innovations, although they may result in structural changes in the organization, are merely adaptations to changing conditions. At the level of action, innovations take the form of conscious strategies of transformation of the conditions of action. Examples here are the expansion of domain of occupational and professional groups and the rationalization of technique, and the imposition of external controls on productive activity by administrative decision makers. Such strategic innovations may come into conflict with each other, since one innovative strategy may be formulated with the practical intent of limiting or blocking the implementation of another or, at a higher level of power, changing the conditions of action of other strategic actors. However, it is only at the level of organizational praxis that innovations are directed not only at transformation, but at self-transformation or the mutual transformation of subject and object. Here, we have not so much an external target of change, but rather a conscious attempt to transform the totality of self/other relationships on a collective level, in other words, to alter the conditions by which all subjective collective actors in a given organization or organizational network are constrained. Rather than being limited to strategic innovations that may result in the domination or elimination of one actor by another, innovations at the level of praxis involve a process of collective self-transformation or self-organization. Mere reactive behavior and proactive strategy are subsumed under a self-active process of organizing for the purpose of minimizing external determination and mutual constraint or domination and maximizing the possibility of self-determination. Innovation becomes a process of true structural transformation that goes beyond the goal of increasing the adaptive capacity of the organizational system vis-à-vis others. It changes the level at which organization/environment relationships are conceptualized and experienced.

A crucial aspect of organizational praxis is that self-organizing innovations involving social groups must overcome the resistance of *both* subject and object, of self and other, of organization and environment (Gramsci, 1971; Korsch, 1938). Hence it is only in this sense that organizational praxis can be said to transform a given social-historical organizational formation and, conversely, that a change from one to another does not occur unless there is innovative change at the level of self-organization. All other forms of change merely continue the organizational status quo with other means, usually resulting in a more or less unstable structure of domination or exploitation. In the analysis of concrete historical cases of such innovative self-organization, one must of course carefully define the unit of analysis in which change is conceptualized and observed (for a review of cases see Hunnius et al., 1973).

In order to put these notions of organizational praxis and innovation into a reasonably comprehensive and comprehensible context, let me briefly spell out my ontological and epistemological assumptions, and then give a concrete example.

ON ONTOLOGY

In terms of ontology, I see social reality as a concrete process of historical emergence in which practical human activity continuously produces and reproduces the material, social, and cultural world in which we live (Marx, 1967). Although this world can be symbolically represented and internalized by human beings, I assume it to have objective historical existence. Yet society is not only a collection of historically produced social structures and patterns of behavior, but is internalized in such a way that self and society cannot be separated except in certain analytic procedures. Specifically, the subjectivity and autonomous activity of human individuals can only be separated analytically from the social matrix and symbolic environment in which they live. As a result, society cannot be seen as merely consisting of socialized individuals; rather, it refers to the totality of relationships in which individuals find themselves (Marx, 1973). Furthermore, human individuals and groups create their own world and history under conditions produced in their historical past, which is to say, they produce the conditions under which they will create their future world. This formulation addresses the dialectical process of transforming and self-transforming activity (Marx, 1967; Sartre, 1968; Freire, 1970; Bourdieu, 1977). This is conceived not as eternal recurrence or as overdetermined bricolage or as an infinite game, but as the creation of historically objective structures and conditions, which, in turn, shape future practical activity (Appelbaum, 1978). From this perspective, the dualistic antinomies of individual and society, freedom and necessity, good and evil, mind and body, subject and object, are subsumed under a broader dialectical and historical process.

This does not mean, however, that human individuals and groups are relieved of moral responsibility and normative constraints; it means only that they can recognize, hence collectively change, the human-made, sociohistorical, and ideological nature of moral values and ethical norms. Thus the historical development of the world community and its moral evolution in terms of civil rights and universal human rights (however uneven) can provide a moral standard. Such a standard is independent of traditional ontological assumptions such as the "world as substance," the priority of mind over body, and validity of absolute truth or natural law, and the existence of supernatural and divine powers.

From the perspective of evolution, I see human culture and civilization as a distinct historical emergent made possible by the symbolic and hence social character of interaction among human beings based on their capacity for language. Here, following the symbolic interactionists (Mead, 1934), I draw the line between animal and human behavior and between the natural and cultural factors in human evolution. Nevertheless, large areas of human behavior must be seen as continuous with animal behavior insofar as human beings share certain needs and limitations of the biological organism with all forms of life, especially the time-ordered character of the life-cycle and the fact of death.

ON HUMAN NATURE

The view of human nature that follows from these assumptions is similarly historical and dialectical. I assume human nature to be neither good (hence capable of absolutely autonomous moral action and altruism, as in anarchism) nor evil and egotistical (hence in need of external social constraint, as in social contract theory), but as historically specific and, above all, evolving in terms of the self-activity and self-production of human capacities. A crucial aspect of this self-production of human nature is the historically developing production of new needs that go beyond both natural-biological needs (food, sleep) and specific sociohistorical needs such as the need for religious redemption or individual property rights. Thus, the production of needs and the institutional means to satisfy them is seen as historical accomplishment involving social praxis, not as the result of a prestructured, transhistorical hierarchy of values giving rise to a predetermined hierarchy of needs.

From this perspective, human nature cannot be classified exclusively in terms of one or another historically specific metaphor, such as *homo ludens, homo faber,* or *homo homini lupus,* or man as zoon politican, economic man, rational man, and the like, except in the very general sense of human nature as self-producing and essentially open ended. The organizational implications of this view are that neither hierarchical authority nor division of labor or any other ordering principle is intrinsic or essential to human nature, and that any organizational form, including unknown future organizational arrangements, can potentially satisfy particular needs and practical requirements. Nor do particular roles or behavior patterns have to correspond to the physical characteristics of human beings, be they racial or sexual ones. In this respect, I assume human infants to be relatively neutral and androgynous, although they may subsequently be socialized into specific behavior patterns, social roles, and differential capacities for self-determination and praxis. Needless to say, such a view transcends the dichotomies of nominalism versus realism and voluntarism versus determinism.

ON EPISTEMOLOGY

Epistemologically, I believe the subject/object dichotomy to be an unnecessarily restrictive construct in the analysis of the process of knowing and cognition. Instead, the mutual transformation of knowing subject and known object implies a dialectical process in which praxis gives rise to knowledge, and knowledge is, within certain limits, used in praxis. An important and complex consequence of this epistemological stance is that there are no fixed, a priori, transhistorical categories, but that the categories of analysis are themselves emergent and historically changing. One example might be the historically emergent conflict between the categories of analytic logic and those of dialectical logic, or the shift from a dualistic ontology to a dialectical one. Another example might be the analysis of a contemporary event, say, the 1980 workers' strike in Poland, as either a struggle of liberal democratic forces against totalitarianism and a reassertion of civil society against the state or, alternatively, as a new form of workers' self-organization with an affirmation of democratic socialism but a rejection of many features of the socialist state. While either interpretation must empirically measure itself against the self-understanding of the strikers, it is conceivable that the older categories of analysis (e.g., state versus society or socialism versus capitalism) are ideologically more limited than are the historically

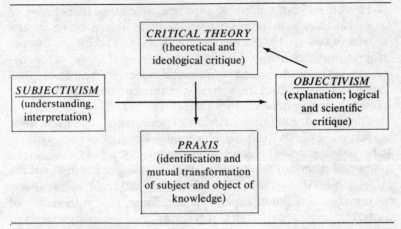

Figure 20.1   Four Moments in Praxis

emergent ones (e.g., self-organization); hence, understanding of and reaction to the events may be more or less incomplete and inadequate depending on the nature and choice of categories involved.

One way of representing the dialectical development of knowledge categories is to postulate praxis as the most complex form of knowledge and consciousness that contains in itself and transcends all previous forms and levels of development — for example, subjectivism, objectivism, and criticism. Alternatively, one could postulate a process of historical-structural development in which subjectivist stances such as solipsism, egocentrism, ethnocentrism, and the purely interpretive-definitionist mode are superseded by objectivist principles such as analytic logic, objectivity, value neutrality, detached scientific description, the logic of explanation, and the criteria of testability and falsifiability. In either case, praxis would constitute the endpoint of a developmental sequence and would provide an experiential link between the ancient, time-honored realms of being, thinking, and doing, as represented in Figure 20.1.

The deadlocked antagonism between subjectivism and objectivism has characterized much of the debate of epistemological issues in analytic philosophy and the logic of science (Habermas, 1976; Bernstein, 1976). However, with the emergence of critical theory, two new criteria of knowledge and knowledge production have become available. One is a new conception of critique as not merely a method of establishing the limits of reason and knowledge and the validity of logical and scientific reconstruction, but as critique of ideology and as a method of taking into account the historical limitations of specific social theories as well as the practical intent and the activist moment in theorizing (Horkheimer, 1976).

This criterion of critique is not to be understood as negation or scepticism designed to reject any dogmatic assertion, be it subjectivist or objectivist. Rather, critique is seen as taking the form of critical theory that incorporates different levels and modes of theorizing such as the positivist and hermeneutic modes. Critical theory thus constitutes a multilevel theoretical structure composed of both substantive theory and metatheory (Habermas, 1973).

The second emerging criterion of knowledge and knowledge production is praxis itself, which contains but goes beyond critique and practical intent (Heydebrand and Burris, 1982). Praxis becomes a source and criterion of knowledge precisely because it transcends the subject/object dichotomy not only in theory and critique, but also in the ontological realm of experience and doing, i.e., in the sense of transformation, self-transformation, and self-organization (Thompson, 1978; Negt and Kluge, 1972). Once again, praxis must be distinguished from the pragmatic-instrumentalist concept of practical action where the problem-solving capacity of goal-oriented activity becomes the criterion of truth. Rather, the self-validating character of praxis is grounded in the possibility of self-transformation (through understanding, explanation, and critique, i.e., through interaction with the object), without which it would regress to mere objectifying action, pluralistic relativism, rote behavior, or automatic reflex. Moreover, this notion of praxis is understood as a unitary, experiential, and concrete dialectical process (Heydebrand, 1981). Therefore, it differs from analytic composites such as the notion of separate economic, political, ideological, and scientific-theoretical practices (Althusser, 1976); work and interaction (Habermas, 1973); and different levels of consciousness such as practical consciousness, discursive consciousness, and unconscious sources of cognition and action (Giddens, 1979).

ON METHODOLOGY

The methodology flowing from these assumptions is neither exclusively qualitative nor quantitative, but a complex of policies and strategies that permit a given problematic to be understood, explained, critically analyzed, acted on, and resolved or transformed. For the study of organizations, this requires an openness for process, totality, contradictions, and social construction (Benson, 1977). Most important, the fundamental dichotomy of history and structure is transcended in the direction of a sociological emergentism in which subjectivity and collectivity are linked not only by experiential and symbolic ties, but also by political safeguards to protect individual autonomy and to ensure ethical procedures of research.

As an example of an attempt to move toward such a methodological stance, let me briefly describe the project I have been involved in for the last few years. The project is designed to study the impact of the so-called fiscal crisis of the state (O'Connor, 1973) on American courts of law and on the judicial system. The theoretical expectation is this: Given the increasing demand for judicial services and the relative decrease in the fiscal resources allocated to the third branch, courts do not have the organizational capability to deal with this crisis and are coming under pressure to rationalize their procedures and to streamline their operations so as to make them more cost-effective (Heydebrand and Seron, 1981). Given further that courts of law are professional organizations dominated by a judicial elite, it is expected that administrative rationalization will either be subordinated to the interests and priorities of judges, or will meet with outright resistance by the dominant professional elite, or will drastically alter the organization of work and the authority relations of courts.

As a result of interviews and observation, it became clear that rationalization could not be described as a functional or merely adaptive process of bureaucratization. Rather, it became useful to view rationalization more as a multifaceted historical movement toward strategic administrative and technical innovations emanating from various sources inside and outside the judicial system, and manifesting itself in a variety of judicial and administrative policies as well as contradictory strategies of reform. Thus to study this emergent historical development of new organizational strategies and structures implied a need to be sensitive to the very process of organizational formation and transformation, to the contradictions and mediations that mark this process, and to the emergence of possibly unknown forms out of older ones with which they coexist (Heydebrand, 1977a). This perspective then required not only a synchronic structural analysis of courts as organizations, but also a comparative historical analysis including the identification of critical events and contradictions, adequate concepts to describe the observational and interview material in terms of the self-understanding of the actors involved, and propositions and theoretical generalizations that would eventually go beyond mere descriptive accounts and conceptual models. Most important, this perspective required locating the event histories in a practical, ideological, and political universe of discourse reflecting the confrontation between the viewpoints and strategies of judges, administrators, and state planners. In other words, empirical observation and analysis had to go hand in hand with the critical evaluation of the conceptual and theoretical content of propositions, and with the identification and evaluation of the ideological programs and practical strategies of real political actors. For example, the goal model of organizations (Georgopoulos and Tannenbaum, 1957) largely corresponds to the views of judges, the bureaucratic model (Weber, 1966) to those of administrators, and the system-resource model (Yuchtman and Seashore, 1967; Eisenstadt, 1959; Parsons, 1951) to the more technocratically oriented state planners and decision makers. Thus these models are neither true nor false in an absolute sense, but only more or less useful in describing different phases of, and perspectives on, a common organizational reality.

The theoretical question of the differential responses of courts to the judicial crisis implied that it would be necessary to analyze the main features of the surrounding political economy of courts, i.e., not only to obtain an economic, demographic, and political profile of each court's jurisdiction, but to do so for an adequate period of time in which changes in the surrounding political economy could be observed (Heydebrand, 1977b). Quantitative data for these profiles were obtained from the Bureau of the Census for the years 1950, 1960, and 1970, and were aggregated to the unit of analysis used in the study, the jurisdictional district of each court. In addition, it was necessary to conduct a more qualitative analysis of policy statements, conferences, speeches, newspaper clippings, and other documentary material to identify the issues of "judicial crisis" and "rationalization of courts" from the perspective of the political-ideological positions of the major groups involved. This analysis, in turn, led to a broadening of the theoretical framework such that changes in the judiciary could be linked to the constitutional relations between the judicial and executive branches and to major changes in the larger political economy (Heydebrand, 1979).

METHODOLOGY AND PRAXIS

What does this methodological approach mean concretely in terms of praxis? Perhaps the best way to begin answering this question is to recall the distinction made earlier between three types of organizational innovation: behavioral-adaptive innovations, strategic innovations, and self-transforming, self-organizing innovations. At the level of behavioral and merely adaptive innovations, the analyst follows a functionalist method of identifying general problem areas in a given organizational system, pinpointing those needs and requirements that are not currently met and suggesting the institution or adoption of new behavior patterns or structures designed to maintain or regain a given level of functioning. This method will work under conditions of structural homogeneity and ideological consensus as to the goals of the organization. But under conditions of structural heterogeneity, organizational contradictions, and conflict among interests such as is true of courts of law and the justice system, in general, the observer-analyst will find it necessary not only to think in terms of strategic innovations, but also to identify a variety of structured interests, each with its own strategy of reform. The three main perspectives, in ascending order of their scope of awareness of organization-wide problem areas and the degree of articulation of crisis issues, are the professional, the bureaucratic, and the technocratic.

In courts, the professional strategy of innovation is carried predominantly by judges and attorneys, who tend to respond to problems and crises by demanding an increased level of legitimacy of professional dominance and an expansion of their domain (including an expansion of resources). The typical practice of research here is the professionally guided commission or research committee that conceives of problems of quality and effectiveness in terms of the goal model of organizations, i.e., maximizing organizational effectiveness by increasing the input of value rationality and substantive rationality (e.g., input of professional service, selection, and control).

The bureaucratic strategy of innovation is carried by administrators and, more generally, by the representative of executive functions (compared here to judicial-professional-service functions). Thus court administrators and prosecutors share common interests in the efficiency of the system, i.e., in using existing organizational and fiscal resources more economically rather than expanding them. In other words, the main target for change is the reorganization and intensification of the labor process in order to increase productivity. Where expansion rather than intensification is advocated, it will tend to serve the expansion of administrative control, e.g., through the adoption of new technologies such as management and information systems. In general, measures of rationalization and cost-effectiveness (i.e., input of functional, technical, or instrumental rationality) come closest to the administrative strategy of innovation.

Both professional and bureaucratic types of innovation are strategic in the sense of seeking to implement a given reform policy, seeking to block others or limiting their conditions of action. Here, the political and ideological (i.e., practical) *content* of strategic innovations is highly articulated. Perhaps for this reason, such strategic innovations are particularistic, one-sided, or class bound and do not lend themselves to concerted action in the face of rapid change, increasing environmental complexity, and endemic crisis situations.

Analysts of the crisis of the judicial system have in the past tended to choose sides, i.e., to advocate either the generally more aggressive management perspective or the generally more defensive professional service perspective. Only recently, since the crises of the 1960s and 1970s, has a third, more encompassing perspective begun to appear in professional service organizations. This type of innovation, which will be called "technocratic," is still strategic since it is singularly oriented toward the overcoming or prevention of crisis situations. But as a strategy of innovation, it contains structural elements (e.g., systems theory, social engineering, broadening the basis of participation) that point to the third level of innovation, namely, self-transformation and self-organization of the system as a whole.

Here, then, is a crucial connection between organizational praxis and methodology, where in the process of analysis, evaluation, and critique, the roles of analyst and political actor tend to merge. Knowing subject and known object are no longer strictly separated. In this process, the articulation of different forms of innovation that are practical strategies of change or resistance to change becomes itself policy oriented and politically active.

TECHNOCRACY: THE EMERGENCE OF A NEW ORGANIZATIONAL FORM

The new theoretical elements emerging from this "reflexive" research process do not only lead to a new level of conceptualizing innovations; they also entail a reconceptualization of the concept of technocracy and a new perspective on technocratic theory (Heydebrand, 1981). From this perspective the concept of technocracy may be understood in a dual capacity: as a concept referring to new strategies of organizational control and to new organizational formations, and also as a concept of critical theory that can help resolve conceptual difficulties in the relations between occupational logic (e.g., professionalization) and organizational logic (e.g., bureaucratization) to provide an intellectual bridge between organizational, occupational, and class analysis, and to serve as an instrument of social criticism and political praxis.

The conventional definition of technocracy emphasizes its character as a system of social control based on scientific-technical knowledge and instrumental rationality in decision making. Ultimate control of all economic and political resources of a social system is seen to be in the hands of scientists, engineers, and technical experts (the "technocrats"). Traditional definitions of technocracy also treat it as an extension of bureaucracy (as in "technobureaucracy") and as the ultimate form of technical rationality and planning, which is defined as a "power" of functional or purposive rationality (Habermas, 1971). In short, technocracy involves highly systematized and codified forms of knowledge ("science") and their systematic application in terms of technical innovation, social engineering, information processing, decision making, work procedures, and behavior control.

There are several problems with this conventional notion of technocracy. First, there is an insufficient distinction between the economic and political dimensions of power, on the one hand, and the assumed autonomy of technical labor and control, on the other. It seems that the purely technical aspects of domination cannot be treated independently of the dynamics of production of the political economy, be it capitalist or state socialist. Second, the notion of technocracy suggests a relatively fixed, one-dimensional system of control, whereas it is probably more useful and closer to contemporary realities to identify specific technocratic strategies. These strategies are flexibly aimed, by corporate and governmental decision makers, at preventing or dealing with crises, reducing uncertainty and complexity, stabilizing the political economy, and facilitating but not necessarily achieving long-term planning. Third, most academic conceptions of technocracy see it as a linear extension of Weber's notion of bureaucracy — as a system of control based on technical knowledge. This is a one-dimensional, unidirectional conception of progressive institutionalization of functional rationality. It does not deal with the fundamental tension between Weber's model of bureaucracy and the theory of social systems (Parsonian and otherwise) or with the potential contradictions and possible dead ends of technocratic strategies of administration in their attempt to integrate service and domination or production and control.

In contrast to accepted definitions of technocracy, the concept is defined here as a historical and structural synthesis of professional administration and bureaucratic administration transcending both forms and implying their gradual transformation, especially deprofessionalization (Haug, 1973) and debureaucratization (Eisenstadt, 1959).

This definition takes account of the historical and dialectical development of technocracy as a new form of organizational control structure that emerges out of, but supersedes, previous forms. Thus generic occupational, crafts, and professional functions can be seen as combining both productive activity and its control within one actor or one collective subject, e.g., the guild or occupational status group. The development of bureaucracy, compared to crafts and professional occupations, is marked by the externalization of control and its separation from productive activity. It is usually conceptualized as hierarchical authority or control of labor. Another aspect of bureaucratization is the differentiation or fragmentation of work activities themselves, usually conceptualized as division of labor. Under technocratic strategies, *both* production and control functions are externalized, but they are no longer strictly separated from each other, but more or less integrated into a systemic synthesis. In other words, in a technocratic system, the structural separation between production and control functions is minimized or even eliminated. As a result, new forms of control tend to appear that are designed to manage the system as a whole, but that also facilitate the reinternalization and reintegration of productive activity and control on a new level involving new organizational arrangements, broader participation, and the emergence of new collective interests and responsibilities. This process can be seen as both resulting from, as well as giving rise to, the conscious creation of new forms of self-organization that may go beyond technocracy.

A crucial new element of technocratic control structures, in contrast to professional and bureaucratic ones, is the involvement of the state apparatus in the delivery of public and professional services on an unprecedented scale, not just in the legitimation of professional mandates and bureaucratic authority. In other words, increasing levels of state intervention in economy and society, frequently initiated or legitimated by various public or private commissions (e.g., the President's Commission on Law Enforcement and the Administration of Justice, or the Carnegie Commission on Higher Education), bestow a distinctly new (technocratic) character on state-wide and nation-wide systems of service delivery.

Another crucial element in this new definition of technocracy is the integration of professional and bureaucratic functions into a comprehensive system of production and control based on systems theory and systems engineering. The far-reaching consequences of this process for the autonomy of professional groups, the separation of constitutional powers, the supersession of Taylorism, and the transformation of bureaucratic management can only be indicated here and are being developed elsewhere (Heydebrand, 1981). Suffice it to say that the process involves both deprofessionalization and debureaucratization, as well as new organizational forms emerging from the integration of production and control, of service and domination, and of substantive and functional rationality. Thus reform-oriented policymaking in the areas of criminal justice or higher education, for example, could avoid trying to make impossible choices between the quality of professional service (the goal model), the efficiency of rational administration (the bureaucratic model), or the balancing of different subsystem goals (the system-resource model). Instead, the real choice may be between technocratic systems engineering and altogether new forms of political control over production and services. Whether this new political control takes the form of democratic self-organization or some other type of organizational arrangement (e.g., neocorporatism) will probably be decided in future crises and conjunctions.

In sum, the idea of organization as praxis involves not only organizational self-transformation, but also of the previous moments of understanding, explanation, and critique. Praxis-oriented analysis merely makes available the articulation of alternative strategies for the resolution of complex and contradictory situations. But each of the strategies represents a practical program that is only part of a resolution. Since the collective actors and their analysts are to various degrees involved in concrete situations, they must achieve a very high level of self-understanding and self-criticism in order to be able to participate creatively in their own self-transformation and self-organization, instead of merely reacting to crises or engaging in particularistic strategies.

About the Author

WOLF V. HEYDEBRAND

My intellectual development owes much to the critical theory of the Frankfurt school of sociology, where I studied in the early 1950s, and to the empirical and interactionist tradition of the Chicago school of sociology, where I took my Ph. D. in the 1960s. Needless to say, these two traditions do not see eye to eye on most issues of theory and research. Indeed, the limitations of the positivist model of social science, on the one hand, and the unquestionable importance of sustaining what E. P. Thompson calls "the empirical mode of intellectual practice," on the other, are the two sides of a contradiction that continues to confront and challenge me in my method and writing.

In addition, having grown up in Germany in the 1930s and 1940s, I developed, like many of my generation, a particular political sensitivity to the authoritarian and antidemocratic tendencies of modern societies, be they fascist, neocorporatist, technocractic, or state socialist.

The political experience of the 1960s and the development of alternative theoretical perspectives in sociology generated new opportunities to reconsider the relevance of the interpretive, historical, and critical approaches in addition to positivism and functionalism. In advocating an empirically grounded but critically oriented sociological approach, I continue to search for a method that might help to interpret *and* change the social world without playing out critique and change against interpretation and explanation.

21

TOWARD A REALIST PERSPECTIVE

William Outhwaite

THE REALIST VIEW OF SCIENCE

"Realism" is used here to refer to a position in the philosophy of science that has roots as far back as Aristotle but has become increasingly prominent in the last ten or twenty years. The most important contributions to this development are those of Mary Hesse (1966, 1974) and Rom Harré (1970, 1972), and in the past few years, the work of Roy Bhaskar (1978). A particular feature of this movement is the intimate link established between the philosophy of science and social theory: both Harré (Harré and Secord, 1972; Harré, 1979) and Bhaskar (1979) have written extensively about the nature of the social sciences, and two other recent contributions to the debate also introduce realism into a discussion of alternative paradigms in social theory (Keat and Urry, 1975; Benton 1977). This chapter is based mainly on Bhaskar's treatment of these issues.

The central principle of realism is its conception of reality. Whereas empiricists have shifted attention from reality to our *knowledge* of reality and analyzed that knowledge in terms of sense impressions, realists stress that what science is really interested in is the structures and mechanisms of reality. The combined tendencies of these structures and mechanisms *may* generate events that in turn

Author's Note: It will be clear from the content of this chapter how much it owes to the work of Roy Bhaskar, who was unable to attend the workshop but has provided constant advice and encouragement during the writing of it. I should like also to thank the other participants in the workshop, and Trevor Pateman, who commented on an earlier version.

may be observed, but the events take place whether or not there is anyone around to observe them, and the tendencies of the underlying structures of reality remain the same even when they counteract each other in such a way as to produce no (directly or indirectly) observable change in reality.

Bhaskar draws a distinction between three "domains": the real, the actual, and the empirical. The empirical is made up of experiences, obtained by direct or indirect observation. This domain must be distinguished from the domain of the actual, which includes events whether or not they are observed. These events may just happen to be unobserved because there is no one around to observe them, or they may be too small/large/fast/slow to be perceived. What happens is not the same as what is observed to happen: "to be" is *not* (*pace* Bishop Berkeley) "to be perceived."

But we need a further distinction between the domain of the actual, made up of events, and the domain of the real, comprising the processes that generate events. The absence of an event — a change in the world — does not necessarily mean that there are no underlying tendencies toward change. It may just mean that they are counteracted by other forces. The tendency of the books on my table to fall to the center of the Earth is counteracted by the presence of the table: The books remain where they are. To take another example: My watch has a mechanism in virtue of which it has the power to, as we say, tell the time. But for this to happen there are three main conditions. First, the mechanism must have its causal powers intact: It must not be, for example, "broken." Second, the mechanism must be activated: I must remember to keep my watch wound up and set to the correct time zone. And third, although the watch will, if these conditions are satisfied, "tell the time" 24 hours a day whether or not I observe it, it will only tell *me* the time if I *observe* the *event* of the hands pointing to 11:15, an event produced by a latent structure or *mechanism*.

Realists, then, see science as a human activity that aims at discovering, by a mixture of experimentation and theoretical reasoning, the entities, structures, and mechanisms (visible or invisible) that exist and operate in the world. How does this apparently common-sense view of science differ from that provided by other philosophies?

Classical empiricism assumes that the real world is unproblematically represented in or (in the phenomenalist variant of empiricism) is identical with the empirical world of our experiences: We have only to record our experiences of the world and summarize them in theories, which characteristically take the form of stating constant conjunctions between observed events. This cosy picture of science is threatened, however, by the realization that the whole idea of given atomic facts that we observe and record prior to our theorization of them is fundamentally unsatisfactory. Observation statements are always made with reference to a set of explicit or inexplicit *theories:* They are "theory laden." Our concepts are produced within theories that confront our sense experience not piecemeal but as whole systems of assumptions, techniques, forms of representation, and so forth (Quine, 1953).

Once one accepts this, the way is open to a radically conventionalist position in which our frameworks, perspectives, or paradigms not only influence what we "perceive" but actually generate it. In Kuhn's notorious formulation, which he admits is a "strange locution . . . after discovering oxygen Lavoisier worked in a different world" (Kuhn, 1970b: 118). But to take this step is to render the choice between alternative theories, frameworks, or paradigms something radically indeterminate, as it is for example with Weber's related concept of value reference *(Wertbeziehung):* It is in terms of a set of values that a certain slice of an infinitely complex reality becomes interesting *for us*. The relations between theories become a matter of shifting perspectives or horizons (Gadamer, 1975: 269ff.). The temptation of relativism becomes hard to resist.

The realist solution is to accept the theory-laden nature of all description but to draw a sharp distinction between scientific concepts, theories, and laws, what Bhaskar calls the "transitive" objects of science and the "intransitive" objects of science — the real structures and mechanisms of the universe to which our theories aim to refer. Intransitivity here means that these structures exist independently of our descriptions of them; what we call the laws of physics and chemistry would exist even if no entities had evolved on the earth with the capacity to discover them. Thus we do not "form reality," as conventionalists would have it. Rather, what we do is formulate descriptions of reality that aim to express its essential properties in the form of thought and language. However difficult it may be to compare alternative theories, there is a "fact of the matter" that they are attempting to represent and their relative success can be, in principle, a matter for rational judgment.

It has been implied so far that these ontological and epistemological claims can be made for all scientific practice, including that of the social or human sciences. Let me now try to justify this assumption by addressing some of the standard arguments that are made for the contrary view, i.e., that there are essential differences of principle between the natural sciences and the social sciences.

First, it is often alleged that the subject matter of the social "sciences" is intrinsically more complex than is that of the natural sciences, and therefore not amenable to scientific investigation. One way of putting this is to say that social laws will be either so trivial or so frequently violated that there is little point in enunciating them. This position can be seen to rest on an empiricist analysis of causal relations as grounded in constant conjunctions of empirical events; we observe a correlation between two variables and postulate some sort of connection between them. The difficulty with the constant conjunction approach is that events in the real world of both natural science and social science take place in "open systems" in which they are subject to a wide range of causal influences. Where two or more tendencies interact, they may neutralize each other such that there is nothing to be observed, as in the example of the books resting on my table, which (under the dual influence of gravitational attraction and the resistance opposed by the table) simply stay where they are. Open systems, then, are the rule rather than the exception even in the natural sciences, and the closure of systems by experimentation in such a way as to generate deductively justified predictions is less common in the natural sciences than philosophers like to assume. It is clear that experimental closure is rarely, if ever, possible in the social sciences; the artificiality of "laboratory" research in social psychology goes to prove this point (see, for example, Harré and Secord, 1972).

For realism, none of this amounts to a problem of principle or a difference of principle between natural and social science. The realist analysis of causal relations is designed precisely to cope with the prevalence of open systems in both the natural and the social world. Open systems must be analyzed as the battlefields of conflicting tendencies; even the best analysis of these tendencies and their interactions may not yield a successful prediction of the outcome. But realists, unlike many positivists, do *not* identify explanation with prediction; a successful prediction is a welcome addition to a successful explanation rather than something intrinsically related to it. This is because, to repeat the point once more, explanation for the realist involves the demonstration, *not* of a constant conjunction of events, but of a powerful tendency, materially embodied in a generative mechanism. (This may be further analyzed in terms of the powers and liabilities of entities — their intrinsic and relational properties; see Harré and Madden, 1975). There are many ways in the different sciences of furnishing logical and empirical support for postulated explanations; prediction is only one of them. Even if experimental closure is *never* possible in the social sciences, this only means that the criteria for theory choice will, in principle, have to be exclusively explanatory rather than predictive.

A second argument for the fundamental distinctiveness of the natural and social sciences also concerns the analysis of causal relations. It is often claimed that the purposive action of human beings (and perhaps of the higher animals) is something radically different from the interaction of causal mechanisms in nature and must be analyzed in terms of motives, purposes, reasons, and so on, rather than in terms of causal influences. Although some realists continue to insist on this distinction, it is also possible, given a realist analysis of causation in terms of entities with causal powers and tendencies, to see a much closer parallel with the analysis of human agency.

One of the weaknesses of the constant conjunction analysis of causation is its inability to give a plausible account of human agency. If causal relations are analyzed in an empiricist way as contingent relations between logically independent events, this analysis hardly seems to fit the relation between, say, my intending to raise my hand and my actually doing so. Interpretive social scientists thus conclude that the analysis of actions in terms of reasons, purposes, motives, and so forth must be something radically different from causal analysis.

Let us look more closely at the hand-raising example. I have the power to raise my hand, and on most occasions when my hand goes up, I am in some sense the initiator of the event, although others can also raise my hand if I allow them to or if they overpower me. We can distinguish further between cases when I raise my hand deliberately to catch the chairman's eye, to salute someone, and so forth, and those where it seems to go up automatically, because it has been held down for a long time or is raised under posthypnotic suggestion or, as in Dr. Strangelove's Nazi salute, from force of habit.

Dr. Strangelove, while working in Nazi Germany, had a good reason to give Nazi salutes, even if he did not enjoy doing so and would have preferred it if some other form of greeting had been equally acceptable. Having transferred his allegiance to the U.S. government, he had no further reason to make Nazi salutes and seems to have experienced embarrassment when the habit persisted. It seems to me reasonable to say that in Germany, his salutes were initially activated by a conscious mechanism (though one that may soon have become habitual), whereas in the U.S. the salutes were always in some sense unintentional. The analysis of Strangelove's salutes seems to me in both situations a causal investigation, and it seems prima facie reasonable to treat his reason for saluting, which was present in Germany and absent in the United States, as a component of those causal sequences.

Bhaskar (1979: chap. 3) provides a more detailed set of arguments for the analysis of agency in causal terms. Harré, on the contrary, has wished to uphold the separation between explaining actions in terms of reasons and in terms of causes, arguing that "reason explanations" are the analogue in the social sciences to the "mechanism explanations" that apply to the natural world (Harré and Secord, 1972; Harré, 1979).

It cannot, therefore, be claimed that realism as such resolves the longstanding dispute over reasons and causes. What is does, however, is change the terms of the dispute by providing a more adequate analysis of causal explanation and at least make plausible the analysis of human beings, together with their reasons for acting in the ways they do, as special kinds of causal agents.

A third argument for a radical distinction between natural and social science is the claim that social situations are constituted, in an ontological sense, by the "meanings" and interpretations of those who participate in them. What is at issue here, from a realist perspective, is basically the question of what sort of case can be made for the intransitivity, in Bhaskar's sense, of *social* structures and mechanisms as opposed to the meanings and interpretations through which they are constituted in everyday practice. Intransitivity, it will be recalled, means essentially that "things exist and act independently of our descriptions" (Bhaskar, 1978: 250). Do social structures exist and act in a sense that is separate from meanings and interpretations? Many interpretivist social scientists would argue no, for although the structure of social relations in, for example, contemporary Britain is hardly affected by *my* conception of it, it is surely not independent of the conceptions of all the social agents who participate in those relations. Once this is conceded, as I think it must be, it may seem that idealism, expelled with a realist fork from the study of nature, is poised to return when we study social structures and processes. Interpretive sociology, especially in its "phenomenological" variant, enthusiastically takes up this possibility.

It does so, however, as the cost of generating its own antinomies, for the "social construction of reality" cannot plausibly be represented except on the basis of some given system of preexisting social relations. Human agency, too, presupposes society as its most important precondition. It does not so much "produce" society as reproduce and transform it (Bhaskar, 1979: 43). To say that social structures are unobservable is a red herring: so are magnetic fields. What matters is that their existence can be demonstrated by their causal effects. Even if we concede that social structures do not exist independently of the activities they govern (Bhaskar, 1979: 48), it is impossible to explain those activities except as, in essential respects, the effects of those structures.

The second section of this chapter will attempt to show how a realist perspective can be applied in social analysis. What I have tried to show so far is that realism is *prima facie* applicable to the domain of the social sciences as well as to that of the natural sciences.

REALISM AS A STRATEGY FOR SOCIAL RESEARCH

What are the implications of this approach for the practice of social research? We can begin to answer this question by reviewing some of the realist principles that have already been mentioned. In the sphere of ontology, we have:

(1) the distinction between transitive and intransitive objects of science: between our concepts, models, and so forth, and the real entities, relations, and so on that make up the natural and the social world;

(2) the further stratification of reality into the domains of the real, the actual, and the empirical (the last of these is in a contingent relation to the other two; to be — either for an entity or structure or for an event — is *not* to be perceived);

(3) the conception of causal relations as tendencies, grounded in the interactions of generative mechanisms; these interactions may or may not produce events that in turn may or may not be observed.

In addition to these three ontological claims, and related to the first one, we have the rejection of both positivist empiricism and interpretivist conventionalism above. The practical expression of this epistemological position is the concept of real definition. Real definitions, which are important for both realist and rationalist philosophies of science (Bhaskar, 1978: 171ff., 246; Hollis, 1977: 177ff.), are neither summaries of existing verbal usage not stipulations that we should use a term in a particular way. Although they are of course expressed in words, they are statements about the basic nature of some entity or structure. Thus a real definition of water would be that its molecules are composed of two atoms of hydrogen and one of oxygen. This human discovery about water comes to be expressed as a definitional property of it. At a more complex level, Marx's *Das Kapital* may be read as an attempt to provide a real definition of the capitalist mode of production.

This notion of real definition serves as a leitmotif to the practice of social research on a realist basis (see Outhwaite, 1983: 36-51). The social scientist directs his or her attention to an object of inquiry that is already defined in certain ways in the world of everyday life and ordinary language. (This is, of course, true of natural objects as well, but with the important difference that natural objects do not have concepts of what they are doing when they fall, collide, melt, die, and so forth). The realist social scientist will typically seek to redescribe this object so as to bring out its complexity, i.e., the way in which it is determined by its internal and external relations as an outcome of a multiplicity of interacting tendencies (see Benson, Chapter 22).

The question is, in other words, what (relevantly) needs to be the case for a particular set of social relations to appear as they do? Classical political economy, for example, was established as an area of inquiry through reflection on categories, such as wages, that were already present as actors' descriptions; it was, in effect, developed by asking, in an essentially realist way, what must be the case for these forms of economic life to exist in the way they do? Marx's critique of political economy carries this process a stage further by reflecting both on the phenomenal forms of economic life (such as the wage-form) and on the ways in which his predecessors had analyzed these forms. How was it possible for these appearances to exist and for classical economists to give a partially accurate, though also deeply flawed, representation of these appearances?

The notion of relevance in the preceding paragraph shows how the conception of the object of inquiry will crucially determine the sorts of methods that are appropriate to its investigation. The ethnomethodological approach of conversational analysis will not help us to understand the rate of profit in a capitalist economy, nor will the law of value explain how one can terminate a telephone conversation without embarrassment. Historical analysis may or may not be relevant to the study of a particular contemporary situation. In other words, the question of what is needed to explain an observable social phenomenon will receive a contextually specific answer. The main point is that in this redefinition of objects of social inquiry, and prior to any choice of methods of investigation, are questions of social ontology. What sort of object are we trying to describe and explain? To what extent is it a product of the interpretations of human beings, and to what extent is it structured by "deeper causes that are opaque to human consciousness"?

Rom Harré, who has argued for an interactionist, interpretivist social psychology, and Roy Bhaskar, who has upheld a more structuralist and materialist approach in the social sciences, can both legitimately construe their proposals in realist terms. Both can claim to be propounding ways of getting at the fundamental structures and generative mechanisms of social life: Where they differ is in their accounts of the constitution of social reality and of how this reality can be known (Harré, 1979: esp. 19ff., 139ff., 237, 348ff., 356; Bhaskar, 1979: chap. 2). Realism does not uniquely license either of these approaches. What it *does* provide, however, is a framework in which these alternative social ontologies can be rationally compared and discussed — in which they are not brushed aside as "mere" definitional assumptions.

The existence of different approaches to a realist research strategy raises the question as to how we can evaluate the real definitions of social phenomena provided by different social scientists. A number of possibilities can be identified. First, they will, of course, have to satisfy certain a priori conditions of self-consistency. Second, there may also be more interesting a priori conditions: A real definition of social or economic systems may, for example, be criticized on a priori grounds if it fails to make room for an adequate account of the reproduction and transformation of that system (Hollis and Nell, 1975: esp. chap. 8). Third, real definitions and other theoretical statements will have to be evaluated a posteriori in terms of "the revealed explanatory power of the hypotheses that can be derived from them" (Bhaskar, 1979: 63). It is necessary to examine, for example, whether postulated structures and mechanisms can explain observable phenomena. The Freudian unconscious, for example, aims to explain such apparently unrelated phenomena as dreams, slips of the tongue, neuroses, jokes, and so on. In order to evaluate the persuasiveness of this explanation, attention must therefore be turned to the negative task of asking whether other possible explanations can account just as well for the explanandum, and to the positive task of seeing what independent evidence can be furnished for the existence of the postulated mechanism. Fourth, the generation of successful predictions may have a part to play in providing further evidential support, though as discussed earlier, the realist social scientist, unlike the positivist, will not wish to make prediction the main criterion of successful theory. Such criteria will more usually be purely explanatory (Bhaskar, 1979: 165).

A realist perspective is now beginning to inspire a growing body of work in social theory, psychology, and linguistics. At the present state of development, it is inappropriate to draw a sharp distinction between realism as research program and realism as the basis of a critique of existing positivist or interpretivist research. However, I do believe that it is appropriate to suggest that realism offers a more adequate philosophy for science, including the social sciences, than do the positivist or interpretivist perspectives that have hitherto been dominant.

About the Author

WILLIAM OUTHWAITE

I am member of the "generation of '68" — the year in which I began the study of philosophy, politics, economics, and sociology at Oxford. I had become interested in Marxism some years earlier and, encouraged by the spirit of the times, identified myself with the fashionable work of Herbert Marcuse and Jürgen Habermas, who was gradually becoming familiar to the English-speaking world.

I moved to the University of Sussex to take my M.A., where Habermas provided the organizing framework for my book on the Verstehen tradition (*Understanding Social Life* 1975). By the time this book was published, I was teaching sociology at Sussex and working on a Ph.D. project on the construction of social scientific concepts, under the patient supervision of Tom Bottomore. The late 1970s brought the publication of a growing body of "realist" literature, discussed in my paper in this volume, and in particular of Bhaskar's *Possibility of Naturalism* (1978), which has convinced me that it is possible to combine the essential insights of the interpretivist tradition and critical theory within a broadly naturalist conception of the (partial) unity of natural and social science and a materialist theory of society. This position is developed in my *Concept Formation in Social Science* (1982) and in my contribution to this volume.

— 22 —

A DIALECTICAL METHOD FOR THE STUDY OF ORGANIZATIONS

J. Kenneth Benson
University of Missouri

For some time I have been developing a dialectical approach to the study of organizations (Benson, 1977). Such an approach can be constructed within the Marxian tradition of dialectics. Central to this task is the formulation of a dialectical method of wide applicability, i.e., applicable to various types of social formations and levels of analysis. The key features of such a method are discoverable in Marx's analysis of competitive capitalism but are capable of extrication from that analysis. The dialectical method can survive the failure of Marx's specific propositions about competitive capitalism and indeed can survive the passing of that social formation. The method should be applicable to a variety of societies, including not only state capitalist but also state socialist systems. The method should also provide an approach to phenomena not specifically analyzed by Marx himself.

In the present chapter I provide a progress report on my effort to formulate such a method and to apply it to the study of organizations. I will first present a brief statement of a dialectical method, then suggest how organizational issues are to be addressed, and finally describe in barest outline a field study.

THE DIALECTICAL VIEW

The dialectical method consists of interrelated ontological, epistemological, and axiological commitments (see, for example, Lukács, 1971; Goldmann, 1969, 1976; Gouldner, 1980; Lefebvre, 1968, 1976; Markovic, 1974; Marx, 1973; McLellan, 1977). In developing the view presented here, I have been particularly influenced by Bernstein (1976), Bhaskar (1978, 1979), and Applebaum (1978). These commitments are embedded in a conceptual framework that is capable of guiding inquiry into specific phenomena. The framework provides a basis for a dialectical form of structural analysis, or perhaps "genetic structuralism," to use Goldmann's (1969) phrase.

The basic ontological commitments stress social production. People produce the social world and are in turn produced by it. The world in which we live and that shapes our development is a product of prior human activity. Furthermore, it depends on human activity every day for its reproduction; it is reproduced in and through the everyday practices of people.

The process through which people create a social world involves the enactment of practices within the context and under the constraint of previously constructed practices. The constructions are shaped by social locations, interests, and constraints or limits. Practices are not merely objective phenomena (as in a set of externally observable routines), but are enactments involving subjectively and intersubjectively shared meanings, purposes, and assumptions. Practices, in this conception, defy classification as either subjective or objective phenomena. As people strive to satisfy their needs (e.g., to overcome scarcity) they generate new forms of social organization (e.g., new divisions of labor, technologies, and modes of control).

Forms of social organization (ensembles of social relations), once in place, have determinate tendencies. A way of organizing social life, which is at root merely an arrangement of the social practices followed by people, has at its core a tendency to develop in predictable directions, so long as the core practices remain in place. In the Marxian view, the core practices center on the production of material goods. Changes in the sets of social practices concerned with the production of material goods tend to occasion changes throughout the total social formation.

Caught within a particular way of organizing social life, people lose control of the production and reproduction of their social worlds. In this fundamental sense, they are alienated. Their alienation is ironic in that the determinate force of the social order rests ultimately on their practices, on the orderliness and predictability of the social relationships they create and then re-create each day. Their alienation stems in part from the assumptions they make about the social world (for example, the assumption that it is necessary or inevitable or natural). These are not necessarily the assumptions built into philosophies or theories, but rather the assumptions that govern routine practices of everyday life.

A form of social organization (or ensemble of social relations), as it develops in accord with its own inherent tendencies, eventually creates contradictions; that is, it generates sets of practices that threaten its own essential character or reach beyond its limits. Contradictions, while not determining outcomes exactly, do force continuing reorganizations of the ensemble.

Dialectical analysis must be concerned with the emergence within a social formation of new, incompatible components. The ongoing process of social production, guided by the essential tendencies of a social formation, generates new forms of social organization that contradict the limits of a particular order. These new forms, although generated by the core tendencies of a given order, gradually undermine the bases of that order. An understanding of these contradictions permits an explanation for ongoing events (e.g., conflicts) and a basis for projecting future possibilities.

The dialectical method locates contradictions in social organization rather than in the confrontation between people and their social arrangements. The arrangements consist of people acting in certain ways, carrying out certain practices. Contradictions are then confrontations between opposing or incompatible ways of arranging social life. The analytical task is to identify the social conjunctures, the combinations of social forces that make change possible or probable. This knowledge may serve an emancipatory function, allowing people to see through the ideological covering of the social order and to understand crises and potentialities for action. People may then act concertedly to contradict the limits of the social order.

Social arrangements must be examined concretely rather than abstractly. This means locating events in their total contexts (totalities) rather than abstracting them from contexts. Since social production always occurs in and is shaped by social contexts, dialectical analysis must always include a totalizing movement. This does not mean that in every study the whole of the social formation must be examined, an impossible dictum anyway. Rather, it means that a prominent feature of the analysis must be the location of observations within total social formations, i.e., in relation to the core structures and tendencies of the social formation. In this totalizing move, the formation itself must be conceived as a historically developing arrangement or ensemble of social relations.

In the totalizing move, the analysis must deal with the relation between the essential, core tendencies of a social formation and its contingent, historically specific forms. Analyses adopting one or the other of these possibilities (the essential or the contingent) are incomplete. Dialectical analysis must grasp the specific, contingent ways in which the essential tendencies of a social formation are displayed. Doing this requires getting past the confusing array of factual observations to a conceptual model of the social formation that sorts out the essential from the nonessential components, locates events within strata or levels, and identifies the main developmental tendencies. There is an ongoing interaction between empirical observation and the formation of a conceptual model. This is not a one-sided interaction dominated by the factual observations (empiricism) or by theory. Rather, there must be a continuing refinement of the model on the basis of more focused observations and of theoretical reflection not simply on the facts immediately at hand but ranging across an array of accumulating knowledge of the social formation. This totalizing move is not completed in a single study (although it should always be present); rather, it continues through a series of studies and ideally characterizes a whole field of study and indeed connects it to other fields (see Bhaskar, 1979: 55-56).

In the dialectical view, knowledge production, including social knowledge, is like other forms of social production, shaped by its context and by the way in which knowledge producers are inserted into the social world. The producers of social knowledge react to a real world but not in a merely passive way (the reflection view). Rather, through their practices, shared within knowledge communities, they actively shape the knowledge they generate. Furthermore, knowledge may be used to change to some extent the realities themselves. The practices through which knowledge is generated are, like other human practices, developed in particular social contexts and are partially shaped by those contexts.

Thus, interests and power bases, institutional settings, and class affiliations affect the concerns of social scientists and their practices. It is not sufficient to recognize with Kuhn (1970b) and others that knowledge communities are guided by, and defensive of, paradigms. Beyond this, we must deal with the insertion of such paradigms in the larger social context through ties to interest and power bases in organizations, institutional complexes, social classes, and so on. Even dialectical analyses are subject to such social conditioning. Contrary to most conventional theorizing, dialectical analysis is concerned reflexively with its own mode of insertion into the social world. Furthermore, dialectical analysis is guided by an explicit concern with praxis, i.e., with the achievement of a reasoned basis for emancipatory action — action that removes unnecessary constraints on the development of human societies and opens new possibilities where human productive activity can more freely realize human potentialities for self-organization (i.e., allowing human societies to overcome alienation, to construct their futures freely and rationally).

Axiologically, the dialectical view is concerned with the production of social change in the direction of praxis. This involves, as one component, formulating theory to guide revolutionary practice by viewing reality from the standpoint of a particular interest and power base (preferably a progressive one) and looking for points of leverage in the social formation. But theory cannot be merely a tool of practice in the way that an organization is a tool of certain controlling interests. Rather, because the value commitment is to praxis in the fullest sense (i.e., to the liberation of human potentiality for free and rational social construction of the social world) rather than merely to efficiency of means, dialectical theory pursues an holistic understanding of the social world that locates various interest and power bases for social construction and accounts for their formation and their capacity to guide social evolution. The relative progressiveness or backwardness of various positions is a matter for continuing analysis, not for doctrinaire attribution. Further, the commitment to praxis entails an ongoing dialogue between theory and practice and between leaders and masses. Revolution, in this view, is not adequately defined by the seizure of power but by the achievement of praxis based on the liberation of consciousness. In this way, the position guards against the replacement of one form of domination by another.

These basic ontological, epistemological, and axiological commitments constitute a distinctive methodological base for a dialectical social science. Most distinctive is its transcendence of conventional dichotomies or dualisms, for example, between freedom and determinism, between subjective and objective conceptions of social reality, and between practical and merely contemplative knowledge. The position is thus quite different from the sociologism of the Durkheim tradition or the subjectivism of the idealist tradition. It grants a large role to choice, intentions, and the like (even envisioning a freely chosen future), but it also recognizes that choices tend to be made within limiting frameworks of assumptions and social structures. It contends that practical knowledge can and should be constructed in a way that incorporates reflexive understanding and so becomes emancipatory. It recognizes that social organization has a determinate influence on the course of events while at the same time insisting that social organization consists of intentional activities and meaningful practices of people that are modifiable.

This distinctive view provides a basis for constructing analytical categories and empirical theories. It does not specify precisely what theoretical concepts will be formed, and, given the view of human society as ongoing social production, any specific analytical system must be continually criticized in the light of social change. In particular, empirical theories (e.g., laws operative within a particular type of society) must be revised in the light of ongoing social evolution. The dialectical view, however, provides a continuing base for the reconstruction of theories as new social realities are carefully examined.

Marx's own approach to dialectical analysis was set within a framework of political economy, analyzing core features of competitive capitalism through concepts such as surplus value, wage labor, capital, profit and exploitation. While political economy remains a useful analytical framework, it requires modification to account for the unique features of advanced capitalism, such as the intervention of the state and monopoly power. This modification evolves through dialectical analysis as analysts attempt to deal with changing forms of social organization. Markovic's (1974) analysis of socialist bureaucracy provides an example. So long as the core tendencies of capitalism remain in place, political economy is likely to provide a useful analytical framework, but in time, may well need to be revised drastically or even discarded.

TOWARD A DIALECTICAL SOCIOLOGY OF ORGANIZATIONS

Developing a Marxian approach to the study of organizations involves a double determination. It must be accomplished in a manner consistent with the dialectical method. It must also be accomplished with some connection to ongoing political economy analyses. (Another constraint, in my own view, is that there must be a continuing contact with the conventional organization literature in an effort to transcend it. A total break with organizational analysis and its associated means of production — journals, departments, and so on — would concede the continued hegemony of the conventional theories).

A program for the development of a dialectical approach to organizational studies should be guided by the following paradigm.

(1) The organization as an object of knowledge is an (incomplete) ensemble of social relations consisting of social practices enacted by participants operating within frameworks of meaning and within structural constraints or limits. The organization is a site of ongoing social production and is produced and sustained by people not only historically but also through their everyday practices. Analysts must be sensitive, then, to the ongoing production of organizational realities in the everyday practices and discourse of participants and to deep-seated tendencies structured into the organization and worked out in practices and discourse. (A position close to this was recently formulated by Ranson et al., 1980).

(2) The ongoing production of social life in organizations generates organizational contradictions, i.e., points at which ongoing human activity encounters fixed limits occasioned by previously produced organizational arrangements. Organizations, then, as ensembles of social relations, develop an internal dialectic in which production according to inherent tendencies of the organization generates arrangements that threaten to override the fundamental limits of the organization. Indeed, the structure of the organization generates the bases not only for its own reproduction but also for organizing action (involving interest structure, power bases, and resource mobilization) that potentially challenges the existing order. A particular arrangement of organizational life always has a substructure of interest and power bases that tends to generate opposing forces. The structural contradictions, then, often are associated with social conflict between groups representing opposing interests, operating from different power bases, and mobilizing different resources (see Heydebrand, 1977a, for an illuminating discussion of organizational contradictions).

(3) The production of organizational life is integrally connected to the social totality. The generative mechanisms, the contradictions, and the organizing actions of the larger totality are involved in the production and reproduction of organizational practices. Dialectical analysis, then, must be concerned with how the developmental tendencies of the organization are guided by the tendencies of the totality. In other words, it involves examining the relationship of the organizational dialectic to the larger dialectical processes. (My earlier paper [Benson, 1977] was weak in this regard, as a number of perceptive critics have pointed out.) The possibilities are numerous. Some organizational transformations may be direct expressions of a larger pattern; others may be independent within some broad limits set by the entanglement of the organization within the totality. Some organizational processes may be loosely coupled to the tendencies and constraints of the larger system, while others are tightly coupled.

In this view the effort of some participants to construct rationally articulated, goal-oriented organizations are seen as precarious undertakings. To a considerable extent, the organization is a site where various forces and tendencies intersect (e.g., occupational movements, technological innovations, and interorganizational dependencies). Maintaining control of these multiple processes may be impossible at the organizational level. Indeed, the organization may be an inappropriate unit of analysis for understanding these processes. Even where a degree of managerial control is possible, we would need to inquire about the power base from which the rational construction proceeds and the function of such constructions in the larger political economy.

Dialectical analysis of organizations, as outlined in these three guidelines, can potentially provide a basis for organizational praxis, i.e., for organizing activities that combat dominance and move toward self-organization and that push toward thoroughgoing change in the practices of the organization and of the social formation. (Organizational praxis is not confined to the official boundaries of the organization. Social movements external to the organization may have substantial openings for changing the organization's practices, e.g., the environment movement.) Support for organizational praxis grows out of the analysis of the conjunction of the essential tendencies and the contingent combinations of practices on the surface of the organization. Such an analysis dereifies the organization, making its mechanisms of production and reproduction transparent. It sorts the hodge-podge of "facts" thrown up by the organization from various depths and times, making clear how the existing conjuncture of practices was formed and distinguishing real generative mechanisms from purely ideological accounts, (in some cases undermining rational, goal-seeking accounts and revealing underlying agendas of domination). It also identifies possibilities for reconstruction of the organization and the ways in which such reconstruction can become a general contestation of the established way of organizing the social formation.

A THEORETICAL CASE STUDY: FORMATION OF A NATURAL RESOURCES AGENCY

In 1974 a number of formerly separate programs of Missouri state government were combined to form a single department of natural resources (DNR) encompassing a wide range of activities (regulation of environmental pollution, geological research, energy development and conservation, parks and outdoor recreation, historic preservation, and others). The reorganization set off a series of negotiations within DNR. I studied these internal negotiations through interviews, field observation, and document analysis. (A detailed summary is in preparation). Here I will show how the analysis of DNR has been guided by and contributes to a dialectical view of organizational life.

The analysis may be termed a "theoretical case study" of reorganization in DNR. The study provided a series of empirical materials. These were subjected to a continuing theoretical anlysis, a repeated cycling between theory, observation, and examination of evidence. At one stage the concept of "logic of action" was adapted from Karpik (1972) and from Callon and Vignolle (1977) to refer to practices and discourse patterned by a central organizing principle. Observations were cast into the logic of action framework. At a later stage the logic of action analysis was assimilated into an emerging argument influenced by Marxian theories of the capitalist state (e.g., Habermas, 1975; Offe, 1975). The data were "rethought" in light of this developing argument and used as a source of insight for further refinement of the emerging theory.

Theoretical work was not confined to the beginning and ending of the research but entered at every step of the analysis. Further, the theoretical work, while in touch with the empirical materials, was not "grounded" in the sense of growing only out of those materials. Theoretical analysis was highly speculative and moved beyond the case at hand to locate it in a larger context (the capitalist state). The result is a model of reorganization based on tendencies present but incompletely realized in the case at hand, tendencies tied into a model of the structure and contradictions of the capitalist state. Explanation of the case was not sought via reduction to microprocesses of interaction or negotiation (as in Strauss, 1978) nor to principles of organization (e.g., cognitive limits on rationality as in Williamson, 1976, or laws of structural differentiation as in Blau and Schoenherr, 1971). Explanation was pursued rather through inclusion of cases in larger wholes.

The logics of action in DNR are divisible into two basic types: (1) logics of control and (2) logics of (substantive) work. Logics of control are concerned with opposing principles for establishing direction over the department. These include: (a) the Administrative Logic (involving the imposition of control via hierarchical authority and procedural rules and routines); (b) the Policy Logic (the imposition of control via expert knowledge, examination of evidence, and assessment of political realities); and (c) the Field Logic (involving the imposition of control based on the maintenance of worked-out routines of everyday work, for the most part negotiated prior to reorganization).

Logics of work are patterns of practice and discourse tending to be realized in the substantive activities and programs of the agencies. Distinct logics of work constitute alternative and sometimes opposing ways of carrying out the substantive tasks. In DNR I distinguished several *dilemmas of work orientation* stemming from opposing logics, as follows:

(1) *Service versus Enforcement:* providing a service by assisting various interests in the use of natural resources and in defending against regulation of this activity versus aggressive enforcement of environmental regulations;

(2) *Application versus Science:* providing a service to various interests by supplying scientific information that they can apply in pursuit of their objectives versus contributing to a body of scientific knowledge through research of general relevance;

(3) *Naturalistic Preservation versus Recreational-Educational Programming:* preserving natural settings by removing them from private use and controlling public access versus conducting programs for public enjoyment and education in natural and manmade settings;

(4) *Development versus Protection:* supporting the exploitation of natural resources in the interest of industrial and commercial development versus resisting such exploitation in the interest of protecting environmental quality. This became the central dilemma faced by DNR with the others either assimilated to it or obliquely aligned with it. Under a variety of political and economic pressures, DNR personnel seem frequently to have conceived their options in these terms (including, of course, the option of maintaining balance between these alternatives).

The opposing logics of work were not simply opinions but interrelated patterns of practice and thought embedded in the agencies that formed DNR. The logics were linked, I theorize, to the positions of the agencies in interorganizational political economies consisting of resource dependencies between organizations.

Prior to reorganization these interorganizational political economies were loosely coupled. They were part of a system of networks I call "interorganizational feudalism." The system involved extensive use of appointed boards and commissions to govern programs, extensive influence of the state Senate over appointments, and a lack of central directive capacity in the governor's office. This apparatus was damaged severely by reorganization although its patterns tended to regenerate in particular agency contexts; that is contacts and dependencies tended to follow old lines and to overflow the channels officially prescribed by the reorganization.

Reorganization brought these opposing logics into a conjunctural but contradictory unity in DNR. Agencies that previously maintained opposing or obliquely related logics of work, depended on partially disconnected political economies, and engaged each other minimally in cooperative ventures were thrown together. They were subjected to a common hierarchy of authority, to a common budgetary process, to a common channel to the legislature, and so forth.

In this situation organizing activity (Heydebrand, 1977a) took place; people operating from positions within opposing logics of action (some structurally tied to now damaged political economies) attempted to construct a new organization. These organizing activities were based on underlying interest structures that provide a foundation for alternative constructions of reality in an organization and involve the mobilization of power resources that are attached to and/or accessible to specific interest structure locations. In organizing activity previously taken for granted logics of action are consciously and systematically formulated and articulated, and ideological appeals made to those in similar structural locations. Thus organizing activity develops from positions in the substructure of the organization, the movement of the substructure opening possibilities for organizing activity but not determining their course.

These substantive mobilizations were conjunctural with the reorganization of control. That is, the reorganization of control (emerging concretely in the rationalizing and policy-forming agendas) created a structural opportunity for pursuing substantive agendas. Proponents of particular views within the DNR (e.g., to move geological survey more toward protection or to move parks toward recreational programming) seized on reorganization as an opportunity to pursue their aims, to build their programs of substantive change into the emerging apparatus of control. In doing so, they were often participating in movements extending well beyond the boundaries of DNR (e.g., professional groups and reform movements).

Analysis of the case must push beyond the level of intra- and interorganizational structures and processes. We must locate the reorganization of DNR in the context of the structure and contradictions of the totality in which it is embedded. This involves a further step in the theorization of the case. Our procedure for accomplishing this step has been to think of DNR in relation to Marxian theories of the capitalist state.

The logics of action in DNR (including both logics of control and logics of work) may be seen as opposing tendencies extending beyond the boundaries of DNR or even Missouri state government. The rise of the administrative logic and the emergence of the policy formation logic and their transformation into political agendas (not only in DNR but throughout the state apparatus) may be seen as responses to rationality deficits in the capitalist system. Specifically, the system confronts challenges that cannot be met without increased intervention by the state apparatus in giving guidance and coordination to the social formation. The challenges are in part endogenous to the capitalist mode of production (CMP). There are varying interpretations of the crises of the CMP; here I will depend on Offe's (1975) formulation. The exhaustion of sources of surplus value available through competitive strategies, Offe (1975) argues, leads to an increased reliance on the state apparatus and a qualitative shift in state activity. The state must engage increasingly in productive activity, involving its direct participation in the production of surplus value including, for example, resource development, manpower development. product development, regional economic development, and so on. The challenges are also in part exogenous (e.g., the actual depletion of worldwide energy resources). The state is also involved in legitimation problems, i.e., those concerned with legitimation of the capitalist mode of production and its institutions. These become entangled with the production problem in two ways: (1) Government programs concerned with legitimation (e.g., equal opportunity, environmental protection, occupational health and safety) generate restraints on accumulation that contribute to rationality deficits; the government is divided against itself. (2) In addition, as Offe (1975) has argued, the state's increasing involvement in productive activity presents legitimation problems, for example, by showing its commitments to the maintenance of the CMP and the defense of bourgeois class interests.

The rationality and legitimation problems make necessary the modernization and fine tuning of the state apparatus. The instruments of government must be coordinated, their drag on private investment controlled, their response to various interests moderated and contained, and so forth. It is here that we can locate the reorganization movement with its coexisting (but eventually contradictory) agendas of rationalization and policy formation. The administrative and policy logics and their associated political economies are brought into play, given expanded resources, and granted new territories to conquer. The modernization of state governments becomes an important project for elites representing the interests not of specific capitalists but of the CMP and the capitalist class. This cause is advanced at the expense and against the resistance of entrenched structures of interorganizational feudalism in state governments.

Following this argument, the reorganization of the machinery of government we would expect to be differentiated rather than uniform across the different policy sectors and levels of government. Some sectors, central to the production problem (e.g., natural resources and energy), might be more thoroughly subjected to the logic of policy formation with allowances for managed participatory mechanisms to deal simultaneously with legitimation problems. Other sectors, more traditional in function (Offe might call them allocative), might be more thoroughly rationalized in pursuit of efficiencies, economies of scale, and the like. Some sectors, not central to current crises, might be left free in a period of reorganization to develop more or less autonomously on the basis of interests and power bases embedded in the sector and not extending outward from it.

Looking again at reorganization in DNR we can suggest interpretations of events within a larger structured totality. The rationalizing and policy-forming agendas (and the underlying logics of control) may be seen as responses to rationality deficits, part of a modernization of the state apparatus demanded by new functions placed on it. In addition a blocking agenda, based on the field logic of action, was defensive of established routines previously negotiated and reproduced within partially autonomous political economies (embedded within interorganizational feudalism). DNR became an arena for the collision of these forces.

The logics of work in DNR relate in different ways to the crises of the CMP. It appears that some of the work dilemmas (alternative logics of work) were tightly coupled to the immediate crises (i.e., rationality deficit). In particular this seems to have affected the sections concerned with the development and/or protection of natural resources. The programs most thoroughly reorganized were those in the environmental protection area, where the threat of excessive regulation of industry centers and legitimation problems also abound. There were also strong efforts to erode the autonomy of the geological survey and some planning and development functions in water resources and energy were withheld from this division's control. Further, a fledgling energy program was at first kept under the close control of the department director and protected by him against claimants to it (including geological survey) and against legislative foes; later it was given division status within the department. The department leaders even sought ways that the Parks division could contribute to "natural resources" functions. It seems then that issues of natural resource development and preservation were central to the reorganization and became the focal points of the rationalizing and policymaking drives. Events in these areas seem in some sense over-determined.

The parks and recreation functions, on the other hand, seem only obliquely related to natural resource concerns. Certainly they are not central to the rationality deficit problem. Their only tie would appear to be in the area of policy decisions about the withholding of land from industrial development. Thus, in areas of land acquisition, wilderness areas, and the like, parks interests are closely linked to natural resource questions. The everyday work of parks personnel, by contrast, does not involve this tie. For this reason, we think, Parks went through an internal reorganization (involving a struggle over naturalistic preservation versus recreational and educational programming logics of work) that was only loosely coupled to the main event. The internal reorganization, we might say, was underdetermined. It was carried out largely by mobilization of forces within the division with little or no outside interference or connection to the struggles underway elsewhere in DNR. It was an interoccupational negotiation within the Parks arena.

It is possible, however, that the conflict in Parks is related more to problems of legitimation than to those of accumulation. The move toward recreational programming then might be seen in the context of urban politics and the effort to provide for collective consumption of urban and suburban populations. In the future these problems may move to center stage rather than be peripheral to the political concerns shaping the department.

This analysis of DNR is highly tentative and at some crucial points is "data thin" (i.e., long on interpretation and short on data). It is illustrative, nonetheless, of a dialectical method in organizational analysis. A model of the CMP and the capitalist state is employed to explain a series of observations in DNR. And the observations are used to refine the model. "Facts" are subjected to a continuous theoretical processing and recycling. The usefulness of the model is confirmed in its ability to provide provocative accounts for events in DNR. The encounter with DNR too becomes a source of new ideas regarding the extension of the model, leading perhaps to a theory of reorganizations.

CONCLUSION

Dialectical analysis of organizations demands detailed empirical studies guided by a dialectical view and in touch with current analyses of the larger political economy in which the organizations are embedded. The purpose is not merely to describe cases in detail nor simply to uncover the deep structural patterns manifest in the organization. Rather, it is to untangle the events on the surface of organizational life by locating them within social relations, in particular power relations that govern the events. These social relations must be conceived dialectically — not as a reified object world — and be stratified into various levels of determination. The core tendencies (generative mechanisms) pushing this ensemble of social relations must be identified. The limits of control exercised at each level must be specified. The ensemble of social relations must be seen as a developing, emerging totality with tendencies (not fully realized at a given time) growing out of the structure of the ensemble, i.e., the way in which social practices making up the ensemble are formed. Such analysis untangles the confusing array of events on the surface of organizational life and reveals the real social relations underlying events. Such analyses over time should show how shifting organizational arrangements are related to the core processes of production and reproduction of the emerging totality, for example, how shifting organizational arrangements are related to the reproduction of the relations of production (Lefebvre, 1976). One possible connection (pursued briefly here) is the relation of organizations, especially those within the state apparatus, to the solution of steering problems or rationality deficits of late capitalism.

Dialectical analysis should not merely strip away surface events and reveal underlying structures. It should also deal with the conjunction of core tendencies and contingent combinations of circumstances, showing how structures orchestrate events and how contingent combinations channel and shape the actual realization of structural tendencies.

Dialectical analysis must grasp, in addition, the emergence of contradictions that, although growing out of the core tendencies of the social formation, tend to push it beyond its fundamental limits.

Rather than simply describing stable structures, then, dialectical analysis searches for those basic contradictions that potentially (not inevitably) destroy a system and bring alternative arrangements into view as possibilities.

Dialectical analysis can be advanced (among other ways) by the in-depth study of strategically selected cases. In the case reported here I studied an organizational crisis (reorganization) in which the underpinnings of the organizations were to some extent visible. Such studies start with the organization as understood by participants and subject that knowledge to a widening and deepening analysis and critique. Then, having untangled events into a complex array of underlying social relations, one can reconstruct the organization (in thought), sorting events into their appropriate contexts and levels.

Dialectical analysis permits the critique of existing organizational realities and the construction (both in thought and in action) of alternative futures.

About the Author

J. KENNETH BENSON

I finished graduate school in the mid-1960s and began a teaching and research career in a time of controversy about social science methods. In the midst of racial conflict, the student movement, and demonstrations against the Vietnam War, sociology and the other social sciences fell into a methodological-theoretical crisis. Positivist methods, in which I was relatively well trained, were challenged from a number of directions. Marxism, phenomenology, critical theory, and structuralism (among other possibilities) were arrayed as alternatives. In this context I taught and initiated research on organizations. I found the prevailing functional and rational approaches to the field unsatisfactory, particularly the failure to deal with power in organizations and the relation of organizational power to larger patterns of dominance. Organization theory, in its prevailing forms, seemed woefully inadequate for dealing with the organizational and interorganizational conflicts displayed each day by the media and personally encountered in the university and elsewhere. In this context I formulated a critique of organization theory. Then, through the 1970s I gradually worked out a dialectical approach based in critical strands of neo-Marxist thought. While events of the 1980s reconfirm the importance of such a theory, I continue to draw on the formative years of the late sixties for a sense of what needs to be explained.

23

CLASS ANALYSIS AND THE STUDY OF SOCIAL FORMS

G. Carchedi
University of Amsterdam

This short introduction to a Marxist research strategy in the social sciences cannot hope to provide either a balanced discussion of all relevant issues or a "faithful" account of Marx's own methodology. The former impossibility is due to lack of space, the latter to the well-known fact that Marx never wrote a methodological treatise. His method is embedded in his writings, and any attempt to present it is necessarily at the same time a reconstruction of it. My reconstruction will hinge on the centrality of class as a unity of both social life and social research. To stress this, I have chosen to call this approach "class analysis."

NONREFLECTIVE MATERIALISM

It will be useful to enunciate right away some basic ontological and epistemological principles.

(1) To live and reproduce themselves, people must transform reality, and first of all material reality. From this follows that:

(a) In a society, which by definition is not made up of social atoms without any relation with each other, this transformation is based on a social division of labor; i.e., the social product is the result of a collective activity, and its parts are the results of the activity of groups of people.

(b) The existence of a social division of labor implies that these groups must enter into relations with each other in the very act of production, through the intermediary of the means of production, i.e., that they must enter into production relations. We call these groups, identifiable in terms of production relations, social classes. A complete definition of a social class encompases not only economic but also political and ideological elements in a relationship of dialectical determination (Carchedi, 1977).

(c) Under capitalism, production relations are antagonistic and asymmetric. They are *antagonistic* because they unite, in a tie of mutual existential dependence, two antagonistic poles defined, for example, as relations between the owner/appropriator/nonlaborer and the nonowner/expropriated/laborer. They are *asymmetric* because in this dependence one aspect (e.g., the owner vis-à-vis the nonowner) is the principal (or determinant) one and the other is the secondary (or determined) one. Consequently, social classes (i.e., the carriers of contradictory aspects of social relations) are antagonistic too, and can exist only in a context of class struggle, i.e. in a constant attempt to dominate each other.

(2) To transform something material, we must gain a knowledge of it, and to know something we must deal with it, transform it. This statement stresses: the *materialist basis of epistemology,* that is, that only those who are engaged in material transformation have the possibility of knowing reality, and the *materialist nature of science,* that is, the principle of the determination of the concrete in thought by the real concrete, and to begin with, of the production of knowledge by material production. From the fusion of this last principle and the principle that the material transformation (production) is carried out by social classes (which moreover are antagonistic to each other), it follows that:

(a) Only classes identifiable in terms of production relations have the objective *possibility* (given their position within the class structure) of an independent knowledge of reality.

(b) The larger the portion of reality dealt with by a class, the greater the objective *possibility* it has to gain a correct knowledge of reality.

(c) Under capitalism, it is the proletariat, defined for our purposes as all those who participate in the transformation of material (and thus also mental) use values, i.e., in the transformation of the social product while not owning the means necessary for this transformation, which deals with an increasing portion of social reality and thus has the objective possibility of knowing it correctly, in all its complexity and interrelations.

(d) In the context of the structurally determined and constant attempt that classes make to dominate each other (1c), the need people (classes) have to know reality in order to transform it can only realize itself through a multiplicity of world views, all of them struggling for domination (that is, it can only realize itself through ideological class struggle).

(3) Therefore: *Ontologically,* we must presuppose the existence not only of material reality but also of nonmaterial real concretes (social relations). We call this position a materialist one, recognizing:

(a) the existence of both material and non-material real concretes and

(b) the primacy of social relations of material transformation (production relations) over other social relations and phenomena, as well as over material transformation.

There is no conflict between the principle of the material basis of life (and thus of society) and the principle of the primacy of the production relations over material transformation. In fact, first, the principle of the *material basis of life* (i.e., that the basis of life is material transformation) expresses the need individuals have (aside from any social conditioning) to transform material reality in order to reproduce themselves. But while the need to transform material reality is not socially determined, the *way* this transformation takes place is socially determined. It is the nature of the production relations that determines the way in which people reproduce themselves by producing their means of reproduction. This is the *social basis of material life*. And, finally, in class-divided societies, classes — identifiable in terms of specific production relations — are the basic units of social life and thus of material transformation. It is for this reason that they also determine all other social relations. This is the principle of the *class basis of social life*.

(4) *Epistemologically,* the primacy of real transformation over the production (transformation) of knowledge implies:

(a) The process of the production of knowledge is a process of mental, active transformation (and not of reflection of the real concrete in thought) and is class determined. There are, in other words, different interpretations of the same reality and all of them are objective (even though not necessarily correct).

(b) These different interpretations/transformations are antagonistic because they are conditions of domination (on the level of knowledge) of antagonistic classes — conditions of reproduction or supersession of inherently antagonistic structures.

(c) There is no incompatibility but complementarity between (i) class determination of knowledge, (ii) the existence of a plurality of objective knowledges, and (iii) the possibility for one of them to provide a correct (but not in the sense of a reflective) vision of reality. More specifically, knowledge is both objective (i.e., determined by the need to transform reality and solve both practical and theoretical problems, and thus independent of the will of the individuals), and class determined (and thus a condition of class domination, since these problems are perceived and solved from a class point of view). This implies, first, that the solution of problems is an aspect of class domination — that problems are never solved to the advantage of the whole of society, of all classes, but only to the advantage of one or some of them; and second, the incommensurability of different knowledges because they are class determined. Therefore, correct knowledge is the correct solution (as shown by the double and interrelated process of practical and logical verification; see Carchedi, 1983) of problems from a class point of view (thus not in a reflective way), of the same but differently perceived problems that in principle can be, but not necessarily are, correctly solved by the class that has the largest contact with all facets of reality. Even if the principle of class determination of knowledge, and thus of the incommensurability of knowledges, prevents verification in terms of comparison with socially neutral theories or data, the materialist basis of epistemology ensures the possibility for one class to produce a knowledge that is not only class determined, but also able to be correct because of that class's position within the social structure. This class perceives reality, and thus problems, in terms of contradictions and has at its disposal a theory that justifies its claim to be able to solve not only localized but also general contradictions.

To conclude: The point of view of the proletariat is that each class secretes its own knowledge as a condition of domination over other classes. From this point of view, absolute or judgmental relativism cannot be defended because it is the proletariat that has the objectively determined possibility of gaining a correct knowledge of reality.

ASPECTS OF THE DIALECTICAL METHOD

The Relevance of Dialectical Determination for Social Analysis

The foregoing ontological and epistemological principles imply a method of inquiry that is dialectical and have general implications for the way social analysis must be conducted.

First:

(a) Points 1 and 2 emphasize the importance of studying material production (a part of reality) as a condition for an understanding of all other aspects of reality. But, at the same time

(b) the principle of the social division of labor (1a) implies the social production of knowledge (i.e., the production of knowledge as an aspect of society's production) and thus emphasizes the study of the whole as a condition for an understanding of all aspects of society, including the economic (i.e., that complex of production, distribution, exchange, and consumption relations — and their forms — in which production has the determinant role).

Second:

(c) The principle of the existence of social relations and thus of social classes (1b) emphasizes the need to study these latter as basic units of society, while the antagonistic character of classes (1c), and thus the antagonistic character of the different knowledges (2d), requires that this study be focused in the context of class struggle, and thus as an epistemological rather than an ontological category. At the same time

(d) given that these classes are expressions of structures (social relations), our approach must empasize the study of those structures, of which classes are but carriers.

Third:

(e) The principle of the interrelation of all parts (1a and 1b) emphasizes the need to study the inner structure, or logic, of that interrelation. At the same time

(f) this interrelation is a process and thus must be studied in its present, conjunctural, as well as past (historical) forms. Therefore,

we must identify the dynamic principle that allows the manifestation of structures.

Consequently, dialectics as a method of inquiry must be able to unify
in an organic and coherent whole, the study of the whole (b) and of the
parts (a), of the essence or structure (d) and of its carriers (c), of the
internal logic (e), and of its concrete, past and present, configurations
(f).

To this end, let us start from Lenin's (1963: 223) concise definition
of dialectics as "the doctrine of the unity of opposites" or, in other
words, as "the splitting of a single whole and the cognition of its
contradictory parts." As Lenin suggests, this notion embodies the
essence of dialectics, but is in need of certain "explanations and
developments." Particularly important for our purposes is the concept of dialectical determination, with its emphasis on the nature of
the determinant and of the determined instances, and on the nature of
the relation between these instances. Since we are basically interested in the social sciences, this question interests us principally in
the view to be taken of the relation among all instances of society. In
the light of what is said in the section on Nonreflective Materialism
above, this means that we are interested, to begin with, in the relation
between the economic and the other instances of society. In an
oft-quoted letter, Engels stresses that "we make our history ourselves, but in the first place, under very definite assumptions and
conditions. Among these the economic ones are ultimately decisive.
But the political ones . . . and indeed even the traditions which haunt
human minds also play a part, although not the decisive one" (Marx
and Engels, 1970: 487). If the economic is the ultimately determining
instance (1a), what then is the relation (1) between it and the other,
determined, instances and (2) among the determined instances?

We have already discarded the "reflection" of the determinant into
the determined instances, and we should, of course, discard also the
opposite view — the simple mutual interdependence of all instances
in which no principal role is given to the economic, either in its more
open form as presented by Weber (1949) or in its more disguised
interpretation as represented by Laclau (1977). Finally, no satisfactory solution can be found in the Althusserian branch of Marxism
either (Althusser, 1969; Althusser and Balibar, 1970), because on this
view determination is a structural condition of existence. This view
thus glosses over the possibility for the determinant instance to determine (1) the conditions of its own supersession and (2) a multiplicity of forms of a certain determined instance. This is an area that still
requires "explanations and developments" and whose importance for
methodology cannot be overestimated.

Before presenting the concept of dialectical determination favored here, we should stress that for us, dialectic is a law of cognition and not an ontological law. To understand means to conceive, to constuct "the peculiar logic of the peculiar object" (Marx, quoted in Geschichte der Dialektik, 1979: 250). Capitalism, a peculiar object, has a peculiar logic that can be understood through a dialectic that is not *the* dialectic but the Marxist dialectic. It becomes thus understandable and theoretically consistent to submit that Marxism, the knowledge of the proletariat, of the direct and indirect *producers,* gives the determinant role to the economic, to *production,* and sees the world through this class-determined perspective. Marxism's class determination (i.e., the application of its epistemology to itself in order to reach self-understanding) becomes thus visible in the double aspect of *historical materialism* (i.e., history becomes the history of several modes of production that take place in the context of class struggle) and of *dialectical materialism* (i.e., the view that the condition for knowledge is to consider reality as the development of opposites). Thus the working class rewrites history as the history of class struggle and considers reality in its own image and likeness — as a movement (no class trying to achieve a radical social change could see reality as static) of two poles that can exist only because the other exists ("in a unity") and yet are in mortal antagonism ("opposites"), just as the struggle between the proletariat and the bourgeoisie is a movement within a unity of opposites. What then characterizes Marxist dialectics? In order to answer this question, we will submit a concept of dialectical determination.

The Construction of a Mode of Dialectical Determination

The following are the basic elements of our model. Let us call A the determinant instance, B and C two types of determined instances (e.g., the state and ideology), $B_1 \ldots B_n$ and $C_1 \ldots C_n$ the several possible forms that can be taken by these two types, and a bar above the capital letter to indicate a certain realized form of a certain type of an instance (e.g., $\bar{C}_x$, where $C_x \in C_1 \ldots C_n$). Then:

(1) *Determination in the last instance.* Determination in the last instance (DLI) means that A calls into existence B and C as a condition of A's own existence or supersession among a range of real possible conditions of existence or of supersession (i.e., among $B_1 \ldots B_n$ and $C_1 \ldots C_n$). We focus here on the functional relation between A on the one hand and B and C on the other. Or, B and C are

considered not in their specific, realized characteristics (e.g., as $\bar{B}_x$ and $\bar{C}_x$) but in their function as necessary conditions of existence (reproduction) or supersession of the determinant instance. For example, an analysis of a certain form of the capitalist state ($\bar{B}_x$) in terms of DLI reveals how that particular form is functional for the reproduction of the capitalist production relations, how other forms $B_1 \ldots B_n$ could be equally functional, and how still other forms ($B_\alpha \ldots B_\gamma$) are not real possibilities (an autocratic state, for example). This thesis is of great political importance since it stresses the significance of the struggle in the superstructure for a qualitative change in the economic basis. It is the struggle in the former that is the condition for a change in the latter. This thesis thus allows us to appreciate Gramsci's (1971) emphasis on socialist political culture without cutting loose its ties with its determination by the economic, or to appreciate the importance social movements not restricted to any specific class (e.g., the feminist movement) can have for a certain class (the proletariat) and for its struggle. To be logically determined does not mean to be politically less important. On the contrary. Only a change in the determined instance makes possible a change in the determinant instance, but no change in the former will be lasting without a change in the latter. But DLI does not tell us yet how and why, among all real $B_1 \ldots B_n$, in that particular historical conjucture B_x has been selected for realization thus becoming (the concrete) $\bar{B}_x$.

(2) *Relative autonomy.* Relative autonomy means that $\bar{B}_x$ and $\bar{C}_x$ are not simple reflections of A since they are the concretization of one or more among the several possible $B_1 \ldots B_n$ and $C_1 \ldots C_n$. We focus here on the possibility that more than one B or C can be the condition of existence or supersession of A, and this is why the determined instances are autonomous. However, their degree of autonomy is limited to the ranges $B_1 \ldots B_n$ and $C_1 \ldots C_n$, and this is why their autonomy is relative.

(3) *Concrete determination.* Concrete determination means that of all possible B's and C's only one (or some) B and C will find concrete realization, will become $\bar{B}_x$ and $\bar{C}_x$ due to the complex interrelation of all instances of society.

(4) *Overdetermination.* Overdetermination means that $\bar{B}_x$ and $\bar{C}_x$ react on $\bar{A}_x$ (i.e., on A now considered in its specificity) and thus tend either to modify it or to prevent its modification (and possibly supersession).

(5) *Correspondence or contradiction.* Correspondence or contradiction between the determinant and the determined instances means that the latter can respectively foster or hinder the reproduction of A. The reproduction of the determinant instance is really

hindered only in case of antagonistic contradiction. We cannot explain here the difference between correspondence, nonantagonistic contradiction, and antagonistic contradiction. Elsewhere it is shown (Carchechi, 1983) that this distinction is fundamental for an understanding of the relation between capitalist production relations and capitalist production forces. For example, it is a lack of this distinction that causes Luxemburg (1968) to mistakenly theorize about the impossibility of the further growth of the productive forces under capitalism.

(6) *Domination*. Domination means that one instance (A, B, or C) plays the fundamental role in the reproduction or supersession of the determinant instance. Thus the dominant role can revert also to one of the determined instances.

(7) *Unity in complex determination*. This means a unity of the determinant and the determined instances tied by a relation as depicted in points 1 through 6 above (i.e., by a relation of complex dialectical determination). Lack of space prevents consideration of the case of the *simple* dialectical determination (see, for example, Mao Tse Tung, 1967: 311-347; Badiou, 1975). For our purposes here it will be sufficient to point out that in a relation of simple determination, one aspect presupposes necessarily another aspect and only that aspect (i.e., there is no plurality of possible determined instances), and the determinant one calls the determined one into existence only as a condition of its own existence (and not of its own supersession).

(8) *Complex dialectical process*. This means the process of development of a complex unity in determination regulated by a specific type of determined instances, the laws of development. These latter will be discussed in a later section of this chapter.

Levels of Complexity of the Model and the Search for the Determinant Instance

The scope of the model is widened by considering an increasing number of instances or, in other words, by descending from the highest level of abstraction to more concrete ones. In this process we consider more and more "details" or, better said by Marx (1973: 102), we consider instead of just the "simplest determinations" the "rich totality of many determinations and relations." But how do we reach the simplest determination or determinant instances? For Marx these are not reached by abstracting the ahistorical essence but, on the contrary, by focusing on, by *condensing* in it what is specific and historically determined (Della Vope, 1969). It is in this sense that the simplest determinations are the outcome of the process of knowledge. (Logical and historical analysis thus complement each other. The former type of analysis provides the scheme for interpreting the relation between different instances; i.e., it provides the concept of determination, but the adjudication of the determinant, dominant, and so on to those instances is a question for historical analysis). And it is because of this specific, historical, and condensed character that the simplest determinations are also those that encompass already *in nuce* all other contradictions and that can, therefore, serve as the point of departure for an increasingly complex depiction of reality (of the real concrete) through the *unfolding* of more and more of those contradictions already *implicit* in them. The final outcome of this process is what Marx calls the concrete-in-thought, an articulated mental construction. To descend to more concrete levels of abstraction means not to add mechanically more and more elements but to unfold the contradictions already implicit in the determinant ones. These contradictions are part and parcel of a method of inquiry that explains reality in terms of contradictions instead of explaining them away as mistakes or anomalies. Here resides the basic difference between a model of social reality based on an assumption of equilibrium and the dialectical model. By starting from equilibrium, all inherent contradictions (e.g., unequal development) are excluded a priori, a standpoint functional to the class whose structurally determined interest is the maintenance of the status quo. And, on the other hand, it is precisely here that the explanatory power of a dialectical model resides, i.e., in its ability to account for more and more elements (determinations and relations) and for its own dynamic from within itself and not through a process of mechanical addition (accretion) of noncontradictory elements.

The Dynamization of the Model

This model is not only a highly simplifed scheme; it is also a static one. It can be turned into a dynamic one only by organically introducing class struggle. In fact society is, as we have seen, a totality of mutually interacting structures (relations) and their forms that could not exist if people did not exist. Structures can exist only because people become carriers of them, of aspects of them, i.e., they exist only because people become carriers of social relations. Now, the capitalist social relations are contradictory because they are, for example, relations of ownership, that is, relations between owners and nonowners of the means of production. Thus this structure cannot exist without agents — carriers of aspects of contradictory production relations — just as its contradictory nature cannot exist except through the struggle between the owners and nonowners of the means of production through class struggle. Class struggle is thus the *mode of existence* of contradictory structures (i.e., of social relations) and consequently of their forms in class divided societies. Class struggle is thus part and parcel of social life and not simply a determined instance as argued for example by Wright (1978). There is therefore no separation, let alone contradiction, between a class-oriented and a structure-oriented social analysis. Thus the dilemma between the essentially idealist view of history as the result of action of classes (e.g., Lukács, 1971) and the structuralist view, which considers history as a succession of structural transformations in which social agents have in fact no role to play (e.g., Althusser, 1969), is a false one.

How the Model Works

We must now account theoretically for the basic features of the model and for the possibility for the determinant instance to determine (1) its conditions of supersession, (2) a plurality of forms of a certain determined instance and (3) the concrete realization of only one (or some) of those forms at one conjuncture and of another at another conjuncture. The discussion of these points — which will have to cover also the issue of overdetermination — implies, as we will see, the clarification and use of the concept of interest.

Let us start by returning to the example of the owner/nonowner relation. These two agents, representing two classes, are tied in a simple dialectical unity. The carrier of the principal (determinant) aspect of this relation is the owner, and he or she is such because he or she carries that aspect that characterizes "the nature of things," which characterizes the nature of that relation (see Mao Tse Tung, 1967: 333). Thus the structure will tend to reproduce itself first of all through the reproduction of its principal (determining) aspect. The secondary (determined) aspect is, of course, necessary, in the sense of being the condition of the principal aspect's existence. In turn, the owner/nonowner simple dialectical unity can reproduce itself only through the production of other unities within the production relations as for example, the exploiter/exploited and the laborer/nonlaborer:

These two latter elements will be tied to the original one (owner/ nonowner) in a complex dialectical relation (the capitalist production relations), which again requires, as conditions of its own reproduction or supersession, distribution, political, ideological, and so forth relations. In this way our model unfolds itself and reaches more and more concrete and detailed levels of abstraction. And since structures exist only through agents — carriers of aspects of social relations and thus representatives of classes — the mode of existence of these contradictory structures is class struggle (e.g., the owner will interact with the nonowner through class struggle).

But if class struggle is the way the contradictory nature of social relations comes to life, it must manifest itself as a *struggle for domination* in all spheres of society. Our thesis is that it is by creating the conditions of their domination on other classes that classes create the conditions of reproduction or of supersession of the structure. In fact, in our example the agent carrying the principal aspect will fight for domination on the agent carrying the secondary aspect and, since the reproduction of the principal aspect through the production of its conditions of existence can take place only through this agent's struggle, will perceive the reproduction of the principal aspect and thus the creation of those conditions of existence (which are also the conditions of existence of the dialectical unity as a whole) *as his or her own interest.* In short, the several forms and types of domination on the proletariat are also the condition for the continuous reproduction of the ownership relation and are also the objective (structurally determined) interests of the carrier of the principal aspects of that relation.

Now the secondary aspect. This is the other pole of the antagonistic relation and is thus *antagonistic to the principal aspect and thus* (given that this latter is the one that characterizes the nature of the whole) *is antagonistic also to the relation as whole.* Consequently, this aspect is antagonistic to itself. This becomes clearer if the carrier of the secondary aspect of the production relations, the nonowner, is considered. As such, he or she too is an agent and represents a class. For him or her too, then, class struggle will be his or her mode of existence and will be directed toward domination over the capitalist class on all levels or, which is the same, toward the abolition of the capitalist domination. But because of his or her antagonistic position, the nonowner will not fight to create the conditions of his or her existence as nonowner since this would perpetuate one pole of the relation and thus the relation itself. The proletariat's fight for domination will have to be a fight for the supersession of the relation and thus of itself, and this fight will be a structurally determined need. But you cannot abolish a mode of production based on exploitation without replacing it with another one: You can abolish an ideological view of the real concrete only by working out another, more correct one. You cannot do away with a political system without at the same time creating another type of political organization. It will be thus a structural need of the carrier of the secondary, antagonistic aspect to introduce new social relations and especially production relations, that is, to create the conditions for the supersession of the existing social relations. In short, the secondary aspect is determined by the principal one but, since it is contradictory to it, it will struggle for domination and, since it is antagonistic, it will attempt to introduce new, different social relations, thus superseding the original dialectical unity (the owner/nonowner relation) and thus itself. These new relations, these conditions of supersession, will be *perceived* by the carrier of the secondary and antagonistic aspect *as his or her own interest*. Both classes are engaged thus in the struggle for domination, the ultimate aim (interest) being the reproduction of the relation (structure, system) for the carrier of the principal aspect and its supersession for the carrier of the secondary, antagonistic aspect. Thus interests are the way the aspects of a relation manifest their nature through agents: They are the personified expression of the aspect's nature, of the nature of the relations binding the agents. If the aspects are contradictory, so will be the interests. If the aspects are also antagonistic, not only will there be contradictory interests; one aspect, the principal one, will tend to reproduce itself and thus the unity as a whole, while the other aspect will tend to supersede that unity and itself. Thus, *interests are the personified expression of the structurally determined conditions of existence or of supersession of the structure.* (This position rejects the idea that interests are the mediating category between basis and superstructure [Sorg, 1976: 23]. Note, too, that if the agents perceive as their interests the creation of the conditions of existence or supersession of the structure as determined by the structure itself, the Weberian dichotomy between value judgments and statements of fact is shown to be false at one stroke. Science can and should help in the choice of ends, that is, in the clarification of interests).

However, given that agents are the expression (carriers) of structures (relations), do not the former first have to change the latter before they can change themselves? And how can agents change something of which they are only an expression? Marx's answer can be found in the "Third Thesis on Feuerbach": "The coincidence of the changing of circumstances and of human activity can be conceived and rationally understood only as a *revolutionary practice*" (Marx and Engels, 1969: 19). But the Third Thesis cannot be understood so long as one persists in choosing "man" instead of agents (classes) as units of social analysis and if one does not stress the contradictory aspects of the relations carried by the agents. Thus, the possibility of a revolutionary change of existing (capitalist) social relations by the proletariat is created by the fact that the proletariat personfies a radical antagonism to those relations, even though, indeed, *because,* it is the carrier of (aspects) of those relations. It is by creating the conditions of its own domination (i.e., by introducing new social relations antagonistic to the ones already existing) that the proletariat creates the conditions for the supersession of the old society, thus changing itself in this process at one and the same time. The conditions for the proletariat's domination within the capitalist production relations (revolutionary practice) thus become the conditions for the supersession of those relations, and thus also for the supersession of the proletariat itself. This is the profound meaning of the Third Thesis. Marx's dialectical genius allows us to escape the false dilemma posed by economism and voluntarism. But the understanding of the Third Thesis is conditional on the understanding that the same structure, by tying together two antagonistic aspects, and thus two radically opposed forces, one of which will work for its maintenance and the other for its supersession, can express the conditions both for its reproduction and for its supersession.

We now come to the problem of relative autonomy, and thus to the existence of a plurality of possible forms of a certain type of a determined instance. To return to a previous example: there can be several forms of the capitalist state (the social-democratic, the fascist, the liberal, the bonapartist, and so on). If we use the symbols CPR for capitalist production relations, CS for capitalist state, and the subscripts a, b, . . . n for the different forms of the capitalist state, then we have to explain that

$$CPR \rightarrow CS_a, CS_b \ldots CS_n$$

The answer is already implicit in what is said above. These several forms are not a priori existing ideas, already formed and waiting to be chosen by some mysterious hand for realization on earth, but are inscribed in the actual composition, structure, and nature of the determinant instance — they are *real* possibilities. By this we do not mean in a structuralist fashion, different combinations of the same, already existing, somewhat presocial elements: They are formless potentials contained in the determinant instance. They can be truly new social forms and yet contained in the determinant instance in the sense that they are conditions of reproduction or of supersession of that instance and thus, first of all, conditions of domination of one of the classes economically identifiable in the economic structure. As Binns (1973) has remarked, "Reality contains, alongside the existents, *coexisting in time*, the world of potentials as well. Practice, in the first instance, does nothing but alter the boundaries between things which are already with us in existence or potential."

Finally, we tackle the problem of the actual concretization of one of the several real possibilities, noting that more than one form can (and certain forms of determined instances, e.g., knowledge, do) find concrete realization at the same time. This complicates but does not change the nature of the problem, and need not be dealt with here. Given that:

$$CPR \rightarrow CS_a, CS_b \ldots CS_n$$

The problem is to account for

$$CPR \rightarrow \bar{C}\bar{S}_x$$

where the bar indicates realization and where

$$CS_x \in CS_a, CS_b, \ldots CS_n$$

Or, how can a certain determinant instance "choose" one form of a certain determined instance (e.g., $\bar{C}\bar{S}_x$) at a certain conjuncture and another form (e.g., $\bar{C}\bar{S}_y$) at another conjuncture?

The answer requires an intermediate logical step. Just as concerning the problem of relative autonomy we had first to postulate and then to explain theoretically the plurality of possibilities, now, before we can tackle the realization problem, we must first postulate and then explain both the possibility of the determined instance overdetermining the determinant instance and the possibility of reciprocol influence among the determined instances. This intermediate step will be a bridge between the plurality of possibility problem and the realization problem and will provide all the elements for the latter's solution. In fact, in order for our model of dialectical determination to have some explanatory power, we must postulate and subsequently explain relative autonomy. This means that we have to postulate a *mediated* tie between the determinant and determined instances because otherwise (in case of a direct, nonmediated tie), the determined instances would be a simple reflection of the determinant one, and there would be thus no relative autonomy. One of the two. Either the determined instance does overdetermine the determinant one and thus reacts on and modifies the other determined instances *as expressions of the determinant instance* (in which case we have to postulate the reciprocal influence of the determined instances), or such a determination and reciprocal influence do not take place because the influence of the determinant instance is overpowering, because either no interrelation occurs among all instances or an interrelation does occur but does not bring about any theoretically significant change (which is logically the same thing). But in this case there would be an immediate and not a mediated tie and thus no relative autonomy. There would be only the economy to determine which determined instances realize themselves. Thus if there is relative autonomy, there must be reciprocal influence.

Having shown why it is necessary to *postulate* overdetermination and the reciprocal influence of all determined instances, how can we now *account* theoretically for them? We have seen that, given that the agents are carriers of aspects of social relations, and given that these agents create the conditions for the existence or supersession of those relations through class struggle, the determined instance is an expression not of the whole of the determinant one in its fullness, but basically of one aspect (interests) rather than of another. It is because of this that the determined instance can acquire, so to speak, a relatively independent life vis-à-vis the determinant whole. The determined instance is not a simple reflection of the whole (this could be possible if the determinant instance were an undifferentiated, unstructured, and noncontradictory whole) but, by being an expression of basically an aspect (part) of the determinant instance, reacts on the determinant instance (contradictorily articulated) by reacting differently on the different contradictory parts (aspects) of the whole. *Overdetermination is thus differential impact on the different structural elements of the determinant instance.* Therefore, each determined instance, since it is a partial and unilateral expression of the determinant instance, will react differently on each of the other determined instances and thus will modify them (or prevent their modification). It is through this interaction — where interaction means the differential impact the determined instances have on the different structural elements of the determinant instance and thus on each other as expressions of the different elements of the determinant instance through this reciprocal modification — that the determined instances (and thus also the determinant, due to overdetermination) take up concrete form. And since, as we know, the contradictory nature of the structure (determinant instance) manifests itself as class struggle, it is through class struggle that the interaction among the several determined instances takes place and therefore, that several instances realize themselves in a specific, socially and historically conditioned, form.

SOCIAL PHENOMENA AND SOCIAL LAWS

Having provided some elements of the dialectical model of re-search, we can now give a few indications of its application to the study of *social phenomena,* i.e., of social relations and their forms. Such an application allows us to formulate what we could call the three basic methodological principles in the social sciences.

(1) *Consider social phenomena as determined both by the totality and by the economic.* In the light of the discussion of complex dialectical determination (i.e., of both DLI and of concrete determi-nation), it should now be clear that there is no incompatibility, but a deep and necessary interpenetration, between these two aspects of determination: Without the complex interrelation of all phenomena, the DLI cannot take concrete form, but without DLI, complex interrelation becomes theoretically meaningless. From this principle we can draw at least two important consequences:

(a) Social phenomena are objective, in the sense that they are inde-pendent of the will of the individuals as such (i.e., taken in isola-tion).

(b) Their "intellegibility. . . develops in proportion as we grasp their function in the totality to which they belong" (Lukács, 1971: 13) as well as their relation to the economic.

(2) *Consider social phenomena as both structure determined and class determined.* Again, the rationale for this principle can be found in the previous discussion concerning structures and their carriers, classes. Again, we can draw at least three important conclusions from this principle:

(c) "Only the class can actively penetrate the reality of society and transform it in its entirety" (Lukács, 1971: 39).

(d) Social phenomena as (partial) expressions of the contradictory nature of the whole (determined by the contradictory nature of the determinant instance), are themselves contradictory.

(e) Since social phenomena come to life through class struggle (i.e., struggle for domination), they can be subdivided by catergories, the most important of which in class-divided societies are the economic, the ideological, and political *because* these are the *basic types of domination* of one class over the others. Each of these three categories is the object of a specific social science. While all social phenomena fall within the scope of *sociology,* the study of the production, reproduction, and supersession of social phenomena, the interrelation of which forms *society,* other social sciences study those social phenomena that fall within specific categories. For example, *economics* studies the production, distribution, exchange, and consumption relations and their forms; or, it studies the production, distribution, exchange, and consumption of material (solid, liquid, and gaseous) and mental products as exchange values. But a complete picture of a social phenomenon can be gained only when it is considered from the point of view of the different disciplines. Thus, sociology is the combined, general, total view of social phenomena and ultimately of society itself.

(3) Finally, since complex determination (i.e., the way structures, and especially economic structures, come to life and create their conditions of existence or supersession through classes in their constant attempt to dominate each other) is by definition a process and thus something in movement through time, we can enunciate our third principle as: *Consider social phenomena as both conjuncturally and historically determined.* Social phenomena must, in other words, be considered *both* in their present complex dialectical determination *and* in their birth, development, and disappearance; we must consider the complex dialectical determination from which a social phenomenon originates not only in its present articulation but also in its birth, development through time, and extinction. The rationale for this is, as we have said previously, that only historical analysis can allow us to judge the determinant or other roles of the various instances/phenomena.

These three basic methodological principles do not constitute a typology of social phenomena, but are a basis for their study and thus for such a typology. We will mention here only one particularly important type — *social laws,* i.e., those social phenomena that *regulate* the production and reproduction of society and thus of the social relations on which that society is based. Our fundamental thesis is that social laws, or laws of development, are the social form taken by natural laws (which are independent of any social/historical determination). Since every society is characterized by certain social (and especially production) relations, these natural laws become social in nature; they take on a specific social nature according to the specific nature of those relations. For example, the labor process, or transformation of use values, is characteristic of all societies, but it takes on a specific nature in a specific society (e.g., it also becomes a surplus value producing process under capitalism). It is because they are the social expression of natural laws that social laws regulate the functioning of the social system, that they become laws of motion of society. Thus natural laws within society can manifest themselves only in specific social forms, by taking up a specific social content, while retaining their character of necessity, of objectivity. Like all social phenomena, social laws have a character of necessity and objectivity only vis-à-vis individuals (and not vis-à-vis classes, which can change them by changing society) and push their way through in spite of the will of individuals (see, for example, Paul, 1978: 192). The difference between social and natural laws is that the latter (but not their interpretation) are independent of the will and action of classes as well.

If this is so, which is the particular way social laws regulate the functioning of the system in class-divided societies, and particularly under capitalism? Since social laws are the "translation" in society and by society of natural laws, and since in class-divided societies this "translation" is determined by contradictory social relations, social laws must regulate the functioning of this type of system in a contradictory way. Let us make the same point in a slightly different way. The fact that social laws are not arbitrarily "chosen," that they are the social form taken by natural laws and that this social form is contradictory, implies that the system is based on fundamental social phenomena that are contradictory in nature, and thus that is is based on fundamental contradictions. Social laws can therefore be regarded as the expression of the fundamental contradictions of a class-divided society. Now, the specificity of social laws' contradictory regulation under capitalism is their being *tendencial,* in the sense that the basic tendency cannot be separated from the several countertendencies: It is this that lends the specificity to the inner contradictoriness of this particular type of social phenomena. Take Marx's law of population under capitalism. The basic tendency is the creation of relative surplus population due to the introduction of capital-intensive techniques, while one of the countertendencies is the absorption of the resulting unemployment by the creation of new branches of production. What determines the contradictory nature of this social phenomenon?

In my view, it is the need capital has to increase the organic composition of capital as the way to increase the production of relative surplus value. It is this latter that pushes the entrepreneur to both replace people with machines, and at the same time, to search for new markets, both internal and external. Thus both production and absorption of relative surplus population are determined by the same determinant instance, which determines both the tendency and the countertendencies. It is precisely because of this logically contemporaneous determination that a certain phenomenon assumes a tendencial nature, that it cannot realize itself (as a condition of reproduction of the determinant instance) apart from the realization of countereffects, equally conditions of reproduction of the same determinant instance. In short, the determinant instance, because of its contradictory nature, can reproduce itself only in a contradictory way, by creating contradictory conditions of its own reproduction. Tendency is thus the particular way dialectical determination acts in those particular social phenomena that are social laws.

About the Author

G. CARCHEDI

Biographical notes are useful only if some light is shed on the features of the work submitted or on the author's motivations. From my point of view this means that the personal trajectory of the author's life should be seen in the light of the social phenomena that shaped it, rather than in the specific terms of his or her personal experiences. For me these have been the affluence marred by the social contradictions of the "economic miracles" of postwar Europe (where I grew up), the tension and almost maddening alienation of life in the huge North American urban centers (to which I have been exposed for many years), and the abysmal poverty of the Third World (which I observe first hand) as well as contact with the European workers' movement, participation in the student movement, and the influence of the great social upheavals of the 1960s and 1970s (all filtered through the study of the classic and moderns Marxist works). These are the milestones and the sources of inspiration that have motivated and will continue to motivate my research.

— III —

CONCLUSIONS

24

TOWARD A MORE REFLECTIVE SOCIAL SCIENCE

Gareth Morgan

York University

> What an immense digestive act you are accomplishing! I'm reminded of the snake which swallowed the elephant in *Le Petit Prince*.

So am I! Bill Torbert's timely comment on my efforts to analyze the nature and implications of the chapters in this volume vividly captures the way I feel as I begin to write these concluding chapters. The boa constrictor in Saint-Exupery's childhood fantasy had the luxury of six months of motionless hibernation to digest its enormous meal. Such respite would prove very welcome to me just now, particularly for the blissful realization that the digestive problems posed by this volume would have disappeared on reawakening. Unfortunately, I cannot lose the problems that easily. Though you, the reader, can absorb its contents at leisure, working bite by bite through its various chapters, I, following the way of the boa, have been obliged to consume it whole, and in this conclusion wish to share my reflections on the digestive process that has ensued.

The diversity of research strategies presented in this volume is clearly overwhelming. While each author advocates a research strategy that is logically coherent and consistent in terms of the assumptions on which it builds, these assumptions vary from chapter to chapter. The phenomenon to be researched is conceptualized and studied in many different ways, each generating distinctive kinds of insight and understanding. In this diversity we find opportunity. Our volume suggests that there are many different ways of studying the same social phenomenon, and given that the insights generated by any one approach are at best partial and incomplete, since something somewhere must always remain undecided (Gödel, 1962), the social researcher can gain much by reflecting on the nature and merits of different approaches before engaging in a particular mode of research practice. It becomes clear from reading this volume that social scientists, like other generators of knowledge, deal in possibilities. They are concerned with the realization of *possible knowledge,* since what is studied and what is learned are intimately connected with the mode of engagement adopted. In developing the interpretive structure provided by one mode of engagement rather than by another, the social researcher directly influences what he or she will "discover" about the phenomenon being researched, realizing one possible form of knowledge within a wider set of possibilities.

The opportunity and choice facing the researcher are very much like those facing a hungry man at a smorgasbord or a visitor to an art gallery. Our volume offers many different ways of doing research, just as a smorgasbord offers many things to eat, and the gallery many things to see. Time can be spent indulging oneself with in-depth involvement in a single area or in reflecting on the diversity with which one is confronted. The chapters presented in this volume merit consideration and digestion in both these ways, as a means of broadening our understanding of the research process and its possibilities, and hence of improving the conduct and quality of research.

However, our discussion must go much further than this. If the question of choosing a research strategy were as simple as that of choosing what to eat at a restaurant or what to see at an art gallery, we would have few problems in engaging in research, for our choice of research strategy could well be justified or defended according to a criterion of personal taste. Insofar as the research strategies are offered as a means of advancing our formal as opposed to personal or tacit knowledge of the social world, then the significance and problems of choosing among the different research strategies fall within a more public domain. The choice of research strategy now becomes a question relating to the issue of what counts as valid social science, to be answered with reference to criteria as to what counts as valid scientific knowledge. Are all the research strategies equally valid? Do they all have a role to play in social research? How are we to understand the relations between them? How can we come to an opinion regarding their significance and merits? Questions such as these become of major concern.

Viewed from this standpoint, the diversity and opportunity offered in this volume present themselves as a problem, for we are obliged to recognize that any attempt to evaluate or judge the significance of different approaches to social research may be framed by assumptions or presuppositions that have no a priori claim to supremacy over those of other evaluative stances. As noted in the introductory chapter, it is fallacious to conclude that the propositions of a system of thought can be proved, disproved, or evaluated on the basis of axioms within that system, since the process becomes self-justifying. This means that it is not possible to determine the validity or contribution of different research strategies in any absolute sense in terms of evaluative stances that draw on the same assumptions as do any of the research strategies examined. Unless it is possible to find an independent point of reference against which the nature and claims of the different research strategies can be assessed, all evaluative efforts encounter a relativism in which it may be possible to say that one research strategy may be more effective for a specific purpose than for another (e.g., for aiding prediction and control, understanding meaningful action, engaging in problem solving), but that ultimately the different research strategies do different things, and that as far as their contributions and knowledge claims are concerned, we should follow Feyerabend (1975) and conclude that "anything goes."

Traditionally, the social sciences, following the natural sciences, have in effect attempted to deal with the above problem by drawing a distinction between the realm of subject and object, and by presuming that scientists are able to represent the external world in objective forms of knowledge. As Rorty (1979) has shown, the traditional conception of scientific knowledge has drawn heavily on visual metaphors that favor the idea that the "Eye of the Mind" sees knowledge in correspondence with, as a representation and a general mirroring or reflection of, the world. This visual conception of knowledge has favored development of the idea that the ultimate criterion for evaluating the claims of competing theories must be through means of empirical tests or predictions that appeal to accuracy of representation— "correspondence with the facts" — as a means of determining objective truth. Theories that contribute most to our knowledge are, from this point of view, those that are able to describe or predict what is happening in the external world. The assumption that subjective mind and external reality are quite separate realms fosters the idea that theories and concepts, the products of the scientist's mind, can be tested against the independent facts of objective reality in a way that allows us to decide quite conclusively which theories provide the truest explanations of that reality. This imagery sets the basis for a science searching for a knowledge that is certain and true in a foundational sense. Science, in effect, becomes a quest for the foundations of knowledge. The external world is used as the ultimate, independent point of reference against which the accuracy of our thoughts and ideas, expressed in terms of theories, propositions, and predictions, can be judged.

However, the "independence" of this external world, and hence its validity as a fixed point of reference against which the claims of scientific theories can be evaluated, begins to break down once we introduce the idea that the independence of subjective mind and objective reality is no more than an assumption. As soon as we entertain the idea that what the "Eye of the Mind" sees in the external world may be as much a consequence of the nature of the eye as it is of the object seen, we create severe problems for the view that the "truth claims" of scientific theories can be judged in terms of a criterion of objective knowledge based on an ability to mirror or reflect the nature of the external world. This line of argument opens the way to the idea that objectivity is as much a part of the observer as it is of the object studied, and that all knowledge of the world is in some degree a socially constructed knowledge, since what the "Eye of the Mind" sees is shaped by the assumptions that frame the scientist's investigation.

The influence of subjective processes on scientific investigation has of course been well recognized (Kuhn, 1970b; Mitroff, 1974) and has attracted a variety of responses concerned with finding a new basis for objectivity. One popular course of action followed by those interested in adhering to the idea that the ultimate reality rests in the nature of the empirical world, and that knowledge ultimately rests in the ability to describe and predict the nature of that world, is to attempt to minimize the influence of subjective processes. Thus the assumptions that shape inquiry are treated as potentially irrational elements, that as far as possible must be purged from the process of inquiry or at least be made explicit (Lakatos and Musgrave, 1970; Kuhn, 1970a, 1974). Another response has been to attempt to anchor knowledge in an understanding of the categories and processes through which the "knowing subject" attempts to structure the world in which he or she lives, as in Kantian philosophy, neo-Kantian phenomenology, and many approaches to the philosophy of language. A third approach has been to argue that since knowledge is a product of the union between subject and object worlds, knowledge is best obtained through a praxis that systematically explores the relation between subject and object.

Each of these approaches to the problem of knowledge in effect searches for firm foundations on which our understanding of the world can be based. As Dewey (1929), Mannheim (1936), and Rorty

(1979) have suggested, the whole history of epistemology can be interpreted as hinging on this quest for certainty in our way of knowing. Yet while the quest has at times shown considerable promise, it has always ultimately run into difficulties because it has been unable to find that independent point of reference necessary to avoid the problem of self-justifying claims. As we have noted, there is a logical contradiction in attempting to argue for the certainty or superiority of knowledge stemming from one set of assumptions if one's argument is based on those assumptions. Hence the positivist's argument that knowledge must be grounded in "empirical data" purged as far as possible of all traces of subjectivism because the world is ultimately an objective reality is in large measure self-justifying. So too the phenomenologist's claim that subjective reality is all-important because the locus of reality rests in the knowing subject. Similarly, the idea that scientific research is a process of "engagement," as argued in the present work, does not of itself establish the supremacy of knowledge that systematically explores the relation between subject and object. In order to be able to make such foundational claims regarding the priority of subject, object, or some relation between the two, one has to be able to see and evaluate their claims from a perspective that transcends the presuppositions that shape the subject/object problematic. Interestingly, this would require that we search for a perspective that places ourselves outside the problematic that defines science, for the unity of science since Descartes hinges on different renderings of the relation between subject and object: Positivist, phenomenological, and praxis-oriented philosophies are best understood as negatory aspects of the same dialectical whole. Phenomenology negates positivism, and philosophies of praxis are concerned with negating the dualism thus created.

REFRAMING OUR VIEW OF KNOWLEDGE

Given the difficulty of finding a unique evaluative perspective from which the claims of different research strategies can be assessed, there seems to be good reason to search for an alternative means of dealing with this problem. Since the difficulties hinge on the relativism that emerges from the inability to find independent foundations for evaluation, an approach that allows us to deal with this relativism is required. Or, to put the matter in a more positive way, we need to find a way of dealing with the *possibilities* that relativism signifies. In order to find such an approach, it is necessary to reframe our view of knowledge in a way that gets beyond the idea that knowledge is in some sense foundational and can be evaluated in an absolute way, for it is this idea that ultimately leads us to try and banish the uncertainty associated with relativism, rather than simply to deal with it as an inevitable feature of the process through which knowledge is generated.

Important ideas on how this task can be approached are found in the work of Dewey (1929, 1933, 1938), Gadamer (1975), Heidegger (1962), and a number of other modern philosophers (see Rorty, 1979) who have sought to understand science and the quest for knowledge as but a specific kind of human practice, to be understood along with other human practices, as particular and partial means of expressing ourselves and our relationship with the world. As Gadamer (1975) has argued, when we engage in research action, thought, and interpretation, we are not simply involved in instrumental processes geared to the acquisition of knowledge but in processes through which we actually make and remake ourselves as human beings. The pursuit of scientific truth is from this point of view a particular way of making and remaking ourselves, or in Heidegger's terms, just one "project" among others, and is of as much significance because of its implications for the development and well-being of all those humans involved with or influenced by this activity as it is for the "knowledge" it generates. Viewed from this perspective, we are encouraged to see the pursuit of formal knowledge as but a particular form of human action, which because of its essentially social nature, must be understood as being as much an ethical, moral, ideological, and political activity as it is an epistemological one. If there are evaluative criteria that can be brought to bear on the nature of knowledge, they relate as much to the way knowledge serves to guide and shape ourselves as human beings — to the consequences of knowledge, in the sense of what knowledge does to and for humans — as to the idea that there are fixed points of reference against which knowledge can be judged "right," "wrong," or unambiguously "better than."

When we approach the problem of dealing with the nature and claims of different research strategies with these considerations in mind, we are encouraged to replace a quest for absolute judgment of their merits with a concern with exploring and understanding their significance. We are encouraged to reflect on the research process as a form of human action, with a view to grasping its nature, its possibilities, and its consequences. In so doing, we are able to obtain a fuller understanding of the way we make and remake ourselves and our world through our research, and possibly, of new and more interesting or more comfortable ways of doing so.

To achieve such a stance, we need to initiate a process that Mannheim (1940) would describe as "substantially rational," Rorty (1979) as "edifying," and Vickers (1965, 1972) as "appreciative." This would emphasize the importance of critical reflection as a basis for action, to help researchers orient their activities in ways that attempt to take full account of the relations within which such action is set, the consequences of that action, and of alternative actions. Such a perspective would reorient the role of the researcher from that of a technical functionary pursuing a prespecified form of knowledge (as the foundational view of knowledge tends to encourage), and place responsibility for the conduct and consequences of research directly with the researcher. Each researcher would carry an obligation to reflect on the nature of his or her activity as a means of choosing an appropriate path of action.

This approach to the conduct of research would replace a concern for evaluation in a foundational sense with a concern for what I will describe as "reflective exploration" or "reflective conversation." I use this term as a metaphor for framing an approach to research inquiry, research education, and the consideration of knowledge claims that facilitates the kind of reflective understanding and action envisaged by Mannheim, Rorty, and Vickers.

EXPLORING RESEARCH STRATEGIES THROUGH REFLECTIVE CONVERSATION

Such an approach commends itself for a number of reasons. First, it encourages us to recognize the research process itself as a form of social interaction in which the researcher "converses" with, and learns about, the phenomenon being studied. Sometimes the conversation takes place on the researcher's terms, and at others, on those of the phenomenon being investigated or in a way that is mutually defined. In reflecting on the particular kind of conversation in which the researcher is engaged, much can be learned about the nature of the research process, which allows us to choose intelligently among alternative strategies or to modify our favored strategy in constructive ways.

Second, we can view different research strategies as but different "voices" in a conversation about the nature and status of knowledge. Thus regarded, the voices can be treated as offering different interpretations of a situation or different arguments in favor of understanding a phenomenon in a particular way. We are encouraged to see that the different voices may be trying to say different things to different listeners, drawing on different vocabularies or even different languages. Some of the research voices may be espousing or defending a conventional wisdom, others trying to say something new. Certain voices may be attempting to shape the agenda of discussion, others to persuade, justify, shock, or merely engage in diversionary talk. And so on. Viewed in these terms we are encouraged to treat knowledge claims as claims, rather than as statements that purport to be foundational, and to pay them the close consideration, attention, and degree of skepticism that we might pay to other claims in everyday talk. In so doing, we render knowledge claims tentative rather than absolute, and render them open to critical discussion from many different points of view (e.g., with regard to their action consequences, ethical implications, psychological significance, aesthetics, sensationalism, or any other theme of interest to those engaged by the particular kinds of claims being made).

Third, we can engage in reflective conversation about the nature and claims of different research strategies in a way that deliberately tries to minimize commitment to a favored point of view. This helps to explore diversity as fully and critically as possible without prejudging the issues involved. Although the idea that we should explore knowledge claims through conversation suggests an image of research as an interpretive process, this does not mean that it necessarily favors interpretive research strategies in the debate that it generates, for as in any conversation, any voice can be given an equal chance to be heard and hence to have an impact on the course that discussion takes. All the research strategies represented in this volume, for example, have something to contribute to such a conversation. The conversation generated may take various turns, leading at different times to synthesis, compromise, consensus, transformation, polarization, or simply clarification and improved understanding of differences. The important point is that such conversation should be allowed to occur in a way that facilitates exploration rather than constraint, encouraging those involved to gain a measure of detachment from their usual presuppositions through reflection on the nature and implications of what they and others do in their research and the consequences of the knowledge they generate. In creating the possibility of exchange based on differences of viewpoint, such conversation offers the promise of edifying dialogue that is not overly concerned with forging premature consensus or arriving at an end point that purports to establish or reveal some foundational truth. Rather, the point is to learn from the process itself, and to encourage the conversation to continue so long as disagreement lasts. In so doing, we are able to minimize the hegemony of a fixed evaluative stance or of any conventional wisdom that seeks to brush disagreement aside under the delusion that it can know what is true and right (except under optimal, controlled circumstances) in favor of an edifying exchange that thrives on self-conscious criticism, challenge, and diversity. Although in all conversations there is always the danger of what Heidegger describes as "idle talk," the way of gossiping, there is also the opportunity to address issues and preoccupations of major concern.

One of the fine, flexible things about conversation is that it can begin anywhere and explore many different themes according to the way it becomes structured by those involved. A conversation usually only needs a starting point. Once this is provided, those whose interest is engaged can usually be relied on to do the rest. Such conversation will prove edifying so long as the participants feel a genuine involvement in the issues being explored and use the course of conversation to confront and reflect on the views they hold and to act on any significant conclusions that emerge.

In creating the opportunity for such conversation in their professional lives, social scientists have the opportunity of confronting their professional "selves" and their role in making and remaking social science as we know it today. The juxtaposition of the different research strategies presented in this volume itself invites such conversation and provides a useful starting point, for the very fact that a researcher favors one strategy rather than another is something worthy of exploration. In many respects, therefore, we could end our discussion here with the call "Let the conversation begin," or where it is already in progress, with an affirmation that it needs to continue.

However, there is an irresistible temptation to do more and to share some of the themes that have captured my interest as this project has developed, particularly as a result of the York research strategies workshop. These themes identify topics that need to be addressed in order to help break the grip that a foundational view of knowledge holds on the way we approach epistemological problems. They are not offered in the spirit of "agenda setting," but as exploratory probes designed to identify issues that will open the way to constructive discussion.

25

THE SIGNIFICANCE OF ASSUMPTIONS

Gareth Morgan

York University

One route to a reflective understanding of research practice lies in exploring the nature and consequences of the assumptions that frame different modes of inquiry. Such assumptions are of crucial importance, especially in the social sciences, where the situations studied are what Ackoff (1979) and Churchman (1979) characterize as "complex" and "ill-structured," or in Ackoff's vivid terminology, as "messes." Assumptions make messes researchable, often at the cost of great oversimplification, and in a way that is highly problematic. As Maurice Landry (1980) reminds us, a system in serial arrangement cannot be better than its weakest part. In scientific research, the assumptions that frame inquiry usually qualify for this role, for even though a scientist may go to great lengths to ensure that a research design meets the stringent controls of scientific method, the assumptions on which the research builds frequently escape scrutiny of any kind. Hence science, fastidiously rational in the care and precision it devotes to the design of relations between detailed means (the research design) and ends (research results), often runs the risk of being fundamentally irrational to the extent that it fails to critique the foundations (and hence ultimate means) on which it builds. This is why Kuhn's (1970b) analysis of the role of paradigms in scientific inquiry is so important, for it demonstrates how scientific communities may be bound together by various bonds and commitments, which, insofar as they build on taken for granted assumptions, are basically unscientific.

In other writings (Burrell and Morgan, 1979; Morgan, 1980) I have attempted to set a basis for the task of analyzing and challenging assumptions through a form of map-making activity designed to increase awareness of the taken-for-granted premises that ultimately shape social research. The authors contributing to this volume help us to do this by presenting their favored approach to research in a way that makes their assumptions evident, and thus open to examination and critique, in a manner that allows us to confront and examine the differences between competing points of view. However, a messy problem still remains: What do we do with the diversity once we have explored and understood it?

The work of Churchman (1971) and Mason and Mitroff (1981) on the design of inquiring systems shows us that a number of different approaches are always possible. The following five adapt and develop ideas drawn from the above sources, pragmatist philosophy, and Feyerabend's (1975) radical approach to epistemology.

Supremacy. One response to the existence of different research assumptions is to call for some form of evaluation or test that will determine their merits. This is obviously foundational, and suffers from the problems to which we have given so much attention in the previous chapter. As we will discuss in detail in Chapter 27, advocates of different research strategies can usually identify distinctive grounds for evaluation that may be as persuasive as any other. In challenging assumptions one may be able to refine a research strategy but may not be able to demonstrate that it is any better than strategies based on other assumptions. This attempt to evaluate different research assumptions in a foundational sense thus encounters the same kind of relativism as that with which it is attempting to deal.

Synthesis. This response is also foundational, concerned with finding an optimal way of conducting research. However, instead of attempting to choose among different research assumptions, an attempt is made to find ways of combining their strengths and minimizing their weaknesses. The search is for an integrated approach, or common ground, that can be recognized by everyone as the superior or most reasonable way to conduct research. Attempts to find an all-embracing paradigm or metaphor for framing inquiry, to translate different strategies into a common language, or to find ways of overcoming traditional dichotomies, provide good examples of such integrative effort. The complexity of different paradigms in social research has in part resulted from this kind of activity, as one viewpoint is synthesized with another (Burrell and Morgan, 1979).

Contingency. A third approach is to appeal to a pragmatist criterion that suggests that the significance of knowledge is ultimately teleological and arises from the needs of human beings to cope with specific problems and concerns (Dewey, 1929, 1933, 1938; Susman, in this volume). This view leads to the idea that assumptions and knowledge should be judged according to their usefulness. Hence assumptions and the specific theories and propositions to which they give rise are treated as tools to be regarded and used in a very practical manner. This typically leads to the idea that there is no one best set of assumptions or tools for conducting research, and that it is appropriate to vary assumptions from one situation to another according to the issues being studied or the problem being solved. The idea that there is an optimal way of conducting research is thus qualified by the principle of contingency: the view that "it all depends." This approach abandons the idea that scientific research is concerned with establishing some foundational truth in favor of the idea that assumptions and the knowledge to which they give rise are of ultimate significance because of their practical use and hence the interests they reflect and serve.

Dialectic. This approach also accepts the diversity of assumptions and knowledge claims as an inevitable feature of research and attempts to use the differences among competing perspectives as a means of constructing new modes of understanding. In contrast to approaches that attempt to eliminate diversity and uncertainty by searching for the best formulation or some kind of synthesis, the dialectical approach deliberately counterposes the insights of different perspectives in the hope that a completely new mode of understanding will emerge from the debate generated by this opposition. This analytical approach stems from Hegelian roots and has been operationalized as a distinctive form of inquiring system by Mason and Mitroff (1981) to bring to the surface and debate the assumptions that guide corporate planning. The assumptions held by different stakeholders involved in the planning process are paralleled in the present work by the assumptions that underwrite different research strategies. By counterposing the assumptions and knowledge claims of different research perspectives, we may be able to learn more about the phenomenon being researched, just as corporate planners can generate new creative plans by adopting different approaches to the planning process. One way in which this methodology can be developed is through the use of dialectical or multisided case studies in which the same situation is analyzed from many different perspectives. Allison's (1971) work on decision making provides an illustration of this approach in practice. My own work advocating a theoretical pluralism in which organizations are studied on the basis of different paradigms and metaphors provides another (Morgan, 1980). The essence of dialectical analysis lies in the idea that we should accept all research strategies as having something to offer but attempt to use their competing insights within the context of a single analysis. The dialecticians believe that we must recognize and *use* diversity in a constructive fashion, learning from diversity by using conflict and debate as a means of exploring and expanding our understanding. Synthesis, if it emerges, only occurs at a final stage of analysis in a form of understanding that attempts to recognize and yet go beyond original formulations of the problem and all the conflicts that these generate.

Anything Goes. A final approach for dealing with the nature and claims of competing assumptions adopts a complete relativism, favoring the idea that every research strategy may have something to offer, and whether or not we attempt to systematize insights is of little real concern. The attempt to evaluate, synthesize, be pragmatic, or engage in dialectical analysis may from this point of view be regarded as useful, but not necessary. Anything goes!

This approach stems from Feyerabend's (1975) advocacy of a theoretical and methodological anarchism in science on the basis that there is no idea, however ancient or absurd, that is not capable of improving our knowledge. Approaches to research that are complementary, contradictory, or proceed counterintuitively in defiance of formal logic are all acceptable because they may generate some form of insight and understanding that cannot be achieved in any other way. Feyerabend's anarchism is committed to a creative humanism that recognizes a potential contradiction between creativity and method and rejects the idea that one form of knowledge can be determined as uniquely superior to another. For Feyerabend, only the individual human being, whether researcher, researched subject, or user of knowledge, is in a position to choose what kind of knowledge or ideology should guide our activities.

These five approaches for dealing with the nature and consequences of different research strategies each offer a concrete course of action. The question now arises as to which, if any, is most appropriate for dealing with the messy problem that diversity presents. Should we attempt to evaluate assumptions, search for common ground, adopt a criterion of usefulness, engage in dialectics, or decide that anything goes?

In attempting to answer this question, we again encounter the problem of relativism that stems from the absence of an independent point of evaluation for judging the merits of different research approaches. While the absence of such a reference point allows us to conclude that foundational approaches that attempt to place knowledge on a certain basis through evaluation or synthesis are likely to be insufficient, we cannot rule these out of consideration. This is because the remaining three approaches are all based on the idea that every approach to social research may have something to offer. Hence even those epistemological stances that are ultimately trying to find the one best way to do research or to assess the merits of research may yield distinctive kinds of insights, even though they pursue an unattainable ideal. There are simply no grounds for saying that a research perspective or approach to evaluating research is not worthwhile. While not necessarily favoring a completely anarchistic theory of knowledge, we are obliged to recognize that no one research strategy or inquiring system can be authoritative or complete and that there is at least some merit in Feyerabend's claim that "anything goes."

This consideration returns us to the idea that since we cannot find any foundational solution to the problem of knowledge, all we can really do is explore what is possible. The conversational model presented earlier provides an important means of doing this. Rather than search for fixed frameworks for settling claims, we are encouraged to accept that research can only ultimately be evaluated and improved through reflective consideration of what we and others do and by identifying untapped possibilities. By reflecting on one's favored research strategy in relation to other strategies, the nature, strengths, and limitations of one's favored approach become much clearer. In seeing what others do, we are able to appreciate much more clearly what we are *not* doing. In this way, we are able to create a means of developing and refining favored research strategies in a way that makes them stronger, yet at the same time more modest. We increasingly realize the limitations of our favored perspective the more we explore others, learning about ourselves through the other. In this way we can learn about and improve research strategies in a manner that is not so much concerned with deciding which is best or with substituting one for another as with encouraging an attitude and activity that is sensitive to the merits of diversity and seeks to explore and enrich research rather than constrain it through a search for an optimum way of doing things.

The one strong element of consensus emerging from discussion at the York research strategies workshop focused on the relevance of this kind of conversational model of inquiry for exploring different research perspectives and as a formal means of approaching and structuring research education. By using conversation to explore the assumptions that guide inquiry, presenting one's own position and listening to others or by presenting what we see as each other's position, we move beyond reproduction of the differences that divide us to an appreciation of why we are divided. In doing so, we arrive at the only powerful means of assessing the nature and limitations of research practice — by acquiring a capacity for knowing what we are doing, why we are doing it, and how we might do it differently if we so choose. In this activity lies the capacity for a substantially rational action in which science is conducted by scientists who actively realize that they make knowledge, and who, through intelligent reflection on the relationship between means and ends, are able to choose appropriate means for achieving what they and others value. The ultimate significance of assumptions rests in this realization: that assumptions ultimately mean choice, and that the exploration of assumptions involves the exploration of choice.

26

KNOWLEDGE, UNCERTAINTY, AND CHOICE

Gareth Morgan

York University

In order to move toward a more reflective social science, it is necessary to replace the notion that assumptions and knowledge can be certain, authoritative, and unambiguously "true" (except under limited, controlled circumstances) with the idea that uncertainty is a defining feature. In so doing, we may be able to replace the popular concern with eliminating uncertainty with the idea that diversity, uncertainty, and perhaps even contradiction are central aspects of the process of knowing with which the scientist must cope and that must be explored.

Uncertainty has always played a fascinating and, in many respects, paradoxical role in the development of science. Science has evolved as a way of knowing that seeks to replace more traditional systems of belief, such as those embodied in folklore, myth, and religion, with a codified knowledge that uses "systematic doubt" as a technique for choosing among different explanations of the phenomenon being studied. In other words, science searches for a knowledge that is certain and reliable by suspending belief in certainty as a means to this end. Indeed, the hallmark of knowledge deemed "scientific" is that belief has been suspended in the way things are, at least temporarily. Under positivism, suspension of belief usually takes the form of hypothesis testing, in which rival hypotheses are subjected to systematic doubt and their respective merits determined through the exercise of reason and disciplined observation. Phenomenological research strategies "bracket" or suspend belief in the way things are or disrupt taken-for-granted settings to reveal the formative influence of the presuppositions and practices through which we structure and filter our everyday experiences. Action research implements the logic of hypothesis testing by examining the consequences of *alternative* paths of action and by reformulating understanding of the situation acted on in terms of the results of this process. In other words, these perspectives search for knowledge by using doubt or uncertainty as a technique for achieving this end.

In recent years, the central importance of uncertainty in the conduct of science has been formulated in a number of ways. Karl Popper (1958, 1968), for example, has suggested that since scientific hypotheses can at best escape refutation — never be proved — the scientist should be guided by a logic of scientific discovery in which he or she systematically attempts to *disprove* the conjectures or hypotheses being investigated. His philosophy suggests that scientific knowledge can never be regarded as definitively true, since even scientific explanations that can command a great deal of evidence in their favor may someday be replaced by better explanations, as illustrated in the way Newton's view of the universe was obliged, after many years of confirmation, to give way to Einstein's. Hence Popper's idea that only by attempting to refute our theories can we systematize the search for better ones. Insofar as scientists dwell on the satisfaction of results that confirm favored hypotheses, science loses its critical edge. Only by attempting to subject theories to the sternest possible tests can science hope to cope with the basic epistemological uncertainty that stems from the realization that we can never ever know that we are correct, except on the premises of a closed system of logical thought in which we remove uncertainty through assumption, or by controlling it in laboratory settings.

Popper's work offers a serious challenge to the way much of social science is presently conducted. The spirit of research is often guided by a desire for affirmation rather than for refutation. The use of social science as a technique for generating knowledge to help sustain, develop, or change society, together with the fact that it is conducted and evaluated within the context of bureaucratic structures, often tends to squeeze out the role of doubt in favor of a production-oriented mentality that emphasizes the importance of achieving significant, useful results. These considerations tend to favor an approach that is basically affirmational, in that the scientist is ultimately concerned with producing findings that add to a stock of knowledge by identifying hypotheses, insights, or explanations that can command some degree of empirical support, however small. The role of doubt or refutation in such investigations is often reduced to a purely technical consideration, incorporated in a rather minimal way, through, for example, statistical tests of significance that examine whether favored hypotheses and explanations beat the laws of chance. Studies that fail to generate clear-cut results are rarely deemed significant, even though they may signify a potential refutation of the researcher's whole frame of reference for interpreting the situation being studied.

However, there are problems in adopting a logic of refutation, since in any research study it is clear that a stance that is in some degree affirmational is always required if any progress is to be made. As we have shown, all research strategies are framed by assumptions that shape the course of inquiry in distinctive ways. If one brings systematic doubt to bear on these assumptions at an early stage of inquiry, it is likely that the grounds of research will be ever changing, with the consequence that substantive research becomes difficult because there is no clear view of what is being studied, and hence, of how it is to be studied. Popper's solution to this problem rests in his advocacy of hypothesis testing, backed by a representational view of knowledge, in which the scientist is able to appeal to the facts of an external world as an independent point of reference against which the claims of competing theories can be judged. The assumptions that frame inquiry become significant because of the hypotheses they generate. Hence affirmation in the design stage of a research project — the process through which we select a model for inquiry — can ultimately be tested in a refutational mode according to the support that its hypotheses generate. In this way, Popper produces an excellent solution to the uncertain nature of knowledge, but only insofar as one accepts the independence of facts and the idea that it is meaningful in the situations being studied to formulate relationships in the simple, clear-cut way that hypothesis testing demands. Clearly, hypothesis testing is a method that scientists have developed to simplify our understanding of reality, converting the ill-structured "messes" we encounter in everyday life into a network of well-structured problems. The paradox this approach raises is thus the familiar one already discussed: that science involves a quest for certainty using uncertainty as a second-order construct or method for achieving this end.

Despite these qualifications, Popper's approach to the philosophy of science helps us to accept the idea that science can never produce definitive statements on "the ways things are" and encourages us to view the claims of science in a more modest and tentative way than is often the case. (See the chapter by Cook in this volume for a related view.) Within the limitations identified above, the logic of his position is forceful and clear — scientists should generate hypotheses, and systematically attempt to *refute* those hypotheses. In this way, scientific activity may improve our ability to explain the world, even though we will never be certain that its explanations are absolutely correct. The method of hypothesis testing he favors has direct relevance for research strategies underpinned by a representational view of knowledge applied in the study of well-structured situations and for those adopting an action research perspective in which the consequences of action can be tested against expected consequences. The challenge to other traditions is to refine the methods through which they bring systematic doubt to bear on the course of their research investigations, for affirmation itself does not capture the spirit of science.

In addition to the "epistemological uncertainties" stemming from limitations in our way of knowing it is possible to identify what I call "ontological uncertainties." These arise from the nature of the situation being investigated and set the basis for knowledges that may be complementary or contradictory. Arguments, which we must regard as suggestive rather than conclusive, favoring the existence of such ontological uncertainties stem from studies of both the natural and social worlds. Foremost among these is the field of quantum physics, where it has become recognized that the building blocks of the material world are by no means as fixed and certain as the Greek atomists and those who have built science on atomic and mechanistic principles have led us to believe. Research on the behavior of subatomic phenomena suggests that reality at this level has a probabilistic character (Heisenberg, 1958; Bohr, 1958; Capra, 1975; Zukav, 1979) and that science is best regarded as an uncertain endeavor dealing with an uncertain world.

Important implications of these discoveries have been formulated in Heisenberg's "uncertainty principle" and Bohr's "principle of complementarity." These related ideas develop the theoretical implications of the indeterminancy of quantum mechanical systems, which cannot simultaneously possess an exact position and an exact momentum since these attributes constantly affect each other. Heisenberg and Bohr have generalized the implications of this finding, suggesting that such indeterminancy is a characteristic of all phenomena but that its evidence is only apparent at the subatomic level, where the minute nature of the constituent elements of reality make the principle of greater significance in its actual effects. They have also formulated the principle that it is impossible to study subatomic phenomena without influencing what is seen, and that what is observed and measured is as much a function of the mode of observation and measurement as it is of the phenomenon being measured. As discussed much earlier, this principle has widespread implications for the conduct of science, for it breaks down the idea that the scientist is able to research something without being part of what is being studied. Hence Heisenberg's suggestion that the scientist does not generate knowledge of an object world, but of his or her *interaction with* that world, and that science tells the scientist as much about him- or herself as it does about the phenomenon being investigated.

A second source of ideas suggesting that science is obliged to deal with ontological uncertainties stems from recent work linking findings in the field of brain and consciousness research to those in quantum physics, through the metaphor of a holographic universe (see Bohm, 1971, 1973; Ferguson, 1980; Pribram, 1977; Watson, 1979). These ideas suggest that the world as we experience it is the result of a process of transformation through which the brain translates the information it encounters from the world "out there" into the forms that we know as objects, sounds, smells, experiences, and so on through mathematical processes that have little common-sense relation to the structure of the world as we know it. The idea is that the brain and world are holographic (i.e., constituted images derived from a totally dispersed information source in which every part of the whole is a reflection of the whole), and that its apparent concreteness is an illusion snatched from a kaleidescopic flux of immaterial frequencies from a dimension transcending space and time. The basic order of this world rests not in the forms we see and know, but in an implicate structure or code, very much as the unfolding reality of physical development in human beings can be understood as resting in the genetic code, DNA. While the research supporting these revolutionary ideas is still very much in its infancy, it is clear that there are important links with the well-established ideas of Heisenberg and Bohr. Common to both is the idea that human beings participate in the construction of what we know as physical reality and that there are very sound reasons to believe that this "real world" is far less certain and concrete than we typically assume. While both strands of research are consistent with the view that there is a basic ordering of the world, even if only of a probabilistic or deep structural kind, the consequences of this ordering render themselves visible to human beings in different ways according to the structures of thought and experience through which they are engaged and known.

Although scientists are usually quite content to use probability theory as a technique for dealing with the uncertainties of our world, there is often a reluctance to accept the full implications of the kind of view presented above. The world we encounter in our daily lives feels far too real and concrete for us to accept that its building blocks are

highly unstable or that is concreteness is an illusion. The usual sentiment is captured in the spirit of Einstein's reaction to Heisenberg's
ideas — "that God does not play dice with the universe." Even
though we may be prepared to entertain the existence of "black
holes" in outer space, which literally make physical reality disappear,
the idea that similar counterintuitive processes may apply here in the
realm of everyday reality is far less readily embraced. There is an
understandable tendency to favor scientific explanations that are
consistent with the world as experienced.

Yet if we examine the social world, we find that these ideas have
much greater intuitive relevance than may first appear. In the social
world we have a realm that is far less concrete than is the physical
world and where the kind of ontological uncertainty identified in
quantum physics and holography can be seen as a defining feature of
everyday reality. For example, it is easy to see that social life has an
unpredictable rather than certain character, in that the actions of
human beings are always drawn from a set of wider possibilities and
the most routine situations are frequently disrupted and transformed
by unexpected circumstances, since realities typically unfold according to the contingencies present in the way circumstances are constructed or develop. We can also see how the very same surface
reality may embody many different meanings, some of which may be
complementary and others contradictory, as when an action signifying genuine friendship on one occasion may on another be hollow and
perfunctory, and on yet another, be used as a manipulative ploy. As we
examine the nature of the social world, we can easily see that the kind
of uncertainty that modern physicists suggest is a characteristic of the
material world has a direct and obvious parallel in the nature of the
social world.

In the very different writings of social philosophers such as Jung
(1954) and Nietzsche (1968) we find clear parallels with the ideas of the
quantum physicists. Take, for example, Nietzsche's idea that human
beings are continually engaged in fixing or freezing a process of
becoming into a state of being, overconcretizing their experience of
reality, treating "frozen" words, concepts, and everyday understandings as the realities to which they relate. This links very closely to the
basic ideas captured by the "uncertainty principle." Similarly, Jung's
view that human beings meet themselves in the symbolic constructions that they use to negotiate their world directly parallels Heisenberg's idea that in science one confronts only oneself, since one is
investigating the way one has engaged one's world. Many social
theorists, like the quantum physicists, have long favored the idea that
what we see and experience as reality is something extracted from a

more complex and fundamental domain. For philosophers such as Nietzsche, human beings transform the flux of becoming into a more concrete state of being for the purpose of governing it. Language and knowledge of all kinds are viewed as instruments of power that impose form and order for the purpose of control. For Jung, human beings form and realize a reality to meet and know themselves. Clearly, such considerations also rest very comfortably with the basic notion underlying the holographic universe — that we live in a world constituted through images of what is real.

Such ontological uncertainties have direct and major implications for the way we should approach social science. For in stressing that what we know is but a partial and incomplete representation of a more complex reality, they emphasize a point made earlier: that social science, like the natural sciences, is concerned with the realization of possible knowledges. Another way of illustrating this point is to see the raw phenomenon being investigated as rich in potentialities. The scientist in engaging the phenomenon in a specific way engages or realizes a potentiality in the phenomenon. Thus as the quantum physicists have illustrated in relation to the study of light, whether light behaves as a wave or particle depends on the way in which it is studied. Light has the potential to reveal itself in both these ways, and in accordance with the principles identified by Heisenberg and Bohr, these potentialities are mutually exclusive because its constitution in the form of waves precludes its constitution in the form of particles. Hence in attempting to study light in one way, the scientist precludes the possibility of knowing it in another. Since incompleteness is a corollary of indeterminancy, the theories of Heisenberg and Bohr thus reinforce the logic of Gödel's theorem, discussed earlier, emphasizing that all theoretical formulations are necessarily incomplete, since something somewhere must always remain undecided.

By applying these ideas to the research strategies presented in this volume, one can see each strategy as offering a way of realizing knowledge of the multifaceted nature of social life. Our discussion suggests that all social phenomena may have many potential ways of revealing themselves and that the way they are realized in practice depends on the mode of engagement adopted by the researcher. Thus the phenomenon "social organization" may at one and the same time lend itself to investigation as structure and process, as configuration, as a learning system, as a socially constructed reality, as a cultural milieu, as a life history, as a text, as otherness, as theater, as a system of communicative distortion, as the concretization of unconscious energy, as a mode of domination, as a form of praxis, as an instrument of class rule, and so on. All these potentialities may rest in the phenomenon; whether they are realized as knowledges of the phenomenon depends on the way in which they are investigated. Our knowledge of social organization is ultimately a product of the researcher's interaction with this multifaceted phenomenon and tells us as much about the researcher and his or her cultural milieu as it does about the phenomenon itself.

All these arguments underscore the central idea that we can learn to approach scientific inquiry in a way that allows us to cope with uncertainty as a defining feature of the enterprise. The epistemological uncertainties that we have identified can best be handled through the development of approaches to social science, and perhaps specific techniques, that enhance our capacities to be consciously self-critical of our favored research strategies, recognizing that while it is necessary to adopt a stance that is in some degree affirmational, it is also necessary to see the weaknesses as well.

The ontological uncertainties we have discussed pose problems that are more fundamental and ultimately more difficult to deal with, at least insofar as the individual researcher is concerned. At a minimum, they suggest the need for a conscious pluralism in research practice, designed to realize as many different knowledges as possible. For what is to be gained by limiting our perspective? Such pluralism will serve to generate complementary and contradictory insights, according to the way the phenomenon is engaged. Given that we can abandon the idea that an unambiguous foundational truth lies waiting to be discovered, we will reduce our trouble in coping with the rival claims of different perspectives. Just as the first act of conciliation from an authoritarian ruler may *at the same time* be understood as an attempt to retain control, there would seem to be no reason why different and contradictory knowledges of the same phenomenon should not coexist in the nature of that phenomenon. All it means is that we need to find a way of dealing with the significance and consequences of knowledge claims in a way that recognizes such uncertainty as a defining feature of knowledge.

These considerations lead us back to the conclusion of our earlier discussion regarding the significance of assumptions in scientific inquiry and the uncertainty that stems from the absence of an authoritative point of reference for judging the merits of different approaches to research: *that uncertainty ultimately involves choice.* The pluralism advocated above ultimately poses choice and the existential dilemma as to what we should do or not do in our research. As Dewey (1929) has argued so clearly, uncertainty is always ultimately of significance because of its action consequences. For us here this hinges on the realization that the scientist must ultimately face the dilemma that a large measure of the responsibility for what we know rests on his or her shoulders. As has been argued, in choosing a research strategy the scientist in large measure determines how the phenomenon being studied will be revealed, and indirectly, the consequences of the knowledge thus generated. In challenging the idea that there can be foundational knowledge that is neutral and objective, our analysis of the uncertainties associated with science thus removes a shield that has traditionally protected the scientist from the dilemma of choice. An advocacy of pluralism means that this problem must be confronted and that the basis and implications of choice must be fully explored.

27

EXPLORING CHOICE

Reframing the Process of Evaluation

Gareth Morgan

York University

In order to confront the full nature and range of choices open to us in research, it is necessary to examine the nature, knowledge claims, and consequences of different research strategies as openly and critically as possible. To do this effectively, it is necessary to examine and reframe the way we typically evaluate research, particularly through the processes of institutional control, since these exert an important influence over the direction of research activity. It is particularly important that we address these issues at the present time, for there is a tendency for the criteria traditionally used to evaluate positivist research to be applied in the judgment of all kinds of knowledge claims. In other words, the kind of knowledge for which positivist researchers seek is seen as defining the nature of knowledge per se. The existence of such a foundational view hinders the development of research strategies seeking to produce different kinds of knowledge and hence hinders recognition and exploration of the full range of choice open to the researcher.

These issues manifest themselves most clearly in debate about the relevance of different paradigms for the conduct of social research and the difficulties that researchers adopting nonorthodox research strategies encounter in publishing their results in mainstream journals. Their research and knowledge claims are often viewed with skepticism because the approaches and methods adopted are deemed unscientific, or stated more accurately, because they do not accord with the standards of science as traditionally conceived. The analysis presented in this volume encourages us to understand that such conflicts may be rooted in different conceptions of scientific inquiry and scientific knowledge and that no single set of scientific standards can claim monopoly over decisions as to what counts as valid knowledge. In everyday life we would not normally dream of applying criteria for judging the quality of a cream cake in the assessment of a slice of roast beef. One wonders, therefore, why we engage in this kind of activity in social science. Different research strategies, though seeking to contribute to a formal body of knowledge described as "scientific," may be qualitatively different in nature and intent and call for different criteria for considering the worth of their claims.

In exploring how different research strategies favor different evaluative criteria, we can help break the grip that a foundational view of knowledge exercises on research. For in rendering evaluation problematic, we open the way to choice. We will proceed by discussing the nature and logic of the positivist view of knowledge, and through discussion of its limitations, move to consideration of some alternatives.

As is well known, mainstream social science has attempted to model itself on practice in the natural sciences, aiming to describe and explain events, processes, and phenomena in the social world in a manner that allows generalizations to be drawn. The quest is for systematic explanations that can be supported with empirical evidence. Within the positivist tradition, this has involved a search for empirical relationships that lend themselves to one of four basic kinds of explanation, described by Nagel (1961) as deductive, probabilistic, functional (or teleological), and genetic.

These approaches to scientific explanation presume a basic regularity in the social world that can be observed and expressed in terms of empirical laws or relationships. Although scientists forewarned by Hume's (1740/1962) famous critique of causality are normally cautious about using the idea of "cause" as a basis of explanation, the quest is for a certainty of knowledge grounded in the idea that just as day is likely to follow night, condition A is likely to be associated with condition B in a regular and hence highly predictable manner. Given this kind of quest, the use of hypothetico-deductive approaches that generate knowledge through the use of predictions to be tested against data generated in controlled experiments and through survey research provides the basis for a very logical and powerful methodology. Similarly, research methods that use an inductive approach, drawing inferences and generalizations from data that are already available, also commend themselves. The task of ensuring that the knowledge thus generated is sound and true becomes a technical one; the research studies using these approaches can be evaluated according to the degree of rigor with which they have designed and conducted their experiments and surveys and the competence with which they have collected and analyzed their data. A main concern is to ensure that the research is reliable and valid in the sense envisaged by Campbell and Stanley (1963) and that the results can be reproduced in similar settings. Hence the forceful logic of Derek Pugh's claim in Chapter 3 that the researcher should be concerned with producing generalizable knowledge based on systematic, comparative, replicative observation and measurement. These are the hallmarks of good positivist research and the criteria that can be used to judge the quality of research generated by positivist and neopositivist research strategies such as those advocated in the chapters by Pugh, Miller and Mintzberg, and Cook — but only insofar as one accepts the assumptions that underwrite the positivist approach.

Once one challenges the assumption that it is possible or meaningful to study the social world as a system of objective, empirical regularities that can be neutrally observed, measured, and predicted, the criteria used to evaluate such research become highly problematic. The reasons are numerous and well known. For example, there is the question concerning the neutrality of observation and the related problem of objectivity. As has been suggested many times in this volume, observations can be seen as theory laden and objectivity as a socially constructed phenomenon. Viewed from this perspective, the protocol of positivist science is rendered as a specific kind of interpretive activity that serves to produce not objectivity, but the myth that one is being objective. The disciplined observation, measurement, and analysis that characterize positivist science produce a form of planned perception. If a group of people agree to see the world in a certain way, it is hardly surprising that they are likely to see the same thing. The protocol of science operates to produce this kind of effect. The process of hypothesis testing breaks down a "messy" reality into sets of clearly structured relationships or what Ackoff and his colleagues would describe as well-structured problems. The method requires that we banish ambiguity and hence implicity assumes that the absence of ambiguity is a quality of the phenomenon being measured. The attempts to develop concepts and measurements for implementing the hypothetico-deductive approach are the actions that attempt to remove this ambiguity. The tests of reliability and validity are the evaluative procedures that judge how well this has been done. In establishing this kind of protocol for the conduct of scientific research, the researcher is, in effect, laying a clear trail for others to follow. If they choose to do so, they structure reality in an identical way and hence improve the chances of seeing the same things and of confirming or rejecting the findings produced by the original research. The objectivity of such research rests as much in the nature of the research instrument used as in the data observed or the conclusions drawn. The replication of such research projects to determine the generalizability of findings is in essence a replication of the socially constructed way of seeing built into the protocol that guides the research.

What then are we to make of the knowledge generated in this way? Clearly, the knowledge produced tells us something about the phenomenon being researched. Thus just as measurements recorded on a seismograph can tell us about the severity of earth movements in a given area, a positivist research project can tell us about variations in organization as revealed by the research instruments used. However, the important thing to realize about such knowledge is that its validity is circumscribed. There is more to an earthquake than simply the severity of the earth tremors, and there is more to an organization than just profiles on a particular set of measuring scales. In other words, the validity of the knowledge generated relates to a specific aspect of the phenomenon studied. Once one recognizes the existence of the phenomenon in a sense wider than that dictated by the research design, the limitations of the knowledge generated within the confines of that design become very clear. This somewhat obvious statement in point of fact identifies a crucial epistemological principle formulated by Heisenberg (1958) in relation to the limitations of knowledge. It is always possible to establish incontrovertible facts and exact solutions to problems, provided one defines and bounds the domain of experience to which they apply. Positivist science does this implicitly in its search for objective knowledge through the use of research designs and instruments that construct an area in which truth and objectivity can be found. Once one begins to relax the constraints of protocol or attempts to extend the realm of applicability, the basis of such objectivity and truth breaks down. The classic, though extreme, illustration of this within the field of organization studies is found in Herzberg et al.'s (1959) well-known "two-factor" theory of motivation, which only seems to attract empirical support when tested through Herzberg's own methodology. The illustration serves to emphasize our point: The generalized knowledge that stems from positivist research and that may be based on systematic, comparative, replicative observation and measurement produces a generalization and objectivity that rests as much in the research design as it does in the situations studied.

Though most social scientists are usually very ready to recognize these problems and limitations of positivist research, their relevance for setting standards for the evaluation of knowledge are not so clearly appreciated. The idea of obtaining a generalized form of objective knowledge based on the positivist ideal of systematic, comparative, replicative observation and measurement is still often used as a point of reference against which *all* research should be judged. These are the criteria that are often used to disparage the worth of a single case study or of qualitative research, in which the researcher as participant in the situation is really the only research instrument used. Such an approach to evaluation is based on a major fallacy and logical error in that rules for conducting research are mistakenly seen as rules of justification to be used in the evaluation of knowledge. The protocol and aims of positivist research prescribe a way of doing research and have much value in this regard. But they have no logical claim to serve as general standards for the evaluation of research. As our discussion suggests, positivist research attempts to create an objective way of seeing that is, at best, partial. The rules that underlie the acquisition of such objectivity are thus of purely local significance. They are rules that help to produce a particular way of seeing, and while they can usefully be used to monitor and control the conduct of research studies designed to reproduce that way of seeing, their significance is no greater than this. While the objectivity of research produced through the use of positivist research strategies may be as valid and reliable as is any other kind of objectivity, it has no special claim to be more authoritative.

Hence research strategies that abandon the positivist standpoint of the detached, neutral observer cannot be fairly judged in terms of the evaluative criteria normally applied to positivist research, for they seek a different kind of insight, adopt different methodologies, and favor different criteria for judging their knowledge claims. Such is the case with interpretive research strategies, which in essence have evolved in an attempt to counter the limitations of positivism. The theorists who laid the foundations of modern interpretive research, such as Wilhelm Dilthey, Edmund Husserl, and Max Weber, sought to remedy weaknesses in the positivist approach by focusing on the rich, socially constructed texture of the social world (Burrell and Morgan, 1979). Reacting against the emptiness or "thin" description produced by the positivist quest for generalized laws and relationships and the tendency of the positivist scientist to impose meaning and explanation on the social world, they advocated an exploration from "within" the phenomenon being studied. In their different ways they laid the basis for research strategies that could achieve a new kind of objectivity in the social sciences that actively takes account of the importance of subjective meaning and individual action in the processes through which human beings construct their world. Their quest, in essence, was for new foundations on which the social sciences could build.

The idea that interpretive social science should replace positivist research is still a popular one among those advocating the interpretive perspective. The argument developed in this and earlier chapters suggests, however, that such an approach, like the argument in favor of a positivist hegemony, gives too much credit to the idea of a foundational knowledge. Interpretive social science certainly offers a brand of insight that positivism cannot achieve, but on the other hand, positivism can also generate forms of knowledge that elude the interpretive approach. A more relativistic view of the research process encourages us to see these different approaches as doing different things and to attempt to assess their contributions with this in mind.

Insofar as interpretive research is concerned, this means that it is necessary to assess research in a way that is sensitive to the requirements of the interpretive endeavor. In order to understand how the social world becomes constructed as a reality that positivist researchers can then observe, it is necessary to get inside the process of social construction, building up from the concepts and actions found in the situation being studied to describe and understand the detailed means through which human beings engage in meaningful action and create a world of their own or one that is shared with others. The chapters in this volume by Denzin, Jones, Smircich, Bougon, Turner, and Cooper attempt to do this, illustrating the basic structure of experience; how meaning is created, sustained, and shared through use of language and other symbolic constructs; how individuals have to negotiate differences between their views of reality and those of others; and so on. By focusing on such issues, it becomes possible to understand how the social world actually evolves from members' interpretations and actions. This approach to research inevitably favors in-depth description and analysis of limited realms of experience through immersion in the contexts in which they occur. Large-scale surveys, extensive comparative research, laboratory experimentation, and measurement of relationships are more or less ruled out or made redundant by the need to be sensitive to the fact that meaning can never be taken for granted and is always context bound. The same phenomenon may have a different significance in different situations, so positivist methods of research immediately encounter difficulties as tools of interpretive inquiry because they typically take for granted the social constructions that interpretive research always treats as problematic.

The positivist aim of a generalizable knowledge based on systematic, comparative, replicative observation and measurement simply does not apply to this kind of interpretive inquiry. While it is true that generalizations are sought, since all inquiry typically presumes the possibility of extrapolation of findings beyond the individual case, the interpretive researcher is more concerned with identifying generalized processes that are not content specific and therefore cannot be characterized in terms of measured relations between networks of fact verified through predictions of outcome. However, there is a contribution to knowledge if the researcher can identify generic processes or patterns through which human beings construct and make sense of their realities, illustrated through the evidence of exemplars or archetypes, rather than through systematic bodies of data in the positivist tradition. The evidence generated by interpretive research is much more likely to be of an evocative rather than comprehensive kind, to be sustained, rejected, or refined through future studies. The conclusions of one study merely provide a starting point in a continuing cycle of inquiry, which may over time serve to generate persuasive patterns of data from which further conclusions can be drawn. Hypothesis testing is simply inappropriate for dealing with research situations that are as "messy" as those in which processes of reality construction are concerned and in which the significant relationships are not manifest in the *content* of detailed empirical evidence, but in the structure or pattern that underlies this. The researcher can do no more than place him- or herself in the role of building up understanding from the raw data through which everyday situations are defined (rather than through the scientist's own concepts) and of adopting the critical attitude that characterizes the essence of science, bringing systematic doubt to bear on all the generalizations that emerge from the research data. The required approach is one that Denzin (1978) describes as "naturalistic," and the style of argument an essentially qualitative one. While considerable attention has been devoted to the development and refinement of interpretive methodology, insufficient attention has as yet been devoted to evolving criteria for assessing the general quality and rigor of interpretive research.

Enough has probably been said to establish the general principle that different kinds of research strategy favor different criteria for judging the nature of their contribution and to discredit the idea that positivist criteria should exercise monopoly over the judgment of knowledge claims. We have made our case by contrasting criteria favored by the positivist and interpretive traditions in general terms, but the argument can easily be extended by considering criteria suggested by other kinds of research strategy.

For example, in many of the research strategies in this volume there is a concern with producing knowledge through action. This is a special consideration in those chapters by Cook, Susman, Schön, Torbert, and Heydebrand, who, despite their differences, seek a form of knowledge *in the process of acting on and changing the situations they are researching*. The idea that valid knowledge must always be action based is a very important one in the history of social thought and clearly recommends itself as an important consideration in the evaluation of knowledge-claims. Action provides the basic means through which we can come to know the world, since it is through action that we ultimately construct and make contact with our reality. It is in attempting to influence and change that reality that we come to understand it most clearly (Dewey, 1929, 1938; Mao Tse Tung, 1936; Piaget, 1971, 1972).

Hence, if we wish to take a foundational approach to the evaluation of research we can argue that action-based criteria have as good a claim to importance as do positivist, interpretive, or any other criteria. However, it is important to recognize the special qualities of this kind of research rather than to argue for its hegemony. The more pressing and appropriate need is to give systematic attention to the contributions it can make and to the principles that can be used to guide and judge its quality. Among these are criteria that assess how action-based learning increases our capacities for effective action and that assess the consequences of such action. Action-oriented researchers are interested in the relevance and validity of what they are doing in their research on a real-time basis. They need to devise means of validating their analyses, intuitions, feelings, perceptions, hypotheses, and actions as they engage the situations in which they are involved, always being open to what is happening and making exploratory probes to test whether their assessment of the situation is timely and relevant. The validity of their research ultimately rests not in abstract explanation or interpretive understanding, though these might indeed be relevant, but in the action capacities and effectiveness of the change that the research creates. Validation also comes from the rate at which effects spread to other situations as the experience becomes diffused and used as a basis for creating yet new forms of action, as much from following any code or protocol.

Closely related to the idea of researching through action is that of using research as a means of empowering human beings to take responsibility and control over their lives. This concern with generating a liberating form of knowledge is particularly evident in the action-based strategies of Torbert and Heydebrand referred to above, and in the chapters by Mangham and Overington, Forester, Wilson, Glennon, White and McSwain, Benson, and Carchedi. The research strategies they advocate attempt to find different ways of empowering humans (e.g., through demystification, critique, changing established power relations, increasing awareness of unconscious processes, breaking the hold of convention and belief, refocusing awareness) so that human beings — as individuals, groups, or classes — can engage in action consistent with their interests.

The empowerment theme thus offers important criteria for the evaluation of research activities that are rarely given direct consideration in debate about the merits of different kinds of research. When we talk about research in relation to the empowerment of individuals, groups, and classes, we explicitly recognize that research has an ideological dimension. Hence we are invited to evaluate how different research strategies may favor and advance different interests, either because of their intrinsic nature or because of the way in which they are used. We are invited to see that research inevitably has an ethical, moral, and political aspect that is relevant in the evaluation of *all* research. Hence individual researchers and institutions involved in the production and publication of research may choose to take heed of the kind of challenge issued by Carchedi's chapter: to see where they stand in the class-based production of knowledge. Whose experience or view of reality does our research express? Whose interests does it serve? Carchedi's challenge is to recognize that knowledge serves interests and to acknowledge directly the human consequences of our research activities. This challenge is particularly relevant at a time when great stress is being placed on the need to develop useful knowledge, and when many research institutions, funding agencies, journals, and publishing houses are favoring research with a problem-oriented stance. Useful for what? Useful for whom? What problem? Whose problem? These become crucial questions in exploring the values and interests that shape the research process.

A related consideration emerges from Wilson's chapter, which draws attention to how the division of labor within the research process expresses a power relationship that distorts the possibility of free and open inquiry. The challenge of his chapter is to examine the institutional arrangements through which we organize research, to remove the distorting influences. The analysis of power relationships offered in the chapter by Forester provides the basis for a critique of current institutional arrangements in a way that supplements the proposals offered by Wilson. In essence, the arguments presented invite individual researchers and those with institutional respon-

sibilities to account for their actions, policies, and general relationships to the process of knowledge production in a way that directly
confronts the political dimension of the research process.

Another crucial issue relating to the evaluation of knowledge
concerns the general status and significance of empirical data. Under
the influence of a representational view of knowledge, appeal to
empirical data as a means of determining the claims of competing
theories has become a major feature of modern social research. Research strategies are often mainly concerned with accounting for
relationships between various kinds of empirical evidence, whether
they be positivist "facts," or patterns of ideas and socially constructed meanings. A number of chapters in this volume challenge the
adequacy of such approaches to understanding and explaining social
life because they do not uncover the deeper structure of relationships
to which the empirical data merely lend a historically specific content
or detailed form. The issues are posed most clearly in Outhwaite's
argument in favor of a realist research strategy, in Turner's exposition
of Lévi-Strauss's approach to structuralism, in Cooper's analysis of
the Other, in White and McSwain's analysis of the unconscious, in
Benson's dialectical analysis, and in Carchedi's class analysis. One of
the important implications of these chapters is that we need to reconsider the way we use and interpret empirical data and the status they
are accorded in our quest for knowledge. In particular, they suggest
that the task of scientific explanation and understanding is incomplete
unless it goes beyond the realm of the empirical and attempts to
account for the pattern of the empirical world made visible by the
researcher within the context of a wider and structurally significant
set of relations that define what Benson, Heydebrand, and others
describe as "totality." Set within this framework, the status of empirical evidence is important, but more modest than is usually the case.
We are encouraged to see facts and relationships as but elements or
illustrations of a significant pattern or archetype in which a more
important relationship can be discovered. The possibility of acquiring
structural approaches to explanation and understanding that deliberately seek to penetrate beyond "surface-empirical" or "literal"
modes of explanation and understanding thus raises an issue of crucial importance for considering the knowledge claims of different
research strategies.

Yet another consideration relevant to the evaluation of different
research strategies concerns the importance of dialectical knowledge
and the relevance of dialectic as a method of research. As will be
apparent from a number of chapters in this volume, the dialectic can

be generally understood as a logical structure that combines opposition and complementarity. This is illustrated theoretically in Cooper's discussion of the Other as a state of "in-one-anotherness," in the contradictions which shape action in Benson's dialectical conception of totality, in Carchedi's class analysis, and in Heydebrand's conception of praxis. In an applied sense the dialectic is well illustrated in Glennon's concern with overcoming the dualism that characterizes common conceptions of gender, in the models of reflective inquiry offered by Torbert, Susman, and Schön, and in all the chapters that attempt to overcome the dualism between subject and object. The notion of dialectic is, at least at an implicit level, one of the unifying themes of this volume. Indeed, it is one of the unifying themes in social thought generally, since different paradigms and schools of thought have produced each other as part of a self-defining whole. Thus positivism can, in effect, be seen to have produced phenomenology, just as the dominance of positivist methodology in the social science of the 1960s and 1970s has tended to generate its own negation in terms of a renewed interest in interpretive inquiry. The opposition thus created is in turn being negated by an interest in action and practice that rejects the positivist-interpretive dichotomy. In a similar way the conservative, status-quo orientation of social science in the 1960s has generated its negation in terms of an interest in conflict, transformation, and change. The paradigms of social thought, though diverse in nature, are bound together dialectically within the same problematic.

The question this discussion raises is whether research strategies that explicitly recognize the structural significance of dialectic are in some way superior to those that ignore it. In Chapter 25 we examined the possibility of dealing with the knowledge claims of different research strategies dialectically, for example, by employing dialectic as a methodology in the manner suggested by Mason and Mitroff (1981). The question now is whether individual research strategies should strive to be dialectical in stance. In seeking to answer this, it is clear that insofar as a research strategy is preoccupied with one aspect of a dialectical relationship (for example, in focusing on objectivity in a way that obliterates the role of the subjective), attention is narrowly and unreflectively focused on one aspect of a whole and hence is inevitably partial in nature. However, such partiality is in large measure the basis of different ways of seeing, so our question hinges on the extent to which we should be prepared to lose difference in pursuit of sameness. Cooper's analysis of how humans construct their realities would suggest that our knowledge is always constructed dialectically, though we are frequently unaware of this, since even an extreme preoccupation with objectivity is mediated by the idea of subjectivity. Hence the debate here is really about whether research strategies should strive to be *explicitly* dialectical. This line of thought takes us back to the question of whether social science should attempt to be foundational, and hence to the problems we encounter in attempting to determine whether dialectical foundations are superior to any other.

If we wish to approach the problem of evaluation in a purely technical manner, we can argue that the rigor with which a particular research strategy is implemented is important. Recognizing that different research strategies try to do different things and call for distinctive criteria for judging their contribution to knowledge, it is possible to try to judge the competence with which research projects are executed using positivist, interpretive, dialectical, action-oriented, or other criteria, as is appropriate. However, as Feyerabend (1975) has shown, it is also possible to argue that there are no standards that are essential because insofar as we are interested in generating creative research, "anything goes." If we choose to follow the former approach, much can be done to investigate and formulate criteria for evaluating different research strategies in ways that are true to the logic that underwrites their practice. If we choose to follow Feyerabend's position, the issue of evaluation hardly matters.

Our approach to the problem of evaluation raises issues that are much broader than this, however. Once we relax the assumption that research is concerned with generating a foundational knowledge we are obliged to recognize that it is inadequate to frame research as a technical process. For this reason it is insufficient to take a stand for or against method, because there is a dimension of research that takes us beyond method. We have shown how it is possible to evaluate the claims and consequences of knowledge in many meaningful ways. Knowledge may serve to explain empirical facts, help us to understand meanings, allow us to act more appropriately, empower in a liberating way, reveal links between everyday reality and the structural logic that produces and reproduces that reality, advance specific political interests, and so on. In broadening our view of knowledge in this way, we are obliged to reframe the process of evaluation in a manner that supplements the purely technical considerations discussed above, with considerations that recognize that the significance of knowledge is not simply epistemological, but ideological, political, ethical, and moral as well. In doing so, we are encouraged to see the process of evaluation as resting not in the application of fixed frameworks or techniques to the end results of research, but as something that should be an integral aspect of the research process itself. In engaging in research, the researcher engages in an activity that inevitably has human consequences of many kinds. It would thus seem that the researcher should be aware of these and attempt to bring them to bear on the selection of research strategies and in understanding the consequences of their use. In doing so, it becomes possible to move toward an approach to the conduct and evaluation of research that is characterized by a continuous process of reflective exploration, rather than by a quest for a certain basis for knowledge, as is now often the case.

28

IN RESEARCH, AS IN CONVERSATION, WE MEET OURSELVES

Gareth Morgan
York University

In this work I have attempted to develop a means of confronting and accepting the diversity of contemporary social research practice in order that we may deal with it. Debates within the social sciences are usually underwritten by a foundational view of knowledge, which results in arguments about the supremacy of one paradigm or research perspective over another or in a search for synthesis or common ground. The search is typically for the "best way" of doing research. In contrast, I have attempted to offer an approach that is antifoundational and is content to see social science develop in many different, and indeed contradictory, directions in the hope that new and more interesting ways of knowing will emerge.

The position I have adopted hinges on the argument that the process of knowing involves a process of forming and transforming, and that in knowing our world, we also form and transform ourselves. Approached in this way, the diversity of social research practice presents itself as a realm of choice of central importance to the way we make and remake ourselves, both individually and collectively. This perspective frames social science as an activity that is not just epistemological, but human in the fullest sense.

My position thus encourages an approach to the conduct and evaluation of social science in a way that explicitly recognizes its human nature and its human consequences. This runs counter to the prevailing ethos, which tends to view and organize research as a technical activity to be controlled and evaluated through bureaucratic mechanisms. This ethos depersonalizes the research process and tends to remove responsibility for what the researcher does from the researcher, often reducing his or her role to that of an agent engaging in the kind of research he or she feels the institutionalized system demands.

In contrast, I have attempted to argue for an approach to research that is substantially rational in the sense that its practitioners develop a capacity to observe and question what they are doing and to take responsibility for making intelligent choices about the means they adopt and the ends these serve. Such a capacity will help us move much closer to the ideal of a social science in which the researcher actively examines the choices that are open to realize the many potential knowledges waiting to be engaged, with active anticipation of the consequences of such engagement.

The process of reflective conversation advocated as a model of inquiry and research education provides a concrete means through which we can initiate this process. For in conversation, as in research, we meet ourselves. Both are forms of social interaction in which our choice of words and actions return to confront us in terms of the kind of discourse or knowledge that we help to generate. This feature of conversation can be actively used to explore our favored approach to research in a way that is constructively critical, in that we systematically attempt to confront and understand the nature and significance of what we do and how we might begin to do it differently. Such conversation allows us to understand the nature and consequences of our research in a way that is exploratory rather than evaluative, in that we can suspend our commitment to favored points of view or have them challenged by others, and in so doing, create an opportunity to enrich what we do in practice. The image that I have in mind is akin to what happens when a group of craftspeople come together and exchange views. They do not necessarily end up agreeing with each other and certainly do not leave the gathering to produce an identical product. Rather, they use the opportunity to make better sense of their own way of doing things and to learn how they may do their own thing better. The call for reflective conversation to improve social research is not a call designed to produce uniformity so much as to promote improved diversity.

In a work that seeks to enhance the capacity for self-critical inquiry, it is appropriate that we should reflect on potential weaknesses in the position advocated above. As in all discourse, there is a danger that we may become trapped by the limitations of the images or metaphors through which we shape inquiry. For us here, the danger is that conversation may be used as a substitute for action, serving to create a measure of self-edification for the researcher, but no more. There is also danger that, in the end, the loudest, most powerful voices will be those with the most to say. It is also possible to object to the relativism of my argument and to the responsibility that has been placed on the shoulders of the individual researcher in shaping the nature of research.

Recognizing that conversation itself may be insufficient, that conversation may need to be democratized by extending it beyond the community of social researchers, and that conversation should always be used in a way that helps us to avoid being trapped by ideas and arrangements already in place, we have a means of exploring such criticisms and acting on them. The position I am offering here does not seek to offer a point of view that will satisfy everyone. Rather, it seeks to present a position that we will be able to criticize and refine, perhaps in a way that takes us beyond conversation.

Bibliography

Abercrombie, N. (1980) Class, Structure and Knowledge. London: Basil Blackwell.

Ackoff, Russell L. (1979) The Art of Problem-Solving. New York: John Wiley.

Ackoff, Russell L. (1974) Redesigning the Future. New York: John Wiley.

Ackoff, Russell L. and F. E. Emery (1972) On Purposeful Systems. London: Tavistock.

Allison, Graham (1971) The Essence of Decision. Boston: Little Brown.

Althusser, Louis (1969) For Marx. London: Allen Lane.

Althusser, Louis (1976) Essays in Self-Criticism. London: New Left Books.

Althusser, Louis and E. *Balibar* (1970) Reading Capital. London: New Left Books.

Anderson, T. R. and S. Warkov (1961) "Organizational size and complexity." American Sociological Review 26: 23-28.

Angyal, A. (1941) Foundations for a Science of Personality. New York: Viking.

Appelbaum, Richard (1978) "Marxist method: Structural constraint and social praxis." American Sociologist 13: 73ff.

Arendt, Hannah (1977) Eichmann in Jerusalem: A Report on the Banality of Evil. Elmsford, NY: Penguin.

Argyris, Chris (1957) Personality and Organization. New York: Harper & Row.

Argyris, Chris and D. A. *Schon* (1974) Theory in Practice. San Francisco: Jossey-Bass.

Argyris, Chris and D. A. *Schon* (1978) Organizational Learning. Reading, MA: Addison-Wesley.

Ashby, W. R. (1940) "Adaptiveness and equilibrium." Journal of Mental Science 86: 478-483.

Ashby, W. R. (1952) Design for a Brain. London: Chapman & Hall.

Ashby, W. R. (1956) An Introduction to Cybernetics. London: Chapman & Hall.

Austin, John (1961) Philosophical Papers. Oxford: Oxford University Press.

Axelrod, Robert (1976) Structure of Decision. Princeton University Press. Princeton, NJ.

Badiou, A. (1975) Theorie de la contradiction. Paris: Maspero.

Bardwick, Judith (1974) "Androgyny and humanistic goals," pp. 49-63 in M. L. McBee and A. Blake (eds.) The American Woman. Beverly Hills, CA: Glencoe.

Baritz, Loren (1960) The Servants of Power. New York: John Wiley.

Barnard, Chester (1967) The Functions of the Executive. Cambridge, MA: Harvard University Press.

Bartlett, Frederic C. (1932) Remembering. Cambridge: Cambridge University Press.

Bateson, Gregory (1972) Steps to an Ecology of Mind. New York: Ballantine.

Bateson, Gregory (1979) Mind and Nature. New York: Dutton.

Becker, Howard (1975) "On methodology," in Howard S. Becker, ed. Sociological Work: Method and Substance. Chicago: Aldine.

Benson, Kenneth (1977) "Organizations: A dialectical view." Administrative Science Quarterly 22: 1-21.

Benton, Ted (1977) The Philosophical Foundations of the Three Sociologies. London: Routledge & Kegan Paul.

Berger, Peter and Thomas Luckmann (1966) The Social Construction of Reality. Garden City, NY: Doubleday.

Berger, Peter, B. Berger, and H. Kellner (1973) The Homeless Mind. New York: Random House.

Bergson, Henri (1896) Matiere et Memoire. Paris: Felix Alcan.

Bergson, Henri (1902) "L'effort intellectuel." Revue Philosophique de la France et de l'Etranger 53: 1-27.

Berkeley, George, Bishop (1709) A New Theory of Vision. Everyman's Library. New York. (1910 reprint).

Berkeley, G. (1910) [1709] A New Theory of Vision. New York: Everyman.

Berkeley, G. (1971) A Treatise Concerning the Principles of Human Knowledge. Marston, England: Scholar Press.

Bernard, Jessie (1978) Self-Portrait of a Family. Boston: Beacon.

Bernard, Jessie (1981) The Female World. New York: Free Press.

Bernstein, Richard (1971) Praxis and Action. Philadelphia: University of Pennsylvania Press.

Bernstein, Richard (1976) The Restructuring of Social and Political Theory. Philadelphia: University of Pennsylvania Press.

Bhaskar, Roy (1978) A Realist Theory of Science. Hassocks, England: Harvester.

Bhaskar, Roy (1979) The Possibility of Naturalism. Hassocks, England: Humanities.

Biddle, Bruce J. (1979) Role Theory. New York: Academic.

Binet, Afred (1894) Psychologie des Grands Calculateurs et Joueurs d'Echecs. Paris: Hachette.

Binet, Alfred (1903) L'Etude Experimentale de l'Intelligence. Paris: Schleicher.

Binns, Paul (1973) "The Marxist theory of truth." Radical Philosophy 4: 3-9.

Bittner, E. (1965) "The concept of organization," in R. Turner (ed.) Ethnomethodology. Baltimore: Penguin.

Black, Mary B. and D. Metzger (1965) "Ethnographic description and the study of law," pp. 137-165 in S. A. Tyler (ed.) Cognitive Anthropology. New York: Holt, Rinehart & Winston.

Blau, P. M. and R. Schoenherr (1971) The Structure of Organizations. New York: Basic Books.

Blumer, Herbert (1969) Symbolic Interactionism. Englewood Cliffs, NJ: Prentice-Hall.

Bogdan, R. (1974) Being Different: The Autobiography of Jane Fry. New York: John Wiley.

Bogdan, R. and S. J. *Taylor* (1975) Introduction to Qualitative Methods. New York: John Wiley.

Bohm, David (1971) "Quantum theory as an indication of a new order of physics, part a." Foundations of Physics 1: 359-381.

Bohm, David (1973) "Quantum theory as an indication of a new order of physics, part b." Foundations of Physics 3: 139-168.

Bohr, Neils (1958) Atomic Theory and the Description of Nature. Cambridge: Cambridge University Press.

Bohr, Neils (1958) Atomic Theory and Human Knowledge. New York: John Wiley.

Boring, Edwin G. (1954) "The nature and history of experimental control." American Journal of Psychology 67: 573-589.

Bougon, Michel G. (1980) "Schemata, leadership, and organizational behaviour," Ph. D. dissertation, Cornell University. Ann Arbor, MI: University Microfilm International Publication, no. 8103006.

Bougon, Michel G., K. Weick, and D. Binkhorst (1977) "Cognition in organizations: An analysis of the Utrecht Jazz Orchestra." Administrative Science Quarterly 22: 606-639.

Bourdieu, Pierre (1977) Outline of a Theory of Practice. Cambridge: Cambridge University Press.

Brecht, Berthold (1964) Brecht on Theatre. London: Methuen.

Brittan, Arthur (1978) The Privatized World. London: Routledge & Kegan Paul.

Brown, Richard H. (1978) "Bureaucracy as praxis — toward a political phenomenology of formal organizations." Administrative Science Quarterly 23: 365-382.

Buber, Martin (1970) I and Thou. New York: Scribners.

Burke, James (1980) Connections. Boston: Little, Brown.

Burke, Kenneth (1965) Permanence and Change. Indianapolis: Bobbs-Merrill.

Burke, Kenneth (1966) Language as Symbolic Action. Berkeley: University of California Press.

Burke, Kenneth (1968) Counterstatement. Berkeley: University of California Press.

Burke, Kenneth (1969a) A Grammar of Motives. Berkeley: University of California Press.

Burke, Kenneth (1969b) A Rhetoric of Motives. Berkeley: University of California Press.

Burns, Elizabeth (1972) Theatricality. New York: Harper Torchbooks.

Burns, James MacGregor (1978) Leadership. New York: Harper & Row.

Burns, T. and G. M. Stalker (1966) [1961] The Management of Innovation. London: Tavistock.

Burrell, Gibson and Gareth Morgan (1979) Sociological Paradigms and Organizational Analysis. London: Heinemann Educational Books.

Callon, M. and J. P. Vignolle (1977) "Breaking down the organization: Local conflicts and societal systems of action. Social Science Information 16: 147-167.

Campbell, Donald T. (1979) "Qualitative knowing in action research," in M. Brenner et al., eds. The Social Contexts of Method. London: Croom Helm.

Campbell, Donald T. and J. C. Stanley (1963) Experimental and Quasi-Experimental Designs for Research. Chicago: Rand McNally.

Campbell, Mary Ann (1982) "Creating feminist sociology." S.W.S. Network 12: 23-24.

Canetti, E. (1962) Crowds and Power. London: Gollancz.

Canetti, E. (1974) Kafka's Other Trial. London: Calder & Boyers.

Capra, F. (1975) The Tao of Physics. New York: Wildwood House.

Carchedi, G. (1977) On the Economic Identification of Social Classes. London: Routledge & Kegan Paul.

Carchedi, G. (1983) Problems in Class Analysis. Production, Knowledge, and the Function of Capital. London: Routledge & Kegan Paul.

Carper, W. and W. Snizek (1980) "The nature and types of organizational taxonomies: An overview." Academy of Management Review 5: 65-75.

Cassirer, E. (1946) Language and Myth. New York: Harper & Row.

Cavan, Sherri (1974) "Seeing social structure in a rural setting." Urban Life and Culture 3: 329-346.

Chandler, A. D. (1962) Strategy and Structure. Cambridge, MA: MIT Press.

Child, J. (1973) "Parkinson's progress: Accounting for the number of specialists in organizations." Administrative Science Quarterly 18: 328-349.

Chomsky, Noam (1968) Language and Mind. New York: Harcourt, Brace & World.

Chomsky, Noam (1980) Rules and Representations. New York: Columbia University Press.

Churchman, C. West (1971) The Design of Inquiring Systems. New York: Basic Books.

Churchman, C. West (1979) The Systems Approach and Its Emenies. New York: Basic Books.

Cicourel, A. V. (1967) The Social Organization of Juvenile Justice. New York: John Wiley.

Cicourel, A. V. (1969) "Basic and normative rules in negotiation of status and role." Recent Sociology 2: 3-45.

Cicourel, A. V. (1972) Cognitive Sociology: Language and Meaning in Social Interaction. Harmondsworth: Penguin.

Collins, Randall (1979) The Credentialist Society. New York: Academic.

Cook, Judith A. (1980) "The development of feminist methodology." Presented at the Great Lakes College Association Women's Studies Conference, Rochester, Indiana.

Cook, T. D. and D. T. Campbell (1979) Quasi-Experimentation: Design and Analysis Issues for Field Settings. Chicago: Rand McNally.

Crenson, M. (1971) The Unpolitics of Air Pollution. Baltimore: John Hopkins University Press.

Cronbach, L. J. and Associates. (1980) Toward Reform of Program Evaluation. San Francisco: Jossey-Bass.

Crozier, M. (1963) The Bureaucratic Phenomenon. Chicago: University of Chicago Press.

Dallmayr, Fred and T. McCarthy (1977) Understanding and Social Inquiry. Notre Dame, IN: Notre Dame University Press.

Darwin, C. (1968) [1859] The Origin of Species (J. W. Burrow, ed.). Harmondsworth: Penguin Books.

de Beauvoir, Simone (1961) The Second Sex. New York: Bantam.

DeGroot, Adriaan D. (1965) Thought and Choice in Chess. Mouton. The Hague.

Della Vope, A. (1969) Logica come scienza storica. Editori Riuniti.

Denzin, Norman K. (1971) "The logic of naturalistic inquiry." Social Forces 50: 166-182.

Denzin, Norman K. (1978) The Research Act. New York: McGraw-Hill.

Denzin, Norman K. (1980) "A phenomenology of emotion and deviance." Zeitschrift für Soziologie 9: 251-261.

Denzin, Norman K. (1981a) "Notes on criminology and criminality." Presented at the 33rd Annual Meetings of the American Society of Criminology.

Denzin, Norman K. (1981b) "The paradoxes of play," in J. W. Loy, Jr. ed. Paradoxes of Play. West Point, NY: Leisure Press.

Denzin, Norman K. and C. M. Keller (1981) "Frame analysis reconsidered." Contemporary Sociology 10: 52-60.

Derrida, Jacques (1970) "Structure, sign, and play in the discourse of the human sciences," pp. 247-272 in R. Macksey and E. Donato (eds.) The Languages of Criticism and the Sciences of Man. The Structuralist Controversy. Baltimore: Johns Hopkins University Press.

Derrida, J. (1978) Writing and Difference. London: Routledge & Kegan Paul.

Deutsch, K. (1963) The Nerves of Government. New York: Free Press.

Dewey, J. (1929) The Quest for Certainty. New York: Minton, Balch.

Dewey, J. (1933) How We Think. Lexington, MA: D. C. Heath.

Dewey, J. (1938) Logic: The Theory of Inquiry. New York: Henry Holt.

Dirac, Paul (1930) The Principles of Quantum Mechanics. Oxford: Clarendon Press.

Dollard, J. (1944) Criteria for the Life History. New York: Peter Smith.

Douglas, J. D. (1970) Understanding Everyday Life. Chicago: Aldine.

Duncan, Hugh Dalziel (1962) Communication and Social Order. New York: Oxford University Press.

Duncan, Hugh Dalziel (1968) Symbols in Society. New York: Oxford University Press.

Duncan, Hugh Dalziel (1969) Symbols and Social Theory. New York: Oxford University Press.

Dunn, W. N. (1982) "Reforms as arguments." Knowledge: Creation, Diffusion, Utilization 3: 293-326.

Durkheim, Emile (1952) The Division of Labor in Society. New York: Macmillan.

Durkheim, Emile (1964) The Rules of Sociological Method. New York: Free Press.

Dyer, W. G. (1977) Team Building: Issues and Alternatives. Reading, MA: Addison-Wesley.

Easterday, L., D. Papademas, L. Schorr, and C. Valentine (1977) "The making of a female researcher." Urban LIfe 6: 333-347.

Edelman, Murray (1971) Politics as Symbolic Action. Chicago: Markham.

Edelman, Murray (1977) Political Language. New York: Academic.

Edinger, Edward (1973) Ego and Archetype. Baltimore: Penguin.

Eichler, Margrit (1980) The Double Standard: A Feminist Critique of Feminist Social Science. New York: St. Martin's.

Eisenstadt, S. N. (1959) "Bureaucracy, bureaucratization and debureaucratization." Administrative Science Quarterly 4: 302ff.

Emery, F. E. and E. L. Trist (1960) "Sociotechnical systems," pp. 83-97 in C. W. Churchman and M. Verhulst (eds.) Management Science, Models, and Techniques, Vol. 2. New York: Pergamon.

Evreinoff, Nicolas (1927) The Theatre in Life. New York: Bretano's.

Ferguson, Marilyn (1980) The Aquarian Conspirary. New York: St. Martin's.

Feyerabend, Paul (1975) Against Method. London: New Left Books.

Filstead, W. J. (1970) Qualitative Methodology. Chicago: Markham.

Foa, U. (1961) "Convergencies in the analysis of the structure of interpersonal behavior." Psychological Review 68: 341-353.

Forester, John (1980) "Listening: The social policy of everyday life." Social Praxis 7: 7-34.

Forester, John (1982a) "Planning in the face of power." Journal of the American Planning Association 48: 67-80.

Forester, John (1982b) "Know your organizations." Plan Canada 22: 3-13.

Foucault, Michel (1977) Discipline and Punish. New York: Pantheon.

Foucault, Michel (1980) Power and Knowledge. New York: Pantheon.

Frank, A. P. and M. Frank (1969) "The writings of Kenneth Burke," pp. 495-512 in William Rueckert (ed.) Critical Responses to Kenneth Burke: 1924-1966. Minneapolis: University of Minnesota Press.

Fraser, R. [ed.] (1969) Work, Vols. 1 and 2. London: Penguin.

Freire, Paolo (1970) Pedagogy of the Oppressed. New York: Seabury.

Freud, Sigmund (1950) The Interpretation of Dreams. New York: Modern Library.

Freud, Sigmund (1957) Standard Edition of the Complete Psychological Works, Vol. II. London: Hogarth.

Friesen, P. H. and D. Miller (1981) "A mathematical model of organizational adaptation." Working Paper. Montreal: Faculty of Management, McGill University.

Gadamer, H. (1975) Truth and Method. New York: Seabury.

Galton, F. (1907) Inquiries into Human Faculty and Its Development. London: J. M. Dent.

Garfinkel, H. (1967) Studies in Ethnomethodology. Englewood Cliffs, NJ: Prentice-Hall.

Gaventa, John (1980) Power and Powerlessness. Oxford: Clarendon.

Geertz, Clifford (1973) The Interpretation of Culture. New York: Basic Books.

Georgopoulos, Basil and A. Tannenbaum (1957) "A study of organizational effectiveness." American Sociological Review 22: 534ff.

Geschichte der Dialektik (1979) 19 bis 18. Jahrhundert: Dietz Verlag.

Giddens, Anthony (1977) New Rules of Sociological Method. London: Hutchinson.

Giddens, Anthony (1979) Central Problems in Social Theory. Berkeley: University of California Press.

Gilb, Corinne (1966) Hidden Hierarchies. New York: Harcourt, Brace.

Glaser, B. G. and A. L. Strauss (1967) The Discovery of Grounded Theory. Chicago: Aldine.

Glennon, Lynda M. (1979) Women and Dualism. New York: Longman.

Gödel, Kurt (1962) On Formally Undecidable Propositions. New York, Basic Books.

Goffman, Erving (1952) "Cooling out the mark" Psychiatry 15: 451-463.

Goffman, Erving (1959) The Presentation of Self in Everyday Life." Garden City, NY: Doubleday.

Goffman, Erving (1967) Interaction Ritual. Garden City, NY: Doubleday.

Goffman, Erving (1968) Asylums. Garden City, NY: Doubleday.

Goffman, Erving (1974) Frame Analysis. New York: Harper & Row.

Goldmann, Lucien (1969) The Human Sciences of Philosophy. London: Jonathan Cape.

Goldmann, Lucien (1976) Cultural Creation. St. Louis, MO: Telos.

Gould, Meredith (1980) "The new sociology." Signs 5: 459-467.

Gouldner, A. W. (1955) Patterns of Industrial Bureaucracy. London: Routledge & Kegan Paul.

Gouldner, A. W. (1959) "Organizational analysis," in R. Merton et al. (eds.) Sociology Today. New York: Basic Books.

Gouldner, A. W. (1973) "Reciprocity and autonomy in functional theory," pp. 190-225 in For Sociology. London: Harmondsworth.

Gouldner, A. W. (1980) The Two Marxisms. London: Macmillan.

Gramsci, Antonio (1971) Selections from the Prison Notebooks. New York: International.

Greiner, L. E. (1972) "Evolution and revolution as organizations grow." Harvard Business Review 50: 37-46.

Guttman, L. (1954) "A new approach to factor analysis: The radex," in P. Lazarsfeld (ed.) Mathematical Thinking in the Social Sciences. New York: Free Press.

Habermas, Jürgen (1971) Toward a Rational Society. London: Heinemann.

Habermas, Jürgen (1972) Knowledge and Human Interests. London: Heinemann.

Habermas, Jürgen (1973) Theory and Practice. Boston: Beacon.

Habermas, Jürgen (1975) Legitimation Crisis. Boston: Beacon.

Habermas, Jürgen (1976) "The analytic theory of science and dialectics," in T. W. Adorno et al. (eds.) The Positivist Dispute in German Sociology. New York: Harper Torchbooks.

Habermas, Jürgen (1979) Communication and the Evolution of Society. Boston: Beacon.

Hallowell, A. I. (1955) Culture and Experience. Philadelphia: University of Pennsylvania Press.

Hannan, M. and J. Freeman (1977) "The population ecology of organizations." American Journal of Sociology 85: 929-964.

Harré, Rom (1970) Principles of Scientific Thinking. Chicago: University of Chicago Press.

Harré, Rom (1972) Philosophies of Science. London: Oxford University Press.

Harré, Rom (1979) Social Being. Oxford: Basil Blackwell.

Harré, Rom and E. H. Madden (1975) Causal Powers. Totowa, NJ: Rowan & Littlefield.

Harré, Rom and P. Secord (1972) The Explanation of Social Behaviour. Oxford: Basil Blackwell.

Harvey, E. (1968) Technology and the Structure of Organizations. American Sociological Review 33: 247-259.

Haug, Marie (1973) "Deprofessionalization: An alternate hypothesis for the future," in P. Halmos (ed.) Professionalization and Social Change. Sociological Review Monograph 20, Keele University, England.

Haug, Marie and M. Sussman (1969) "Professional autonomy and the revolt of the client." Social Problems: 151-161.

Head, Henry (1920) Studies in Neurology. Oxford: Oxford University Press.

Hegel, G. W. F. (1931) The Phenomenology of Mind. London: Macmillan.

Heidegger, Martin (1962) Being and Time. New York: Harper & Row.

Heidegger, Martin (1966) Discourse on Thinking. New York: Harper & Row.

Heilman, Samuel C. (1976) Synagogue Life. Chicago: University of Chicago Press.

Heisenberg, W. (1958) Physics and Philosophy. New York: Harper Brothers.

Helson, H. (1964) Adaptation-Level Theory. New York: Harper & Row.

Herbert, Simon (1957) Models of Man. John Wiley.

Herbst, P. G. (1974) Sociotechnical Design. London: Tavistock.

Herzberg, Frederick, B. Mausner, and B. Snyderman (1959) The Motivation to Work. New York: John Wiley.

Hesse, Mary (1966) Models and Analogies in Science. Bloomington: Indiana University Press.

Hesse, Mary (1974) The Structure of Scientific Inference. London: Macmillan.

Heydebrand, W. V. (1977a) "Organizational contradictions in public bureaucracies: Toward a Marxian theory of organizations." Sociological Quarterly 18: 83-107.

Heydebrand, W. V. (1977b) "The context of public bureaucracies." Law & Society Review 11: 759ff.

Heydebrand, W. V. (1979) "The technocratic administration of justice," in S. Spitzer (ed.) Research in Law and Sociology, Vol. 2. Greenwich, CT: JAI.

Heydebrand, W. V. (1981) "Die Technokratisierung des Rechts und der Jistizverwaltung." Jahrbuch fur Rechtssoziologie und Rechtstheorie, Vol. 8. Oplander: Westdeutscher Verlag.

Heydebrand, W. V. and B. Burris (1982) "The limits of praxis in critical theory," in Z. Tar and J. Marcus (eds.) The Frankfurt School Revisited. New York: Columbia University Press.

Heydebrand, W. V. and C. Seron (1981) "The double bind of the capitalist judicial system." International Journal of the Sociology of Law 9: 407-436.

Hickson, D. J. and C. J. McMillan [eds.] (1981) Organization and Nation: The Aston Programme IV. London: Gower.

Holdaway, E. A., J. F. Newberry, D. J. Hickson, and R. P. Heron (1975) "Dimensions of organizations in complex societies." Administrative Science Quarterly 20: 37-58.

Hollis, M. (1977) Models of Man. Cambridge: Cambridge University Press.

Hollis, M. and E. Nell (1975) Rational Economic Man. Cambridge: Cambridge University Press.

Horkheimer, Max (1976) "Traditional and Critical Theory," in P. Connerton (ed.) Critical Sociology. New York: Penguin.

Hoy, David C. (1978) The Critical Circle. Berkeley: University of California Press.

Hughes, E. C. (1951) "Work and the self," in J. H. Rohrer and M. Sherif (eds.) Social Psychology at the Crossroads. New York: Harper.

Hume, David (1962) [1740] Enquiries Concerning the Human Understanding and Concerning the Principles of Morals. Oxford: Clarendon.

Hume, David (1967) [1748] A Treatise on Human Nature. Oxford: Clarendon.

Hunnius, Gerry et al. [eds.] (1973) Workers Control. New York: Vintage.

Hunt, R. G. (1970) "Technology and organization." Academy of Management Journal 13: 235-250.

Husserl, Edmund (1960) Cartesian Meditations: An Introduction to Phenomenology. Atlantic Highlands, NJ: Humanities.

Husserl, Edmund (1962) Ideas. New York: Collier.

Husserl, Edmund (1973) Experience and Judgment. Evanston, IL: Northwestern University Press.

Ingalls, John D. (1976) Human Energy. Reading, MA: Addison-Wesley.

James, William (1890) The Principles of Psychology. New York: Henry Holt.

Jowell, Jeffrey (1975) Law and Bureaucracy. Port Washington, NY: Kennikat.

Joyce, James (1978) Finnegans Wake. New York: Garland.

Jung, C. G. (1954) "The difference between Eastern and Western thinking," in pars. 759-787 Collected Works, Vol. 11. London: Routledge & Kegan Paul.

Jung, C. G. (1966) The Collected Works of J. C. Jung. London: Routledge & Kegan Paul.

Jung, C. G. (1968) Analytical Psychology. New York: Pantheon.

Kaplan, A. (1964) The Conduct of Inquiry. San Francisco: Chandler.

Karpik, Lucien (1972) "Les politique et les logiques d'action de la grande enterprise industrielle." Sociologie du Travail 1: 82-105.

Katz, D. and R. L. Kahn (1966) The Social Psychology of Organizations. New York: John Wiley.

Keat, Russell and J. Urry (1975) Social Theory as Science. London: Routledge & Kegan Paul.

Kegan, R. (1981) The Evolving Self. Cambridge, MA: Harvard University Press.

Keller, H. (1954) The Story of My Life. Garden City, NY: Doubleday.

Kirkhart, Larry and Orion F. White (1977) "The practice or transformational organization development." Presented at the American Social Psychology Association Conference, Atlanta, Georgia.

Klapp, Orrin E. (1962) Heroes, Villains and Fools. Englewood Cliffs, NJ: Prentice-Hall.

Klatzky, S. P. (1970) "Relationship of organizational size to complexity and coordination." Administrative Science Quarterly 15: 428-438.

Knight, Everett (1960) The Objective Society. New York: George Braziller.

Kohlberg, L. (1972) "Stages of moral development as a basis for moral education," in

C. M. Beck et al. (eds.) Moral Education: Interdisciplinary Approaches. New York: Paulist-Newman.

Korsch, Karl (1938) Karl Marx. London: Chapman & Hall.

Korzybski, Alfred (1941) Science and Sanity. Lakeville, CT: Institute of General Semantics.

Kuhn, Thomas S. (1970a) "Reflections on my critics" pp. 231-278 in I. Lakatos and A. Musgrave (eds.) Criticism and the Growth of Knowledge. Cambridge: Cambridge University Press.

Kuhn, Thomas S. (1970b) The Structure of Scientific Revolutions. Chicago: University Press.

Kuhn, Thomas S. (1974) "Second thoughts on paradigms," pp. 459-482 in F. Suppe (ed.) The Structure of Scientific Theories. Urbana: University of Illinois Press.

Lacan, J. (1977) Ecrits. London: Tavistock.

Laclau, E. (1977) Politics and Ideology in Marxist Theory. London: New Left Books.

Lakatos, Imrie and A. Musgrave [eds.] (1970) Criticism and the Growth of Knowledge. Cambridge: Cambridge University Press.

Landry, Maurice (1980) "Must We Analyze or Design Complex Problems?" Working Paper 80-19. Quebec: Université Laval.

Lasky, Melvin J. (1980) "1917 and all that." Encounter 54: 79-82.

Lawrence, P. R. and J. W. Lorsch (1967) Organization and Environment. New York: Irwin.

Leary, T. (1957) Interpersonal Diagnosis of Personality. New York: Ronald Press.

Léfebvre, Henri (1968) Dialectical Materialism. London: Jonathan Cape.

Léfebvre, Henri (1976) The Survival of Capitalism. London: Allen & Busby.

Leiss, William (1974) The Domination of Nature. Boston: Beacon.

Lenin, V. I. (1916) State and Revolution. Moscow: Foreign Languages Publishing House.

Lenin, V. I. (1963) Collected Works, No. 38. Moscow: Progress.

Lévi-Strauss, Claude (1963a) Structural Anthropology. New York: Basic Books.

Lévi-Strauss, Claude (1963b) Totemism. Boston: Beacon.

Lévi-Strauss, Claude (1963c) Tristes Tropiques. New York: Atheneum.

Lévi-Strauss, Claude (1966) The Savage Mind. Chicago: University of Chicago Press.

Lévi-Strauss, Claude (1967) The Scope of Anthropology. London: Jonathan Cape.

Lévi-Strauss, Claude (1969) The Elementary Structures of Kinship. London: Eyre Spottiswode.

Lévi-Strauss, Claude (1981) The Naked Man. New York: Harper & Row.

Lewin, K. (1935) "The conflict between Aristotelian and Galileian modes of thought in contemporary psychology," in A Dynamic Theory of Personality. New York: McGraw-Hill.

Lewin, K. (1938) The Conceptual Representation and Measurement of Psychological Forces. Cambridge: Cambridge University Press.

Liberman, A. M. (1970) "Some characteristics of perception in the speech mode." In A.R.N.M.D. 48: 238-254.

Loevinger, J. (1976) Ego Development. San Francisco: Jossey-Bass.

Lukács, Georg (1971) History and Class Consciousness. London: Merlin.

Lukes, Steven (1974) Power: A Radical View. London: Macmillan.

Luxemburg, R. (1968) The Accumulation of Capital. New York: Monthly Review Press.

Mangham, Iain L. (1978) Interactions and Interventions in Organizations. Chichester: John Wiley.

Mangham, Iain L. (1979) The Politics of Organizational Change. London: Associated Business Press.

Mannheim, Karl (1936) Ideology and Utopia. New York: Harcourt, Brace & World.

Mannheim, Karl (1940) Man and Society in an Age of Reconstruction. London: Routledge & Kegan Paul.

Manning, Peter K. (1979) "Metaphors of the field — varieties of organizational discourse." Administrative Science Quarterly 24: 660-671.

Manning, Peter K. (1980) "Topics and tropes." Contemporary Sociology 9: 670-672.

Mao Tse Tung (1936) On Practice. Beijing: Foreign Languages Press.

Mao Tse Tung (1967) "On contradiction," Selected Works, Vol. 1. Beijing: Foreign Languages Press.

March, J. G. (1981) "Decisions in organizations and theories of choice," in A. Van de Ven and W. Joyce (eds.) Perspectives on Organization Design and Behavior. New York: John Wiley.

March, J. G. and H. Simon (1958) Organizations. New York: John Wiley.

Marcuse, Herbert (1964) One Dimensional Man. Boston: Beacon.

Markovic, Mihailo (1974) From Affluence to Praxis. Ann Arbor: University of Michigan Press.

Marx, Karl (1904) Contributions to the Critique of Political Economy. Chicago: Kerr.

Marx, Karl (1957) Capital, Vol. 1. Moscow: Foreign Languages Publishing House.

Marx, Karl (1963) The Eighteenth Brumaire of Louis Bonoparte. New York: International.

Marx, Karl (1967) Writings of the Young Marx on Philosophy and Society (L. D. Easton and K. Guddat, eds.). Garden City, NJ: Doubleday.

Marx, Karl (1973) Grundrisse: Foundations of the Critique of Political Economy. New York: Vintage.

Marx, Karl and F. Engels (1969) Selected Works, No. 1. London: Laurence & Wishart.

Marx, Karl and F. Engels (1970) Selected Works, Vol. 3. Moscow: Progress Publishers.

Mason, Richard O. and Ian I. Mitroff (1981) Challenging Strategic Planning Assumptions. New York: John Wiley.

Mauss, Marcel (1967) The Gift. New York: W. W. Norton.

McCall, George J. and J. L. Simmons (1978) Identities and Interactions. New York: Free Press.

McCarthy, Thomas (1978) The Critical Theory of Jurgen Habermas. Cambridge, MA: MIT Press.

McGuire, W. J. (1968) "Personality and social influence," in E. F. Borgatta and W. W. Lambert (eds.) Handbook of Personality Theory and Research. Chicago: Rand-McNally.

McKelvey, W. (1975) "Guidelines for the empirical classification of organizations." Administrative Science Quarterly 20: 509-525.

McKelvey, W. (1978) "Organizational systematics: Taxonomic lessons from biology." Management Science 24: 1428-1440.

McLellan, David [ed.] (1977) Karl Marx, Selected Writings. Oxford: Oxford University Press.

Mead, G. H. (1932) The Philosophy of the Present. Chicago: University of Chicago Press.

Mead, G. H. (1934) Mind, Self and Society. Chicago: University of Chicago Press.

Merleau-Ponty, Maurice (1962) Phenomenology of Perception. Atlantic Highlands, NJ: Humanities Press.

Merleau-Ponty, Maurice (1964a) Primacy of Perception. Evanston, IL: Northwestern University Press.

Merleau-Ponty, Maurice (1964b) Sense and Non-sense. Evanston, IL: Northwestern University Press.

Merleau-Ponty, Maurice (1964c) Signs. Evanston, IL: Northwestern University Press.

Merleau-Ponty, Maurice (1969) The Visible and the Invisible. Evanston, IL: Northwestern University Press.

Merleau-Ponty, Maurice (1970) The Structure of Behavior. Evanston, IL: Northwestern University Press.

Merleau-Ponty, Maurice (1973a) The Prose of the World. Evanston, IL: Northwestern University Press.

Merleau-Ponty, Maurice (1973b) Adventures of the Dialectic. Evanston, IL: Northwestern University Press.

Merton, R. K. (1957) "Bureaucratic structure and personality," in Social Theory and Social Structure. New York: Free Press.

Merton, R. K. and E. Barber (1967) "Sociological ambivalence," pp. 91-120 in E. A. Tiryakian (ed.) Sociological Theory, Values, and Sociological Change. New York: Harper & Row.

Miles, R. and C. Snow (1978) Organizational Strategy, Structure and Process. New York: McGraw-Hill.

Milgram, Stanley (1965) "Some conditions of obedience and disobedience to authority." Human Relations 18: 57-76.

Miller, D. (1978) "The use of multivariate 'Q-Techniques' in the study of organizations." Academy of Management Review 3: 515-531.

Miller, D. (1979) "Strategy, structure and environment: Context influences upon some bivariate associations." Journal of Management Studies 16: 294-316.

Miller, D. (1981) "Toward a new contingency approach: The search for organizational gestalts." Journal of Management Studies 18: 1-27.

Miller, D. (1982) "Evolution and revolution: A quantum view of structural change in organizations." Journal of Management Studies 19: 131-151.

Miller, D. and P. Friesen (1978) "Archetypes of strategy formulation." Management Science 24: 921-933.

Miller, D. and Friesen, P. (1980a) "Archetypes of organizational transition." Administrative Science Quarterly 25: 268-299.

Miller, D. and P. Friesen (1980b) "Momentum and revolution in organizational adaptation." Academy of Management Journal 123: 591-614.

Miller, D. and P. Friesen (1982a) "Structural change and performance: Quantum vs. piecemeal-incremental approaches." Academy of Management Journal 25: 867-892.

Miller, D. and P. Friesen (1982b) "The longitudinal analysis of organizations: A methodological perspective." Management Science 28: 1013-1034.

Miller, E.J. (1959) "Technology, territory, and time: The internal differentiation of complex production systems." Human Relations 12: 243-272.

Miller, J. G. (1965) "Living systems: Basic concepts." Behavioral Science 10: 193-237.

Miller, Jean Baker (1976) Toward a New Psychology of Women. Boston: Beacon.

Millman, Marcia and Rosabeth Moss Kanter [eds.] (1975) Another Voice. Garden City, NY: Doubleday.

Mills, C. Wright (1959) The Sociological Imagination. New York: Oxford University Press.

Mills, C. Wright (1963) "Situated actions and vocabularies of motive," pp. 439-452 in Irving L. Horowitz (ed.) Power, Politics and People. New York: Oxford University Press.

Mintzberg, H. (1979) The Structuring of Organizations. Englewood Cliffs, NJ: Prentice-Hall.

Mitroff, Ian I. (1974) The Subjective Side of Science. New York: Elsevier.

Mitroff, Ian I. and R. H. Kilmann (1978) Methodological Approaches to Social Science. San Francisco: Jossey-Bass.

Morgan, Gareth (1980) "Paradigms, metaphors and puzzle solving in organization theory." Administrative Science Quarterly 25: 605-622.

Morgan, Gareth and Linda Smircich (1980) "The case for qualitative research." Academy of Management Review 5: 491-500.

Nagel, Ernerst (1971) The Structure of Science. New York: Harcourt, Brace & World.

Negt, Oscar and A. Kluge (1972) Offentlichkeit und Erfahrung. Frankfurt: Suhrkamp Verlag.

Neisser, Ulric (1976) Cognitive Psychology. New York: Appleton-Century-Crofts.

Nelson, Benjamin (1969) "Conscience and the making of early modern cultures." Social Research 36: 4-21.

Neumann, Erich (1969) Depth Psychology and a New Ethic. New York: Harper Torchbooks.

Nietzsche, Friedrich (1968) The Will to Power. New York: Vintage.

Norman, Donald A. (1976) Memory and Attention. New York: John Wiley.

O'Connor, James (1973) The Fiscal Crisis of the State. New York: St. Martin's.

O'Neill, John (1972) Sociology as a Skin Trade. New York: Harper & Row.

O'Neill, John (1974) Making Sense Together. New York: Harper & Row.

Oakley, Ann (1981) "Interviewing women: A contradiction in terms," pp. 30-61 in Helen Roberts (ed.) Doing Feminist Research. London: Routledge & Kegan Paul.

Offe, Claus (1975) "Policy Formation," pp. 125-144 in L. Lindberg and R. Alford (eds.) Stress and Contradiction in Modern Capitalism. Lexington, MA: D.C. Heath.

Outhwaite, William (1983) Concept Formation in Social Science. London: Routledge & Kegan Paul.

Overington, Michael A. (1977a) "Kenneth Burke and the method of dramatism." Theory and Society 4: 131-156.

Overington, Michael A. (1977b) "Kenneth Burke as social theorist." Sociological Inquiry 47: 133-141.

Parkinson, C. N. (1957) Parkinson's Law. London: John Murray.

Parsons, Talcott (1951) The Social System. Glencoe, IL: Free Press.

Parsons, Talcott (1960) Structure and Process in Modern Society. New York: Free Press.

Parsons, Talcott and R. F. Bales (1955) Family, Socialization and Interaction Process. Glencoe, IL: Free Press.

Parsons, Talcott, R. F. Bales, and E. A. Shils (1953) Working Papers in the Theory of Action. Glencoe, IL: Free Press.

Paul, H. H. (1978) Marx, Engels und die Imperialisus — Theorie der II Internationale. Hamburg: VSA Verlag.

Penfield, Wilder (1968) The Excitable Cortex in Conscious Man. Liverpool: Liverpool University Press.

Pennings, J. M. (1975) "The relevance of the structural-contingency model for organizational effectiveness." Administrative Science Quarterly 20: 393-410.

Perrow, C. (1974) "Is business really changing?" Organizational Dynamics: 31-44.

Perls, F., R. Hefferline, and P. Goodman (1951) Gestalt Therapy. New York: Delta.

Peter, Laurence J. (1969) The Peter Principle. New York: William Morrow.

Pfeffer, J. and G. Salancik (1978) The External Control of Organizations, New York: Harper & Row.

Phillipson, M. (1972) "Theory, methodology and conceptualization," in P. Filmer et al. (eds.) New Directions in Sociological Theory. London: Collier MacMillan.

Piaget, Jean (1936) The Origins of Intelligence in Children. New York: W. W. Norton.

Piaget, Jean (1961) Mechanisms of Perception. New York: Basic Books.

Piaget, Jean (1967) Biology and Knowledge. Chicago: University of Chicago Press.

Piaget, Jean (1971) Genetic Epistemology. New York: W. W. Norton.

Piaget, Jean (1972) Psychology and Epistemology. New York: Viking.

Pinder, C. and L. Moore (1979) "The resurrection of taxonomy to aid the development of middle range theories of organizational behaviour." Administrative Science Quarterly 24: 99-118.

Pirandello, Luigi (1952) "Six characters in search of an author," in Eric Bentley (ed.) Naked Masks New York: E. P. Dutton.

Polanyi, M. (1958) Personal Knowledge. Chicago: University of Chicago Press.

Pondy, L. R. (1969) "Effects of size, complexity and ownership on administrative Intensity." Administrative Science Quarterly 14: 47-60.

Pondy, L. R., P. Frost, G. Morgan, and T. Dandridge [eds.] (1983) Organizational Symbolism. Greenwich, CT: JAI.

Popper, Karl (1945) The Open Society and Its Enemies. London: Routledge & Kegan Paul.

Popper, Karl (1957) The Poverty of Historicism. London: Routledge & Kegan Paul.

Popper, Karl (1958) The Logic of Scientific Discovery. London: Hutchinson.

Popper, Karl (1968) Conjectures and Refutations. New York: Harper & Row.

Porac, Joseph F. (1981) "Causal loops and other intercausal perceptions in attribution for exam performance". Journal of Educational Psychology, 73(4):587-601.

Pribram, Karl H. (1977) "Some comments on the nature of the perceived universe," in R. Shaw and J. Bransford (eds.) Perceiving, Acting and Knowing. New York: John Wiley.

Progoff, Ira (1973) Jung's Psychology and Its Social Meaning. Garden City, NY: Doubleday.

Pugh, D. S. (1966) "Modern organization theory: a psychological and sociological study," Psychological Bulletin 66: 235-251.

Pugh, D. S. [ed.] (1969) Organization Theory. Harmondsworth, England: Penguin.

Pugh, D. S. (1981) "The Aston Programme of research," in A. Van de Ven and W. Joyce (eds.) Perspectives on Organization Design and Behavior. New York: John Wiley.

Pugh, D. S. and D. J. Hickson (1972) "Causal inference and the Aston studies." Administrative Science Quarterly 17: 273-275.

Pugh, D. S. and D. J. Hickson (1976) "Organizational structure in its Context: The Aston Programme 1, Farnborough, England: Saxon House.

Pugh, D. S. and C. R. Hinings (1977) Orginizational Structure: Extensions and Replications, The Aston Programme II. Farnborough, England: Saxon House.

Pugh, D. S. and R. J. Payne (1977) Organizational Behaviour in its Context: The Aston Programme III. Farnborough, England: Saxon House.

Pugh, D.S., L. Donaldson, and P. Silver (1976) "A comparative study of the processes of organizational decision-making." London Business School Working Paper. London: School of Business.

Pugh, D.S., R. Mansfield, and M. Warner (1975) Research in Organizational Behaviour: A British Survey. London: Heinemann.

Pugh, D.S., D.J. Hickson, C.R. Hinings, and C. Turner (1968) "Dimensions of organization structure." Administrative Science Quarterly 13: 63-105.

Quine, W.V.O. (1953) From a Logical Point of View. Cambridge, MA: Harvard University Press.

Ranson, S., C.R. Hinings, and R. Greenwood (1980) "The structuring of organizational structures." Administrative Science Quarterly 25: 1-17.

Rapoport, R.N. (1970) "Three dilemmas of action research." Human Relations 23: 499-513.

Reeves, T.K. and J. Woodward (1970) "The study of managerial control," in J. Woodward (ed.) Industrial Organization: Behavior and Control. London: Oxford University Press.

Riecken, H.W. and R.F. Boruch [eds.] (1974) Social Experimentation. New York: Academic.

Rorty, Richard (1978) "Philosophy as a kind of writing: An essay on Derrida." New Literary History 10: 141-160.

Rorty, Richard (1979) Philosophy and the Mirror of Nature. Princeton, NJ: Princeton University Press.

Roszak, Betty and Theodore Roszak (1969) Masculine/Feminine. New York: Harper & Row.

Routamaa, V. (1980) "Organizational structuring." Acta Wasaensia (Finland) 13.

Rueckert, William [ed.] (1969) Critical Responses to Kenneth Burke: 1924-1966. Minneapolis: University of Minnesota Press.

Rushing, W.A. (1967) "The effects of industry size and division of labor on administration." Administrative Science Quarterly 12: 273-295.

Ryle, Gilbert (1968) "The thinking of thoughts." University of Saskatchewan University Lectures, No. 18. University of Saskatchewan, Regina.

Ryle, Gilbert (1971) Collected Papers, Volume II. New York: Barnes & Noble.

Saint-Exupery, Antoine de (1943) Le Petit Prince. New York: Harcourt, Brace & World Inc.

Sartre, Jean-Paul (1939) Nausea. Paris: Gallimard.

Sartre, Jean-Paul (1966) Being and Nothingness. New York: Washington Square Press.

Sartre, Jean-Paul (1968) Search for a Method. New York: Vintage.

Sartre, Jean-Paul (1976) Critique of Dialectical Reason. London: New Left Books.

Saussure, F. de (1955) General Course in Linguistics. New York: McGraw-Hill.

Sayer, Derek (1979) Marx's Method. Atlantic Highlands, NJ: Humanities Press.

Schaef, Ann Wilson (1981) Women's Reality. Minneapolis: Winston.

Schechner, R. (1973) Environmental Theater. New York: Hawthorne.

Scheffler, Howard W. (1970) "Structuralism in anthropology," in J. Ehrmann (ed.) Structuralism. Garden City, NY: Anchor-Doubleday.

Schein, E.H. (1972) Process Consultation. Reading, MA: Addison-Wesley.

Schon, Donald (1972) Beyond the Stable State. New York: W.W. Norton.

Schrank, Robert (1978) Ten Thousand Working Days. Cambridge, MA: MIT Press.

Schroyer, Trent (1973) The Critique of Domination. New York: George Braziller.

Schutz, Alfred (1967a) Collected Papers (3 vols.). The Hague: Martinus Nijhoff.

Schutz, Alfred (1967b) The Phenomenology of the Social World. Evanston, IL:

Northwestern University Press.

Schutz, Alfred and T. Luckmann (1973) The Structures of the Life World. Evanston, IL: Northwestern University Press.

Schwartz, H. and J. Jacobs (1979) Qualitative Sociology. New York: Free Press.

Searle, John (1969) Speech Acts. Cambridge: Cambridge University Press.

Silverman, David (1970) The Theory of Organizations. London; Heinemann.

Simmel, Georg (1950) The Sociology of Georg Simmel. Glencoe, IL: Free Press.

Simon, H. A. (1947) Administrative Behavior. New York: Macmillan.

Simon, H. A. (1969) The Sciences of the Artificial. Cambridge, MA: MIT Press.

Smircich, L. and G. Morgan (1982) "Leadership: The management of meaning." Journal of Applied Behavioral Studies 18: 257-273.

Smith, Dorothy (1979) "A sociology for women," in J. A. Sherman and E. T. Beck (eds.) The Prism of Sex. Madison: University of Wisconsin Press.

Smith, Dorothy (1981) "A method of inquiry for a sociology of women." Presented at the American Sociological Association Meetings, Toronto.

Sorg, R. (1976) Ideologietheorien. Berlin: Kiepenheuer und Witsch.

Spradley, J. P. (1979) The Ethnographic Interview. New York: Holt, Rinehart & Winston.

Starbuck, W. H. (1965) "Organizational growth and development," in J. G. March (ed.) Handbook of Organizations. Chicago: Rand McNally.

Starbuck, W. H., A. Greve, and B. Hedberg (1978) "Responding to crises." Journal of Business Administration 19: 111-134.

Steiner, Jean-Francois (1967) Treblinka. London: Weidenfeld & Nicolson.

Strauss, A. (1959) Mirrors and Masks. Glencoe, IL: Free Press.

Strauss, Anselm (1978) Negotiations. San Francisco: Jossey-Bass.

Suchman, E. A. (1971) "Action for What? A critique of evaluative research," in R. O'Toole (ed.) The Organization, Management and Tactics of Social Research. Cambridge, MA: Schenkman.

Sudnow, David (1978) Ways of the Hand. New York: Alfred Knopf.

Sudnow, David (1979) Talk's Body. New York: Alfred Knopf.

Susman, G. I. and R. D. Evered (1978) "An assessment of the scientific merits of action research." Administrative Science Quarterly 23: 582-603.

Talbot, Michael (1981) Mysticism and the New Physics. New York: Bantam.

Terkel, S. (1974) Working. New York: Pantheon.

Terrien, F. W. and D. L. Mills (1955) "The effect of changing size upon the internal structure of organizations." American Sociological Review 20: 11-13.

Thompson, E. P. (1978) The Poverty of Theory and Other Essays. New York: Monthly Review Press.

Titchener, Edward Bradford (1910) A Text-Book of Psychology. New York: Macmillan.

Torbert, W. (1973) Learning from Experience: Toward Consciousness. New York: Columbia University Press.

Torbert, W. (1974) "Doing Rawls justice." Harvard Educational Review 44: 459-469.

Torbert, W. (1976a) Creating A Community of Inquiry: Conflict, Collaboration, Transformation. London: John Wiley.

Torbert, W. (1976b) "Inquiry, fraternity, liberty, equality." Unpublished Paper.

Torbert, W. (1980) "Initiating an institutional self-study." Working Paper Chestnut Hill, MA: Boston College School of Management.

Turner, B. A. (1971) Exploring the Industrial Subculture. London: Macmillan.

Turner, Stephen (1977) "Complex organizations as savage tribes." Journal for the Theory of Social Behavior 7: 99-125.

Turner, Stephen and Frank J. Weed (1983) Conflict in Organizations. Englewood Cliffs, NJ: Prentice-Hall.

Van Maanen, J. and E. Schein (1979) "Towards a theory of organizational socialization," in B. Staw (ed.) Research in Organizational Behavior. Greenwich, CT: JAI.

Vickers, G. (1965) The Art of Judgement. New York: Basic Books.

Vickers, G. (1972) Value Systems and Social Processes. London: Tavistock.

von Bertalanffy, Ludwig (1950) "An outline of general systems theory." British Journal of Philosophical Science 1: 134-165.

Ward, James (1886) "Psychology." Encyclopedia Britannica 20: 37-85.

Ware, James (1978) "Student perception of causality in the academic environment," Ph.D. dissertation, Cornell University.

Warner, W. and A. Havens (1968) "Goal displacement and the intangibility of organizational goals." Administrative Science Quarterly 12: 539-555.

Watson, Lyall (1979) Lifetide. New York, Simon & Schuster.

Watts, Alan (1975) Tao: The Watercourse Way. New York: Pantheon.

Weber, Max (1946) From Max Weber (H. H. Gerth and C. Wright Mills, eds.) New York: Oxford University Press.

Weber, Max (1947) The Theory of Social and Economic Organization. Glencoe, IL: Free Press.

Weber, Max (1949) The Methodology of the Social Sciences. Glencoe, IL: Free Press.

Weber, Max (1966) Max Weber on Law in Economy and Society. Cambridge, MA: Harvard University Press.

Weick, Karl E. (1969) The Social Psychology of Organizing. ("First edition"). Addison-Wesley. Reading, MA.

Weick, Karl E. (1977) "Enactment processes in organizations," pp. 267-300 in B. Staw and G. Salancik (eds.) New Directions in Organizational Behavior. Chicago: St. Clair.

Weick, Karl E. (1978) "Cognitive processes in organizations," in B. Staw (ed.) Research in Organizational Behavior. Greenwich, CT: JAI.

Weick, Karl, M. Bougon, and G. Maruyama (1976) "The equity context." Organizational Behavior and Human Performance 15: 32-65.

Weick, Karl E. (1979) The Social Psychology of Organizing. Reading, MA: Addison-Wesley.

Wheeler, J., R. Mansfield, and B. Todd (1980) "Structural implications of organizational dependence upon customers and owners." Organization Studies 1: 327-348.

White, Hayden (1978) Tropics of Discourse. Baltimore: John Hopkins University Press.

White, Leonard D. (1958) The Republican Era. New York: Harper Colophon.

Whitmont, Edward C. (1969) The Symbolic Quest. New York: Harper Colophon.

Wiener, N. (1954) The Human Use of Human Beings. Garden City, NY: Doubleday.

Wilden, A. (1972) System and Structure. London: Tavistock.

Wilensky, Harold (1964) "The professionalization of everyone?" American Journal of Sociology 70: 137-158.

Wiley, Norbert (1979) "Notes on self-genesis: From me to we to I," pp. 87-105 in Norman K. Denzin (ed.) Studies in Symbolic Interaction, Vol. II. Greenwich, CT: JAI Press.

Williamson, Oliver (1976) Markets and Hierarchies. New York: Free Press.

Wilson, H. T. (1973) "Rationality and decision in administrative science." Canadian Journal of Political Science 6: 271-294.

Wilson, H. T. (1976a) "Science, critique and criticism: the 'open society' revisited," in John O'Neill (ed.) On Critical Theory. New York: Seabury.

Wilson, H. T. (1976b) "Reading Max Weber: the 'limits of sociology.'" Sociology 10: 297-315.

Wilson, H. T. (1977) The American Ideology. London: Routledge & Kegan Paul.

Wilson, H. T. (1979) "The meaning and significance of 'empirical method' for the critical theory of society." 3: 57-68.

Wilson, H. T. (1981a) "Technocracy and advanced industrial society: Remarks on the problem of rationality and social organization." Presented at a Conference on Organization, Economy and Society, Brisbane, Australia.

Wilson, H. T. (1981b) "Values: On the possibility of a convergence between economic and non-economic decision making," in K. Weiermair and G. Dlugos (eds.) Management under Differing Value Systems. New York: Walter de Gruyter.

Wilson, H. T. (1982) "Science, technology and innovation: The role of commonsense capacities." Methodology and Science 15: 167-200.

Wilson, H. T. (1983) "Notes on the achievement of communicative behaviour and related difficulties." Dialectical Anthropology (Spring).

Winch, P. (1958) The Idea of a Social Science. London: Routledge & Kegan Paul.

Wittgenstein, Ludwig (1922) Tractatus Logico-Philosophicus. London: Routledge & Kegan Paul.

Wittgenstien, Ludwig (1969) Philosophical Investigations. New York: Macmillan.

Wolin, Sheldon (1960) Politics and Vision. Boston: Little, Brown.

Woodward, J. (1965) Industrial Organization: Theory and Practice. London: Oxford University Press.

Wright, E. O. (1978) Class, Crisis and the State. London: New Left Books.

Yeats, W. B. (1933) "Crazy Jane Talks with the Bishop" pp. 294-295 in Collected Poems. London: Macmillan.

Young, Michael (1958) The Rise of the Meritocracy. Harmondsworth: Penguin.

Yuchtman, Ephraim and S. E. Seashore (1967) "A system-resource approach to organizational effectiveness." American Sociological Review 32: 891ff.

Zimbalist, A. [ed.] (1975) Case Studies on the Labor Process. New York: Monthly Review Press.

Zollschan, G. K. and M. A. Overington (1976) "Reasons for conduct and the conduct of reason," pp. 270-317 in K. Zollschan and W. Hirsch (eds.) Social Change. New York: John Wiley.

Zukav, Gary (1979 The Dancing Wu-Li Masters. New York: William Morrow.